Civic Innovation in America

The publisher gratefully acknowledges
the generous contribution to this book provided
by the General Endowment Fund of the Associates
of the University of California Press.

Civic Innovation in America

Community Empowerment, Public Policy,
and the Movement for Civic Renewal

Carmen Sirianni
and Lewis Friedland

UNIVERSITY OF CALIFORNIA PRESS
Berkeley · Los Angeles · London

University of California Press
Berkeley and Los Angeles, California

University of California Press, Ltd.
London, England

Library of Congress Cataloging-in-Publication Data

Sirianni, Carmen.
    Civic innovation in America: community empowerment, public policy, and the
movement for civic renewal / Carmen Sirianni and Lewis Friedland.
        p.   cm.
    Includes index.
    ISBN 0-520-22636-4 (cloth: alk. paper).—ISBN 0-520-22637-2 (pbk.: alk. paper)
        1. Political participation—United States.   2. Citizens' associations—United
States.   I. Friedland, Lewis, 1952–   II. Title.
JK1764.S543   2001
323'.042'0973—dc21   00-031628

Printed and bound in Canada.
09   08   07   06   05   04   03   02   01   00
        10   9   8   7   6   5   4   3   2   1

The paper used in this publication meets the minimum requirements
of ANSI/NISO Z39.48-1992 (R 1997) *(Permanence of Paper)*.

To
David Walsh-Sirianni
and
Samuel Oliker Friedland

Good citizens, great sons!

CONTENTS

ACKNOWLEDGMENTS

Writing this book together has been a process of genuine discovery and relationship building, and we are indebted to many people. Lewis Coser, distinguished elder statesman of sociology, had asked one of us to write a book about participation and democracy for a new series he was editing, which would extend some of the comparative (primarily European) historical and theoretical work we had previously done, but in a form suitable for the non-specialist reader. But a funny thing happened on the way to the publisher! As we began examining recent American experience, we were quite unexpectedly struck by some of the participatory innovations that we found. And as we began telling some of the stories for a general audience—one that included community activists and undergraduate students as well as professors and policy wonks—it became clear to us that civic innovation was a slow, often invisible and convoluted process of social learning extending back to the "participatory democracy" of the 1960s and 1970s, however problematic and contested that experience might have become. This learning was evident in the biographies of activists, as well as professional practitioners in nonprofit and government organizations, and even in some corporate organizations seeking new forms of partnership with citizens and communities. It was evident in the emergence of networks that promoted innovation, and in fresh democratic practices suitable to addressing complex problems and stubborn conflicts. And it was evident in increasingly sophisticated democratic theory wedded to an everyday civic language of collaborative problem solving by citizens building a shared commonwealth. We thus jettisoned the original volume, already two-thirds complete, to focus on the contemporary United States, though we are most grateful to Lew Coser for helping us get started.

Richard Sinopoli gave one of our early papers to William Galston, who had recently become a deputy assistant for domestic affairs in the White

House in 1993. Bill invited one of us to become research director of the Reinventing Citizenship Project and later to serve as senior advisor to the National Commission on Civic Renewal. The Reinventing Citizenship Project was convened jointly with director Harry Boyte of the Center for Democracy and Citizenship at the University of Minnesota and Benjamin Barber of the Walt Whitman Center at Rutgers University. All of them, and Richard Schwartz of the Syracuse University College of Law, who helped convene the initial group, provided much insight. Harry, in particular, whose path had first crossed our own in the democratic community and workplace-based movements of the 1970s, has served as a close colleague, whose practical, theoretical, and personal wisdom about citizen democracy we count as an invaluable treasure of friendship, as well as an indispensable legacy of contemporary American civic culture. More than anyone we have ever met, Harry understands deep in his bones that civic democracy entails organizing public space in every nook and cranny of institutional life and doing public work in every niche and corner of our societal division of labor that might require public reasoning and civic trust in order to produce the kind of goods and services, communities and people to which we aspire.

The Reinventing Citizenship Project, as well as a series of related action research projects over the next several years, enabled us to convene teams of leading activists, professional practitioners, academic policy experts, and government officials, and to conduct more than four hundred and fifty formal interviews with innovators from many settings. These people shared their time and insight, as well as much archival and current organizational material (strategic planning documents, project evaluations, community action guides, minutes of meetings), which provided invaluable windows on civic innovation. Clearly, we cannot thank all of these people individually, though many are referenced throughout the book. To these reflective practitioners of civic democracy we owe our greatest debt, and we look forward to years of further collaboration. It is on their shoulders that we stand.

Among our academic colleagues, Jenny Mansbridge provided rich insight over many years, as well as critical feedback at the final stage. Iris Young provided a detailed, incisive critique of some of our early efforts—the kind that only a dear friend would undertake or could hope to get away with! We learned much, but undoubtedly still have our differences. David Plotke and Ian Shapiro hosted a most fruitful discussion of our work at the political theory luncheon among the faculty of the Yale Political Science Department and Law School, which helped us reorient some of our early thinking. Robert Putnam invited us to present our analysis of civic innovation as social learning to the Wequessett conference on social capital in 1994, and has provided lively exchange on these issues at various other professional panels. Margaret Weir and Marshall Ganz engaged us in a spirited debate on the relationship of civic renewal to party renewal, an issue we take up at some length in our concluding chapter. Despite our persisting disagreements, we have learned enormously from both these friends over many years. Paul Light helped us think about the importance of a civic renewal movement, as did Helen Ingram, Steven Rathgeb Smith, and Anne Schneider at their American Political Science Association panel on policy designs for democracy, and Steve and Anne provided invaluable comments on the entire manuscript. Frank Fischer provided insight, contacts, and healthy initial skepticism about policy learning theory, and we have learned much from his own work on democracy and technocracy over years of collaboration. Zelda Gamson helped us frame our argument on the civic renewal movement for innovators determined to renew the civic mission of higher education itself. And though we regret not having been able to help more in the vital work that she and other innovators such as Elizabeth Hollander and Barry Checkoway have been doing, or to include our most recent research on youth and civic engagement, they have further deepened the general conclusions we have drawn. Jay Rosen invited one of us to engage in research on the emerging public journalism movement through a variety of projects and seminars. Kevin Mattson provided detailed reflections on the improbability of a civic renewal movement. When we were in between projects, Michael Walzer, Joan Scott, and Albert Hirschman provided one of us with an idyllic intellectual setting at the Institute for Advanced Study at Princeton, which in hindsight was our initial spur to study civic democracy in the United States. Michael Walzer's work on civil society and spheres of justice has been an inspiration for a long time.

Other academic colleagues have provided valuable comments on various parts of this manuscript: Mark E. Warren, Jean Cohen, Mark R. Warren, Jeff Isaac, Jack McLeod, Jon Cruz, Hemant Shah, Jo Ellen Fair, James L. Baughman, and Michael Pfau, as well as George Ross and Peter Conrad, who also provided welcome support as chair of the Brandeis University sociology department. Several graduate students at Brandeis provided useful research leads and critical feedback, including Tony Vogt, Bob Irwin, and Tina Taylor. Debra Osnowitz read the entire manuscript with the eye of a professional sociologist and experienced editor. And another of our Brandeis students, Claire Reinelt, was the first to convince us that relational power in the women's movement was important to our story. Melissa Bass brought a wealth of experience in developing curricula on active citizenship for AmeriCorps, University Extension, and National 4-H, and much insight into the emerging civic renewal movement, especially among youth. She also provided invaluable research assistance and editing for the Civic Practices Network (CPN; www.cpn.org), which we have published together from Brandeis and the University of Wisconsin, and she helped maintain the editorial network of academics and innovators too numerous to name here. Many Brandeis undergraduates have also contributed to the CPN research enterprise, including Maya Holtz, Sharon Abramowitz, Sierra Matula, Eric Percher, Jessica Salerno, and Mira Zaslove. We would especially like to thank Abigail Lawrence and Lisa Geller for their excellent research and editorial work. Jack Shonkoff, dean of the Brandeis Heller Graduate School for Social Policy, as well as Susan Curnan, Andy Hahn, Alan Melchior, and Dale Morse, provided a welcome home for several of our projects at the Center for Youth and Communities. And the Heller inequality seminar convened by Robert Reich provided critical feedback on one of our chapters. Judy Hanley and Elaine Brooks of the department of sociology provided more forms of everyday support than we could ever enumerate.

Kathryn Campbell sustained the research enterprise on civic journalism at Wisconsin, and David Kurpius and Katie Daily spent months in the field interviewing public journalists and several years analyzing data in the course of becoming public scholars. Naewon Kang conducted valuable studies of community. Sandra Nichols analyzed the archives of the Pew Center for Civic Journalism. Without Sheila Webb, there would have been no Civic Practices Network. Her work has sustained ours over many years, and we owe her enormous thanks. Richard Zauft's excellent design gave CPN and our other civic websites their visual identity. Eliza Tanner, Benjamin Wutt, Randall Ramig, and others provided the web savvy to keep CPN and ONline@UW going.

At the Committee on Degrees in Social Studies, an interdisciplinary honors concentration at Harvard University where one of us has taught the junior tutorial on civic democracy for more than a decade and has had the privilege of supervising and examining many wonderful senior theses in this area, we owe a special debt of gratitude to Judy Vichniac. As director of studies, Judy has shaped this program into what is arguably the most exciting, theoretically informed, and empirically productive undergraduate social science department in the country, and the opportunity this has provided us to test ideas and learn from young scholars—and, in some cases, future community organizers—has been invaluable. Seyla Benhabib and David Landes, former chairs of Social Studies, provided us with a welcoming intellectual home away from home, and their own work on deliberative democracy and the organization of time, respectively, has informed two of our long-standing research interests.

We would also like to thank several foundations, which supported various projects that enabled us to deepen our research enterprise. Ed Skloot and Robert Sherman of the Surdna Foundation provided support and wisdom for the Civic Practices Network for several years, which enabled us to convene teams of academics and practitioners to survey best practices, and which put us in contact with many innovators in the field. Michael Lipsky of the Ford Foundation's program in Governance and Civil Society provided funding for the Reinventing Citizenship Project and incisive questions throughout. Gigi Sohn of the Ford Foundation, and Pamela Meyer, former director of Media, Arts, and Culture at Ford, supported our work on the civic uses of the new telecommunications media. And although the constraints of space do not permit us to discuss these at any length in this book, they have deepened our general perspective and equipped us for further work in this area, as did support from Stephen Elkin at the University of Maryland for our collaboration with him on the New Information Commons. Christopher Beem and Boyd Gibbons of the Johnson Foundation, as well as Carla Johnson and Charles Bray, formerly of Johnson, hosted several important meetings at the Wingspread conference center in Racine, Wisconsin, in which we collaborated, and they have helped make Wingspread one of the critical venues for nurturing innovative civic renewal strategies. Chris gave us helpful comments on the manuscript as well.

The Pew Charitable Trusts has provided support for various projects. These include our primer for foundation staff on "Critical Concepts in the New Citizenship." On this, as well as on our evaluation of civic journalism projects funded by the Trusts, we worked with Page Snow. The guidance and support of Ed Fouhy and Jan Schaffer of the Pew Center for Civic Journalism were critical to this research. Suzanne Morse, director of the Pew Partnership for Civic Change, offered wisdom and support at various stages. Michael Delli Carpini, who serves as Pew's Public Policy Program director, has provided support for extending our analysis to youth leadership networks for civic renewal, and has provided important feedback on our book and insight into the emerging renewal movement. The Kettering Foundation has provided support for an evaluation of public journalism projects, the study of community networks, and a broad analysis of the civic renewal movement for activists and practitioners. David Mathews, president of Kettering, has provided many forms of intellectual support and wisdom, and a vital context for thinking about the foundations of democracy, as have John Dedrick and Ed Arnone throughout various projects. We have enjoyed a number of most productive exchanges with the Kettering board, and have benefited from lively discussions at Dayton Days meetings. April Lanzilotti was tireless in providing us with material from the Kettering archives. In all cases, as with innovators outside the foundation world, we have been fortunate to find individuals who have a broad vision, think strategically, and can be brutally critical and self-critical in discussions about ongoing projects, as well as on the big questions of what it will take to revitalize communities and renew democracy for the twenty-first century.

We worked with the National Civic League on a number of projects and would especially like to thank Chris Gates, president, Gloria Rubio-Cortés, former vice president, and John Parr, the League's former president, for opening so many doors and sharing so many insights. In our work with the Public Broadcasting Service and Wisconsin Public Television's series *Citizens '96* and *Citizens State of the Union*, we would especially like to thank David Iverson, Byron Knight, Maria Alvarez Stroud, James Steinbach, and Ellen Hume, then director of PBS's Democracy Project. Martha McCoy and Matt Leininger of the Study Circles Resource Center provided lively discussion and innumerable contacts. Bruce Jennings of the Hastings Center for Bioethics introduced us to much interesting scholarly work and many innovators in health care. Our collaboration with Dr. Harold Hassin on the bioethics subcommittee of the Senate Labor and Education Committee helped us think about the challenges of values-based deliberation in health reform. And Carolyn Lukensmeyer, director of America Speaks, provided critical insight into the emerging civic renewal movement.

At the University of California Press, Reed Malcolm has brought good judgment to the project as a whole, and the final product has benefited much from his editing—though we still miss those fifty pages of additional references that had to be cut! We would also like to thank Marielle Leon, Dore Brown, and Jacqueline Volin at the press, as well as Nick Murray for his fine copyediting.

Our congregations, Christ Church Cambridge and Congregation Emanu-El B'ne Jeshurun, nurtured us and reminded us how and why we first became committed to building a more just and democratic world where citizens take on direct responsibility for public work. The Greater Boston Interfaith Organization provided a model of faith in action close to home.

We are forever indebted, once again, to our wives, Andrea Walsh and Stacey Oliker. They made considerable sacrifices in the course of this research, which took us to many cities on more occasions than we might have initially planned. But we have been fortunate also to have partners who are accomplished sociologists and who read the manuscript with careful and critical eyes, and engaged us in fruitful discussion on countless occasions. To each other, we owe years of good friendship that have sustained this and related enterprises. We first met nearly three decades ago while founding a community newspaper and reading social theory together, and this book enabled us to continue both types of work. Our sons, David Walsh-Sirianni and Samuel Oliker Friedland, supplied inspiration, joy, and no small dose of humor. They kept us engaged in soccer and basketball coaching and Sunday school teaching, and have shown us time and again what good young citizens can do. Their wit, reason, and deep sense of justice offer hope for a democratic future. To them we dedicate this book.

Somerville, MA, and Milwaukee, WI
August 2000

ONE

Civic Innovation
and American Politics

Over the past several decades American society has displayed a substantial
capacity for civic innovation, and the future of our democracy will depend
on whether we can deepen and extend such innovation to solve major public problems and transform the way we do politics. To be sure, the obstacles
are forbidding and the outcomes uncertain. But important foundations have
been slowly built through the painstaking public work of citizens, as well as
through networks of professional organizers and practitioners who have
learned to catalyze and support their work in progressively more refined
and effective ways. Americans at the turn of the century face serious strains
in their democratic institutions and worrisome signs in their everyday civic
life, yet they have never stopped reinventing democracy. Indeed, over the
past several decades they have created forms of civic practice that are far
more sophisticated in grappling with complex public problems and collaborating with highly diversified social actors than have ever existed in
American history.

The analysis that leads us to these conclusions will appear welcome to the
thousands upon thousands of people who have been engaged in building
communities and renovating the democratic foundations of American society for much of their adult lives. Indeed, it derives from a deep apprecia-
tion of their work, as well as from an attempt to learn from the paths they
have taken as civic innovators. Our analysis might also provide a hopeful set
of intellectual and practical handles for many others who seek new ways to
become effectively engaged amid pervasive beliefs that nothing works. But
our claims will undoubtedly appear contentious and counterintuitive to many
others. Before laying out a fuller case for these claims and qualifying them
with appropriate critical analysis, let us give a few examples of what we have
in mind.

A TALE OF TWO CIVIC ASSOCIATIONS

The first story concerns Save The Bay, a statewide civic environmental organization in Rhode Island, which has transformed itself over thirty years from a local oppositional group to one that combines advocacy, policy design, education, and habitat restoration. The second is about Communities Organized for Public Service, in San Antonio, a largely Mexican American coalition of congregations dedicated to transforming poor and working-class communities that has evolved over twenty-five years from a confrontational style of community organizing to one based on collaborative public relationships rooted in faith, family, and democratic accountability.

Save The Bay

In the early 1970s citizens of the Narragansett Bay Homeowners Association and Save Our Community formed Save The Bay to stop the construction of an oil refinery in Tiverton, Rhode Island, and twin nuclear power plants at Rome Point. The bay had been degraded during two centuries of industrial development, initially by woolen and cotton mills, then by fertilizer plants and paint factories, and more recently by jewelry manufacturing and electroplating. Urban development and suburban sprawl added new sources of nonpoint pollution, such as roads and shopping malls, and sewage systems needed major upgrading. As citizen efforts expanded, Save The Bay emerged over the next decade as an effective statewide citizen action group that repeatedly engaged in legal and political confrontation with local and state agencies and polluting corporations. Its initial strategies were advocacy and opposition: advocate strong enforcement of command-and-control regulations and oppose any actions that might further degrade the bay. While it made its case in the court of public opinion, Save The Bay did not shy away from taking cases to the courts of legal enforcement.

The National Environmental Policy Act of 1970 and the Clean Water Act of 1972 granted citizens important rights to participate in decision making and considerable leverage to compel compliance, but these were not power enough to protect and restore the bay on a long-term basis. For this, a broader civic strategy would be needed. Save The Bay thus began to identify common interests and to highlight the aesthetics of the bay and inland areas. Its new strategy emphasized the recreational and fishing uses available to all citizens and the need to preserve the environment for the children of the community. Rather than drawing stark lines between the evil polluters and the good guys in green hats, Save The Bay chose to downplay conflicting interests and ideologies and to avoid purely obstructionist methods that stopped short of solutions. It began to build new public relationships with boating and fishing groups, schools, civic associations, businesses, and regulators.

The U.S. Environmental Protection Agency (EPA) itself began to encourage such a shift, as the Chesapeake Bay Program in 1983 and the National Estuary Program in 1987 provided a framework for local collaborative action with the aim of nurturing a "protective ethic" and a "sense of ownership" among the public. EPA's reasoning was that standardized, technology-based approaches provided very limited tools for protecting integrated ecosystems. Citizens needed to understand the consequences of their own actions, such as the use of lawn fertilizers and household chemicals, if nonpoint pollution was to be effectively reduced. And citizens needed to develop new sources of voluntary and collaborative action, because regulators could do only so much and could never generate sufficient legitimacy on their own to make the hard choices, such as passing major new bonds to upgrade sewage treatment systems.

Having established an independent organizational base and impressive educational capacities, Save The Bay positioned itself in the 1980s to become the lead organization for public education in the Narragansett Bay Project, for which EPA provided funds and technical assistance. EPA also helped Save The Bay to organize the first national conference of estuarine groups in 1987 to develop a detailed activist agenda for protection and restoration. In the years since, Save The Bay has developed substantial organizing, technical, and educational capacities, with a staff of twenty-nine and an annual budget of more than 1.5 million dollars. More than half of its funding comes from member contributions and program revenues. It now counts more than twenty thousand members and supporters, with an average of one thousand or so volunteering during any given year. It has an ambitious, volunteer Citizens Monitoring project, built partly upon existing citizen efforts on many ponds and rivers, that includes computerized mapping, a public hotline, training of volunteers, and the operation of the specially equipped Narragansett Baykeeper boat and crew, part of the national Keepers Alliance. Save The Bay's business outreach strategy has included a cooperative effort with local businesses to develop employee education and leadership initiatives to reduce toxics. It has developed an array of local projects in Rhode Island and western Massachusetts, which is part of the larger watershed.

Habitat restoration work became increasingly important for Save The Bay in the latter half of the 1990s, and it now combines sophisticated scientific capacities with direct work by citizens themselves. In its initial assessment of habitat health across the bay, it recruited nearly one hundred citizens from shell fishermen's associations, scuba diving clubs, neighborhood associations, land trusts, town councils, environmental advocacy groups, country clubs, "friends of the stream" groups, and local conservation commissions. They were trained to do local interviews with homeowners to reconstruct the history of salt marsh degradation over many decades. They collected old photographs and maps, and developed computer mapping and databases through diving and aerial photography. Now these and other volunteers are engaged in restoration projects, such as growing and transplanting eelgrass, removing invasive plants, and doing periodic cleanups. Their stories of public work, of the "blood, sweat, and tears" shed in hauling sandbags and building fish ladders, inspire engagement well beyond what the staff itself is able to enlist.

Save The Bay also trains volunteer "docents" and classroom teachers to work with youth groups and schools on extensive environmental education at every level, using methods that include creative puppet shows and on-line games. Its new capital campaign aims to raise 6.5 million dollars to expand bay education centers around the state, with an emphasis on urban schools with minority and working-class populations. Without a much broader public understanding of habitats, Save The Bay reasons, people will not engage in restoration on a sufficient scale, nor will they adequately pressure the state legislature to pass the habitat restoration bill with enough funding to enable citizens to do their work. Save The Bay also provides information to local families on environmentally sound yard care, household toxics reduction, and "green" energy choices within the new deregulated market. It nurtures civic friendships and celebrates community achievements through a continuous array of fairs, festivals, yacht races, bay swims, Mother's Day sails, kayak tours, seal watches, and On the Dock of the Bay dances. Its innovative approaches have been featured in leading national and local newspapers, and it was awarded the seventy-sixth Point of Light by President Bush in 1989.

Save The Bay nonetheless continues to engage in building strong advocacy coalitions with local urban toxics groups and national organizations, such as the Environmental Defense Fund and the Conservation Law Foundation. In the interests of sustainable development with democratic stakeholder involvement, these coalitions stopped the recent Army Corps dredging project on the Providence River and the Quonset container port. As Curt Spalding, Save The Bay's executive director, puts it, "As we move into the next century, advocacy for the bay will be much more than preventing more damage. It will be a process of repairing and restoring the vital connections between bay and community." And for this, a "civic organizing strategy" based on education and restoration by citizens themselves "must come first."

Save The Bay has thus developed a model of an independent citizen organization that can collaborate with regulatory agencies and industry without being coopted and can define its essential mission as ongoing civic education and the public work of restoration without losing the capacity to engage in conflict, if need be. Through a process of extended social learning, it has generated new civic capacities that build upon its organized power of advocacy, legal norms favoring public participation, and existing associational networks. Its own learning "on the ground," so to speak, has ramified upward and outward to federal and state agencies and to other estuary and watershed groups throughout the country. It has provided critical local experience and national advice in the policy-learning process that is manifest at EPA and other federal and state agencies, as well as among policy intellectuals, who urged much greater emphasis on place-based strategies during the 1980s, and then inscribed "community-based environmental protection" (CBEP) as central to reinventing environmental regulation during the 1990s. Along with its eleven regional coalition partners in Restore America's Estuaries, Save The Bay has shaped the basic policy design and advocacy strategy for the Estuary Habitat Restoration Partnership Act, which Senator John Chafee of Rhode Island was able to shepherd through the U.S. Senate before his death in 1999. This bill would require the Army Corps of Engineers to help build local capacity and work collaboratively with community groups in restoration projects.

In Rhode Island itself, Save The Bay was instrumental in passing the first mandatory curbside recycling law in the nation. It also campaigned successfully to democratize the selection process for the Coastal Resources Management Council, on which its own founder and former director, Dr. William Miner, served as chairperson during the 1980s. Trudy Coxe, executive director of Save The Bay during this period, brought its experience in civic environmental approaches to her later position as secretary of the executive office of environmental affairs in Massachusetts during the 1990s. She collaborated extensively with a statewide network of more than sixty watershed associations to develop the Massachusetts Watershed Initiative and worked with a national network of self-described "watershed innovators" to learn from best practices nationwide. Today, hundreds of watershed "associations," "councils," and "alliances" identify as part of a larger "watershed movement," and many share a vision of "watershed democracy" as a core component of effective problem solving and civic engagement.[1]

Communities Organized for Public Service

Our second tale comes from San Antonio, Texas. In the early 1970s Mexican Americans had become the majority of the city's population but remained shut out of the Anglo power structure and deprived of decent services. Their neighborhoods were deteriorating, and they were vulnerable to repeated floods that damaged property and killed residents as a result of the city's failure to invest in adequate drainage systems. When delegates from twenty-seven churches gathered in the summer of 1974 to address this problem, someone facetiously suggested that they call themselves COPS—"You know, they're the robbers, and we're the cops." Since they were engaged in a battle with the city's Public Service Board, another suggested that the "PS" could stand for real public service, and they thus fashioned the name Communities Organized for Public Service to fit the acronym. Behind this playful inventiveness, however, was a serious attempt to innovate by coming to grips with the failures of previous organizing in San Antonio, including the antipoverty and Mexican American civil rights organizing supported by private foundations and the federal government during the previous decade. On another level, however, COPS represented a systematic effort by leaders of the Industrial Areas Foundation (IAF), the nation's oldest community-organizing network, founded by Saul Alinsky in 1940, to reflect on the strengths and limits of its own organizing traditions, as well as those of other movement-based models that had emerged in subsequent years. Ernesto Cortés, Jr., who was in the swirl of Mexican American organizing in the 1960s, had returned to his native San Antonio after several years of training and organizing with the IAF in Chicago, Milwaukee, and Lake County, Indiana. He and other IAF leaders then began to redefine the core principles of a new organizing model based on deeply shared values of faith and family, and oriented to building long-term public relationships and leadership capacities in communities.

Over the next twenty-five years in San Antonio, COPS refined this model continuously. It has enriched its leadership training with a powerful mixture of biblical text, contemporary theology, and democratic theory, and it has articulated a robust conception of the citizen as more than mere voter, client, taxpayer, or consumer. It has expanded its network of Mexican American churches and has developed extensive collaboration with its predominantly African American sister organization on the east side of the city, Metro Alliance, which it helped to found. COPS's organizing and voter registration work transformed the political culture of the city and made it possible in 1981 to elect its first Mexican American mayor, Henry Cisneros. It has helped to reverse the decay of the central city after decades of neglect. Close to one billion dollars of community development funds have been invested in the inner city for infrastructure and housing as a result of COPS's innovative model of distributing Community Development Block Grant (CDBG) funds, which it does through a process of participatory planning and negotiation among COPS leaders from different neighborhoods and between them and city councilors from their respective districts. Increasingly, COPS has been able to leverage its organizational power, based on strident confrontational tactics in its early days, into complex collaborative projects with leaders in banking, industry, education, and politics.

In the 1990s, for instance, COPS and Metro Alliance developed a highly innovative job-training program called Project QUEST (Quality Employment through Skills Training) on the basis of what they describe as a "new social compact" founded on collaborative relationships among employers, workers, and the community, and a "culture of accountability, negotiations, respect, and compromise" forged over the preceding two decades of organizing. The design for Project QUEST grew out of an intensive research process on models of job training and local labor markets, which a core committee of forty community leaders from COPS and Metro Alliance conducted with academic experts and others, such as former Secretary of Labor Ray Marshall. The process was designed to build productive relationships, not just to gain knowledge. It was complemented by extensive "house meetings" in which members of the community told stories of their own experiences in employment searches and the job-training system, especially in programs under the Job Training and Partnership Act (JTPA). These house meetings also built support for a design that would guarantee a specific number of jobs from local employers paying a living wage, secure stipends that would permit two years of training, and coordinate social services to support trainees through the rigorous process.

With strong community support and solid preliminary research, COPS and Metro Alliance leveraged the previous trust they had built with selected business leaders in campaigns on school reform and infrastructure improvement to convene a broader meeting on the future of employment in the city—the first such meeting in which employers themselves actually came together to exchange their views. COPS and Metro Alliance worked to identify the self-interest of employers—bankers interested in the continued general vitality of the city, health care employers concerned with filling skilled positions, and all employers interested in getting a supply of responsible trainees. To respond, COPS and Metro Alliance agreed to staff fifteen neighborhood centers with volunteers committed to doing eighteen thousand hours of outreach and initial screening in the first year alone. This effort would not only utilize relationships as a key source of information and continued personal support, but also build trainees' sense of obligation to the community and promote a desire to give something back in return for the opportunity the community had created.

The struggle for funding was complex and leveraged a significant amount of CDBG funds controlled by COPS and Metro Alliance, as well as relationships built over time with Governor Ann Richards, City Council President Nelson Wolff, and leading bankers, such as Tom Frost, an early adversarial target of COPS in the 1970s. And while continued changes in labor markets have made it difficult to treat employers' job pledges as anything more than moral commitments, Project QUEST has emerged as a broker of relationships among a variety of labor market institutions and actors, from employers and community colleges to churches and families. QUEST has catalyzed institutional changes, such as employer involvement in the design of training and the identification of future labor market needs. It has helped transform the relationship between the community college and employers, so that both are active partners in this process. It has also spurred extensive changes in curriculum design and flexibility to meet student needs and provide supportive team-building practices. In its first few years of operation, its results have been substantial: annual salary increases between $4,923 and $7,457, compared to $900 for the typical trainee in JTPA programs, and success in moving single mothers off welfare. In that first meeting, recalls Virginia Ramirez, a COPS leader,

> I realized all these important people were sitting there, and they had never talked to each other about what jobs were available. And I realized we had brought them all together to talk about jobs. I remember thinking, "Here's Virginia Ramirez, who a few years ago could only get a job sweeping floors. Most of our people never finished high school. And now we were telling these men how we are going to change the face of San Antonio." It was powerful, so powerful.[2]

Like Save The Bay, COPS has learned to leverage power based on effective advocacy into complex civic partnerships and innovative policy designs. As part of a larger IAF network, it has been able to diffuse innovative practices on the state and national level, as well as learn from other groups within the network. Several other national and regional networks of congregation-based community organizations have manifested similar developmental dynamics, sometimes borrowing lessons and models directly from IAF. Today, nearly two hundred such organizations are active in cities across the country, as are hundreds of other faith-based community development groups with different organizing models. They possess increasingly sophisticated training and funding supports and growing capacities for interracial community collaboration based on shared religious values and an organizing model that builds upon what unites people rather than what divides them. Theirs is a vision of collaborative citizen politics based on faith and the power of public relationships, rooted in ongoing reflection on the deepest traditions of American democracy. And, as both COPS and Save The Bay like to quote from the book of Proverbs, "Where there is no vision, the people perish."[3]

CONNECTING CITIZENS TO PUBLIC LIFE

Our task in this book is to understand such civic innovations as social learning extending over the past several decades and to explore their role in democratic revitalization. In recent years such learning has accelerated on a number of levels, even as the stresses on our democratic institutions have deepened. Indeed, a broader *civic renewal movement* has begun to emerge, with common language, shared practices, and networked relationships across a variety of arenas. When we first presented this argument in 1993, the debate on whether Americans' stocks of social capital were in decline had not yet begun. We thus set the task of understanding this process of innovation not in response to a discovery of the possible erosion of social capital in American life but in response to an increasingly complex set of public problems that have proven resistant to traditional policy solutions and

institutional routines, and have elicited vigorous search and experimentation by ordinary citizens and civic associations, supported by professional
practitioners within and outside government. The initial interviews Sirianni
conducted in 1994 as research director of the Reinventing Citizenship Project, funded by the Ford Foundation and convened in conjunction with the
Domestic Policy Council at the White House, provided further evidence for
civic innovation. In attempting to understand the process, we invariably stand
on the shoulders of those whose reflective practice has been driving it forward, and we hope to contribute to the policies and politics that might help
innovations to flourish in the coming years.[4]

At the same time, we are deeply aware of the many obstacles that exist
and the great uncertainty—even profound disagreement—about what a vital civic democracy might mean at the beginning of the twenty-first century.
The story we tell is thus not only one of innovation and learning, but also
one of roadblocks and detours, struggles and failures. Some of these failures, to be sure, have provided occasion for further learning, but others
demonstrate the difficulty of bringing innovations to scale, embedding
them in policy design, and creating a politics that will sustain them. Much
more work will be needed over the course of the next several decades if civic
innovation and renewal are to have a major impact on American politics and
public problem solving. Nonetheless, civic innovators from all walks of life
have laid indispensable foundations upon which to build.

The dynamics of innovation are quite specific to each arena, as we shall
see, yet they operate amid broader trends that shape the search for new forms
of civic engagement. Perhaps the most important underlying trend is one
that Ronald Ingelhart has identified in his extensive cross-national analyses
of contemporary advanced industrial democracies. As he argues, the potential for political action among mass publics in the West has been gradually
but steadily rising because the individual-level preconditions for participation have been increasing. These include dramatically higher education levels over the course of the last half-century, which enhance the skills citizens
need to cope with political life and shift the balance in the distribution of
these skills among elites and the general public. The increase in postindustrial job skills that favor autonomy, innovation, and collaborative problem
solving in complex environments further add to this potential. Political information has also become much more available, and relative shifts in value
priorities favor self-expression and the participation of women and other previously excluded groups. These changes underlie a long-term shift away from
elite-directed modes of participation and towards elite-directing ones. While
voter turnout may have declined, mass publics are "far from apathetic; these
publics are becoming *more* active than ever in a wide range of elite-challenging
forms of political participation."[5]

In San Antonio, for instance, COPS was able to emerge because the

Catholic diocese was searching for ways to respond to the Vatican II (1962–65) mandate for lay participation, itself a response to long-term changes in values, education, and civic skills within church communities. Save The Bay not only drew upon new legal norms of participation in the environmental arena but could also leverage access to technical information and political skills among educated middle-class supporters to enable the organization to challenge regulators and industry on their own terms. A generation earlier, citizens in each of these arenas were not nearly as favorably situated relative to elites as they had become by the 1960s and 1970s.

This powerful underlying trend favoring participation, however, occurs amid the increasingly manifest limitations of a variety of organized forms for connecting citizens to public life. Indeed, the two are related in complex ways. Political parties, the regulatory state, and the welfare state are especially problematic. First of all, the profound and systemic disintegration of parties has continued for more than a century and is manifest in popular partisan dealignment and a declining capacity of parties to aggregate the interests of an increasingly diverse citizenry. The historical factors that account for party decline include the rise of a nonpartisan civil service, the shift from generalized distributive policies to new regulative channels, the emergence of the administrative presidency, and the increase in the number and activities of specialized, nonpartisan interest groups. This trend has been exacerbated by the post-1960s explosion of public interest and consumer groups capable of lobbying and setting agendas independent of party organizations, as well as by participatory reforms in party rules and changes in political means of communication that favor direct communication between candidates and voters independent of locally organized and party mediated interaction. Television advertising and polling techniques have played critical roles here. In the process, parties have been transformed largely into service organizations for candidates. Party loyalty has become increasingly conditional on performance, and "cognitively mobilized nonpartisans" are a growing group within the electorate.[6]

Second, the New Deal regulatory state, characterized by industry capture, became delegitimated in both scholarly and public opinion alike in the 1960s, especially under the onslaught of new participatory claims. But the public lobby regulatory regime that succeeded it has come to manifest serious limits along a variety of dimensions. On the positive side, citizens have gained new rights of participation as a result of changes in administrative law and legislation that have accompanied the new social regulation. The proliferation of new citizen and public interest groups has permitted much greater precision in the representation of individual and group preferences through issue-oriented lobbying and has provided a more even balance in the pluralist representation of interests than existed previously. But the advocacy explosion has also manifested many drawbacks for democratic politics. It encourages a hyperpluralism driven by increasing incentives to organize and lobby along narrow interest and issue lines and to protect programs even when they may have outlived their usefulness. It displaces political discourse to narrow administrative arenas where complex procedural requirements and institutional coalitions among agencies, courts, congressional subcommittees, public interest groups, and industry lobbyists are much less comprehensible to the general public. Public interest groups often exacerbate the decline of trust in government because membership recruitment and mobilization emphasize not-yet-achieved goals, or even mandate unachievable standards, such as those in some environmental regulations which, when repeatedly unmet, breed public cynicism. Organizational incentives for public interest groups favor Washington-based and professionally driven lobbying over local engagement. And when they do mobilize locally, they tend to do so around narrow interests rather than broader forms of public deliberation and community building. As Robert Dahl has argued, the proliferation and fragmentation of interest groups that shape policy making has not yet been matched by a corresponding set of integrating political institutions that encourage conflicting groups to negotiate with one another, as well as with political actors more representative of the general public, in search of mutually beneficial policies.[7]

Third, while the crisis of the welfare state derives from a variety of sources, it is manifest in no small measure as a profound public disillusionment with the continued extension of professional dominance and client dependency. This view is due, in part, to the expansion of clinical authority in solving problems despite the relative intractability of many problems to therapeutic techniques. Social welfare policy and practice by government and nonprofit agencies alike do not foster independent, responsible citizens or self-governing communities capable of mobilizing their own knowledge and associational assets. Policy for poor and disadvantaged communities, in particular, tends to be driven by a deficit model that focuses on the deficiencies of individuals and communities, rather than building upon the individual, associational, and institutional assets and networks that already exist. Categorical funding designed to address each specific "problem" with a matching "program" often results in a jerry-built and fragmented set of antipoverty bureaucracies and serviced neighborhoods whose programs are defended by their personnel even when they produce no appreciable improvement in the community's capacity to deal with its problems. As John McKnight argues, "As the power of profession and service system ascends, the legitimacy, authority, and capacity of citizens and community descend. The *citizen* retreats. The *client* advances."[8]

The "rights revolution," which defines nearly every public issue in terms of the legally protected rights of individuals and groups, has gone hand in hand with the expansion of the welfare state and the public lobby regulatory regime. Indeed, divided government and institutional fragmentation in the United States may have increased the competition for policy innovation that is filtered through a rights discourse. On a number of important levels, as many of our cases reveal, the rights revolution has helped to drive civic innovation. Procedural rights to participate have been critical, if often blunt, tools for broadening the range of stakeholders willing and able to collaborate in searching for new ways to solve public problems. And substantive rights claims, such as rights to housing and health care, which underlay struggles for community development and community health centers in poor neighborhoods, have contributed to local innovations that mobilize civic resources and relationships. Here we agree with Michael Schudson that "the rise of the rights-regarding citizen has done more to enhance democracy than to endanger it."[9] Nonetheless, a rights discourse often tends to frame issues as nonnegotiable and in no need of balance among relative costs and other worthy claims. The expansionary logic of rights that become translated into noncompetitive and open-ended entitlements conflicts with other crucial virtues of a civic republic, namely, responsibility and deliberation. Within this framework, citizens do not have to consider their own responsibilities and assets for solving problems or enhancing the broader public good and do not have to deliberate about costs and trade-offs involved in achieving their specific programmatic goals.[10]

The risk of citizens becoming disjoined from public life comes, however, from yet another direction that may ultimately be the most corrosive of all: the market. To be sure, America has been a vital civic republic only to the extent that it has always been a vital commercial republic. When Save The Bay works with regulators and corporations on environmentally sustainable methods of production that can ensure dynamic market growth, and when COPS works with businesses to upgrade the skills of poor and working-class communities so that they can compete for postindustrial jobs, they opt for a commercial republic, albeit one more deeply embedded in a vital civic infrastructure. But in recent years, corporations have pushed decisions upwards, to national and global headquarters, and executives have fewer incentives to build relationships with particular communities. Unions have been weakened, and capital has become globally footloose, sometimes devastating local communities. The market can thus rend the very fabric of civic life upon which it once depended. And as some of our public institutions go through difficult struggles to restructure themselves, the metaphors of the market become increasingly dominant and threaten to turn nearly every public good into a consumer choice. Even our attempts to reinvent government invoke the language of "serving the customer" more often than "engaging the citizen" as a vital coproducer of public goods in a commonwealth.[11]

Increasing awareness of the limitations of these ways of connecting citizens to public life underlies the search for ways to enrich and refine elite-directing approaches to participation, especially by orienting them more toward deliberative democracy, community building, and collaborative problem solving among multiple stakeholder groups. Indeed, the growing social complexity, differentiation, and interdependence of postmodern societies generate increasing policy problems for which regulatory enforcement, programmatic entitlement, market incentive, and professional intervention are inadequate unless coupled with new forms of civic trust and cooperation. And many older forms of civic involvement also tend to be devalued in the face of increasing complexity and social differentiation, which raise the relative requirements of citizen expertise, the scope of relationships, and the cognitive preconditions for trust building, and increase the opportunities for "exit" to secure valued social goods. Civic innovation seeks to mobilize social capital in new ways, to generate new institutional forms, and to reinforce these through public policy designed for democracy. And it aims to provide citizens with robust roles — in their professional and nonprofessional roles, institutional and volunteer activities alike—for doing the everyday public work that sustains the democratic commonwealth.[12]

SOCIAL CAPITAL AND CIVIC INNOVATION

Social capital refers to those stocks of social trust, norms, and networks that people can draw upon to solve common problems. Networks of civic engagement, such as neighborhood associations, church groups, and sports clubs, represent important forms of social capital. The denser these networks, the more likely are members of a community to cooperate for mutual benefit, even in the face of persistent problems of collective action, because networks of civic engagement foster sturdy norms of generalized reciprocity by creating expectations that today's favors will be returned later. These networks facilitate coordination and communication and thus create channels through which information about the trustworthiness of other individuals and groups can flow and be tested and verified. They embody past success at collaboration, which can serve as a cultural template for future collaboration on other kinds of problems. And they increase the risks to those who act opportunistically and so jeopardize their share in the benefits of current and future transactions. Social capital is productive. Two farmers exchanging tools can get more work done with less physical capital, and rotating credit associations can generate pools of financial capital for increased entrepreneurial activity. As a "moral resource," social capital also tends to accumulate when it is used and be depleted when not, thus creating the possibility of both virtuous and vicious cycles that manifest themselves in highly civic—as well as terribly uncivic—communities.[13]

Civic innovation, as we use the term in this book, mobilizes social capital in ways that promote broad democratic norms, enhance responsible and in-

clusive citizenship, and build the civic capacities of communities and institutions to solve problems through the public work of citizens themselves, often in collaboration with various market, state, and professional actors and
through policy designs that foster self-government. Indeed, civic innovation
often emerges from the initiative of state actors or is sustained through various kinds of government supports—a pattern not dissimilar to earlier periods in the growth of civic associations in America, as Theda Skocpol has
argued.[14] And innovation often draws upon the expertise of "civic professionals," ranging from the public administrators who collaborate with Save
The Bay and the professional organizers who train local community leaders
in COPS to the parish nurses in coalitions for healthy communities and the
civic journalists transforming their newsroom practice in profound ways.[15]
Our treatment of civic innovation is thus broader than that arising strictly
"from the bottom up" but is also delimited quite intentionally. It draws upon
certain traditions within normative democratic theory, as well as upon
specific analytic frameworks for understanding the problems of democratic
institutions, viable communities, and effective policies in the contemporary
United States. We do not cast the net so broadly as to include all forms of
social capital, each dimension of civil society, or every mode of citizen participation. Why do we make the choices that we do?

One reason, of course, is that not all forms of social capital lend themselves well to public problem solving, and some forms work in the opposite
direction by fostering deep distrust of outsiders or fundamentalist beliefs that
brook no compromise with adversaries. The world is filled with forms of social capital that promote ethnic hostility and erode capacities for democratic governance. It is also replete with social capital that lies relatively dormant
as a resource for democratic politics or community problem solving. Thus,
the organizational forms and strategies for mobilizing social capital matter
a great deal. COPS represents an important civic innovation, for instance,
because it mobilizes religious norms and church networks—and, through the
latter, family networks—in such a way as to increase the power of disadvantaged communities in the larger polity, build trust across racial boundaries,
develop new forms of collaboration with other political and institutional actors, and generate policy and program designs that enhance human capital
in the face of a changing postindustrial economy. Civic innovations in health,
environment, and social services also mobilize the social capital of congregations to develop new problem-solving capacities. But many congregations,
while performing important functions, have not made their social capital
available for community problem solving on a broader scale, and some have
mobilized so as to make collaboration with diverse others extremely difficult.

The same can be said for other kinds of social capital. Some neighborhood
associations function primarily to maintain exclusivity, while others become
broadly representative, collaborate with all sorts of civic, community devel-

opment, and environmental groups, and even evolve into citywide systems with formal powers of spending and governance. Some sporting clubs remain focused on recreation, while others take upon themselves larger tasks of conservation and restoration, and work in complex partnerships with environmental groups, agricultural associations, businesses, and public agencies. We do not mean to deny that those associations with less ambitious or explicitly public tasks do many good things or provide a reservoir of trust, norms, and networks available for various challenges of social cooperation. The youth soccer league that is just a soccer league can still teach kids the value of teamwork and respect for diverse skill levels and cultural backgrounds, and it can still link parents in ways that may prove helpful for addressing other community problems. As active (if not always competent) soccer coaches ourselves, we know this. Our focus here, however, remains on those forms of social capital that are mobilized for broader tasks of civic collaboration.[16]

We also delimit the story of civic innovation in this book by not including new social movements or public interest groups per se, though clearly by any comprehensive and purely descriptive classification they represent important innovations within civil society in recent decades. To be sure, new social movements such as the environmental movement and public interest groups such as the Sierra Club play an important role in our story. As we have noted, public interest groups expand citizen representation and power considerably. And movements generate new values, identities, and networks critical for civic innovation. They creatively disrupt set ways of seeing and doing, mobilize new power resources, and win new rights to participate, without which other kinds of civic innovation would often be unable to emerge. Thus, social movements and public interest groups play an important role in the social learning processes we analyze. Nonetheless, public interest groups also contribute to problems of governance and often constrain or displace effective community problem solving. And movements can generate the kinds of value fundamentalism and fragmented identities that impede those collaborative and deliberative designs at the heart of our story, which emerge often as a way of moving beyond the perceived limits of existing movement approaches.[17]

We do not wish, however, to draw the boundaries too rigidly. Many forms of civic environmentalism, for instance, emerge within the broader environmental movement, even as they challenge some of its emphases. Some community innovations draw from the relational organizing legacies of feminism, even as they have little or no formal connection with women's organizations or agendas. Many leading innovators formed their core civic identities in a range of participatory democratic movements of the past four decades, even as they later significantly revised their action frames and practices. And many of the innovations upon which we focus have come to adopt movement labels and traits themselves. This is true for the "watershed movement," the "community development movement," the "healthy communities movement," and the "civic journalism movement." To complicate our story still further, we analyze an emergent "civic renewal movement" and make an argument for building this further as a way of rechanneling some of the vital democratic energies of recent social movements while holding in check some of their more problematic features.

What role can civic innovation play, however, if overall trends show a serious depletion of stocks of social capital in the United States over the past several decades and if Americans are increasingly "bowling alone," as Robert Putnam has argued? For Putnam, many measures of formal associational membership show clear declines. Participation in church-related groups and regular attendance at church services are down by at least one-fifth over the past twenty years. The percentage of parents involved in Parent-Teacher Associations (PTA) or unaffiliated parent-teacher organizations has suffered substantial decline since the 1960s. Union membership has steadily eroded since the 1950s, falling to less than half its peak. Membership in the General Federation of Women's Clubs is down by 59 percent since 1964, and in the League of Women Voters by 42 percent since 1969. And membership in fraternal organizations like the Elks, Lions, and Jaycees is also down significantly. Especially worrisome is the collapse of the activist membership core of civic organizations of all sorts, which witnessed a 45 percent drop from 1985 to 1994 alone. Thus, as Putnam argues, by this measure "nearly half of America's civic infrastructure was obliterated in barely a decade." Neither self-help groups nor social movements have effectively counteracted these trends. The former are not closely associated with other forms of community involvement, and the latter have generally resulted in professionalized, direct-mail organizations with little or no active membership. Even when mass membership in "tertiary" organizations that do not rely on face-to-face interaction among members, such as the Environmental Defense Fund, are included, as well as professional associations that have increased along with rising occupational levels, total associational membership has declined significantly between 1974 and 1994 within all educational categories. Other forms of associational ties, such as family and informal neighborhood socializing, have also eroded, as has generalized social trust, which is highly correlated with associational membership.[18]

Deep social changes underlie these trends, according to Putnam. Women's increasing entry into the labor force makes them less available for community activities, and suburban sprawl draws people away from local involvements. But the biggest factors are the technological shifts in leisure that lead to the private listening and viewing habits associated with the walkman, the CD player, and especially television, and the replacement of the generation whose civic identities were formed by the World War II ethos of national unity and patriotism. But even if some of the other causes are still uncertain, he argues, "Every year over the last decade or two, millions of citizens more have withdrawn from the affairs of their communities," and the civic generation born between 1910 and 1940 is now being displaced by baby boomers and generation X-ers who are much less engaged.

The data that Putnam presents are undoubtedly worrisome. If he is correct—and his most recent data are considerably more compelling than his earlier data—the task of renovating civic capacities to grapple with the kinds of public problems and policy challenges that face communities and the nation at the beginning of the twenty-first century will indeed be daunting. But even if aggregate levels of social capital prove to have eroded much less than he claims, perhaps even to have increased when other measures are included, the task is still quite formidable, because the question is ultimately not one of quantitative aggregates of social capital. Rather, it is one of qualitative forms of civic democracy that, when combined with other tools of governance, can provide effective responses to the increasingly complex and obdurate problems we face and can help to form a nation of effective citizens. In simple terms, the issue is not absolute levels but qualitative kinds and complex mixes in specific community, institutional, and policy contexts.

By some measures, levels of citizen involvement still provide relatively robust foundations upon which to build. Verba, Schlozman, and Brady's massive study of civic voluntarism presents data that support Americans' deserved reputation for high levels of involvement in voluntary associations. Of particular note is the evidence that participation over the past several decades has modestly increased at the level of community and local problem-solving activities and that the decrease in voter turnout has not been accompanied by a general decrease in citizen activism, even on campaign-related activities.[19] When Baumgartner and Walker redesigned the standard survey question on membership in voluntary associations to allow for the new types of groups that had emerged after the 1960s, as well as multiple memberships in any one type of group, they found not only 187 percent more group affiliations than would have been reported with the standard question but that "the overwhelming majority of people's connections with the associational world are through groups that operate mainly in their immediate communities."[20] The Pew Research Center for People and the Press found a sharp contrast with Putnam's findings in its survey of citizen involvement and trust in Philadelphia and its surrounding counties. Philadelphians remain actively involved in community affairs and are meaningfully linked to social support networks. Seven in ten reported confidence in their abilities to have a big or moderate impact on their community, including 50 percent of those who displayed very low levels of interpersonal trust. Of the 41 percent who tried to get neighbors to work together to improve their neighborhoods, 85 percent reported success.[21] Robert Wuthnow's survey and in-depth interviews show that, while many traditional civic associations struggle to remain relevant and viable, citizens continue to generate new ways of engagement based on "loose connections."[22] Other survey and comparative data show relatively strong levels of associational membership and volunteerism in the United States.[23] However, the National Commission on Civic Renewal's composite Index of National Civic Health (INCH)—which includes political, family, trust, membership, and security components—reveals a weakening of our overall civic condition between 1984 and 1994, with an upturn since then.[24] Alan Wolfe's *One Nation, After All* establishes strong support for the American political creed and its core values of civic responsibility among the broad middle class, regardless of race.[25] And James Davison Hunter and Carl Bowman's survey research shows this to be true even for poor people, who are often thought to be far more alienated than other citizens.[26]

Everett Ladd, former director of the Roper Center, contests Putnam's findings in broad terms, declaring that "not even one set of systematic data support the thesis of *Bowling Alone*." PTA membership may have declined but largely because parents have created new local parent-teacher organizations (PTOs) unaffiliated with the national organization, so that they could keep a greater portion of dues and engage in local improvement efforts independent of the PTA's advocacy agendas and organizational ties. Parental engagement is energetic, expansive, and increasing. Affiliations with old, mainline Protestant denominations may be declining, but other denominations are increasing membership, and overall church participation remains strong and may be rising. Adult volunteers in groups like the Girl Scouts and youth soccer have risen very substantially in the past two decades, and there is a "vast proliferation of community service groups."[27]

Our analysis of innovation in specific arenas reveals a variety of patterns of social capital formation and depletion. In the environmental arena, new forms of social capital have been generated on an extensive scale, and old forms mobilized for environmental problem solving in ways previously unknown. Thus we witness the proliferation of "lake watches," "stream teams," and "friends of the river" groups that perform volunteer monitoring of water quality. We see "land trusts," "stewardship networks," "watershed associations," and "ecosystem partnerships" engaged in restoration work, and "environmental justice" groups developing strategies to reduce toxics and protect minority health. Virtually all of these are new civic forms created in response to emergent problems and alternative frames for thinking about them. But we also observe the mobilization of social capital from traditional civic associations, such as local Leagues of Women Voters, Scout troops, fishing clubs, and religious congregations. Even if one were to subtract mere dues-paying members and groups devoted purely to advocacy, the level of community involvement and civic innovation in the environmental arena has advanced enormously in the wake of the contemporary environmental movement and federal and state regulation over the past three decades.

The significant innovations and expanding networks in community organizing and community development, on the other hand, have progressed amid other indicators of the depletion of social capital in inner-city communities. Some causes of this depletion are well known: urban renewal policies that led to the concentration and isolation of the poor in inner-city housing projects, the exodus of the black middle class once discriminatory housing barriers were lowered, and the flight of jobs to the suburbs or abroad. These left inner-city African Americans, in particular, with fewer cross-class associational ties and other resources for maintaining their communities, and the resulting crime increases left them more fearful of congregating in public spaces. But the depletion of social capital has also elicited energetic experimentation in mobilizing those forms still remaining. On the broader urban level, neighborhood associations, crime watches, and community-visioning projects have spread considerably over the past several decades.

In health, where patient empowerment and community involvement were virtually nonexistent in the face of professional dominance until the early 1960s, significant innovations in community organizing, citizen representation, self-help groups, and healthy community coalitions have arisen, though these appear weaker than in the urban development and environmental arenas. Generating new civic capacities to address the problems that health care poses in a society with high-tech medical options, rapidly escalating expectations, an aging population living longer with chronic illness, and the persistent lack of universal insurance coverage will be particularly daunting, whether older forms of social capital have eroded or not.

Civic innovation in journalism—which is the latest to emerge among our four cases, though one that can serve as a critical complement to the others—is a response to the crisis of newspaper readership and the debasement of public discourse in the media. It attempts to achieve more robust forms of civic deliberation and agenda setting and to link these to the decision making of elected public officials and other institutional actors. In some cases, however, the innovative deliberative models of civic journalism are directly coupled with associational networks that might assume some of the tasks of community problem solving. They creatively join deliberative democratic and social-capital-enhancing strategies to renew civic life, without compromising professional norms of journalistic objectivity and public accountability.

On the question of overall trends in social capital, we count ourselves among the worried, though we disagree with some of Putnam's calculations and explanations. And on the ultimate outcomes of civic renewal, we must remain agnostic. Indeed, even if innovation becomes considerably more robust, there is no guarantee that the problems posed by an increasingly complex and global society will not continually outrun our civic and political capacities. But amid the worrisome signs, there is already clear evidence of the kinds of civic innovation that could anchor and instruct broad revitalization strategies in the coming years.

Obstinate inventiveness, indeed, often produces genuine surprise. Michael Schudson, one of our most renowned sociologists of the American press, recently noted at the James Batten Awards for civic journalism that, had someone asked ten or fifteen years earlier whether a significant movement to reform the press was possible, he would have cautioned that it was highly unlikely. In fact, he would have told the leading innovators to "Go home" and counseled their foundation supporters to "spend their money doing something more useful."

And, he adds, "I would have been wrong."[28]

SOCIAL LEARNING

By looking at civic innovation as an extended learning process over several decades, we are able to examine how engaged citizens, community organizers, and professional practitioners of various sorts have grappled with a new set of complex problems within changed political and organizational contexts, how they have mobilized old and new forms of social capital, and how they have attempted to link these to innovative policy designs that enhance democracy. In studying the process of social learning, we draw from three analytical traditions: (1) policy learning, (2) organizational learning and regulatory culture, and (3) participatory democratic theory.

Policy Learning

Policy learning refers to relatively enduring alterations of particular policy instruments or broader policy paradigms, which result from experience and complex feedback loops. In one influential version of this approach developed by Paul Sabatier and Hank Jenkins-Smith, policy learning can occur within or across the multiple advocacy coalitions that have typically come to characterize specific policy subsystems since the 1960s, when the latter became accessible to a much wider variety of groups than at any time previously. Such advocacy coalitions include an array of interest groups, policy analysts, journalists, and government actors from all levels of the federal system, without any presumption of innovation proceeding from top-down institutional initiative ("Potomac fever"). The time frame most useful for examining the learning process is a decade or more, often through multiple policy cycles, if policy research is to fulfill its enlightenment function, since "numerous studies have shown that ambitious programs which appeared after a few years to be abject failures received more favorable evaluations when seen in a longer time frame; conversely, initial success may evaporate over time."

Policy learning is an ongoing process of search, experimentation, and adaptation motivated by the desire to realize core policy beliefs, including a "deep core" of fundamental normative beliefs about power and justice. It builds upon the cumulative impact of findings from analytic studies, as well as upon the ordinary "usable knowledge" of citizens derived from everyday problem solving. And it responds to disturbances and failures in the larger social and economic system, as well as to shifts in the distribution of political resources and governing coalitions. Learning from experience, however, proves messy and difficult because experience is itself ambiguous in a world where

> performance gaps are difficult to measure, well-developed causal theories are often lacking, controlled experimentation is virtually impossible, opponents are doing everything possible to muddle the situation and otherwise to impede one from learning, and even allies' motives are often suspect because of personal and organizational rivalries.[29]

But policy learning can nonetheless be studied, its theorists insist, by examining individual career profiles and biographies, as well as through group and network analysis, content analysis, and the sociology of ideas.

Policy learning is important to our story to the extent that "public policy for democracy" emerges over time in conjunction with innovative civic practice. Public policy for democracy, according to Helen Ingram, Steven Rathgeb Smith, and Anne Larason Schneider, is designed "to empower, enlighten, and engage citizens in the process of self-government."[30] In contrast to most policy, designing for democracy aims to strengthen civil society and build community capacities, rather than lodge ever-greater power and initiative in the hands of experts and administrators. It motivates action through self-regulation and self-learning, rather than through forms of authority that breed dependence. To the extent that all policies are teachings, policy for democracy aims to teach civic responsibility, community initiative, and the arts of public deliberation, and it encourages citizens to weigh relative costs and possible trade-offs, rather than appeal to substantive rights that are non-negotiable. It does not deceive citizens about the cost of public goods, or manipulate them through simplistic slogans or symbols. It encourages them to mobilize the hidden assets of their communities and institutions, to define common values, and to collaborate across divisions wherever this might prove fruitful. And it enables and requires bureaucrats to facilitate deliberative and collaborative civic practice by providing appropriate resources and technical assistance.

In our story, civic innovation and policy learning for democracy represent a process of search, experimentation, and adaptation motivated by deep norms of democratic participation and power. These norms have a long history in the United States and have been reinforced and reinterpreted in recent decades in the wake of democratic social movements, changes in administrative law, and legislated rights to participate in many policy arenas. Learning has responded to problem-solving knowledge generated by ordinary citizens in their communities and by practitioners from various kinds of civic and business organizations and at various levels of government. It has also responded to scientific paradigm shifts and technical knowledge accumulation in some arenas, such as ecosystem science and epidemiology, which have helped to legitimate community-based environmental and health strategies. And learning has been triggered by changing configurations of power and conflict in local arenas, as well as in national governing coalitions, and in response to new opportunities as well as perceived failures in policy tools and participatory programs themselves. Networks that support innovation and policy learning for democracy have developed considerably over the past several decades. Such networks share information, reflect on problems and failures, diffuse best practices, provide technical assistance, and fund local projects. They include multiple constellations of grassroots organizers; foundation program officers and centers; agency officials at local, state, and federal levels; university institutes and consulting firms; professional staff in banks, businesses, health systems, and newspapers; mainline civic associations; and social movement organizations.

Learning is clearly evident in the activist biographies and professional career profiles of many leading innovators over several decades. Like the former head of a major regional chapter of Students for a Democratic Society (SDS) who has spearheaded various community partnerships on the environment at EPA, or the former antirape and antinuclear organizer who has convened tens of thousands of citizens in deliberative health values forums in California, or the former antiwar and community development activists who have pioneered statewide watershed associations and volunteer stewardship restoration networks and strategies, many civic innovators have drawn upon a deep core of participatory beliefs at various junctures in their ensuing careers, even when they have substantially revised their approaches so as to emphasize collaboration and trust-building more than they may have initially done.

Organizational Learning and Regulatory Culture

A second helpful analytic tradition, organizational learning theory, has emerged with the crisis of bureaucratic organizations in an information society characterized by dynamic complexity, where performance increasingly depends on the capacity to learn amid uncertainty, experimentation, and inevitable error, rather than on the application of formal procedures and lines of authority. While this approach has been applied to many different kinds of organizations, participatory mechanisms have been repeatedly identified as key to facilitating the learning process. These include openness of information, self-directed work teams, and voluntary learning networks as a parallel organizational architecture. They also include building shared vision and consensus through dialogue and leadership that promote adaptive work. And, as Paul Light argues, flatter hierarchies and democratization are essential for sustaining innovation in nonprofit and government organizations that engage the public as citizens, partners, and coproducers.[31]

Organizational learning theory also holds that, under certain conditions, deliberative and collaborative regulatory cultures can emerge in response to the limits of command-and-control, expert-dominated, and adversarial approaches. Among the key factors driving the learning process have been protest from citizens and public interest organizations, as well as the establishment of citizen participation rights, which balance power dynamics by giving citizen groups new capacities to punish and reward other parties. This balance of power—along with continued interdependence and everyday interaction among adversaries confronted with strategic decisions about reducing transaction costs that threaten valued outcomes—can eventually produce enough trust to sustain deliberative and collaborative searches for mutually beneficial solutions. The result can transform regulatory cultures. Empowered citizen and public interest groups are more likely than weaker actors to relinquish their commitment to inflexible, command-and-control regulation and to become capable of learning collaboratively with corporate and regulatory officials. Community right-to-know laws can further extend the influence of broader social networks on the "theories in action" within firms and bind managers to the norms of the larger community. Administrators, for their part, can redefine their role as one of enabling a process of "civic discovery." Self-organizing and polycentric systems of common-pool resource governance capable of adaptive learning and experimentation often emerge with regard to forests and fisheries. And the constitution of the administrative state can be shifted fundamentally towards a "democratic experimentalism," as Michael Dorf and Charles Sabel argue in their analysis of new forms of self-government within regulatory arenas.[32]

Participatory Democratic Theory

A third tradition that emphasizes learning is participatory democratic theory itself, which stresses the educative function of participating in community and political affairs for creating the kinds of citizens capable of sustaining democracy. Through active participation, citizens become more knowledgeable about the political system, develop a greater sense of their own efficacy, and widen their horizons beyond their own narrow self-interest to consider a broader public good. This tradition rightly begins with Alexis de Tocqueville, whose visit to America in the nineteenth century prompted him to recognize how participation in town meetings and voluntary associations permits the citizen to practice "the art of government in the small sphere within his reach." Participation engenders a sense of ownership and responsibility for improving local conditions, and refines the "passions that commonly embroil society" so as to interest "the greatest possible number of persons in the common weal." For Tocqueville, town meetings "are to liberty what primary schools are to science; they bring it within people's reach, they teach men how to use and how to enjoy it."[33] These arguments were taken up as part of the 1960s movements for participatory democracy and were further developed in an influential book by Carole Pateman in 1970 and later by Benjamin Barber and others.[34]

Jane Mansbridge's important book, *Beyond Adversary Democracy*, has enriched this approach enormously by theorizing unitary and adversary democratic processes in the context of specific participatory communities' understandings of their practice and their emergent capacity to reflect and learn. Specifically, she argues that participation can provide experiential knowledge and opportunities to deliberate so that citizens can come to recognize when their interests converge and when they conflict. They can thereby develop appropriate forms to manage their affairs democratically under each set of circumstances and to switch between different practices when this serves them best.[35]

Sirianni has extended this learning model by examining how participatory democracy within the feminist movement and various women's organizations and networks over the past three decades has prompted a sustained process of critical self-reflection that might be characterized as "learning pluralism." The early movement, especially in the small groups, suffered from a variety of participatory ills: the tyranny of structurelessness, false consensus, imposed sisterly virtue, lack of democratic accountability, and the marginalization of those unwilling or unable to make totalizing time commitments. A process of learning, however, emerged rather quickly. It drew upon internally generated movement resources, such as small-group skills and an ethic of careful listening and empathy. It also utilized pluralist democratic theory in the writings of those, such as Robert Dahl and Michael Walzer, who were sympathetic to the goals of participatory democracy yet poignant in their critique of its deficiencies.[36]

Because of a variety of methodological obstacles, such as the difficulty and expense of doing massive before-and-after studies that measure the effect of participation on people's characters, Mansbridge argues that no one has been able to prove definitively whether participation makes better citizens, even though she remains convinced that it does.[37] This question, however, cannot be answered apart from the specific organizational forms and reflective practices of participation, and these evolve as part of a broader social learning process. Compare, for instance, the concrete models and tools for consensus seeking and dispute resolution available to both grassroots groups and diverse institutional stakeholders in the 1980s and 1990s with those available in the 1970s, when unitary democracy first became a focus of research. The earlier period was a vital seedbed but with relatively crude methods and uncertain results. The current one is flourishing with considerable success; it systematically incorporates lessons from the field and insights from theory and is sustained by vibrant and ever-growing networks of practitioners and institutional centers.[38]

Compare also those neighborhood associations that are part of well-structured citywide systems and those that are not. The former show a greater impact of face-to-face participation on citizen learning as evidenced by political knowledge, sense of political efficacy, and ability to look beyond the interests of one's neighborhood. And these educative effects are especially strong among low-income groups, which generally suffer from a variety of forms of participatory inequality.[39] Or compare the disciplined and highly reflective IAF evaluation sessions, which analyze the preceding action's impact on long-term public relationships with power holders, to many other forms of community organizing that haphazardly attend to such issues. In short, the structure of participation systems, deliberative democratic designs, and organizing models matters. It matters because it determines whether and how participation is educative and cultivates good citizens. And these forms and practices themselves evolve as part of a larger historical learning process, as we shall see.

The continued development of participatory and deliberative democratic theory since the late 1960s has served as an intellectual resource for critical reflection and learning within various networks, though practice has often run considerably ahead of theory. Public participation staff in federal agencies in the 1970s were often recruited from graduate programs in political science, where they had completed dissertations on practical and theoretical aspects of citizen participation. Conferences among federal officials and citizen participation groups regularly included reflections from democratic theory. This was evident already in the mid-1970s, with the Interagency Council on Citizen Participation (ICCP).[40] Democratic theory has also been utilized for learning within the IAF, civic journalism, health decisions, community planning, and other networks. Many innovators have drawn inspiration from the pragmatist tradition of John Dewey, a resource for democratic experimentation that should never be underestimated in the American context. They have utilized the German critical theory tradition of Jürgen Habermas on issues of communicative competence and discursive democracy, and incorporated insights from the lively debates on pluralism and democracy within contemporary American political theory. Other theorists and activist intellectuals, such as Harry Boyte, Benjamin Barber, David Mathews, Jean Bethke Elshtain, Robert Bellah, and Amitai Etzioni refined many of the themes of civic democracy and raised them to new levels of public accessibility. They were widely read among civic innovators in many arenas and, in turn, began to formulate theory with an eye to ongoing practice at the grassroots. Thus, not only does participatory democratic theory itself develop very significantly as a critical resource over the course of the past several decades, but its relationship to the world of practice also becomes increasingly more direct and reciprocal.[41]

These three analytical and theoretical traditions—policy learning, organizational learning and regulatory culture, and participatory democratic theory—can help us understand civic innovation in the United States. Of course, learning proceeds along varied and complex paths in response to political opportunities and constraints specific to each arena, as well as to recognized limits and failures within participatory organizations and projects themselves. Often learning becomes blocked, organizations dissolve, and practitioners disperse, though many carry a set of critical lessons to other venues as they renew their work. Sometimes learning is considerable at the level of local activity, but bureaucratic resistance or a change in administration obstruct further progress or steer it along more circuitous routes. And, needless to say, there is no guarantee that it will all "add up," either in a decisive paradigm shift within any given policy domain or in civic renewal on a larger scale. But a cumulative process is evident along a variety of dimensions that can serve as a substantial, indeed indispensable, foundation upon which to build.

THE CONTESTED LEGACY OF PARTICIPATORY DEMOCRACY

Our interpretation of civic innovation as an extended process of social learning over several decades beginning in the 1960s differs in important respects from a number of other interpretations of the participatory democracy of this earlier era. Most notable are our differences with many New Left scholars, as well as Samuel Huntington and James Morone.

First, Left scholarly proponents of participatory democracy, such as Doug McAdam, James Max Fendrich, Jack Whelan, and Richard Flacks, who have analyzed the careers of sixties youth activists, do recognize important continuities between earlier and later stages, but primarily in activists' sustaining personal commitments. Despite their own evidence that many activists have thoughtfully redefined their commitments so as to place more emphasis on community problem solving or civic involvement through congregation-sponsored activities, these authors see broader historical continuity predominantly in terms of movement politics and an awaited upsurge of Leftist activism. James Miller, whose compelling account of Students for a Democratic Society initially pointed out how sixties veterans modified participatory democracy in light of their mature experience, seems to have retreated in the face of his Left critics by restricting his understanding of continuities to women's, gay, and green movements and to the legacy of the "wild culture" of the period. The civic republican approach to participatory democracy, which the student leaders of SDS had derived from Tocqueville and Dewey and which competed with a more volatile existentialist version during the sixties, now seems to have lived on for Miller only in political theory. Some interpreters of the sixties, such as Meta Mendel-Reyes, dismiss any life-cycle and maturation analogies, while others, such as Stuart Burns, see the inevitable life-cycle imperatives of family and jobs as simply a drag on participatory commitments, rather than as an opportunity to modify and ramify them in less totalizing ways through other community networks and institutional settings. The analytical frame of repression and/or cooptation in many Leftist accounts reinforces the overriding sense of historical discontinuity in the participatory democracy of earlier and later periods, with the exception of a few ideologically preferred grassroots movements.[42]

Our research, by contrast, reveals that, for an important set of civic innovators in subsequent decades, there occurred considerably greater and quite self-conscious learning and revision that have built upon their often profound and identity-forming experiences in a broad range of earlier settings: the "participatory democracy" of SDS, the "beloved community" of the Student Nonviolent Coordinating Committee (SNCC), the citizenship schools of the Southern Christian Leadership Conference (SCLC), the "maximum feasible participation" of Community Action, Head Start, and Neighborhood Health Center programs, the "widespread citizen participation" of Model Cities, the "broadly representative citizen participation" of Health Systems Agencies, the consciousness-raising groups and community-based rape crisis and battered women's shelters of the feminist movement, the self-help groups of the disability rights and independent living movements, the urban ministries of mainline Protestant and Catholic denominations, old-style Alinsky organizations, and all sorts of democratically run collectives and other grassroots efforts. The self-conception of the great majority of activist innovators whom we have interviewed is one of having matured and learned from experience.

These innovators view themselves as having become more strategic and effective over time, as manifested in how they structure their organizations and choose their tactics. They place much greater emphasis upon building relationships of trust with diverse stakeholders and adversaries and much less upon personalized fulfillment or intense and ideologically pure identity-forming activities. They see themselves as having reached out to broader sections of the American public and as having become more richly enmeshed in their local communities. They do not feel burdened by the guilt of not having been able to maintain their previous forms of radical and totalizing commitment but are generally hopeful and energized about the pragmatic work and commitments that they can sustain. Nonetheless, they worry deeply about the state of American democracy and agonize over how to make their own work more effective and broadly relevant. Perhaps most important, they see themselves as having progressively learned to do democracy in ways more consistent with their original ideals and more appropriate to the complex political and institutional environments and policy conundrums that they face. As we hope to demonstrate, the pragmatic choices that underlay these self-perceptions can be reasonably viewed as, by and large, wise ones that testify to the coming of age of a civic generation—or, more accurately, an important segment of one whose work continues to manifest broad democratic possibilities and to engage younger and more politically diverse activists not directly socialized by the movements of the 1960s.[43]

A second influential interpretation of the participatory democracy of the 1960s and 1970s is that of Samuel Huntington, who argues that this period of "creedal passion" has produced an "excess of democracy" that not only has eroded capacities for governance, but has also had deleterious effects on participation itself. A highly educated, mobilized, and participatory society, Huntington argues, generates a "demand overload" and weakens institutions such as parties and the presidency charged with aggregating interests. Expectations rise much faster than they can be met; political authority declines; and citizens' sense of political efficacy and trust actually declines as well. Participatory overload also produces increased policy polarization and further exacerbates the tendency of voters to withdraw. Huntington's analysis has served as an important filter in intellectual and policy circles and helped to dampen official enthusiasm for citizen participation. While anathema to participatory democrats of all stripes at the time, his argument has no small measure of truth, especially at the level of impacts on political institutions and the policy process. Highly mobilized public interest groups, hyperdemocracy in the use of initiative and referendum, the diffusion of power in Congress, and the proliferation of presidential primaries have exacerbated the problems of governance and have likely discouraged the participation of citizens with moderate views.[44]

Examining civic innovation as an extended learning process, however, permits us to recognize how some of the creedal passion became tempered over time and how in a variety of arenas, if not those upon which Huntington focused, there began to emerge new participatory innovations for aggregating interests, resolving conflict, and solving practical problems in communities. These were still largely invisible when Huntington first developed his analysis in the mid-1970s, and it is thus hardly surprising that a powerful argument about the excesses of democracy would become so influential. It is even less surprising in view of the dominant public philosophy of rights-based liberalism at the time and the role played within it by those such as Ralph Nader, whose claims for direct participation tended to emphasize those forms with the least potential for deliberation and problem solving, such as the initiative and referendum or constitutional rights empowering consumers, workers, and communities to take direct action in the courts.[45]

Our analysis also differs in important ways from a third influential inter-pretation of the participatory democracy of the 1960s and 1970s, that of James Morone. In *The Democratic Wish,* Morone presents a sweeping rein-terpretation of American state building from the early Republic to the con-temporary period in terms of repeatedly disappointed cycles of reform based on attempts to realize the "myth of communal democracy." This myth, which presumes the direct participation of a united people, reasserts itself with great regularity in response to the institutional stalemate and fragmentation char-acteristic of American liberalism. As this myth gathers force and attempts to implement new political institutions, however, the united republican people dissolves into a clash of interests and struggles for representation by new groups. Reformist energies are channeled away from more radical goals and real political authority. And innocence of organizational dynamics is super-seded by crude organizational maintenance as the basic logic of develop-mental learning within participatory settings. The ironic result is new ad-ministrative power but a state still too weak and fragmented to pursue genuine common interests and communal needs. The communal myth proves itself chimerical. The search for direct democracy simply builds up bureaucracy.[46]

Morone's analyses of the seven episodes since the early Republic in which this dynamic is supposed to have played itself out have much to recommend them, and the two post-1960s cases (Community Action and Health Systems Agencies) inform our own thinking in certain ways. Yet the general model displays a tendency to exaggerate strongly the extent to which participatory reformers presumed a myth of a united people with an already established consensus rather than a more realistic view in which consensus had to be forged in practice and often through conflict. It draws the temporal and or-ganizational boundaries of the narratives in such a way as to miss any evi-dence of learning or refinement of practice that does not fit the stylized poles of participatory innocence and organizational maintenance. And it leaves one wondering from whence the practical wisdom needed to "marry dem-ocratic wishes to contemporary institutions" in a realistic way could ever come.[47] By examining civic innovation as an extended process of social learn-ing rather than an endlessly repeated cycle of disappointed myth making and by recognizing civic actors as capable of critical and reflective revisions in practice, our framework is designed to provide a potentially more fruit-ful way for answering just this sort of question.

A NOTE ON METHOD

We have employed a variety of methods to understand the process of civic innovation in the United States over the past four decades. From October 1993 to January 2000 we interviewed 738 individuals, of whom we classify

467 as innovative civic practitioners: community organizers; founders, leaders, and staff of major organizing networks and intermediaries; neighborhood association activists; civic journalists; consultants and technical assistance providers; foundation officers; and federal, state, and local agency staff responsible for citizen participation programs. Our practitioner interviews included, wherever possible, biographical information about formative participatory experiences and ideas, critical turning points, formal and informal network ties, and changing perspectives and practices in individual careers and organizational development. They also included reflections on current practices and anticipated challenges.

We attended and took extensive field notes at 141 practitioner conferences, trainings, strategic planning retreats, and board meetings of various networks, as well as neighborhood association and town meetings. We examined participant lists and biographical data from these meetings, where these were provided, as well as directories of specific organizations and organizational fields. We kept detailed logs or summary notes of approximately nine hundred additional telephone conferences and planning calls. We also examined the publications, strategic planning documents, annual reports, websites, and board membership lists of various associations and networks. We reviewed approximately 280 community action guides and training manuals and videos, which provided important insight into how participatory models and techniques have changed over time, as did government agency handbooks and field guidances, especially when triangulated with other sources that testify to how such manuals were utilized and modified in practice. We examined primary sources, such as government, foundation, and consultant reports; evaluations and case studies; video and audio tapes of projects; and conference proceedings dating back to the 1970s. Our analysis of public journalism projects included field observation, print, and broadcast analysis, and interviews with editors, journalists, civic leaders, public officials, neighborhood associations, and citizen panels in ten cities. Secondary historical sources and social science studies of participatory organizations, networks, programs, and ideas also proved indispensable throughout.[48]

To help build further capacities for learning and innovation in various organizations and networks, and as part of a broader movement for civic renewal, we have approached our work from a participatory action research framework.[49] To this end, we have served in various roles as advisors, evaluators, trainers, faculty, awards jurors, website developers, and steering committee and executive board members for a variety of organizations and projects.[50] As noted earlier, one of us served as research director of the Reinventing Citizenship Project in 1994, which was funded by the Ford Foundation and convened in conjunction with the Domestic Policy Council at the White House. This project provided an opportunity to consult with and interview leaders in federal agencies who wanted to explore how to make active citizenship a central component of reinventing government and how their strategies might be informed by some of the best practices developed to date both within agencies and especially in the civic sector. A number of participants in this and subsequent projects joined us in convening teams of leading practitioners and academics to further survey best cases in various arenas and develop strategies for learning and capacity building (some of these projects are discussed in chapter 6).

This is a book about social learning and capacity building over several decades, not a systematic analysis of the results of civic approaches to problem solving in comparison to other approaches. Thus, our methods do not attempt to measure outcomes directly. To be sure, learning is partly driven by the search for better outcomes, as measured by indicators of ecosystem restoration, job-training effectiveness, housing production, and community health, and it responds to the perceived relative ineffectiveness of other approaches under changing conditions. Some studies have generated systematic quantitative and comparative evidence of hard measures, as well as softer ones, such as the sense of political efficacy, and we cite these where they are relevant. But we do not try to do this for any particular model or arena as a whole, nor for the four arenas combined. Our intention is different, since it includes learning in the face of limits and failures, as well as successes, and since it raises issues about effective citizenship that are normative and political, as well as empirical.

OVERVIEW OF THE BOOK

The next four chapters analyze civic innovation within four arenas: urban development, environment, health, and journalism. The first three represent major arenas characterized by local mobilization and federal action since the 1960s but also reveal distinct dynamics and policy challenges. In the fourth arena, civic journalism has emerged only over the past decade and is independent of local organizing and government initiative, though its mission to create a more vital public sphere complements work in the other three and engages local government and civic actors in new ways. Innovation in each of these four arenas has also been important to the emergence of a broader civic renewal movement over the past decade. The concluding chapter examines this movement and some larger theoretical and political questions bearing upon its future.

Chapter 2 analyzes community organizing and community development in urban areas, beginning with the Community Action Program of the War on Poverty and the heritage of Alinsky organizing, which extended back several decades further but was given new life in the context of African American and Latino movements of the 1960s and neighborhood movements of the 1970s. We focus on three broad streams of innovation: congregation-based community organizing, which emerged directly out of the Alinsky tradition; community development corporations and revitalization strategies; and neighborhood associations and other forms of community visioning and collaboration at the urban and metropolitan level. Finally, we consider how these various approaches define ecologies of local organizing—whether they complement or conflict with each other, whether they can become components of different kinds of urban regimes, and what kinds of larger policy challenges remain.

Chapter 3 analyzes citizen participation as it came to be mandated in environmental legislation and administrative law in the 1970s and the gradual emergence of various civic, community-based, and collaborative approaches in the 1980s and 1990s. We examine the dynamics within three distinct policy arenas: (1) water and watersheds, (2) forest planning and ecosystem restoration, and (3) toxics and environmental justice. We attempt to develop an understanding of the complex relationships among innovative local projects, mainstream civic associations, and the environmental movement, including its professionalized and more radical wings. Finally, we examine recent proposals to restructure environmental policy and the EPA so as to build directly upon civic and community-based approaches, and the continuing obstacles to this reorientation.

Chapter 4 begins by examining the Neighborhood Health Centers and Health Systems Agencies that emerged, respectively, from the War on Poverty and federally mandated public participation in health planning. While each of these proved to be a limited foundation upon which to build, they nonetheless made important contributions, and a variety of other civic and community-based approaches emerged from them. Among subsequent models in the 1980s and 1990s, we examine the "health decisions" model of public deliberation in several states, with an extended case study of the Oregon Health Plan. Here, independently convened community meetings about underlying health values were utilized to educate the broad public and policy makers over an extended period, and were later incorporated as a key feature in the formal development of a plan by the legislature and an appointed Health Services Commission. We also examine the emergence of a "healthy communities" movement in the 1990s, which defines health broadly within community contexts and develops multisided partnerships among health care institutions, public health agencies, community, church and other groups. Healthy communities projects also build upon various other community-based and self-help approaches from the women's health movement, the disability rights and independent living movements, and AIDS/HIV prevention and care. Finally, we examine some of the opportunities and obstacles confronting deliberative and community-based approaches to health reform under managed care in a marketplace that is continually restructuring itself, yet is unable to stem the growth of the uninsured.

And we consider some of the civic lessons that might be drawn from the failure of the Clinton plan.

Chapter 5 analyzes the emergence of public journalism in the 1990s in response to the crisis of the press and politics in the United States. We examine the intellectual stirrings and entrepreneurial initiatives within academia, foundations, a major corporate newspaper chain, and local newsrooms that gave birth to this movement within journalism. We explore a range of practices that have been developed in print and broadcast media for enhancing the kind of public deliberation in which citizens are center stage and for fostering active forms of community problem solving and collaboration. Our analysis develops in-depth case studies of media institutions and partnerships in three cities—Madison, Wisconsin; Norfolk, Virginia; and Charlotte, North Carolina—and draws upon further analysis of projects in various other cities. We examine how these institutions have attempted to transform themselves into self-described "learning organizations" capable of sustaining civic innovation, and how journalists and editors have attempted to reinvent themselves as "civic professionals." We also look at the broader movement and its networks, as well as several national projects, and examine the controversy that civic journalism has sparked within the press. Finally, we analyze its potential in relation to other civic renewal efforts and within the larger political economy of the media and the information revolution.

In Chapter 6, the concluding chapter, we analyze the emergence of a civic renewal movement in the United States in the 1990s. This movement builds upon the various themes, models, and networks in community organizing and development, civic environmentalism, healthy communities, civic journalism, and other kinds of work such as community youth development and the civic engagement movement within higher education. But it also attempts to raise these themes to greater prominence in American politics and to define the contours of a much grander mission: revitalizing American democracy for the twenty-first century. The civic renewal movement seeks to build relationships across different associational networks and policy arenas, to further cultivate common language, and to catalyze mutual learning. It has also attempted to bridge some familiar ideological divides of left and right. We analyze core texts of the movement to discern how it has developed a collective action frame that attempts to reimagine what it means to be a citizen and how citizens act in the world. This constitutes the fundamental symbolic work of all movements in reconstructing identities and reframing the scope and meaning of civic action. We also examine the organizations and networks that are at the core of the movement and the role of key movement entrepreneurs.

Without a powerful movement capable of shifting the tides, too much of the vital public work and innovation of citizens analyzed in our core chapters will remain invisible and segmented, unable to inspire broad and vigorous commitment, and unable to redefine the underlying dynamics of "politics as usual." In contrast to those who would link civic renewal directly to party renewal, however, we argue for a principled nonpartisanship in building the movement, and we sketch a set of challenges that it must confront in the coming years if it is to develop into a robust movement with the capacity to have a major impact on American society and politics. In many ways, the civic renewal movement is an unlikely movement, and it diverges significantly from other recent democratic movements for civil rights and social justice, even as it builds upon their accomplishments in creating a more inclusive and participatory polity. The civic renewal movement thus does not have available to itself much of the rhetoric and repertoire of rights and justice movements. In other ways, however, the civic renewal movement can draw upon some of the deepest traditions of democracy in America and can leverage many important institutional and cultural resources to carry the great work of democracy forward. We conclude with an ambitious, albeit eminently practical, proposal for building the movement on the basis of its existing networks and distinctive repertoires, while nonetheless enabling it to make a dramatic new claim to authority within the political culture that might capture the public imagination. We call this a National Civic Congress convening annually or biannually on the Fourth of July.

TWO

Community Organizing
and Development

Amid the many familiar indicators of social and economic decline in the nation's cities over the past several decades, we see a substantial degree of innovation in community organizing, community development, and other forms of urban democracy. The evidence is clear if we contrast the early 1960s with the end of the century. In the early 1960s, the Community Action Program in the War on Poverty had not yet been devised, and only a few experiments in the Ford Foundation's "gray areas" program and Mobilization for Youth existed. The community-organizing projects of Saul Alinsky's Industrial Areas Foundation were alive and well in only a handful of cities, and their philosophy and techniques were quite crude by the IAF's own contemporary standards. Few, if any, community development corporations (CDCs) existed, and support from city governments for community-based development was virtually nil. Neighborhood participation in local government had either been radically reduced by professional city management or was channeled through local parties evidencing long-term decline.

Today, by contrast, several thousand CDCs across the country are engaged in housing and neighborhood revitalization, with an elaborate network of intermediary institutions to support them at the local, state, and national levels. They have formed increasingly dense and productive relationships with local banks, corporations, religious institutions, city agencies, and community foundations. Not only have they been growing considerably, but they have also been diversifying into activities such as commercial development, job training, and day care, and some have begun to take on new challenges of comprehensive community development. Congregation-based organizing inspired by Alinsky now has close to two hundred local coalitions in more than one hundred cities, with several thousand participating local congregations and important networks within and across denominational hierarchies. Religious congregations have generated national and regional support networks, as well as capacities for community leadership development and collaboration with government and business leaders far beyond what was imaginable in Alinsky's day. Other noncongregational scions of the Alinsky model have substantial membership and influence. Far more multiracial community organizing and development occurs today than ever before. Many cities have expanded their capacities for community development and have recruited innovative leaders of community organizations to staff housing, planning, and other agencies, helping to transform professional and technocratic practices. Many cities have also developed formal systems of neighborhood associations where citizen participation is regular and relatively robust, and these often work with other civic and local environmental groups to build livable and sustainable communities. An increasing number of cities and metropolitan areas engage in long-term community visioning and strategic planning, including stakeholders from many sectors to enhance civic infrastructure. The capacity of community-based organizations to engage in complex public-private partnerships and the availability of workable models are substantially greater than at any previous time in American history.

Yet, as we noted in chapter 1, urban social capital has also eroded in other ways. Many in the black middle class deserted urban ghettos once the civil rights revolution lowered employment and housing barriers, thus thinning out cross-class networks and community assets for neighborhood revitalization. Capital flight, postindustrial development, and federal housing policy have contributed to further isolation and concentration of the urban poor.[1] The dispersion of second- and third-generation ethnic communities in many cities, as well as the decline of local union halls, party clubs, and women's clubs has further depleted important forms of urban social capital. In addition, the gap between cities and suburbs has grown wider, and the political power of cities weaker.

In this chapter we attempt to make sense of these developments as part of a complex historical dynamic in which substantial civic capacity building and policy learning have taken place since the 1960s, and continued opportunities for further progress present themselves, even amid broad indicators of urban decline and deep political obstacles to community revitalization. We first examine the mixed legacy of Community Action and Model Cities programs in the 1960s and early 1970s and then analyze three sets of subsequent developments in which new organizing strategies, institutional forms, and policy designs have emerged: (1) congregation-based community organizing; (2) community development; and (3) neighborhood associations, often in conjunction with other forms of participatory planning and community visioning. We conclude by considering some of the obstacles to building alternative urban regimes and developing national policy supports that are more consistently empowering to urban neighborhoods.

COMMUNITY ACTION AND MODEL CITIES: LIMITS AND LEGACIES

On January 8, 1964, President Lyndon Johnson declared an "unconditional war on poverty," and by mid-year Congress had passed the Economic Opportunity Act with a bold, if never very well-funded, mandate for community action. The act aimed to mobilize public and private resources for a coordinated attack on poverty. A community action program (CAP) was defined as a program "which is developed, conducted, and administered with the maximum feasible participation of residents of the areas and members of the groups served."[2]

This emphasis on participation, which set a precedent for much subsequent legislation, derived from two key sources. First, despite the lack of direct legislative input by civil rights and poor people's organizations for mandated participation, imposing new programs on the poor without their having a say in them was clearly no longer feasible by the mid-1960s. The civil rights movement had simply progressed too far for the president's advisors to imagine that they could fashion a new form of welfare colonialism or white paternalism for the poor. As two of the earliest and most astute observers of community action have noted, the Office of Economic Opportunity (OEO) "was surely right to believe that the days when poor people would passively accept what they were given were numbered everywhere." Whatever the legislative wording or administrative policy, citizen participation would have appeared on the agenda in any war on poverty or inner-city development initiative, and conflict over its meanings would have been inevitable. Indeed, "the most abiding achievement of the war on poverty may prove to be that it helped to articulate this issue."[3]

Second, the president and his advisors fully recognized that the language of participation and community resonated with deep American traditions of self-help, local initiative, and Jeffersonian democracy. As Johnson put it, "I propose a program which relies on the traditional methods of organized local community action." An OEO administrator articulated its main purpose: "To assist communities to mobilize their own local resources to improve the capacities of the poor in their midst." And the *Community Action Program Guide* issued by the OEO put it thus: "The long-term objective of every community action program is to effect a permanent increase in the capacity of individuals, groups, and communities afflicted by poverty to deal effectively with their own problems so that they need no further assistance."[4]

The language and strategy of community action were designed to fit a set of political opportunities and constraints. An appeal to community could legitimate action in terms that did not have to confront racial divisions directly. Self-help contrasted favorably with welfare. Community action could appear boldly imaginative, yet without either massive budget outlays or an ambitious full-employment strategy, and could build a constituency for further efforts.

Community action could also be used to move around the entrenched urban power structure and racialized welfare agencies to open opportunities for minorities, even as its stated mission of forging new forms of collaboration among the poor, city officials, and private social welfare agencies resonated with the norms of American pluralism.[5]

On the ground, community action was interpreted in many ways. Some viewed it primarily as self-help. Others viewed the poor essentially as consumers of services who would provide advice and feedback on the most effective types of programs through neighborhood councils and advisory committees. Still others viewed the provision of jobs through the CAPs, especially in subprofessional positions such as health workers and teaching aides, as a means of generating new opportunities and changing individual motivation as well as educational and social welfare agency practices. Employing the poor in this way would thus help unravel the culture-of-poverty cycle and simultaneously undermine the model of professional social work that treated the poor as passive recipients of services.[6] Finally, those adopting a social action model explicitly viewed poverty as a problem of powerlessness. They saw the goal of community action, in the words of the *Community Action Workbook* issued in 1965 and subsequently withdrawn from circulation under pressure, as organizing the poor into "autonomous and self-managing organizations competent to exert political influence on behalf of their own self-interest." It was this model that drew most from sociological analyses of conflict and power, articulated by engaged social work academics such as Richard Cloward and Warren Haggstrom, by the community-organizing approach of Saul Alinsky, and by a great variety of civil rights, religious, and New Left organizations that had begun to focus significant attention on the new arena opened up by community action programs.[7]

Federal support for the Community Action Program, and a variety of other programs that grew around it, promoted the development of new forms of social capital. For all its problems and controversy, community action turned out to be a vast incubator for involving new neighborhood actors, teaching participatory skills, and spurring local self-help. It stimulated local association building, forged broader networks, and laid the foundations for new forms of collaboration between local groups and city and service agencies. Much of this effort took place more slowly and less visibly than the political drama surrounding community action, and often followed initial stages of conflict and confrontation. Viewed from the level of city politics in the late 1960s, community action may often have appeared to have been captured by the dynamics of political and racial struggle. At the grassroots level, however, it was almost always much more, and poor people demonstrated time and again that they were primarily interested in participating pragmatically to solve problems in their communities and families.[8]

The mechanisms through which capacities developed in the wake of the community action programs of the 1960s are varied and complex. For many, participation on Community Action Agency (CAA) boards and neighborhood councils proved to be an important educative experience. It provided skills in running meetings, collaborating with other community-based organizations, and mobilizing neighbors to get involved. It nurtured and broadened their community-caretaking skills and self-help efforts. Service on a CAA board tended to expand organizational participation in the community, as did related community action programs, such as Head Start and neighborhood health centers. Thousands of affiliated civic organizations grew up around the CAAs nationwide. Leadership training was an implicit and sometimes an explicit goal, and tens of thousands of new community leaders emerged. Neighborhood women, who traditionally performed much of the everyday community caretaking, gained relatively equal access to board positions allocated to the community and filled a disproportionate number of staff positions in neighborhood centers. Leadership networks were strengthened, and CAP activity often provided a framework for organizational collaboration in the black community when other parts of the movement experienced severe fragmentation.[9]

The challenges of building new organizational forms that could involve grassroots participants, mobilize community assets, develop program capacities, and forge collaboration with more powerful and often hostile city officials and private welfare agencies were daunting. Meeting them would inevitably have required a protracted process of learning in even the best of circumstances. In the context of the political conflicts of the 1960s and early 1970s, however, they exposed the entire effort to considerable attack and helped lead to the demise of community action. For instance, the process of deciding "What *demos*?" or who is part of the community and can represent the poor on the CAA boards was often controversial. Civil rights groups preferred to select community representatives at their own meetings or at neighborhood conventions, though this process meant that middle-class and already active citizens such as teachers and civil servants with substantial knowledge of the city and its educational and social welfare bureaucracies would be selected disproportionately over poor and previously uninvolved citizens. For civil rights groups, substantive representation of the poor was more important than descriptive representation, and the everyday fabric of community life as they experienced it was woven from cross-cutting networks, not segmented by bureaucratic categories or income classifications. Mayors, on the other hand, preferred to make the selections to CAA boards themselves or to use an election based on income criteria, as this process strengthened their own relative power. Special elections could take a year or two to organize, typically had low turnout, and excluded many experienced community activists who did not technically meet the poverty income criteria. The OEO continually struggled to ensure one-third representation of the poor, though it eventually excluded the election procedure as undermining the legitimacy of the entire effort. The poor who were selected had high turnover rates, and those without other organizational affiliations tended to campaign on a narrow "friends and neighbors" basis. Ethnic conflict, especially among African Americans and Latinos, was also disruptive to forming CAA boards, and white community representatives were underrepresented or often effectively excluded. In the absence of any broader full-employment policy, conflict over the distribution of jobs in nonprofessional, professional, and summer Head Start positions further compounded the problems of establishing effective community representation and repeatedly paralyzed and distorted deliberation on the CAA boards.[10]

By the time community delegates were chosen, the representatives of the city and private agencies on the boards had often already submitted proposals to the OEO, and directors and staff tended to monopolize these channels of communication and information. Community representatives seldom met together before board meetings or had staff at their disposal. They were often given information only a few days before proposals were due. They thus found themselves rubber stamping staff decisions in a frantic deadline-beating process because getting something was viewed as better than getting nothing. Quick and visible results were needed to legitimate federal programs, ever-vulnerable to public scrutiny for not using federal monies effectively to solve tangible problems of the poor. Concrete results were also needed to motivate active participation at the neighborhood level, yet time was required to develop community capacities in a careful and deliberate manner, thus confronting the programs with a temporal paradox also evident in early efforts to achieve citizen participation in environmental regulation. Congress and the OEO increasingly shifted funding priorities to "national emphasis programs" within CAPs, such as Head Start and Legal Services, which further limited the scope of local innovation. But these programs had developed important local constituencies of their own, while many CAA boards had great difficulty establishing priorities for their communities.

All of these "liabilities of newness"[11] in building capacities for community action were compounded by additional challenges. The first major federal policy in the 1960s to mobilize participation and to begin a long process of generating new forms of urban social capital was overloaded with two other major, indeed historic, tasks: securing black *political* empowerment in urban politics and creating an equal-opportunity *welfare* state to replace the highly racialized policies of the New Deal.[12] Community Action made enormous and lasting contributions to each of these tasks, training thousands of new political leaders and securing the first beachhead for blacks in urban politics, from which they went on to contest for office. Community Action helped to bring minorities into the social services and into its leadership positions, thereby radically reducing discrimination in service practice. But because

Community Action was so tightly linked to the struggle for racial justice, it contributed to the backlash that undermined its support. Head Start, Legal Services, neighborhood health centers, and other programs that had developed distinct constituencies could be given new bureaucratic homes, so that when President Nixon unceremoniously abolished the OEO in 1973, "no one challenged his action. The demise of the OEO wiped the inner cities off the legislative agenda for the next twenty years."[13]

The shift away from Community Action had actually begun earlier, when President Johnson announced his Model Cities program for the newly created Department of Housing and Urban Development (HUD) with the Demonstration Cities and Metropolitan Development Act of 1966. But a mandate for "widespread citizen participation" remained, and despite intentions of confining participation to agency frameworks, officials yielded to well-organized local pressure and accommodated or even encouraged engagement through preexisting CAAs. While HUD remained ambivalent about how much participation there should be, local administrators improvised in response to citizen demands for "partnership" and their own common-sense concerns about outcomes that could legitimate programs in citizens' eyes. Local administrators also improvised to develop means of conflict resolution among the many contending claims of community groups. HUD's chief advisor on citizen participation, Sherry Arnstein, strongly criticized programs where participation remained ritualistic and manipulative and was able to get approval for advisory guidelines and best practices for all Model Cities, as well as a technical assistance fund to build citizen capacities. Municipal agencies confronted well-organized and militant community leadership in perhaps 20–30 percent of cities. As James Sundquist argued after an extensive review of programs in fourteen states, Model Cities *had* "mobilized an extraordinary degree of resident participation in the formation and execution of plans to attack the deep-seated problems of slum neighborhoods— despite the difficulties of organizing participation in the initial year."[14]

Model Cities reached beyond social service agencies to a broad range of municipal services and for the first time established extensive participation in land-use planning, such as housing demolition and construction, transportation routes and freeway construction, industrial site preparation, school building, and rezoning. Model Cities took up issues of community and economic development and brought homeowners into the process. While it encouraged the participation of the poor, and hence confrontation with existing agencies, it required conflict resolution on a Model Cities plan as a condition for continued support. It provided a transition from the categorical social welfare programs of the War on Poverty to revenue sharing and block grants under Nixon's "new federalism."

But Model Cities also laid the basis for a set of strategic choices that would prove significant for future learning. In cities where citizens deeply distrusted municipal authorities, their representatives on the City Demonstration Administration—sometimes known as the Community Development Agency— often refused to give their federal dollars to existing local agencies and instead set up independent community development corporations. Citizens also began to conclude that they needed formal powers decentralized to neighborhood associations so that they could have a legitimate neighborhood government with normal political processes of representation, and so that they could take up a full range of issues more systematically, "rather than dancing a new jig for each different federal program tune."[15] Local citizens and staff, in effect, voted with their feet as they "soon discovered that careful exploration of the labyrinths of the federal government was a poor investment of their time," and that other strategies for community development and neighborhood governance were available to them.[16]

Because Community Action and Model Cities were caught up in the struggles of the broader civil rights movement, in conflicts with mayors and social service agencies, and in the polarized national politics of race, the process of social learning and capacity building that had begun to occur was largely obscured in both scholarly and public opinion alike. Daniel Patrick Moynihan's scathing attack on maximum feasible participation in his 1969 book, despite its many factual inaccuracies, did serious damage to the prospects of further federal experimentation in participatory democracy for the inner city.[17] Scholars who appreciated the contribution made by Community Action to the development of black political capital had no framework for understanding its contribution to the development of social capital, or how the former might help facilitate the latter in subsequent years.[18] Conservative thinkers had yet to develop a focus on "mediating structures," which came only later, in the 1970s.[19] Left-wing scholars appreciated local participation, but their dominant frame of radical change versus cooptation tended to belittle self-help and to obscure the development of collaborative problem-solving and trust-building strategies that had clearly emerged. Nor did they recognize that alternatives to such strategies might have resulted in even weaker or nonexistent community-based organizations in some cities, as well as heightened conflict and increased repression in others, thus reducing community capacities still further.[20]

The organizational and political challenges facing community participation in the 1960s did not bode well either for maintaining many existing forms of social capital or for developing coherent policies that would engender new forms. Community-based development strategies in urban ghettos could probably not have been expected to build primarily upon the cross-class networks that had been held in place by previous racial policies that excluded middle-class blacks from moving outward. The changing nature of manufacturing and the gradual shift to postindustrial patterns of development were not well understood at the time, nor were they much amenable to existing policy tools or grassroots strategies. The problems associated with these changes, such as loss of population and fiscal crises in major cities of the frostbelt, would be further exacerbated as the 1970s wore on. Cross-race network building was impeded by some of the very forms of social capital that existed in white working-class communities, such as craft unions and ethnic associations. No extant models of citizen governance in community and municipal affairs effectively addressed these emergent issues. Reform elites at the national level and within the civil rights movement were overwhelmingly oriented toward civil rights and equal opportunity strategies that paid little direct attention to issues of social capital within urban minority communities and that arguably depleted existing stocks further in white working-class communities through busing and white flight. In addition, the dominant rights-based strategies further fueled the expansion of a therapeutic welfare state, in which minority and white social workers alike proceeded to refine the professional practices that so often erode community problem-solving knowledge and networks.[21]

Looking back on this period when participatory democracy first appeared on the federal urban agenda, we can see that the knowledge base for policies to promote the development of social capital and complex community problem solving was poorly developed. Political conflicts would also inevitably have captured much of the local efforts to build community capacities. Whether other realistic policy options at the time might have altered this balance to favor more robust development of social capital in white working-class and minority urban communities alike and still have been able to secure the basic democratic gains of the civil rights revolution remains an open question. Substantial learning did, however, emerge from the participatory projects in and around Community Action and Model Cities, often building directly upon its network of activists and organizations, but also drawing critical lessons and mapping new directions. The neighborhood movements of the 1970s spurred further and much richer community development strategies, as well as democratic neighborhood associations, which continue to be refined, as we shall see below. But first we examine congregation-based community organizing, which developed on a track largely independent of Community Action and Model Cities.

CONGREGATION-BASED COMMUNITY ORGANIZING

"Alinsky is to community organizing as Freud is to psychoanalysis."[22] Indeed, Alinsky's *Reveille for Radicals,* theorizing his experience in the white, ethnic Back of the Yards area of Chicago in the 1940s and his later pioneering efforts in the largely black Woodlawn area of Chicago in the early 1960s, inspired Richard Boone and others on the initial Community Action task force to campaign for "maximum feasible participation" in the War on Poverty.

Alinsky himself, to be sure, called that effort a "prize piece of political pornography" because of the dependence of Community Action on government sponsorship and the ensuing scramble for patronage.[23] His own aim was to renew the Jeffersonian tradition of participatory democracy as a way of life based upon independent local organizations capable of generating access to power for poor and working-class citizens. He appealed to the homegrown American radicalism of Tom Paine, Patrick Henry, and Sam Adams and to the vision of town-meeting democracy in Tocqueville to rescue America from its growing dependence on large corporations, government bureaucracies, and national trade unions.

The IAF model brought together local institutions (churches, unions, block clubs) into a unified, pragmatic, and nonideological organization with indigenous leadership. The model was refined over the next three decades by talented organizers such as Fred Ross, who pioneered the house meeting as a way to bring people in a community together to share their stories and build relationships. But Alinsky's approach had been quite out of sync with social and political developments in these years. The New Deal belied his early Jeffersonian ideals, and postwar boom and suburbanization substituted tea parties for power-oriented block clubs. The civil rights movement, Black Power, and Community Action were more characteristic of resistance and representation in the 1960s than were unified, independent community organizations. At the time of Alinsky's death in 1972, the IAF consisted of less than a half dozen projects, which remained quite fragile or sustained themselves only by becoming narrow ethnic organizations or community development groups dominated by their staffs. As Manuel Castells notes, "Only in the 1970s did the new citizen movement, based upon collective consumption issues and neighborhood interaction, and focused on the local government level, discover the interest of the populist model of community organizing."[24]

In the years since, several derivative Alinsky models of organizing, a growing network of intermediary institutions for training and funding, and thousands of local organizing projects have emerged. Here we focus on congregation-based organizing because, in our view, it represents the most robust form of community organizing in its capacities to enrich the vision of democracy, develop leadership in communities, and mobilize social capital for complex partnerships and broad empowerment strategies. Although it seems more likely to thrive under some conditions than others, and thus tends to fill certain niches in the ecology of local organizing, the congregation-based model also appears to be more effective in achieving results and building power than other organizing models in communities with similar or identical urban political structures and demographic characteristics. But other models have made many important contributions and have catalyzed the community reinvestment and community development movements.[25]

Upon Alinsky's death, Ed Chambers, an ex-seminarian and first director of the IAF training institute, took over the IAF national office. His leadership, along with especially innovative local organizing and theorizing by Ernesto Cortés of COPS, as we saw in chapter 1, began to transform the IAF. Today, the IAF consists of approximately sixty-five local federations, each composed of several dozen or more congregations with relatively dense relational networks extending into tens of thousands of families.[26] IAF's learning and capacity building is especially evident in three broad dimensions of its work: (1) connecting vision and values to power and interest in the organizing process and mobilizing congregation-based social capital for broad strategies of community empowerment and interracial collaboration; (2) refining community leadership development and trust-building strategies in a participatory yet sustainable and professional organizing model; and (3) developing complex public partnerships and policy initiatives.

Vision and Values

Under Alinsky, the language of narrow self-interest had gradually displaced the language of civic republicanism, and the image of citizens claiming power came to be those "who have some, want more" of what materialist American culture had to offer. Religious values had never been central to organizing, and Alinsky resisted efforts to link them by Father Jack Egan, an original key supporter of the IAF in Chicago in the 1940s who went on to found the Catholic Bishops' Campaign for Human Development (CHD) in 1970. As Alinsky is reputed to have said, "You take care of the religion, Jack, we'll do the organizing." But organizing gradually became reduced to technique; community disappeared as a common space of shared values; and the positive power of citizens to act became divorced from a larger vision. A substantial number of clergy from various denominations, including some who had initiated community organizing, urban mission, and clergy-training programs in the 1950s and 1960s, remained skeptical or outright hostile to the Alinsky model's confrontational tactics and its neglect of the spiritual dimensions of congregational life, as IAF leaders in Chicago were well aware. Alinsky organizing had become increasingly incapable of asking the question, as Harry Boyte has argued, "Power for what?"[27]

Chambers, Cortés, and a host of other organizers and community leaders from the ranks of the clergy began to reverse this process by drawing increasingly on biblical language and storytelling as resources for organizing. Religious faith came to serve as a key medium for building relationships and establishing trust, beginning with the one-on-one meetings at the core of IAF organizing and extending to the interracial collaboration of leaders across denominations and residentially segregated sections of the city. The stories of Moses and Paul are used to model the basic challenge of organizing to recruit many leaders from the community willing to share the responsibility. A group of hundreds of "Gideonites" organize among parishioners of St. Paul's, a core IAF congregation in East Brooklyn, to mobilize the community's assets in the battle against church debt, so that weekly offerings can be used for youth programs. The call of the prophet Nehemiah to "rebuild the walls of Jerusalem, so that we may no longer suffer disgrace," originally part of an ordinary sermon by the Reverend Johnny Ray Youngblood, is echoed in hundreds of community meetings by clergy and lay leaders alike, and eventually throughout the IAF and other congregation-based networks to mobilize support for innovative low-cost housing. The Nehemiah story framed the public discourse that eventually compelled New York City mayor Ed Koch to deliver on his pledges and led to a national Nehemiah housing program at HUD.[28]

Biblical language and storytelling in everyday congregational life and one-on-one organizing—as well as at leadership meetings, trainings, mass actions, and even public negotiations—frame the struggle for community power. They provide a recognized narrative for talking about dignity, equality, and justice in today's world and inspire commitment and confidence in ordinary people to take action. Across individual congregations, whose diversity stretches from various Protestant denominations to Catholic, Jewish, Muslim, and Buddhist, community leaders and organizers have continually refined their use of religious language to embrace all as equally "children of God" and to avoid potentially divisive theological themes. This, along with IAF emphasis on choosing issues that unite rather than divide people and training in broad democratic thinking and traditions, makes deep religious commitment a source of strengthening public life, rather than splintering or polarizing it around non-negotiable fundamentals.

If religious language represents the cultural dimension of social capital that IAF has learned to mobilize for broad community empowerment, the congregations and other religious organizations represent the institutional dimension. As Mark Warren's perceptive study of the Texas IAF shows, over the past two decades the network has gone far beyond Alinsky in learning to mobilize congregation-based and often ethnically and racially homogeneous forms of social capital, generate new and heterogeneous forms across diverse congregations and racially segregated neighborhoods, and link horizontal forms to vertical ones among church, business, and political leaders.[29] The IAF has built upon the foundations of the post–Vatican II encouragement of lay participation in the Catholic church, as well as commitments of the Conference of American Bishops to economic and social justice, to recruit leaders further downward in the parishes, including lay women and nuns, rather than relying primarily upon official clerical leadership. As Sister Maribeth Larkin, an IAF organizer, has noted, "After Vatican II there was a move for Catholic pastors to share responsibilities with lay people in their congregations. But most pastors didn't know how to do it. Then COPS came along and showed them how."[30]

The IAF has also utilized church hierarchies to encourage and reward such organizing and has helped to build an interlaced network within dioceses, as well as across them through the Campaign for Human Development, to generate financial and political capital for local projects. Catholic parishes and dioceses, for their part, began to recognize their strategic self-interest in having IAF projects that improved sewers, streets, and schools, as the flight of parishioners to the suburbs was ballooning church debt just when new churches and schools had to be built and the place-based parish structure committed them to maintaining the existing sites. As the late Father Dan Hennessey said to his fellow pastors in San Antonio, "Joining COPS is good economics. And it's good religion. I'm paying three thousand dollars a year to the chancery for insurance on these buildings; fifteen hundred dollars [COPS' dues for his parish] is cheap to keep them from becoming a cemetery."[31]

While Mexican American Catholic parishes in Texas may provide the densest networks into neighborhoods, family, and kin systems that can be tapped for leadership recruitment, program development, and mass actions, the Texas IAF has steadily expanded its work with African American Protestant congregations. Because these have fewer supports from church hierarchies and less dense and place-based social capital, IAF has developed organizing strategies that encourage cross-race collaboration and leverage multiracial social capital in the political arena. Allied Communities of Tarrant (ACT) in Fort Worth is a good case. In the late 1970s, ministers formed a multiracial and multidenominational sponsoring committee to explore the possibility of bringing in IAF organizers and for the next five years built trust across separate ministerial networks. Once formed, ACT combined a focus on neighborhood issues and racial autonomy in segregated sections of the city with a variety of strategies to encourage active collaboration across racial lines at the grassroots. Hispanics, African Americans, and Anglo clergy work together on strategy and action teams in the framework of common citywide issues that are defined nonracially, such as strengthened families, improved schools, job training, and infrastructure. They travel to each other's neighborhoods to meet, negotiate quid pro quos when there are limited resources to distribute, and periodically reinforce their interracial identity in citywide ecumenical celebrations and services. And they affirm this identity publicly each time they meet with political and business leaders. Their active collaboration reaches further down to the grassroots than most multiracial coalitions typically do. Like other IAF groups, ACT deliberately chooses not to become involved in racially charged issues. Thus it decided not to join a protest against the lenient sentencing of a white skinhead convicted of killing a black man, though several African American leaders in ACT participated as individuals in planning the protest and simultaneously hold membership in the NAACP as another avenue for their civic involvement. But as one

African American lay leader explained, "Religious values help keep racism down. It's key to unity along race lines. At every meeting we talk of our values. Religious values are even more important than the common goal."[32]

Leadership Development

Over the past two decades, the IAF has also expanded and refined its capacities for developing community leadership far beyond what occurred under Alinsky. First, it has developed the one-on-one meeting as "the art of listening" for all organizers and community leaders. One-on-ones are meetings generally lasting a half-hour to an hour in which two individuals share personal stories with public significance. Their purpose is to build relationships, establish trust, and uncover the deeper personal sources of interest, anger, love, and faith that might motivate them. A deceptively simple yet powerful technique, the one-on-one is emphasized relentlessly as the core of all organizing work. It is used to identify potential leaders in the community who might be willing to share responsibility, as well as build public relationships with institutional and political leaders who are sometimes adversaries, yet also potential allies.

Secondly, IAF has fashioned an intensive system of long-term mentoring of leaders by organizers and of new leaders by those more experienced. Such mentoring occurs in the context of practical action, continual challenge, and critical evaluation designed to support the self-development of those who may have never before played a political role in their communities. This "developmental perspective," which views citizen empowerment as a form of extended adult learning with its own distinct developmental challenges, emerged more broadly in the 1970s, though it became most carefully formalized in the IAF. Relational organizing and intensive mentoring have also been designed to tap the potential of women who are everyday community builders in their neighborhoods and churches but were once on the margins of Alinsky organizing. Indeed, IAF's language of "power with," in contrast to "power over," is shared by many feminist organizers and thinkers. Women leaders in IAF, including housewives once terrified of public speaking, have assumed prominent organizational roles where they negotiate with business and political leaders and address thousands at public assemblies.[33]

Third, IAF has developed extensive educative capacities through its training institute, which conducts ten-day sessions several times every year. In addition, there are weekend retreats, shorter trainings, seminars and, in Texas, what some community leaders have called "the University of COPS." These trainings focus on key principles of organizing and major concepts essential to public life: power, self-interest, pluralism, social capital, quid pro quo, political accountability, public and private life. They examine the contrast between the idea of "citizen," with shared power and responsibility to act in common with other citizens to solve public problems, and the array of competing language that tends to strip citizenship of its full meaning: consumer, taxpayer, client, plaintiff, victim, voter. And they teach and dramatize over and over the "iron rule of organizing": "Never do for others what they can do for themselves. Never!" Leaders read and discuss biblical texts and contemporary theological statements, such as Pope John Paul's encyclical on the dignity of work and Paul Tillich's *Love, Power and Justice.* They learn core ideas from democratic theorists such as Thomas Jefferson, Alexis de Tocqueville, and Hannah Arendt. And they engage these ideas at a profound experiential level that challenges their most fundamental proclivities to defer to authority and expertise. Conceptual work is complemented with skills training: how to negotiate and compromise, how to conduct meetings large and small, how to build coalitions, how to research an issue, form relationships with academics, and assess options. But technique is always related to core principles and ideas, with the goal of making IAF organizations genuine "schools of public life."[34]

Fourth, leadership development in the IAF has entailed an increasingly self-conscious redefinition of the professional work that people do. This is perhaps clearest among the clergy. As a number of pastors testified at a meeting at St. Paul's Cathedral in Boston in January 1999, they had been trained at seminary to be counselors and therapists, but their work in IAF projects in Baltimore, Philadelphia, and Boston had enabled them to reorient fundamentally their daily tasks. They no longer view their parishioners as clients whom they serve, nor do they limit their contacts for fear of building up an unmanageable client base. They no longer do outreach based on superficial chatter that bored them to tears for years on end. Rather, they conduct their one-on-ones to share the kind of pain and anger that can lead to public action and expand the base of parish leaders who can share their responsibilities, not add to their therapeutic burden. For many, the one-on-ones have literally revived their sense of vocational mission and even rescued them from well-deserved retirement. Teachers and principals in IAF education projects, such as the Alliance Schools in Texas discussed below, likewise have reconceived their work with parents and other public actors as a process of building new kinds of relationships to tackle educational problems in the larger fabric of community life. The work of the educator now looks and feels different.[35]

Fifth, IAF has steadily refined an organizing model that combines professionalism and structure with participation and consensus building in the community. Professional organizers trained by the IAF receive decent middle-class salaries and benefits, as well as opportunities for career advancement, enabling them to refine their own skills over time, rather than burning out. Staff are therefore not continually turning over, and they avoid the psychology of sacrificial heroism, which can serve as the breeding ground for staff dominance and oligarchy. Continuity also allows staff to mentor community leaders in a long-term process of development. The community, through its local organizing committee drawn from participating congregations, contracts with the IAF for a lead organizer, and perhaps others, for several years at a time and for services that include periodic visits by other IAF organizers and a certain number of slots for the ten-day trainings. The contract entails agreement with IAF organizing principles, which are not open to debate. These include nonpartisanship, nonracial definition of issues, combining confrontation with negotiation, and internal consensus-seeking to define issues that unite the community rather than divide it.

Organizers and more experienced leaders continually recruit new leaders from the community, and they provide conceptual, relational, public speaking, and research skills that allow them effectively to represent and negotiate for the broader membership of the congregations that pay the organizers' salaries and turn out for mass rallies and conventions. Leadership is collective; co-chairs are periodically rotated; and no community leader ever goes alone to negotiate with political and business leaders. While professional organizers clearly play an influential role, they tend to be held in check by the very skills and concepts they teach, as well as by techniques such as extensive house meetings in the community to develop an issue campaign. In turn, the tendency of community leaders themselves to develop oligarchic enclaves of power is held in check by accountability rules that prohibit leaders from running for political office, taking administrative positions in programs developed by the organization, or serving on government boards and commissions. Leaders who choose to move on in this way are expected to resign their official position in the IAF organization, though they are encouraged to maintain ties in their new work. Virginia Ramirez, a community leader and co-chair of COPS, displays the self-confidence of her training: "I'm not dependent on an organizer; I'm dependent on other leaders. My role is to teach new leaders to draw on others. . . . By the time they [organizers] leave here, they can organize anywhere—because we train them well!"[36]

Complex Partnerships and Policy Initiatives

In recent years, the IAF network has progressively developed strategies and capacities for engaging in complex partnerships and policy initiatives. These have emerged in direct response to the limits of confrontational strategies in winning significant gains or even maintaining the support of core constituents. IAF has learned to couple the language of power with one of collaboration that recognizes the varied and legitimate interests of other public actors, including those who have been defined as adversaries in the past—and may again be in the future. It has designed strategies for extended negotiation and partnership building within a broader context of mutual public accountability by political, business, educational, and its own community leaders alike. Indeed, organizers and veteran leaders challenge activists to understand the legitimate self-interests of their adversaries and partners, as well as the complex institutional conditions in which they operate. They challenge them to refine their anger and combine their advocacy with ongoing productive work that directly adds value to the community and facilitates the work demanded of their partners. IAF "accountability nights" with public officials have undergone a significant shift, from confrontational meetings intended to embarrass and expose leaders in the 1970s to forums designed to consolidate incipient relationships in full public view. The IAF has also refined its capacities for collaborative research that combines locally generated knowledge with sophisticated policy analysis and has devised innovative ways to link organizing and relationship building with program implementation. To be sure, given the complex interplay of power on the municipal and state levels, its partnership strategies face serious conundrums and periodic failure, but none seem to have undermined its capacities to continue organizing and learning either locally or throughout the larger network.

Baltimoreans United in Leadership Development (BUILD), for instance, has grown into what is arguably the largest and most effective, predominantly African American community organization in the country. Established in the late 1970s in a campaign against bank redlining, it achieved increased mortgage lending for low-income families. But when it began to confront the issue of jobs and leverage its potentially embarrassing research on employment discrimination in the city, BUILD also recognized that it would need to repair its relationships with the Greater Baltimore Committee (GBC), which represented a powerful voice of business and a potential partner with whom to negotiate. BUILD thus sought to identify common interests in having well-prepared workers entering the labor market from the neighborhoods, as well as the political interest of business in improved relations with a strong organizational partner from the African American community. BUILD engaged in extended trust building in its meetings with the GBC and brought GBC leaders into the churches to meet with congregants. Having been largely unsuccessful in focusing mayor William Schafer's attention on the problems of schools and neighborhoods, BUILD forged an effective voter registration and agenda-setting strategy for the 1987 election, which included highly visible accountability sessions with both major candidates, and then set out from a strong position to move the newly elected Kurt Schmoke to bring the city school system into the emerging partnership.

Drawing upon a model from Boston, BUILD then worked out the Baltimore Commonwealth Agreement with the corporate community for guaranteed job interviews with at least 3 of GBC's 150 member organizations for students with 95 percent attendance records in their last two years of high school. In another partnership with BUILD, Project College Bound, GBC promised to raise 25 million dollars in scholarship funds for high school graduates, with matching funds from local universities. BUILD's own organizing reached not only to churches and parents but also to the Baltimore Teachers Union and the Public School Administrators and Supervisors Association. These groups joined as BUILD member organizations and began to rethink teaching as a democratic craft. They also began to reconceive of schools as centers for after-hours community activity, such as adult education, community service, and the development of public leadership skills. But when Mayor Schmoke insisted on contracting to Educational Alternatives, Inc., to manage the public schools, BUILD moved into opposition and helped defeat the plan. The cost, however, was the erosion of its relationship with the mayor and a shift away from school issues.

BUILD also instituted Community Building in Partnership (CBP) with the Enterprise Foundation, the Sandtown-Winchester Improvement Association, the Urban League, and city, state, and federal governments to develop Nehemiah housing. Yet when CBP did not invest adequately in organizing and instead set a top-down agenda to show quick results, BUILD again pulled back. This response sent a strong signal to the community and to CPB leaders, and after several years of lost momentum, the project has placed renewed emphasis on participation at the grassroots. Former Mayor Schmoke, who continued over the course of his three terms to play a dynamic role in developing one of the more sophisticated and coherent frameworks for community development of any city in the nation, still attributes some of his most critical learning to his early relationship with BUILD, despite its strains.[37]

In San Antonio, as we saw in the previous chapter, COPS and Metro Alliance leveraged their organizing capacities to develop Project QUEST as a complex partnership among congregations, banks, industry, a community college, and political leaders at the local and state levels. And through the Texas IAF they extended the model to other cities. In the area of education reform, as Dennis Shirley shows in his masterful study, a similar set of partnerships emerged as the Texas IAF has "matured from the role of outsider mobilizing for change to insider negotiating with school districts, business leaders, and foundations to hammer out realistic, winnable strategies for improving education."[38] The struggle began in San Antonio by compelling the school district to make its budget public and then defeating an initiative to spend 1.6 million dollars for a new administrative building while dilapidated classrooms housed thousands of the city's poorer kids. When the state legislature created the Select Committee on Public Education headed by H. Ross Perot in the early 1980s, Valley Interfaith, an IAF group in the lower Rio Grande, invited him to a meeting with over two thousand congregants to hear their views of the failures and inequities of public education. Perot subsequently asked IAF community leaders to make a formal presentation to the committee with specific recommendations on financing, which were then largely adopted. But only a further rally by thousands of IAF supporters reversed attempts by the House Public Education Committee to gut every substantive recommendation made by the Select Committee. As a result, IAF was credited with saving the reform that added 2.8 billion dollars to enhance teacher/student ratios across the state.

Local IAF groups then began to work on building capacities for parental engagement and power sharing on a school-by-school basis. They utilized one-on-ones, house meetings, and accountability sessions, but they also instituted Walks for Success involving teachers, clergy, alumni, sympathetic college students, and school students themselves in block-by-block home visitations. This local organizing helped to establish the Texas IAF Vision for Public Schools: Communities of Learners, which borrowed many of the innovative models of school reformers around the country, including those of Ted Sizer, Deborah Meier, Howard Gardner, and James Comer, but embedded them in a conception of genuine parental power. Parents thus become fully engaged change agents in the schools and surrounding neighborhoods. In San Antonio, COPS and Metro Alliance developed an Educational Partnership, based partly on BUILD's model, and worked with Mayor Cisneros and the Chamber of Commerce to enable more than three thousand young people to attend college. They collaborated with police to ensure neighborhood safety around the schools and established an ambitious after-school program with the help of city councilors, whose reluctance gave way in the face of increased voter registration at the schools. Part of the reform process at the Herff Elementary School involved stabilizing the neighborhood through expanded home ownership. Teachers, bankers, and the principal collaborated with the low-income parents on housing fairs, and COPS and Metro Alliance developed a citywide strategy with banks, realtors, and public officials that made ninety-five million dollars available to low-income families. As parent Edna Rodriguez noted, "the bankers have been great. They didn't just come to our housing fair, but they've been coming in every week for one-on-ones with the parents. It's creating a whole new vision for our community."[39]

Governor Ann Richards, elected in 1990, appointed former COPS chair Sonia Hernandez as Director of Education Policy at the state level, as well as a new superintendent, Skip Meno, to head the Texas Education Agency. All worked in partnership with the Texas IAF to develop Alliance Schools on a statewide level, beginning with twenty-one schools and then doubling and tripling this number in the following two years. This partnership proved critical not only in providing institutional credibility, innovation funds, and needed waivers, but also in navigating the many political and bureaucratic obstacles that invariably arise to stifle even the best of reform efforts emerging within individual schools. Innovators need protection, as much experience in school reform outside of Texas also shows, and IAF leaders and organizers have repeatedly been able to draw upon the relationships they have painstakingly built at many different levels of the political and institutional systems. When George W. Bush was elected governor in 1994 and removed Meno, the Texas IAF was able to convince the legislature to double the funding for Alliance Schools and other community-based organizational reform efforts, even though the superintendents of the large school districts tried to keep control over every last dollar of compensatory education budgets.

While IAF remains the most influential of the congregation-based organizing networks and has led the way in transforming the Alinsky model, other networks display parallel processes of learning. The Pacific Institute of Community Organizing (PICO) was founded in 1972 by two Jesuits trained in the old approach. By the early 1980s its neighborhood-based organizing had stagnated, and a key defeat of the Oakland Community Organizations (OCO), the premier project in its home city, confronted PICO with a choice to transform itself or dissolve. PICO organizers began a process of serious reflection on strategic and ethical questions, including their moral uneasiness with the Alinsky model's tendency to instrumentalize both religion and relationships. They perceived new opportunities in the commitment of religious institutions to fund community organizing, and they borrowed from recent IAF practice. Much of this crystallized at a staff retreat in 1984, and the decision to pursue an institutional and cultural strategy rooted in the churches led in Oakland to dramatic increases in organizational capacity and political effectiveness within a year and a half, and capacities soon developed elsewhere as well. Over the next decade and a half, PICO has grown from four neighborhood-based federations with the ability to turn out one or two hundred community participants for major public actions to thirty-two federations capable of turning out several thousand at a time. It now draws upon extensive church resources and networks, recruits new organizers from within minority communities, and significantly affects urban political power and reform in cities across the country. As Richard Wood shows in his richly textured study of OCO and PICO, the main vision of participatory democracy has become embodied in an ethos of "ethical democracy" and a fundamentally pluralist organizing model that balances the moral authority of pastors, the expert authority of organizers, and the legitimacy and structural authority of lay leaders in ways that build upon the complementary strengths that each brings to the process.[40]

The Gamaliel Foundation, a network with affiliates in nearly every major metropolitan area of the Midwest, as well as California, New York, and Pennsylvania, has undergone a similar process of learning as it evolved from the Contract Buyers League, an African American group founded in 1968 to fight discrimination in housing. Since 1986 it has launched more than forty-five congregation-based federations, a national clergy caucus of more than one thousand members, and a women's leadership program. Gamiliel uses the language of the common good, economic justice, and care of the land within a "true metropolitan community" that addresses disparities between cities and suburbs. Other primarily regional networks include Direct Action and Research Training, with sixteen federations in Florida, Kentucky, and Ohio; the Regional Council of Neighborhood Organizations in Pennsylvania; the Organizing Leadership Training Center in New England; and the ORGANIZE Training Center in California and Colorado.[41]

The funding infrastructure within major religious denominations to support community organizing has grown substantially over the past three decades, and congregation-based projects have received increasing support since the 1980s as they have refined their own methods and proven their effectiveness relative to other competing models. The most important funding organization, the Campaign for Human Development (CHD), was set up by the Catholic Bishops Conference in 1970. In response to the Second Vatican Council, which encouraged lay participation and placed a renewed emphasis on social justice, various dioceses, church networks, and interfaith projects established their own programs to fund community organizing in poor neighborhoods and to modify the model of traditional charity. In their 1968 statement on the urban riots, a committee led by Bishop Francis Mugavero of Brooklyn developed a plan to lead a crusade against poverty based on Alinsky-style self-help, and the crusade borrowed the theme of human development from Pope Paul VI's social justice encyclical, *The Progress of Peoples*. The first annual, nation-wide parish collection for CHD raised 8.5 million dollars, at the time the largest single collection in the history of the American Catholic Church, which has maintained its grassroots funding support at substantial levels every year since. CHD has also campaigned actively to educate middle-class Catholics on issues of poverty and justice. Borrowing lessons from the congregation-based federations it has funded, CHD has built relationships with an increasingly dense network of supportive clergy at the parish and diocesan levels. Other religious funding sources have been established by the Presbyterian Self-Development of Peoples Program, the Unitarian Universalist Veatch Program, the Evangelical Lutheran Church, the Episcopal Church, and others. Private foundations have also increased funding for congregation-based community organizing.[42]

A burgeoning number of other interfaith and church-based projects are now utilizing much of the religious language and relational organizing strategies of the IAF, PICO, and Gamaliel networks, sometimes directly borrowing from them, though more often learning on separate but parallel tracks. The Christian Community Development Association, for instance, was founded in 1989 by thirty-seven groups that had been devising a holistic, faith-based vision since the early 1970s and has now expanded to nearly four hundred organizations. The National Council for Community Economic Development (NCCED), the trade association for CDCs, now also has a faith-based community development program. Some groups have utilized relational organizing to set up an array of ministries, spin-off corporations, and partnerships that promote health, economic development, housing renovation, job training, education, and parent involvement in schools. Churches have conducted a series of gang reconciliation projects based on street-level one-on-one evangelism, and are networked through organizations such as Sojourners in Washington, DC. The National Center for Neighborhood Enterprise has helped to train hundreds of community leaders around the country in utilizing faith-based approaches to neighborhood and family violence, drugs, teen pregnancy, and other problems, and a recent national effort led by the Reverend Eugene Rivers, based on successful organizing in Boston, is doing likewise. Independent Sector's 1993 national survey of the community service activities of congregations shows robust involvement in health and social welfare activities (over 90 percent of congregations). Nearly half partner with other organizations, and three-fifths lend their facilities to other community groups. One-fifth of all congregations are involved in community and economic development activities of one sort or another, indicating a substantial potential of congregations to support community organizing and relationship-building strategies in the coming years. As one participant in the Naugatuck Valley Project in Connecticut has put it, "You have to become involved and help with creating your community, because if you don't you are a victim, and God didn't make us victims. He made us co-creators."[43]

COMMUNITY DEVELOPMENT

In the wake of federal Community Action and Model Cities programs, a community development movement emerged and has continued to grow steadily. This movement is distinct from congregation-based and other forms of Alinsky organizing, though they share important areas of convergence. The initial spur to the movement came when the 1966 amendment to the Economic Opportunity Act established a Special Impact Program (SIP) for community development organizations, and Senator Robert Kennedy's active support for the Bedford-Stuyvesant Restoration Corporation in Brooklyn brought national attention to the idea of local nonprofit corporations engaged in housing renovation and construction, as well as local business development. In the first decade, one hundred or so community development corporations (CDCs) were formed, mostly by black activist groups, with the bulk of support coming from SIP and the Ford Foundation. Many of these grew quickly into sizable organizations with ambitious housing and commercial ventures and social service programs that they often could not sustain. The emerging community development movement, however, built strategically upon this initial set of national policies and helped to fashion other policy and institutional supports at national, state, and local levels to further strengthen CDCs in the late 1970s. When the policy environment shifted substantially with the election of Ronald Reagan in 1980, the community development movement generated a further set of strategic responses that enabled it to expand considerably and build new capacities.

The movement's focus on housing has always been an implicit, if not explicit, strategy to preserve social capital by enabling a critical mass of responsible residents to maintain their relationships through stable and affordable abodes on safe and neighborly streets. Housing development was also a rational strategy that responded to the availability of abandoned or neglected property at low or no cost and to the opportunity to build a set of individual and institutional skills, from coordinating the sweat equity of neighbors to project planning and contract management. Restoring housing markets could also lead to reestablishing commercial activity. And housing development permitted residents and CDC staff to make visible to each other and the larger society the products of their public work and commitment, and to "symbolize community resurrection."[44] Indeed, they often marked project completion with neighborhood ceremonies celebrating their achievements and invited the press and politicians to pay heed to their determination to continue the work of rebuilding. Many CDCs have always had ambitious neighborhood-organizing strategies as well. While the "bricks and mortar" approach has often become narrow, especially as CDCs have tried to fill the void created by massive federal housing cuts in the 1980s, the past decade has witnessed increasingly diversified and comprehensive efforts, as well as a renewal of community organizing and the diffusion of assets-based community development strategies. These represent substantial learning and have become institutionalized in an increasing number of local projects, community and national foundations, government programs, and intermediary associations and support networks.

The 1970s proved to be a key period for learning and capacity building. While the first wave of CDCs found it difficult to sustain their most ambitious agendas, they did establish the viability of the CDC as an institutional model that could work with corporate and government partners, generate significant community support, and develop innovative approaches to land use, housing reinvestment, and job training. The second-wave CDCs of the late 1970s were smaller and leaner but far more numerous, and they had roots in a range of urban protest movements, tenant associations, social service organizations, churches, and immigrant support groups. As John Mollenkopf has argued, "The community revolution significantly altered both the urban political terrain and the practice of federal urban development programming."[45] The neighborhood movement established a political rhetoric of citizen participation, community review, and participatory planning that challenged the politics of downtown development at the expense of local neighborhoods. It established a new constituency base for urban coalitions that was more sensitive to neighborhood development and the politics of community, and virtually ended massive urban renewal projects. In many cases, these new constituencies elected mayors friendly to community organizations, and some have subsequently been able to tie downtown development to neighborhood housing and other "linkage" programs. An extensive network of leaders emerged from these organizations and has since become progressively incorporated into many levels of city government that provide organizational and political support for community development, including housing authorities, planning commissions, and development agencies. Others became program officers and leaders of local and national foundations. The shift from categorical funding to revenue sharing and Community Development Block Grants (CDBGs) under Nixon's "new federalism" further facilitated CDC development. The movement at the local level received increased federal funding, as well as administrative and legislative support, under President Carter in the latter half of the 1970s through the Community Services Administration, HUD's Office of Neighborhood Development, and from various other programs that funded local organizers. The Neighborhood Reinvestment Corporation, which was established in the wake of the Community Reinvestment Act (CRA) of 1977, also provided significant support.[46]

Under President Reagan in the 1980s, federal housing budgets were massively cut, and support for core CDC operating expenses and organizing activities was radically reduced. The administrative capacities of HUD were decimated, only to be slowly rebuilt under Jack Kemp during the Bush administration and then more substantially under Henry Cisneros and Andrew Cuomo during the Clinton administration, albeit in the face of threats of radical dismantlement by the Republican Congress. Federal aid to the cities was cut by 60 percent from 1980 to 1992, and urban development all but disappeared from HUD's mission. As deep federal subsidies for low-income housing dried up, private developers largely withdrew from the field. The community development movement, rather than withering away as some predicted, responded to these challenges in a third wave of growth that expanded the number of CDCs to two thousand, further buttressed local capacities, broadened the array of partners, and built institutional networks of support at city, state, and national levels. CDCs were also able to capitalize on the successes of a parallel community reinvestment movement that used the CRA to shift over 60 billion dollars in more than 300 agreements to community reinvestment by the early 1990s. And the community development movement helped to mobilize local coalitions for housing and services, which eventually coalesced into state and national coalitions to win policy victories that further helped build capacities.[47]

These victories included the strengthening of CRA financial disclosure requirements in the 1989 Financial Institutions Reform, Recovery, and Enforcement Act, and the 15 percent set aside for comprehensive housing development organizations in the 1990 National Affordable Housing Act. Low Income Housing Tax Credits (LIHTC), which were introduced by the 1986 Tax Reform Act, generated substantial new flows of capital and created the opportunity and necessity for collaboration among banks, state tax credit and bond-issuing agencies, city subsidy providers, foundations, and others to ensure systemic support affecting all tax credit deals. Effective advocacy extended many of these policies under Clinton and achieved other advances, such as the Community Development Financial Institutions program, which built upon a network of more than three hundred such institutions in forty-five states that had emerged by 1994. This program has provided technical and financial assistance to community development banking operations and has encouraged other banks and credit unions to develop and expand community lending divisions. CDC advocacy also shaped the Empowerment Zone and Enterprise Community legislation, including the key criterion of strategic partnerships among community-based organizations such as CDCs.

By building extensive new capacities in the 1980s, the movement established a new policy paradigm for community-developed affordable housing as an alternative to both for-profit housing for the poor through tax incentives to private developers and top-down housing of the poor through over-scaled and bureaucratic HUD projects.[48] While these are by no means secure achievements and can hardly address issues of housing and urban development on their own, they nonetheless represent important advances occurring in a political climate largely hostile to cities and the urban poor.

Building CDC Capacity

Learning and capacity building are evident within the community development movement along various dimensions. The numerical growth of CDCs accelerated considerably in the 1980s and has continued throughout the 1990s. The number of CDCs now stands at 3,600, according to the criteria established by the National Congress for Community Economic Development, but it may be as high as 8,000 by somewhat looser standards. Leadership and staff development have become steadily more refined over the years, and practitioners are immeasurably more skilled and networked than three decades ago. As federal funds contracted in the 1980s, state and city funding increased substantially, and program design now follows the lead of community-based housing innovators. While cities with distinct and identifiable neighborhoods, such as those more typically found in the Northeast and Midwest, have generated the most CDCs, their number is now increasing throughout the country.[49]

The movement has generated an elaborate set of support networks and intermediary organizations that provide technical, financial, and political assistance. They leverage increasingly dense relationships of trust and reciprocity in multilevel local community development systems, and they transfer learning increasingly effectively among local actors and across cities. Perhaps the single most important factor in the development of CDCs in the 1980s and 1990s, these networks and intermediaries draw in new partners and sources of capital, legitimate CDC projects, facilitate risk sharing, and nurture a local culture of charitable giving supportive of participatory values and community-based social and economic development. The most important national intermediaries include the Local Initiatives Support Corporation (LISC), established by the Ford Foundation and six corporate sponsors in 1979, which has worked with more than 1,700 CDCs in 38 cities; the Enterprise Foundation set up by Jim and Patty Rouse in 1981, which has projects in 150 locations and works with 500 neighborhood groups; and the Neighborhood Reinvestment Corporation created by Congress in 1978, which has worked with 180 local Neighborhood Services Organizations. The National Congress for Community Economic Development (NCCED), established in 1970, serves as the trade association for CDCs nationwide.

The Center for Community Change, which has helped thousands of community-based organizations since its founding in 1967, brought together practitioners from Community Action, unions, civil rights groups, and the Kennedy family under the initial leadership of Richard Boone, the presidential advisor most directly responsible for the "maximum feasible participation" language in the federal legislation. The Development Training Institute, the Coalition for Low-Income Community Development, and the Institute for Community Economics (ICE) have also provided critical training and support. Program officers in national and local foundations serve to facilitate critical learning across the field through informal networks, as well as through forums such as the National Neighborhood Funders Group, and in recent years they have begun to fund CDCs to enhance their capacities for strategic planning. National intermediaries and training centers have helped to catalyze some two dozen state-level CDC associations, as well as many regional and local intermediaries. The latter have worked relatively effectively to overcome tendencies toward neighborhood parochialism. Through such supports, cities such as Boston, Cleveland, San Francisco, Chicago, Minneapolis, and New York have nurtured vibrant CDCs for two decades, and a number of cities in the South and Southwest have recently become engaged in substantial capacity building. The web of relationships and partnerships facilitated by such intermediaries has become progressively denser and more productive, and the channeling of capital from banks, corporations, foundations, churches, and the low-income housing tax credits through them to local groups has become quite substantial.[50]

The dramatic improvement of CDC capacities in the 1990s has been partly due to the National Community Development Initiative (NCDI), an un-precedented national philanthropic collaboration begun in 1991, which now includes eighteen major foundations, banks, corporations and HUD committed to work together until 2001. Led by LISC and Enterprise, NCDI has operated in twenty-three cities with some three hundred CDCs to build capacities for strategic planning, resource development, internal governance, and networking. As a result, the number of "capable" CDCs in the cities doubled by 1997, and the number of "top-tier" performers increased by 45 percent. The number of new local partners among corporations, banks, foundations, government agencies, universities, and other institutions increased substantially and produced what Walker and Weinheimer describe as a "revolution of local institutions" that includes new lending and operating support collaboratives, more coherent public strategies, and a narrowing of the gap between cities with long community development experience and the relative newcomers.[51]

Growing diversification of CDC activities is also evident. While housing remains the core activity, some 20 percent of CDCs have become active in commercial and industrial development, and a good number are involved in providing venture capital, loans, and technical support for local entre-preneurial activity. Some are part of networks collaborating in workforce development. Others have created industrial parks composed of dozens of businesses and retail stores, sometimes employing hundreds or thousands of people. Still others are involved in developing and coordinating family services, such as day care cooperatives that provide licensing, training, and networking for in-home providers and link these to home renovation programs so that providers can improve their facilities and meet all code requirements for safety. CDCs have also established partnerships with YouthBuild programs that combine on-the-job construction training with public leadership development for school dropouts, as well as with other "community youth development" groups networked through a range of organizations such as the National Network for Youth and the International Youth Foundation.[52] In some cities, CDCs have mobilized thousands of volunteers for urban reforestation, landscaping, weatherization, and home repair projects. Many are engaged in an array of senior citizen programs, anticrime and antidrug activities, and health care and teen pregnancy programs.[53]

Some of these activities have characterized CDCs from the beginning but were de-emphasized in the 1980s in favor of zealous housing development. They have returned, however, as CDCs' increased stake in maintaining investments in housing and their role in property management have made holistic community development imperative. Investment in housing thus not only aimed initially to preserve social capital in local neighborhoods, but also has continued to elicit more elaborate community-building strategies to protect investments in physical capital. As with Catholic churches, whose investment in land and physical structures prompted them to invest in leadership development through congregation-based organizing, a virtuous dynamic between investments in physical and social capital has emerged in the community development arena.

The trend in recent years is also a renewal of grassroots organizing. The community development movement has always had a grassroots vision, though the "bricks and mortar" emphasis has often pushed it to the side, and the elimination of such federal programs as the Community Services Administration and CETA in the 1980s ended important sources of funds for organizing. Intermediary organizations and new corporate partners have tended to stress the "hard" measures of success, such as number of units produced, and have shown only limited willingness to support organizing. Staff have oriented themselves to these requirements and have favored recruitment of board members with external clout rather than local organizing capacity. Even when volunteers have been successfully mobilized, they have experienced little extended leadership development or input into the design of projects. And nonprofit directors and building managers have been more likely to rely on shared vision of resident/management cooperation than on formal resident empowerment organizations.[54]

Such criticisms, however, are sometimes exaggerated. As Tony Robinson argues, the claims that CDCs lose touch with their constituencies, foster gentrification, deny housing to the neediest tenants, and co-opt or neutralize neighborhood activism simply do not fit much of the evidence. The increasing power and professionalism of CDCs makes government and private developers increasingly dependent on the political and economic resources that CDCs can bring to the table. CDCs tend to formulate careful managed-growth strategies that include guaranteed low rents, and they resist property-owner organizations that seek to gentrify neighborhoods. They have been leading innovators in developing housing for such hard-to-place tenants as ex-convicts, people with AIDS, the homeless, war refugees, indigenous peoples, and runaway teenagers. Rather than co-opting and depoliticizing neighborhood activism, CDCs across the country have "created tenant management councils, nurtured neighborhood leaders, placed residents and clients on the CDC governing board, and allied with all variety of neighborhood protest movements."[55] They have recognized, and often promoted, a differentiated set of organizations with distinct advocacy and development functions, and they have learned to work in progressively complementary fashion with the community reinvestment movement, whose grassroots advocacy had initially emerged on a separate track.

In recent years private foundations have placed increased pressure on CDCs to demonstrate widespread community support as part of a larger strategic planning process for community revitalization and have been willing to provide funding to make this possible. Funders have mandated training for community board members and required board reorganization to represent local residents better. LISC, for example, has provided support for CDCs in various cities to hire organizing staff, as various city and state coalitions have also done. LISC has nurtured the "consensus organizing" model devised by Michael Eichler in the Monongahela Valley around Pittsburgh in the 1980s in response to the failures of old Alinsky organizing to generate constructive responses to the collapse of the steel industry. The model develops broad, independent community organizations and grassroots leadership, but with the explicit goal of building trust and relationships with downtown interests to foster collaborative ventures.[56]

Asset-Based Community Development

An increasing number of community development projects over the past decade have incorporated into their work the "asset-based" approach of John McKnight and John Kretzmann at the Asset-Based Community Development (ABCD) Institute of Northwestern University. This approach emerged slowly over a twenty-five year period as McKnight and Kretzmann worked with community groups in Chicago and then in the 1980s began a broader inventory of effective practices in twenty cities. As McKnight insists, "We were chroniclers. It was the community groups who were the inventors over a long period. Then a grant gave us the opportunity to generalize and name what the most effective of them were doing." McKnight and Kretzmann distill five key sets of assets that even the poorest communities possess, and that can be systematically mapped and mobilized in new ways to support "an internally focused, relationship-driven process of community development." These include (1) the capacities of individuals; (2) the work of associations; (3) the resources (not current outputs) of local institutions, public, private and nonprofit; (4) land as physical space; and (5) monetary values and exchanges, including the purchasing power and preferences of local residents. This approach also derives from a trenchant critique of a deficit model of communities and a professional model of intervention, which see residents primarily as clients with deficiencies in need of outside professional remedy and often convince local leaders to denigrate their own community and broker its defects for grants-in-aid, rather than recognize and build upon its strengths.

McKnight, originally a community organizer trained by Alinsky in the 1960s, is also critical of contemporary congregation-based approaches. He sees them as narrowing the range of local associations mobilized for action, and he faults them for tying their leadership training predominantly to a justice model that seeks outside resources, rather than combining this admittedly very necessary strategy with a producer model that seeks to make individuals and local associations themselves productive in the community development process. Yet several PICO and Gamaliel affiliates are currently experimenting with an asset-based approach, as are numerous local organizing groups and neighborhood associations. In the first three years after its publication in 1993, the ABCD Institute's extensive manual, *Building Communities from the Inside Out,* sold eighty thousand copies with no commercial distribution outlets, and its toolkits for local communities have since been further refined and expanded. A substantial number of community foundations, state extension services, local United Ways, settlement houses, healthy community coalitions, and national foundations funding health and human service reforms have undergone training and incorporated elements of the asset-based approach into their work. Various programs at the Department of Health and Human Services (public health, substance abuse, health promotion), the Corporation for National and Community Service, and the Peace Corps have done likewise.[57]

Comprehensive Revitalization Strategies

Over the past decade, comprehensive community revitalization, or "community-building," strategies have emerged from both critical learning within the community development and human service fields and from a search for other sources of funding besides housing dollars. In 1993 the National Community Building Network (NCBN) formed to exchange lessons and promote this approach further, with Angela Blackwell of the Rockefeller Foundation providing critical support and leadership. By 1996 there were some fifty foundation-funded, comprehensive community-building projects around the country, ranging considerably in emphasis and size. LISC also developed a Community Building Initiative with thirty-nine CDCs in eleven cities because "CDCs themselves demanded it."[58] They recognized that they could not maintain thousands of units of housing without simultaneously addressing such issues as drugs and crime. Comprehensive strategies attempt to move beyond categorical approaches in human service delivery, which may bring limited improvements in the lives of specific individuals but have not been effective in addressing systemic problems with many interactive effects (joblessness, low education, poor housing, ill health, limited access to networks of power). Comprehensive community-building strategies also reject deficit models in favor of assets-based approaches, and draw upon a variety of service innovations of recent years that engage clients as coproducers of services and responsible citizens contributing to their communities. As such strategies move systematically away from staff-driven community development models focused solely on housing, they build partnerships with local agencies and engage residents in active participation.[59]

The Comprehensive Community Revitalization Program (CCRP) in the South Bronx, initiated by the Surdna Foundation's Edward Skloot in 1992 in collaboration with other foundation and corporate funders, and now an independent entity, exemplifies a comprehensive revitalization strategy that leverages the capacities of four "mature" CDCs. These include the Mid-Bronx Desperadoes (MBD) Community Housing Corporation, organized in the mid-1970s to respond to widespread arson and abandonment of residential buildings; Mid-Bronx Senior Citizens Council, founded in the late 1970s to serve elderly residents stranded in poor housing with few services; Mt. Hope Housing Company, organized in the mid-1980s by residents and churches to combat neighborhood decline but originating a decade earlier as an Alinsky group among clergy; and Phipps Community Development Corporation— West Farms, a citywide low- and middle-income housing developer that has worked in West Farms since the early 1970s. CCRP chose these four (and two other CDCs that subsequently left) because their existing organizational capacities and perspectives positioned them to become even more energetic entrepreneurs in creating a collaborative set of ventures that would significantly increase resources and mobilize assets across many different networks horizontally within the community and across the city. Anita Miller, who has worked to refine community development strategies since her involvement in Model Cities, served as the project director until 1998, when CCRP, Inc., was created, and she has played a key role in linking the CDCs to a broad range of organizations and opportunities at the local, state, and federal level.

CCRP develops no comprehensive plan or top-down coordination, but provides the venture capital and organizational assistance that permits the CDCs to generate new initiatives quickly and establish new partnerships strategically. These complement the work of other programs and are integrated at the bottom by residents and practitioners from various settings according to their own needs and strengths. Resident participation, which had been neglected by the CDCs, has increased significantly, especially after widespread involvement in the initial visioning processes that formulated Quality-of-Life Physical Plans for the neighborhoods. Participation does not focus upon political activism or formal representation on policy-making boards, though both of these occur. Rather, CCRP recognizes that most members of the community have little time for these activities and thus encourages residents to do work of value to revitalization through civic associations and CDC programs. Here CCRP is responding to lessons of previous political battles for community control of schools in New York City, where control often resulted in low turnout, corruption, and failure, with genuine reform occurring later as a result of site-based collaboration between teachers and parents. This strategy self-consciously emphasizes social capital building based on resident engagement and everyday efficacy rather than political empowerment and impact on large, impersonal forces.

Thus, in responding to neighborhood safety, residents become resources to create safe corridors for school children and work collaboratively with the police through crime watches, while also holding the police accountable. A men's group provides mutual support to participants who are seeking employment, and tenant groups provide support for victims of domestic violence. The Health Realization program encourages people to see themselves as problem solvers and community builders rather than mere victims. Residents and corporate volunteers work with middle school students to clean up the Bronx River and develop a greenway corridor to the Bronx Zoo.

In its first six years, the CDCs have generated many new initiatives. These include the New Bronx Employment Service, with job resource centers in CDC buildings; five new family health care practices with prevention workshops and screening programs; a 108-bed residence for AIDS patients and a home health care enterprise for AIDS/HIV services based on experience with long-term senior care; a shopping center and farmers market; a Beacon School with one thousand youth involved each month in a broad range of after-school and weekend cultural and recreational activities; a Head Start center with innovative training for home-based child care; a catering business; adult education programs; intergenerational gardens; and more. The CCRP, of course, has had its disappointments and has yet to sustain engagement with the larger public systems, such as welfare, foster care, and juvenile probation, in a way that helps transform street-level bureaucracy. But it has provided critical lessons for comprehensive community initiatives, and some are adapting its model in other cities.[60]

Empowerment Zones and Public Housing Authorities

Policy learning and capacity building in community development are clearly reflected in the design of two federal programs of the 1990s, the Empowerment Zones (EZs) and Enterprise Communities (ECs) program and the HOPE VI public housing program. The competitive application process for EZ/ECs emphasizes capacities to develop strategic plans and forge community partnerships, including ties with business. It requires local applicants to inventory assets in the process of developing a vision for sustainable community development that integrates jobs, health, social services, environment, neighborhood safety, and related concerns. National CDC intermediaries lobbied heavily for this design, and they funded local CDCs to assume leading roles, which they did in the application process and after EZ/EC designation. CDCs, established since the original Community Action legislation, were now the dominant community players wherever their infrastructure was moderately strong. Where they were newer or more tenuous, the EZ/EC design, along with complementary efforts by the National Community Development Initiative, has encouraged CDC development. In addition, parallel learning has occurred among many Enterprise Zones formed during the Reagan and Bush years. As Richard

Cowden, executive director of the American Association of Enterprise Zones, has noted, Enterprise Zones were just state and local tax incentives at first. But little by little, with experimentation, people realized tax incentives alone do not work. "Good planners and administrators said, 'What we have here is a bull's-eye. Let's see how much we can hit it with,' and they began adding day care, crime programs, small-business incubators, job training, tax-exempt bond financing."[61]

Six urban EZs were named in 1995 (Atlanta, Baltimore, Chicago, Detroit, New York, and Philadelphia/Camden), along with three rural and two Supplemental EZs (Los Angeles, Cleveland). ECs numbered ninety-five, with four designated Enhanced ECs (Boston, Houston, Kansas City, and Oakland). The six urban EZs will receive 100 million dollars each over ten years and are eligible for 100 million dollars in social service block grants, various tax incentives, and employee wage credits. These zones have priority status for a variety of other federal grants to complement their work through community policing, environmental justice, family services, and the like. Regular ECs receive 3 million dollars in grants but also have priority status for more, while the four Enhanced ECs receive 25 million dollars each. Fifteen new urban EZs were added in a second round in the FY 1997 budget. Many had engaged in strategic planning and partnership formation during the first round, as intended by the program's design.

CDCs and other neighborhood associations have struggled with city halls over the extent and nature of community participation, both in the planning process and after receiving designation, and the outcomes have varied with local political culture. For example, Atlanta, with relatively weak CDC and NPU (Neighborhood Planning Unit) structures, had to fight to get representation alongside city officials, business, and traditional social service agencies. In contrast, Philadelphia, Detroit, and Cleveland have had activist CDCs at the table from the beginning. Baltimore, with few CDCs but a good working relationship among the mayor, Community Building in Partnership, and the Historic East Baltimore Community Action Coalition, has designed Village Centers to become self-sustaining CDCs at the neighborhood level.[62]

It is still too early to tell whether the EZs and ECs can sustain community participation against the tendency of city halls to reign it in or whether the dominant CDCs can accommodate more diverse participation by other community actors. Nonetheless, this federal initiative builds upon the foundations of much greater community capacity, more robust partnerships with other established players, and more complementary programs and resources at federal, state, and local levels than existed at the time of the last major initiatives of the 1960s.

Public housing authorities around the country have also been progressively applying and refining community-building approaches, especially through the HOPE VI program created by the Urban Revitalization Demonstration Act of 1993. HOPE VI resulted from the first fresh look at public housing in decades. It was guided by a number of earlier grassroots innovations and by a recognition of the importance of building human and social capital among resident communities contained in the 1992 reports of the Commission on Distressed Housing and the Cleveland Foundation Commission on Poverty. As of 1997, seventy-five public housing authorities were formally involved in HOPE VI programs. And many others are learning from their experiences in applying three core principles: (1) engage residents in the community, (2) set community standards, and (3) increase access to opportunities. Residents engage in planning for demolition and redesign, and are provided leadership training and dispute-resolution skills to run meetings, whose attendance has been boosted enormously. They develop self-help projects ranging from parenting and health education to community policing and building maintenance and repair, and they have the authority to allocate savings from the latter to other resident priorities. Through Ameri-Corps, Learn and Serve America, Civilian Conservation Corps, and locally developed programs, they perform community service as teacher's aides, work on community education teams, and engage in graffiti removal and landscaping. They devise initiatives to reunite families, as in the Hartford Housing Authority's program to bring men back into their families' lives by guaranteeing employment in its modernization program. Residents in Baltimore's Step Up Program have worked with construction unions and the American Federation of State, County, and Municipal Employees (AFSCME) to establish apprenticeships, and others have developed innovative computer-learning and job-networking projects, and have generated various small business ventures and home ownership strategies.

Central to all these efforts, however, have been the setting and enforcement of community standards of acceptable behavior by residents themselves. These range from everyday norms of not walking on the grass to more difficult rules on crime and drugs that can result in eviction. The residents of Renaissance Village in Cleveland, for instance, all sign a "covenant" to acquire the knowledge and skills to promote prosperity and community, maintain families, ensure safety and security, obey the rules and ordinances of the community, and live as models and leaders. Police calls at Renaissance Village, once regarded as the most dangerous public housing community in the city, fell from 1,046 in 1993 to 239 in 1995, and only three evictions were necessary because of crime. And in the words of the residents' covenant,

> We further commit to watch over one another; to be mindful of one another in our prayers; to assist one another in times of need; to respect and hold one another in the highest esteem as evidenced by our courtesy in speech, our slowness to anger, our readiness for conciliation and mediation. . . . This, our Covenant, is our solemn and joyful commitment.[63]

NEIGHBORHOOD ASSOCIATIONS AND COMMUNITY VISIONING

Urban civic innovation has occurred in a variety of other forms as well over the past few decades, most notably in formal neighborhood governance, participatory planning, and community visioning. These have often been complemented by community organizing, community development, and other forms of civic initiative, though with some dynamic tension and competition among the different forms and the strategies associated with them.

Neighborhood participation in city governance was the focus of the National Citizen Participation Development Project at Tufts University, which was conducted over a ten-year period by a research team headed by Jeffrey Berry, Kent Portney, and Ken Thomson. Four cities—St. Paul, Portland, Dayton, and Birmingham—have especially well-developed participation systems, though a good number of other cities have introduced similar components.[64] In each of the four, federal mandates in the 1960s and early 1970s served as critical catalysts in moving mayors and agency officials to respond to rising citizen demands for participation with a citywide initiative. Portland built upon neighborhood associations active from the 1950s and 1960s and upon Community Action and Model Cities Programs.[65] Dayton likewise built upon its Model Cities Planning Council and on neighborhood councils, which delegated significant decision-making authority to citizen groups but drew lessons from the limits of citizen participation systems confined to selected areas of the city.[66] The Association of St. Paul Communities participated in a committee appointed by the mayor, which had issued its "Making Democracy Work" report in 1973 outlining what has since become its basic institutional reforms, although the catalyst for the attempt was the community development program, which specified that federal funds could be used for citizen participation. In Birmingham, HUD officials established strict participation guidelines for its Community Development Department as a result of the city's past record of racial discrimination.[67] Even in San Antonio, the fifth core city in the study, which differs from the others in having especially strong congregation-based organizing rather than a formal citywide system of neighborhood associations, it was the federal mandate to replace a discriminatory, at-large city council system with district elections that permitted COPS to affect city politics so significantly. And the Community Action Program had also provided an important framework for the Catholic hierarchy and local priests to mobilize church participation earlier in the 1960s, as Archbishop Robert Lucey worked directly with his fellow Texan and friend Lyndon Johnson and appointed a diocesan priest to head the principal Community Action Agency in the city.[68]

The four core cities were able to establish vibrant systems of participation capable of substantial learning over the next two decades because local political entrepreneurs responded to these favorable conditions with major innovations capable of demonstrating benefits to neighborhood groups and city officials alike before federal mandates were weakened and local fiscal constraints became much more stringent. These innovations have taken a variety of forms but have a number of traits in common. They cover all neighborhoods, not simply poor or minority neighborhoods targeted for community development or other funding. Strictly nonpartisan by ordinance, the neighborhood associations cannot directly mobilize resources or dedicate their media to partisan campaigns for city council or mayor. They have extensive two-way information channels with city hall and multiple points to exercise voice, though they tend to be most effective on local land-use issues and least effective on citywide issues such as metropolitan transit, downtown development, and school reform. They have staff paid by the city, though many also raise other funds as incorporated nonprofits with quasi-autonomous standing.

Perhaps most important, these neighborhood participation systems accommodate, complement, and even encourage a wide range of other forms of independent citizen organizing and self-help. Indeed, the existence of multiple organizational forms increased the vitality of participation in the seventy participatory projects studied by the Tufts team. Independent groups initiate action more often, but the neighborhood associations play a strong role in the outcome. They work with the Sierra Club, Audubon Society, and other local environmental groups; with senior and youth organizations, CDCs, local Leagues of Women Voters and United Ways; and with many informal self-help efforts. They have established community mediation projects, "good neighbor plans," and crime watches. They have had a clear impact on trust building within neighborhoods and with government officials, and have helped to develop a sense of community at every income level. And they neither coopt nor supplant various independent forms of citizen action.

All of these developments represent substantial learning and refinement beyond the initial designs implemented in the mid-1970s, and have made these cities more governable. As we noted in chapter 1, the well-structured citywide systems show significantly greater impacts of face-to-face democracy on individual citizen learning. This was measured by indices of political information, sense of political efficacy, and broad community perspectives beyond narrow neighborhood boundaries, which the Tufts team used to compare these cities to comparable communities lacking citywide systems. Learning was especially noteworthy for low-income groups; indeed, in the three core cities of Portland, St. Paul, and Dayton, the participation system produced a responsiveness bias in their favor. Nonetheless, there is significant concern at the local level and among some national innovators and scholars that these formal systems can become gatekeepers limiting civic initiative and constituting citizen bureaucracy.[69] At this point, the evidence is not clear whether such concerns are cause for serious alarm or a trigger for further learning, as some neighborhood associations broaden the range of their civic efforts; shift emphasis from planning to problem solving and self help; and experiment with newer approaches, such as the asset-based model.

Portland: Redesigning the System

In Portland, Oregon, continued vitality and the capacity to learn are especially evident. In the 1990s, the Office of Neighborhood Associations (ONA) was significantly restructured in response to a variety of concerns. Many low-income people, renters, minorities, and families with young children felt poorly represented within some neighborhood associations and angered by their resistance to the siting of social services in their areas. A number of District Coalitions did not appear to manage internal conflict very well or had become staff driven. Activists and leaders grew weary of the customer service model in which citizens simply make demands on government. And in North Portland, major conflict erupted over neighborhood association governance. In response, the city's commissioners established a task force of twenty-five people to conduct a fifteen-month participatory review that included visits to the neighborhood associations, surveys, public meetings, and an opportunity for all associations and District Coalitions to review the draft recommendations and debate them in further public meetings. They also studied citizen involvement models in other cities, including Seattle, which we examine below. The city council adopted the final recommendations in January 1998.

The ONA was renamed the Office of Neighborhood Involvement (ONI) to recognize its new role in promoting greater diversity, representativeness, and accountability. Its mission is not only to support the work of the neighborhood associations but also to include ethnic associations, multicultural organizations, and other "communities beyond neighborhood boundaries," as well as neighborhood business district associations (NBDAs). ONI is designed to facilitate greater communication and partnerships among all these forms of civic association and to develop trust building and mediation capacities in the interests of long-term win-win solutions. It also seeks to ensure greater accountability of neighborhood associations and District Coalitions to each other and to the diversity of associations in their areas. ONI provides training and continuous leadership development to promote diverse participation, generate community dialogue on race, ensure compliance with the Americans with Disabilities Act, encourage day care at meetings, and foster informal neighborhood socializing. Nondiscrimination on the basis of sexual orientation was also strongly reaffirmed for all officially recognized associations, including the NBDAs. And resources have been shifted to support neighborhoods with greater socioeconomic needs, despite the resistance of some neighborhood associations to their own relative loss. Indeed, commissioner Gretchen Kafoury, her chief aide, Nancy Biasi, who formerly served as director of ONA, and mayor Vera Katz, who like many others in Portland began her career as a neighborhood activist, have all supported greater focus on poorer neighborhoods, low-income housing development, and conflict resolution to site social services in resistant neighborhoods. This support, buttressed by the efforts of the National Community Development Initiative, has helped the city make very substantial CDC system gains during the 1990s.

Various other components of Portland's political culture have complemented these efforts. Michael Harrison, chief planner for neighborhood and community planning, once a citizen activist in the early 1970s, has transformed the culture of planning in the city by working closely with neighborhoods and by recruiting activists through Portland State University's graduate program in regional and urban planning. In Oregon, a strong state framework for comprehensive planning and controlled growth established "core values," such as water quality and the preservation of forest lands, which were reinforced in the civic culture through a multitude of media and could help citizens focus on shared goals in their many—and often very intense—disputes over the specifics of land-use plans. The Portland Metropolitan Service District is the only elected regional land-use agency in the country, dating from a 1970s law limiting urban sprawl. The culture of participatory planning forms the backdrop for the Portland Option, which encourages federal, state, and local cooperation and regulatory flexibility around benchmarks for education, workforce development, reduction of dependency, and maternal and child health. Citizen forums have been essential in developing, refining, and prioritizing the benchmarks in the Portland area and across the state. The District Attorney's Office, challenged by citizen anticrime efforts that have received assistance through ONA and ONI over the years, has developed an innovative system of Neighborhood DAs. These serve in partnership with citizens as local facilitators, legal counselors, problem solvers, and community advocates—but not litigators—to reduce the kinds of low-level crime that threaten public safety and breed more serious criminal activity.

Neighborhood associations have also provided a template for environmental problem solving and the formation of watershed associations. They serve as partners along with churches, schools, soccer leagues, and little leagues for innovative projects, such as Naturescaping for Clean Rivers and the Downspout Disconnection Program. The latter is designed to lessen stormwater runoff and the combined sewer overflows that pollute the Willamette River and Columbia Slough. Some five hundred middle school students have learned how to do downspout disconnections on neighbors' homes. They pool what they earn from the city's incentive program to fund other community projects of their own choosing. And they utilize these practical skills in the context of a school curriculum developed to meet the Oregon Benchmarks in Math, Science, and Language Arts.

Some community groups remain critical, to be sure. The IAF's Portland Organizing Project is profoundly skeptical of citizen involvement that is funded through the city, and its organizing has been an important factor in strengthening commitments to affordable housing. Some neighborhood associations still resent their symbolic loss of status as ONA became ONI. Nonetheless, the breadth and depth of citizen participation in Portland have continued to grow over the decades, and innovative forms have emerged in a great variety of arenas. And many in leadership positions recall their roots in the organizing of the 1960s and 1970s. As former ONA director Nancy Biasi, who was an organizer in both the student and women's movements, put it, "Every time we had a meeting about whether to have a bike path or some other neighborhood issue, we utilized the skills we learned from women's organizing in the 1970s."[70]

St. Paul and Minneapolis:
Competition between CDCs and Neighborhood Associations

In some cities, however, conflict between neighborhood associations and CDCs has emerged as the problems of the concentration effects of poverty have achieved greater prominence in policy circles and popular media, and as homeowners have sought to limit further low-income rental development to protect their property values. In both St. Paul and Minneapolis this dynamic emerged in the 1990s after a twenty-year period in which CDCs had dominated the housing policy subsystem and had collaborated effectively with neighborhood associations.[71] As Edward Goetz and Mara Sidney's studies show, the increasing fear of crime, rise of regionalism, and concern for a fair distribution of urban/suburban responsibilities for affordable housing catalyzed greater action by homeowners, especially where they already constituted a decided minority. In Minneapolis, the Neighborhood Revitalization Program also raised the stakes as substantial funding became available. New resources could enhance the development of home ownership and help retain or attract middle-class residents, thus enabling a more mixed-income neighborhood to improve its schools, bring in new businesses, and build social capital across class lines. Or new funding could reinforce low-income rental strategies and social service spending. Homeowners received support from city officials and regional planners who supported poverty deconcentration, though a "fair share" subsidized housing bill passed by the legislature was vetoed twice by the governor. The familiar participation biases in favor of educated, higher-income, and homeowning groups enabled them to secure majorities on some neighborhood association boards, and several voted for moratoria on CDC-sponsored rental housing, especially where rentals were already 90 percent of the market.

Each institution challenged the other's claim to represent the neighborhood. Neighborhood associations argued that CDCs represented only a narrow constituency of those who benefited from CDC-developed, low-income rental housing and were not open to broad grassroots participation. Renters, they claimed, were more transient and had less of a stake in the neighborhood, whereas their own property investments and long-term residency gave them a greater stake in neighborhood revitalization. CDCs countered that neighborhood associations, though formally open to all, had come to be dominated by small, insular groups of homeowners and failed to represent people of color, newer residents, and the poor. While Goetz and Sidney conclude that these conflicts diminish the potential of the neighborhood movement in these two cities, considerable room for policy dialogue and mutual learning remains among CDCs and neighborhood associations seeking strategies for poverty deconcentration. Indeed, leaders in the effort for the Comprehensive Choice Housing Act in the legislature developed an extensive coalition with community development groups and church congregations within and outside the inner city, as well as with the League of Women Voters and the Citizens League.[72]

Seattle: Matching Grants for Public Work

The City of Seattle was a relative latecomer to a formal system of neighborhood associations, though organizing there goes back decades. As issues of growth and crime heated up in the 1980s, and citizens demanded greater voice, however, city officials began to study St. Paul and Portland and then hired Jim Diers in 1988 to direct the newly established Department of Neighborhoods. Diers had been trained in old-style Alinsky organizing through PICO and the MidAmerican Institute, and he had come to Seattle in 1975 as a "peace and justice organizer" in the low-income neighborhoods of Rainier Valley. "We were confrontational. We were NIMBYs. We'd stop the incinerators, and block more low-income housing where there already was too much. But we did get recycling as a result. And we now have good scatter-site housing." But as the new director of the Department of Neighborhoods, Diers was charged with establishing a system of thirteen District Councils built around little city halls with representatives of all the resident and business neighborhood associations in each area. By 1999, he oversaw a staff of one hundred, mostly serving in neighborhood service centers and providing local leadership training. A budget of 10 million dollars addresses neighborhood planning to meet the requirements of the state's growth management act of 1990.

Early on, however, Diers devised a self-help project that has since become a model for public work by citizens themselves and is being transferred to an increasing number of cities. The Neighborhood Matching Grant program is a policy design simple in concept. The city provides grants on a competitive basis to neighborhood associations, now numbering 230 across the city, that agree to match the dollar value of the grant with donated labor (at $10 per hour), donated materials, or cash. Most are "small and simple" grants under $10,000, but larger grants can run as high as $100,000. Any democratic neighborhood association can qualify, including environmental organizations, ethnic associations, gay and lesbian groups, and historical preservation societies. Applications are judged by peers from the thirteen District Council representatives who make up the City Neighborhood Council. The criteria include self-help, diversity, citizen participation, environmental sustainability, and collaboration. The matching grant program has been a phenomenal hit, funding more than 1,500 projects as of 2000, and its budget, which recently doubled to $3 million per year, will increase further over the next several years, making it the largest funder in the city.

The grants have elicited creative and constructive self-help projects of all sorts. Parents, children, and local architects have built or redesigned over 150 playgrounds and maintain them with a deep sense of community ownership and ongoing civic education. For instance, the beautifully designed "salmon slide" is part of a trail for kids that teaches them the salmon's upstream migration. The trail is linked to a creek restoration project similar to others now funded through matching grants. The frightening Fremont Troll sculpture, which sits under a park overpass, helped to galvanize adults and kids alike to defend their view of public art against a prominent local art critic, who later held the troll up as emblematic of engaged citizens designing public space. The grants have enabled Southeast Asians and other minorities to build community gardens in partnership with local schools and public housing projects. The Involving All Neighbors program helps integrate citizens with developmental disabilities into the productive work of creek restoration projects, the wooden boat center of the Floating Homes Association, and any number of other neighborhood activities to which they can "contribute their gifts."

Indeed, the Floating Homes Association's Lake Union campaign, led by Terry Pettus in the 1960s, established a model of citizen action as productive work in the creation and preservation of public wealth, and this model directly influenced neighborhood and environmental organizers in subsequent decades. Diers still believes that citizens need an independent power base and that they often need to "beat up on the city." But he has managed to utilize his earlier organizing skills in a way that elevates relationship building and public work to a new level and to diffuse this model very broadly across the city through the dozens of staff he has recruited from various community groups. In the process, the neighborhood movement has become much stronger and more diverse in its participants and activities. Rather than a reactive movement, Diers notes, the neighborhood movement is one that now takes responsibility to create public space and public culture—a material, ecological, artistic, and civic culture.[73]

Professional Networks and Intermediaries

Many other cities have developed and refined neighborhood associations and councils over the past several decades. Some built neighborhood-planning systems on the foundations of Community Action and Model Cities agencies and CDBG mandates, surpassing their requirements for citizen participation. By 1984, over fifty cities were doing so, and by 1990, over 60 percent of all cities with a population of a hundred thousand or more had established neighborhood associations. Seventy-three percent of these cities reported an increase in the number of neighborhood councils over the previous decade, and only 6 percent noted a decrease. Seventy percent of cities with councils utilized officially recognized neighborhood councils, though most of the rest reported close working relations between city hall and councils regardless of official recognition. The introduction of participative mechanisms is related to city strategies to retain or attract middle-class residents or to reduce exit by providing voice. And as John Clayton Thomas argues in his study of Cincinnati, the development of neighborhood councils over several decades represents a "long learning process" that eventually "reformed the reforms" of the technocratic planners of the Progressive era.[74]

Several national associations have been especially important in helping to diffuse neighborhood innovations and broader community visioning projects on the urban and regional level. Neighborhoods USA, which was founded by Howard Hallman with funding from the Ford Foundation in 1975, has continued to grow over two decades, even as several other organizations with similar missions have declined. NUSA's members include grassroots activists, neighborhood associations, and city agencies, and the national association is beginning to develop several regional associations in the Midwest and Florida. Despite its relatively weak organizational infrastructure that runs with only one paid staff person, NUSA manages to hold large annual meetings of up to one thousand people that generate a useful exchange of practical tools and models. For instance, quite a few cities have learned how to develop neighborhood matching grants like those in Seattle, and neighborhood leadership colleges like those in Hampton, Virginia, from the workshops and networking they find at the NUSA conferences. They have also learned about assets-based community development, congregation-based community organizing, parish nursing, environmental justice, sustainable development, and healthy communities. NUSA uses its annual conference as an opportunity to enhance collaboration and mutual education among local organizations and officials in its host city, a condition for its signing a contract with the city to host the conference.[75]

Professional associations such as the National League of Cities, American Planning Association (APA), International City/County Management Association (ICMA), National Association of Counties, and Conference of Mayors have become increasingly active in recent years in promoting participatory models. While citizen participation is hardly their main mission, such organizations have repeatedly been compelled by grassroots activists to confront the limits of their own professional and technocratic practices and have been challenged by innovative practitioners within their own ranks to develop new programs and recognize innovative models in the field. Norman Krumholz, former director of the City of Cleveland Planning Commission, brought his rich experience in equity planning, based on relationship and trust-building strategies among agency officials and community groups during a period of intense conflict, to his role as president of the APA. The APA gave its first Presidential Award to the Comprehensive Community Revitalization Program in the South Bronx for its extensive grassroots planning to develop quality-of-life physical plans, and the APA has become increasingly interested in civic renewal as a vital component of effective planning. Dan Kemmis, mayor of Missoula, Montana, brought his innovative community-building practices to the National League of Cities as director of its Leadership Training Institute, and executive director Donald Borut and others have focused increasingly on developing learning resources to help members design and implement participatory strategies. Academics, such as John Forester and John Friedmann, have helped shift the theoretical paradigm of planning and its teaching toward a model of learning collaboratively with citizens.[76]

The Pew Partnership for Civic Change serves as another critical leadership development and learning network. Established in 1992 at the initiative of Rebecca Rimel and the board of the Pew Charitable Trusts, and directed by Suzanne Morse, the Pew Partnership initially provided grants and training to collaborative projects in fourteen smaller cities of 50–150,000. These projects included HandMade in America, a twenty-two-county sustainable community development partnership based on regional handmade crafts in Asheville, North Carolina; neighborhood organizations and regional leadership in Longview and Tyler, Texas; a community-wide youth mentoring program in Eugene, Oregon; a comprehensive affordable housing strategy in Santa Fe, New Mexico; and other initiatives on children, families, and workforce development. The Pew Partnership is designed to foster learning, innovation, and civic capacity building for long-term community change beyond specific projects and to develop a national network to share lessons among and beyond these communities through national trainings and resources. It has enabled communities to benefit from a range of approaches, such as assets-based development and community visioning, and it has been especially attuned to issues of equity, diversity, and inclusion. As most of the initial fourteen cities established ways to sustain their work beyond the 3–4 year grant period, the Pew Civic Entrepreneur Initiative began to provide training for teams of twenty civic entrepreneurs from each of ten medium-sized cities ranging in population from 150,000 to 400,000, who would, in turn, mentor another twenty in a subsequent phase. And the Pew Partnership's most recent initiative, Wanted: Solutions for America, is developing participatory action research in up to fifty communities to foster, document, and diffuse innovations in a broad range of arenas.[77]

Perhaps the most important national nonprofit helping to catalyze innovative partnerships and new forms of community visioning at the local and regional levels has been the National Civic League (NCL), headed by Chris Gates, its president. We discuss NCL's own organizational transformation in the 1980s more fully in chapter 6, where we consider its critical role in building a broader civic renewal movement across the United States. In the years since it reinvented itself, however, NCL has steadily developed new and more sophisticated tools to enable communities to build civic capacity, and NCL has helped to stimulate parallel efforts in other organizations. Its Civic Index enables local civic and government actors to assess their community's current performance on the basis of various indicators of citizen engagement, community leadership, and intergroup collaboration. The Civic Index also serves as the basis for community visioning and strategic planning in an increasing number of communities willing to bring a broad range of stakeholders to the table. NCL has itself facilitated visioning in dozens of cities and regions, such as Charlotte-Mecklenburg, North Carolina; Atlanta, Georgia; Sioux Falls, South Dakota; and Lee's Summit, Missouri. A growing network of consultants does similar work, spun off from NCL or influenced by its practice. Indeed, the demand for these kinds of services has been steadily growing. NCL's Program in Community Problem Solving has provided assistance to scores of community-building projects and local and national foundations, as well as intellectual tools to help guide innovators in government and nonprofits alike. The All-America City Award, which NCL hosts every year in conjunction with Allstate Insurance, provides a wonderfully festive—if rigorously demanding—occasion to evaluate and honor thirty outstanding finalists from cities, counties, towns, or neighborhoods that have engaged in at least three innovative civic projects and have attempted to rethink basic ways in which they conduct their affairs. NCL also uses the award strategically to educate scores of other cities and towns that apply, or even consider applying, by helping them think through the Civic Index and analyze their own accomplishments. The richness of innovative work in many settings, even when we discount self-promotion for the purposes of winning an award, is quite striking, as is the widening circle of local officials and nonprofit applicants who have progressively internalized core civic ideas over the past decade.

NCL's role has been central in linking like-minded practitioners within many of these other professional associations and, indeed, in challenging them to rethink core practices. To be sure, this step was not easy at first. For instance, when Donald Borut, then the deputy director of the ICMA, invited

John Parr, then president of NCL, to address three hundred ICMA members at a workshop in the late 1980s on how city managers need to learn how to work collaboratively with empowered citizens, the very first question from the group was, "So, are you saying that I should take all my education and throw it out the window?" When Parr replied with his wry Midwestern humor, "You're getting warm," sixty people stood up and marched out of the room. Over the course of the 1990s many more rejoined the conversation.[78]

CONCLUSION

The numbers of congregation-based community organizations, CDCs, visioning projects, and neighborhood associations with a significant role in urban governance have grown substantially over the past several decades and have become increasingly diverse in their regional distribution. An extensive array of intermediary institutions and support networks has emerged at national, regional, state, and local levels. These networks have progressively become more sophisticated in their capacities for leadership development and critical learning from best practices and in their ability to put together complex funding and technical assistance. Many innovative tools—from one-on-ones and public accountability sessions to community land trusts and asset inventories—have been developed, refined, and diffused. Various networks have established robust professional norms and practices while continuing to expand their capacities for local organizing. They have mobilized old forms of social capital, such as religious congregations, for new purposes and with fresh democratic methods, and they have carved out new niches for civic organizing. They have devised effective ways to maintain and deepen core participatory democratic beliefs—to "keep the faith," as one CDC leader has put it—and have utilized these core beliefs as important resources in strategic search and experimentation at critical junctures of organizational growth.

Community-based projects have also enhanced their capacities for complex partnerships with an increasingly diverse set of actors, including banks, corporations, major religious and educational institutions, and municipal and state housing, planning, and economic development agencies. Their "relational density," as organizational ecology refers to it, has increased as these participatory innovations have embedded themselves in relationships with a broad set of established governmental and nongovernmental actors in their communities.[79] Indeed, key staff in many local agencies received critical experience and value socialization while themselves first working in community organizing and development groups, and candidates for citywide elective office sometimes come up through the ranks of formally recognized neighborhood associations. But even where this is not the case, significant mutual learning between community groups and established institutions occurs, often triggered by phases of conflict. And strategies for developing financial, physical, social, and human capital for community revitalization have become progressively interlaced as many groups have continued to diversify their activities and connect them to broader community building in partnership with other actors.

The extent of capacity building and learning is evident, even if its full significance is open to considerable debate. At the beginning of the 1960s only a handful of congregation-based community-organizing projects existed. There were no community development corporations, few extant models of citizen governance other than New England town meetings, virtually no community involvement in urban planning and public administration, and not even the remotest inkling of strategic visioning projects for entire cities and regions.

Community-organizing and development groups have continued to refine their local political strategies to shape agendas, design policy, and develop trust as responsible partners, while keeping a critical distance from partisan campaigns. The fears of cooptation, though often exaggerated, have prompted internal reflection on core values and continued practical learning. In view of the inability of academic Left critics of cooptation to proffer a realistic alternative strategy of confrontational mobilization that could have been sustained, or that could have produced comparable results valued by community members themselves, the strategic decisions of congregation-based community organizing networks, neighborhood associations, and CDCs appear, on the whole, to have been politically astute and democratically responsive.

The community development movement reacted strategically to shifts in federal policy after the demise of Community Action and Model Cities. With renewed vigor and critical insight, it leveraged the 1970s neighborhood activism and the relatively favorable policy environment of the early Carter years so that it could respond to Reagan-era cutbacks and devolution with significant new growth in collaboration with local, state, corporate, banking, religious, and foundation partners. Federal cutbacks in economic development funding to cities—such as Urban Development Action Grants and other programs that enabled many cities to develop new entrepreneurial roles for themselves in the late 1970s and early 1980s—also prompted a substantial increase in local public-private ventures that in many cases complemented or incorporated community development agendas.[80]

Local organizing and national advocacy have helped to establish significant policy supports: the Community Reinvestment Act, with its legal leverage for community groups to elicit collaborative investment activity from financial institutions; the Low-Income Housing Tax Credit, with its financial incentives for specific investments and for collaboration among the broad range of corporate, agency, and philanthropic actors to protect the general framework of all tax credit deals; the 1990 Housing Act, with its 15 percent set-asides for comprehensive housing development organizations; HOPE VI legislation, with its support for community building and self-help in public housing; the Community Development Financial Institutions program, with its technical and financial assistance for new community lenders; and Empowerment Zone legislation requiring community participation and strategic partnerships among a broad range of actors. All represent significant policy learning built upon a foundation of substantial capacity building at many levels, strategic responses to a changing environment, and a sustained long-term commitment to participatory values extending back to the 1960s.

Many innovative forms of urban community participation have come to play complementary roles and employ common language, though with considerable dynamic tension and even outright competition in some areas. Neighborhood associations often collaborate with CDCs and other local civic and environmental organizations or with innovative elder health programs such as the block nurses in St. Paul and healthy communities groups in Indianapolis. Neighborhood associations and CDCs have often been critical catalysts and partners of community-policing initiatives and the broader "community justice movement," which have shifted the policing paradigm from a detached professional model to one of community involvement, co-production, and collaboration in problem solving.[81] And the presence of multiple organizational forms seems to increase the overall vitality of participation in many settings. CDCs often establish differentiated organizations to pursue various advocacy and development roles. The Empowerment Zones and Enterprise Communities have built upon existing CDCs, and the community reinvestment movement has progressively converged with the community development movement. Some congregation-based organizing federations, such as the IAF groups in Boston and Chicago, now include CDCs as core members, and leaders such as Ernie Cortés bring the message of renewed organizing to national CDC venues, such as the 1992 Beyond Bricks and Mortar: Building Healthy Communities conference of NCCED. Furthermore, the language of "relationship building" initially developed by IAF, "building upon assets" of the ABCD Institute, and "community building" of NCBN and other networks, has been diffused widely across many different kinds of projects, as have specific techniques (one-on-ones, asset inventories) related to them. This common language has made collaboration easier, even as much variation persists.

Nonetheless, civic organizations face considerable competition over funding, local resident commitment, relative legitimacy of specific organizations and models of organizing, and access to valued partnerships and power brokers. CDCs and neighborhood associations can develop different approaches to the deconcentration of poverty, the importance of home ownership, and the class and racial implications of these. Organizing networks, such as ACORN in its home city of Little Rock, can resist efforts by LISC to establish a community development system where none previously existed. The

IAF organizes through trust-building consensus among congregations and forms selective strategic relationships with corporate and government power brokers, but it eschews more inclusive citywide visioning, neighborhood planning, or community-building projects that might dilute its political leverage and challenge its relative legitimacy in the local ecology of organizing. IAF assemblies serve as public dramas that make visible its systematic work in forging relationships and generating accountability, but these are not designed to provide open forums for democratic deliberation among the broadest spectrum of community stakeholders. Top-down community-building efforts, such as the Atlanta Project, can elicit indifference or opposition from preexisting neighborhood associations or networks of black clergy, even as they engender some creative partnerships between neighborhoods and corporations. Smaller and newer civic associations can resent Empowerment Zones designed to leverage the already existing capacities of mature CDCs. And innovative civic journalism projects, such as Taking Back Our Neighborhoods in Charlotte (see chapter 5), can generate resentment by government and nonprofit actors who feel that they distort priorities previously established at the community level.

In many cities, strategic brokering and niche guidance occur within and across sectors through formal and informal efforts by community foundations, citywide community-building initiatives, and, of course, everyday consultation and bargaining. Common national funding sources, such as the Campaign for Human Development, also function to establish informal norms regulating competition among different kinds of organizing projects. While they face no fixed limit on resources nor a zero-sum distribution of power, community-based organizations and projects are nonetheless vulnerable to a relative scarcity of access and legitimacy, and their models of organizing constitute different, and in some cases incompatible, ways of imagining community and democracy. Such conflicts are, of course, inevitable in settings where significant opportunities and underutilized community assets are present to support new initiatives, yet considerable uncertainty about what works—or even what counts as working—remains. And, as in a thriving small business sector, competition and failure are often the preconditions for innovation and learning.[82]

Successful strategies of community organizing and development that build collaborative relationships with government and other institutions enhance the possibilities for a shift from what Clarence Stone calls "development regimes" to alternative urban regimes oriented to greater opportunity and participation among low- and middle-income constituencies. Urban regime theory is premised upon a "social production model of power" that highlights the relative capacity of local governments to elicit relationships of "civic cooperation" with business and civic actors and generate the appropriate level and kind of resources for ends that appear achievable. Regime theory helps explain the overwhelming dominance of development regimes in the post-war period without at the same time succumbing to a deterministic version of "city limits" that shrivels the space of genuine urban politics and closes off significant policy choices.[83] Development regimes are easiest to organize because they offer an abundance of selective incentives and small opportunities (jobs, contracts), meet the political need for quick and visible action, rely mainly on elite coordination, and can manage conflict through insider transactions. But growth coalitions have been challenged from the 1970s onwards by resistance to urban renewal, the emergence of environmental and quality-of-life organizing that highlight the hidden costs of many developer-driven projects, and by the expansion of opportunities for citizen participation and veto. In addition, it is becoming clearer that inner-city distress threatens important economic assets tied to investments in productivity-enhancing infrastructure and the social relationships of commitment and trust that are generated in the daily rounds of urban space, and that these assets, in turn, anchor economic growth in the suburbs. Thriving regional economies and suburbs need viable cities, and inner cities have important competitive advantages upon which to build.[84]

Under these conditions, community organizing and development strategies that establish multisided partnerships for realizable goals and that accommodate core interests of business and political leaders can help generate alternative urban regimes. This shift is at least partially evident in cities such as San Antonio, where COPS and Metro Alliance exercise a strong presence; in Baltimore, where BUILD and a variety of other community development and neighborhood associational networks are influential; in Chicago under Mayor Harold Washington and Boston under Mayor Ray Flynn; and in a range of other "progressive cities" such as San Francisco, Minneapolis, and Burlington, with some combination of strong environmental, community development, historical preservationist, and racial justice organizing.[85]

Needless to say, we cannot underestimate the obstacles to fashioning urban regimes more conducive to community and economic development in inner cities or to developing regional strategies that challenge some of the disparities between cities and suburbs. Elite-dominated cities, such as Atlanta and Houston, marginalize community organizing and development groups, and patronage politics in cities such as New York and Chicago foster inordinate dependence on local politicians.[86] Despite significant learning within various organizing and policy networks, federal policy towards cities has been massively contradictory and has lacked the institutional memory to prevent community development strategies from perennially "swimming against the tide."[87] Changes in the structure of federal programs to consolidated block grants may further enhance those community-based organizations operating in robust institutional settings where local agencies have well-developed capacities for working with them in planning and program design. But others may be overwhelmed, especially as welfare reform fully kicks in and funding competition intensifies, thus heightening the challenges of collaboration in the nonprofit sector. Generating political support for a federal housing policy that further enhances capacities for community development, but at a scale much more appropriate to the vastly unmet needs, will perhaps require broader strategies that expand home ownership for young middle-class families shut out of the home-buying market.[88] Significantly increasing investments in human capital and infrastructure development to strengthen workers' position in an information economy has been constrained by the politics of federal deficits and now competes at a severe disadvantage with many other claims on the newly realized budget surpluses. In response to the challenges of globalization, capacities for regional governance and economic development that include robust forms of civic collaboration are beginning to emerge. But these are still in their formative stages, as are more concerted strategies for business leadership to support community building.[89] And if the problem of disparities between central cities and suburbs will ultimately have to be addressed, there is still, in the words of one policy analyst, "an ominous lack of consensus [about] how to create a viable political strategy to persuade the majority of Americans who are not poor and who do not reside in cities to respond to the needs in those areas."[90]

Despite these and other obstacles to community revitalization and the perennial struggle to enhance participation in even the best projects, considerable opportunity exists to leverage the substantial learning and capacity of congregation-based organizing, community development, neighborhood associations, and other forms of urban and regional democracy in America in the decades ahead. Complementary developments in the arenas of environment, health, human services, and media will also be critical. And while it is important to recognize that various types of policies will be needed to address issues of poverty and racism and to develop solidarities among suburban middle classes and the urban poor, we must also recognize that other initiatives are unlikely to have the requisite impact unless they are accompanied by efforts to strengthen community capacities and social capital. As Marc Bendick has put it, "Community building alone will not revitalize distressed communities, but no initiative will succeed without it."[91]

Indeed, we would argue, the political support of middle America is unlikely to materialize without a sustained public conversation regarding the collaborative work of building a commonwealth that citizens themselves are doing in our urban areas—as congregants and clergy, parents and educators, residents and police, nonprofit housing developers and bankers, youth and elders. Absent this, many of the claims to social justice for urban inner-city residents are likely to fall on deaf ears.

THREE

Civic Environmentalism

In recent years, as the problems of top-down regulation have become increasingly apparent, and as citizens have progressively refined the practices of participatory democracy and collaborative problem solving, civic environmentalism has emerged as an important paradigm. In 1970, when the Environmental Protection Agency (EPA) was established and the National Environmental Policy Act (NEPA) went into effect, the limits of command-and-control styles of regulation were not well understood, nor did significant institutional capacities exist for an alternative civic approach. By the 1980s, these limits had become increasingly evident, especially in dealing with non-point sources of pollution, ecosystem management, and pollution prevention. Citizen and environmental groups, as well as agency and industry officials, had gained valuable experience in programs requiring public participation and had begun to develop valuable networks and trust, despite their many early disappointments. They also generated substantial organizational capacities at the state and local level, so that when federal policy stalled during the Reagan years, innovative practitioners began to fashion fresh strategies.

As an emerging approach, civic environmentalism embodies a variety of different emphases and methods. As DeWitt John has argued, it serves as a complement to, not a substitute for, regulation. A strong federal role is often required to trigger civic approaches.[1] Among the characteristics of civic environmentalism, we include some combination of the following: (1) collaboration among various communities, interest groups, and government agencies, often initiated by a period of adversarial conflict; (2) deliberation about relative risks and costs, democratic and just ways of allocating these, and common values and interests that might help reframe them; (3) a place-based focus on improving the real places and ecosystems in which people live, rather than on merely reducing statistical risk; (4) public work that directly engages citizens in monitoring, improving, and restoring real places; (5) learning communities among practitioners who share information and best practices horizontally; (6) a federal government role that catalyzes local problem solving within a broad regulatory framework, and policy designs that encourage civic education and responsible action; and (7) extensive use of nonregulatory tools, such as voluntary agreements negotiated through stakeholder participation.

Civic environmentalism has today become manifest in community problem solving, state and local government projects, and a variety of federal programs. It has progressed to the point where it now forms a key component of various influential reports among prominent institutional stakeholders and policy communities that would fundamentally reorient regulatory paradigm and practice. It operates through many specific forms, such as watershed alliances and land trusts, community dispute settlement and good neighbor agreements, volunteer monitoring and stewardship, sustainable community initiatives and design-for-the-environment projects. And civic environmentalism has increasingly engaged the energies of long-established environmental groups and civic associations, as well as community development groups and neighborhood associations.

In this chapter, we examine the context in which citizen participation initially became part of the regulatory regime in the 1970s, and we identify some of the conundrums it faced. We then look at the emergence and diffusion of a range of civic environmental approaches during the 1980s and 1990s in three policy areas: watersheds, forests, and toxics. We conclude by analyzing the relationship of civic environmentalism to the environmental movement and the opportunities for, as well as obstacles to, a more consistently civic policy framework at the federal level.

CITIZEN PARTICIPATION IN ENVIRONMENTAL REGULATION:
THE FIRST DECADE

Civic environmentalism has gradually emerged in a context that has promoted citizen participation on a scale unprecedented in the regulatory arena before the 1960s, but in rather limited forms that have confronted it with substantial learning and capacity-building challenges at various levels. Environmental leaders and activists in the new movement received their political socialization in and around the New Left, inherited its deep commitments to participatory democracy, and strove to realize these ideas in the shape of the new regulatory laws and institutions.[2] But in doing so they faced a distinct set of opportunities and constraints.

The first set of these was provided by administrative law and legislative politics. The New Deal regulatory regime, characterized by industries' capture of the agencies designed to regulate them, came under widespread attack in scholarly and public opinion alike in the 1960s, and over the next decade administrative law was profoundly transformed. Emergent legal norms buttressed core participatory beliefs of the new movements. Citizens gained access through liberalized standing, and courts applied a "hard look" doctrine that required more detailed rationales for administrative action, consideration of alternatives, and effective participation of relevant interests. Courts no longer deferred to agency judgment and actively sought to ensure a pluralist representation of interests in an open deliberative process. Congressional and state passage of sunshine and advisory commission laws, as well as specific environmental laws and environmental impact statement (EIS) requirements, gave citizens a broad array of actionable standards by which to measure agency behavior and get their own views represented. Environmental groups, determined to avoid the fate of winning battles in legislation that would later be lost in implementation, thus found their best opportunity in the courts. And the decentralized congressional committee structure provided them with ample opportunities to ally with sympathetic staffers to ensure a favorable, nonstatutory legislative record upon which judicial interpretation had come to place considerable significance.[3]

Environmental groups themselves, while generally in favor of participatory democracy, began the period without a coherent set of ideas about what this might mean in the regulatory arena. Neither New Left movements nor participatory democratic theory available at the time could provide much concrete guidance. Environmental constituencies were not well organized at local levels, and those groups that did have state and local chapters, such as the National Audubon Society or the Sierra Club, were not well equipped to support effective participation in the myriad jurisdictions that might, for instance, be involved in water pollution issues. There were some attempts to develop an equitable and sustainable "ecology of cities" in the early 1970s, but funders appeared wary of community action. Furthermore, the calculus of steep organizational maintenance costs and potentially foregone political opportunities did not encourage environmental groups to place a priority on citizen involvement. As Berry, Portney, and Thomson argue, "In deploying their organizational resources, they were entirely rational to emphasize lobbying and litigation, run out of the Washington office, rather than to try to build a strong grassroots network that could actively participate in agency rule making and project planning at the regional or local level."[4]

These strategies made even more sense in the face of industry opposition to environmental regulation and conflicting signals on enforcement from the Nixon and Ford administrations that portended regulatory gridlock in the early years. In addition, citizen participation programs began with weak executive support under Presidents Nixon and Ford, and they remained an issue of political contention, which disrupted learning and capacity building. The lack of support was manifest in pitifully small initial budget requests for staff training, the impounding of funds by Nixon, and the passing over of those with experience in previous participation programs to head the Office of Public Affairs at EPA. Instead, public relations people with clear political agendas assumed authority, which alienated those career civil servants most predisposed to participatory program development and caused some to leave the agency. In its first year only fifty thousand dollars were spent on public participation programs out of a total agency budget of some two billion dollars. And in the six major water pollution programs authorized by the 1972 Clean Water Act, with its strong mandate for citizen participation, not a single staff member was assigned to work full time to facilitate the process.[5]

William Ruckelshaus, EPA's first administrator, lent official support to public participation in EPA as essential for citizens to decide the "kind of life [they] want and the risks they will accept to achieve it."[6] But he chose a law enforcement strategy over a participatory strategy as the simplest way to legitimate the agency under a Republican administration viewed suspiciously by environmentalists. The EPA administrative structure itself was pieced together from fifteen units in three federal departments and several independent agencies, each operating under various media-specific statutes, which EPA inherited and which Congress continued to authorize in this form. For a variety of political reasons, Nixon chose to create EPA by executive order rather than ask Congress to write overall authorizing legislation. As a result, EPA emerged primarily as a strong command-and-control advocate and enforcer of a fragmented array of media-specific statutes.[7]

State and local government capacities for environmental regulation and for collaboration with citizen groups were also quite weak in the early years. It took a concerted strategy by the EPA to develop these by mandating state and local action, providing grants to cover much of the costs of mandates, and helping to build management capacity.[8] States, however, were initially resistant to citizen participation programs mandated by federal environmental law and initiated by regional offices of the EPA and other agencies. Such programs could upset bureaucratic routines, delay or derail public works projects, and make meeting federal deadlines difficult. In turn, failure to meet deadlines might very well lead to a court challenge by organized environmental groups, thus revealing a temporal paradox that characterized Community Action Programs in the 1960s as well: the need for quick and visible results to motivate continued grassroots participation and public support and the much slower processes required to develop capacities for meaningful community deliberation and collaboration.

Federal agency staff charged with determining "what *demos*" should be represented in public participation programs of the 1970s, especially those engaged with national rule making, also applied a set of rational criteria that favored national environmental groups with professional staffs and dues-paying mass memberships. These criteria included (1) broad democratic legitimacy, which mass membership organizations with extensive communication channels, democratic election of leaders, considerable mobilization capacities, and voluntary dues contributions could provide more readily than could ad hoc local groups with less stable membership and more questionable representativeness; (2) adequacy and continuity of representation in complex rule making, which well-resourced and professionally led organizations could more effectively provide to balance the influence of regulated interests; and (3) high marginal costs to increase representation beyond those constituencies already active.[9] Of course, these criteria resulted in confining representation largely to the educated, white middle class, the group most active in environmental movements of the 1970s. Furthermore, in the face of vague congressional mandates for participation, mixed signals from the White House, and a variety of risks—including increased public *dissensus* and strained relations with key congressional supporters if favored environmental programs were delayed or disrupted—federal agencies tended to accord citizen participation programs low priority. They developed slowly, even haphazardly. Their budgets were very modest and were often cut at the first sign of general fiscal tightening. They were assigned few staff, and these were poorly integrated into core agency missions and authority structures. Much of the citizen support work was farmed out to consultants who, though often deeply committed and highly skilled, had little impact on agency routines. Programs tended to be recommended rather than required, and the official guidance issued to field staff was often further watered down. All this helped maintain bureaucratic discretion in the face of the political risks of the new regulatory framework in which agency officials at many levels bore responsibility for unprecedented regulatory programs with uncertain technologies and yet explicit deadline dates.[10]

Support and funding for citizen participation at EPA and other environmental agencies increased substantially under President Carter. Critical learning in the late 1970s progressed significantly among local participants, across networks of consultants, and through specific projects. The Interagency Council on Citizen Participation (ICCP) was established in 1976 by voluntary initiative of federal agency staff responsible for public involvement programs and had active participants from all the environmental agencies. As it expanded its network over the next several years, it evaluated existing programs and diffused best practices across the federal government, including dispute-resolution and stakeholder consensus models that would eventually become quite widespread.[11] The EPA engaged civic activists in reflecting on the lessons of the citizen participation programs of the Clean Water Act to aid in the design of effective programs under Superfund and to give voice to the newly emerging community actors in the toxics movement. Its report proved quite prescient and sophisticated, although its potential went largely unrealized in the face of an unsupportive Reagan appointee to head Superfund and the program's flawed overall policy design.[12]

Other major aspects of EPA leadership and strategy during the Carter administration, however, undercut the agency's own capacities to foster balanced deliberation among citizens, and among itself, Congress, the courts, and other branches of the federal government. Administrator Douglas Costle decided to downplay ecological, recreational, and cost concerns, which would have required more complex education and deliberation among citizens living in real places and confronted with complex choices. He pursued instead a strategy that employed simple notions of risk to arouse the public and that utilized the rhetoric of "rights to safety" to establish unconditional claims on public attention and resources.[13] In addition, mid-term elections in 1978 signaled a conservative backlash that helped defeat the Kennedy bill to provide more consistent funding for citizen participation programs. And the Reagan administration's initial hostility to public participation programs in general, together with its strong warnings against even voluntary unpaid work by agency staff in the ICCP, also proved disruptive to the learning that had begun to emerge. To this day, many active ICCP members still refer to the Reagan response as a "purge."[14]

It now appears increasingly clear that effective environmental programs require complex partnerships among diverse government, civic, and business actors at the local, state, and federal levels, and that states and local communities can become innovative in this regard. In the 1970s, however, institutional capacities and political opportunities for civic approaches were limited. Neither the dominant liberal public philosophy nor the conservative deregulatory philosophy anticipated the contours of civic environmentalism. Genuine capacity for civic responses to environmental problems would require years of building organizations, forging new relationships of trust, and testing public problem-solving methodologies and nonregulatory tools. Some critics, with a good deal of evidence on their side, lost confidence in the ability of federal environmental agencies to carry on trial-and-error learning.[15] But as federal environmental policy stalled in the early 1980s, state and local government agencies began to develop collaborative relationships with citizen groups and nonprofits, as well as "shadow learning communities" that could advance the approaches of civic environmentalism and eventually elicit the support of federal agencies.[16] Some of the activist partners had gained critical experience and perspective in mandated participation programs, though at the time participants and scholars alike often saw them as failures.

And, it should be stressed, the participatory rights of the 1970s helped greatly to establish the power of environmental and citizen organizations to impose costs on corporate managers and agency officials in the form of delay, uncertainty, and embarrassment. Such power was a precondition for being accepted as an equal partner at the table and for developing forms of collaboration based on mutual trust within regulatory communities, as we noted in chapter 1. Corporate managers, for their part, were politicized in ways that led to their acceptance of the basic legitimacy of social regulation, and that acceptance eventually led to greater mutual respect between them and the public interest groups with which they were now required to interact on a regular basis. Managers built environmental affairs staffs whose professional training and future careers were linked to effective environmental problem solving. President Reagan's frontal assault on the new social regulation and its participatory fundamentals during his first two years in office was defeated not only by environmental and public interest movements, but also by politicized corporate managers who had made important investments in responding to regulatory requirements, which they did not wish to see devalued or disrupted, and who had developed more collaborative relationships with other actors in these regulatory communities in the process of negotiating more flexible responses. For those who had not reached this point in the early 1980s, the defeat of Reagan's rollback sent a powerful signal that helped reorient their actions significantly in subsequent years. In the aftermath of the draining campaigns against the radical agenda of Reagan's initial environmental appointees and his reelection in 1984, an increasing number of environmentalists also began to appreciate the need to collaborate with industry and seek more pragmatic solutions to address economic and ecological concerns together.[17]

CIVIC ACTION FOR WATER AND WATERSHEDS

As the Conservation Foundation began conducting a series of workshops on water quality for citizens in each of EPA's ten regions in 1974, it called attention to the fact that the Clean Water Act of 1972 "contains one of the strongest requirements for participatory democracy in the whole federal statute book."[18] Over the rest of the decade, thousands of citizens took part in such workshops and trainings, and participated in state and local water-planning projects. Most were organized amid bureaucratic confusion and general lack of consistent support by EPA regional offices and other state and local officials. Some, however, were reasonably well organized, and even noteworthy models, celebrated and discussed more broadly within the networks of agency staff and consultants. Scholarly analyses and formal evaluations generated important practical lessons and theoretical insights informed by the "nonlinear planning and learning processes" occurring among the various stakeholders in these programs.[19] For many local civic groups, these programs provided their first in-depth introduction to the technical issues of water quality and the multiple institutional and constituency viewpoints brought to the table. Even where citizen participants were out-numbered in representation and disappointed with the outcomes, the planning process opened new communication channels among themselves and a broader array of representatives from agriculture, business, and myriad local, state, county, and federal agencies involved in water control. And it educated them about the diverse interests and perspectives of ordinary citizens like themselves, whose economic circumstances and residential choices placed them in quite different situations of potential gain and loss vis-à-vis water planning and flood control decisions. Some homeowners, for instance, stood to pay significantly higher taxes while others made windfall profits, as was the case with the failed Johnson Creek participatory flood control planning in Portland, Oregon. Participants gained experience with a diverse array of interactive dialogue techniques and problem-solving methods, though these generally emerged only after adversarial public hearings and policy stalemate. And the planning process itself provided new incentives and opportunities for local groups to organize and build their own capacities to educate broader constituencies, who initially accorded water quality issues relatively low salience in most places.[20]

The Chesapeake Bay

In the 1980s the EPA developed new efforts to educate and involve the public in pollution control, cleanup, and preservation of the nation's waterways. As part of a slowly emerging shift of emphasis toward specific ecosystems, EPA funded the Chesapeake Bay Program, which included a coalition of nonprofit organizations that could educate a broader public, build political support for EPA's efforts, and develop additional voluntary monitoring and pollution control capacities. If such citizen programs could help nurture a "protective ethic" and a "sense of ownership" among the public, EPA began to reason, then consensus could emerge on pollution control measures. The 1987 revision of the Clean Water Act established a National Estuary Program to facilitate local estuarine constituencies in cooperating to develop long-term protection plans, as in our case study of Save The Bay in chapter 1. Rather than relying on standardized and technology-based solutions, local "management conferences" were to design approaches tailored to each estuary as an integrated ecosystem. With local responsibility a key component of environmental protection where diffuse, nonpoint sources of pollution are significant, citizens would be encouraged to take responsibility for their own actions within local ecosystems, such as the use of lawn fertilizers or farm pesticides. Citizens would then be more willing to assume the costs of cleanup, as well as more equipped to judge where best to spend limited financial resources for long-term improvement. EPA would provide the organizational umbrella and technical expertise for working partnerships among various local, state, and federal interests, but, it reasoned, "the programs to manage estuarine resources—and the political will to protect them—must come from the local users."[21]

Since its inception in 1983, the Chesapeake Bay Program of the EPA has steadily expanded its capacity to facilitate a broad array of volunteer efforts within a framework of formal and informal local partnerships among government agencies, conservation groups, fishing and boating associations, farms and businesses, schools and universities, neighborhood associations, and other civic groups. The program was initiated in response to pressure by environmentalists, who had set up the Chesapeake Bay Foundation to litigate and lobby for the bay in 1966. A subsequent seven-year EPA research study commissioned by Congress a decade later showed the extent to which the bay, the largest and most productive estuary in the country, had begun to deteriorate quite precipitously in the 1960s and 1970s. The states of Maryland, Pennsylvania, and Virginia, plus the District of Columbia and the EPA, signed the Chesapeake Bay Agreement in December 1983 after seven hundred legislators, administrators, scientists, public interest groups, and bay users met at the Governors' Summit. EPA administrator William Ruckelshaus (who had returned to head the agency for the remainder of Reagan's first term after Anne Gorsuch Burford's forced resignation) worked to achieve joint resolutions from many other federal agencies to assist in the restoration efforts. Communities in Delaware, West Virginia, and New York have even involved themselves in collaborative projects as part of the 64,000-square-mile drainage area with 150 rivers and streams that supply the bay's freshwater flow.[22]

The Chesapeake Bay Program, which is fully voluntary and relies on reputational sanctioning, has a variety of key civic and governmental components that have emerged over the past two decades. States have developed new legislation based on collaborative planning processes involving multiple stakeholders and extensive public meetings and workshops. One example of this is Maryland's Chesapeake Bay Critical Areas Law, which establishes criteria regulating development in what the planning group designated as intensely developed areas, limited development areas, and resource conservation areas. The Chesapeake Bay Trust serves as a general funder for many volunteer efforts and local partnerships and raises money from a variety of sources, including voluntary state income tax check-offs and the sale of special license plates. The Alliance for Chesapeake Bay, founded in 1971, coordinates the Citizens Advisory Council and provides educational and technical support for community projects within a nonadversarial framework. The Alliance's Citizen Monitoring Program trains volunteers and facilitates the work of homeowner associations, service organizations, schools, and families that have formed Stream Teams and River Watches to provide citizens and government agencies with essential data on unusual discharges, trash dumps, fish kills, algae blooms, and sewage leaks. The Alliance also administers the Chesapeake

Bay Program's small grants that fund local restoration efforts, as well as the formation of new watershed associations and other civic organizations. The Local Government Advisory Committee provides technical assistance to help local authorities manage growth and form alliances with other organizations. Its Participation Action Plan and Partnership Initiative are designed to support watershed associations, civic organizations, and land trusts in building the constituencies needed for effective governance, and its Partner Communities Program awards Gold, Silver, and Bronze designations to communities meeting specific benchmarks. By the mid-1990s approximately one thousand community-based projects had emerged in the watershed.

The Anacostia Watershed Society (AWS), for instance, has mobilized over seven thousand volunteers to remove some two hundred tons of debris from the Anacostia River running through inner-city Washington, DC, and has planted thousands of trees and shrubs, along with wetlands vegetation. It has worked with the local Sierra Club to bring environmental education into local schools, and with the Izaak Walton League to train students in water quality monitoring. AWS has collaborated with an AmeriCorps group, under a grant from EPA, and has developed projects neighborhood by neighborhood to sustain further efforts. Groups as diverse as the Jewish Community Center Youth Group, the Seafarers Yacht Club, St. Mary's Church, and America Outdoors work on cleanups and conduct canoe trips together. The AWS's work in the predominantly African American community of River Terrace has been complemented by that of business and government partners in the Bladensburg area of Maryland, who identified clear commercial interests in restoring the river. Robert Boone, the activist president of AWS, who approaches river restoration as a "sacred task," argues that the initial focus on trash has sent "an electric message of hope throughout the community." As the river is cleaned up, more people visit it and develop a stake in further restoration work. And while AWS collaborates with various government agencies that came together through the Anacostia Watershed Agreement, signed shortly after the original Chesapeake Bay Agreement, it challenges them to eschew high-priced contractors, whose steep estimates breed defeatism among ordinary taxpayers, and to rely much more upon the restorative work of citizens themselves.[23]

In Pennsylvania, the Donegal Fish and Conservation Association has collaborated with the Lancaster County Conservation District to reduce stream degradation resulting from cattle by helping farmers develop individual work plans and by bringing in scout troops, churches, and schools to help with forest buffer strip establishment. Local contractors donated materials, and Trout Unlimited provided a small grant. Farmers in Adams County, Pennsylvania, hold twilight meetings and open houses as part of the Conservation District's voluntary program to introduce best farm management practices. In Harford County, Maryland, volunteers in a similar partnership walked ninety-six miles of the Swan Creek identifying potential problems, such as bank erosion and fish migration, and school teachers have developed ecology curricula around stream protection. The Gut Road Cleanup Project in East Manchester, Pennsylvania, has brought together the township, the local chapter of the Izaak Walton League, and volunteers from the Jaycees, Lions, and Cub Scouts to clean up several hundred tons of garbage in yearly events since 1990, with utility, food-vending, and refuse-collecting companies providing materials and donated labor. The Juniata chapter of the National Audubon Society has worked with Girl Scouts, Boy Scouts, and their parents to create a riparian buffer along Sinking Creek in Tyrone, Pennsylvania. Several towns and counties have developed eco-industrial parks as part of a larger vision for sustainable development, and have utilized community charettes to help design the parks. The Magothy River Association in Anne Arundel County, Maryland, and community volunteers in Downs Park built a nursery to grow a hundred thousand young oysters, which were then transferred to a reef sanctuary by volunteer divers from the community college, who continue to monitor them. The Elizabeth River Project, with over one hundred active members on its Watershed Action Team, has developed a pet oyster program in which community volunteers help raise baby oysters donated by local businesses and then introduce them into the bay as a way of restoring one of nature's most effective filtration systems. These local efforts have recently helped to spark a general civic restoration strategy for oysters on the bay, where thousands of citizen "gardeners," including boat owners and school children, nurture young oysters at home and dockside, and then transplant them by hand to the reefs.[24]

On the basis of such efforts over the course of two decades, the Chesapeake Bay Program has continued to refine its protection and restoration strategies. These now include building semi-autonomous "tributary teams" composed of government officials and scientific experts, agricultural and industry representatives, educators and realtors, environmental groups, and citizen volunteers capable of authoring and implementing context-specific strategies through an iterative learning process linked to a broad conception of "citizen stewardship." Indeed, the profound change in consciousness among these various stakeholder groups, who regularly visit and work with each other to learn how to situate their own actions in the preservation of the bay's treasures, is recognized as the most important change of all, and the change that makes it a model for restoration across the country in the eyes of regulators and estuary groups alike.[25]

Civic and Sporting Associations

Many other kinds of water protection projects have blossomed in recent years, some falling within the parameters of federal programs such as the National Estuary Program, others emerging at the state level, and many coming from a variety of innovative local initiatives. A noteworthy example combining all three levels is provided by Leagues of Women Voters across the country. When the 1972 Clean Water Act mandating public participation was passed, local Leagues, aided by their national and state offices, claimed representation on a scale perhaps unmatched by any other environmental or public interest group at the time and gradually built the skills and networks that would allow them to play a role in developing broad civic partnerships community by community. In the 1980s, the innovative role of local Leagues became much more evident, and the national office expanded the educational resources it made available on groundwater and other environmental issues. In the early 1990s, the League of Women Voters Education Fund (LWVEF) raised this learning process to a new level with its community groundwater education project, funded in cooperation with EPA's Office of Ground Water and Drinking Water. The project began with an inventory of innovative efforts by eighteen local Leagues published in a beautifully prepared and widely distributed citizen action manual. This initiative has since been followed by other training efforts, including a national town meeting via teleconference among some 350 local and state Leagues in 1997.

Leagues emphasize a process of public education that will enable citizens and institutional actors to take responsibility for local groundwater, help generate volunteer efforts and new forms of collaboration, and build support for stronger and more effective local and county ordinances. In Enid, Oklahoma, the League developed a Retired and Senior Volunteer Program (RSVP) as part of its Well Watchers Program to survey the town's five well fields, all of which were under privately controlled land owned by the petroleum industry and farmers. Well Watchers educate ordinary users and advocate for clean water, and they use the power of public reputation to get voluntary agreements with petroleum companies to change their salt water injection practices, which can contaminate groundwater. In Winnebago County, Illinois, the League collaborated with the local College of Medicine and a local television station, which contributed $5,400 worth of time and materials to produce a half-hour video on local groundwater issues. This video was shown on the network and used in luncheon presentations that the League scheduled with realtors, developers, county supervisors, city planners, and just about any other civic and business association that would agree to invite them. Luncheons were often preceded and followed by one-on-one meetings to establish trust and share information. The video has also been purchased for public education by schools, park departments, health departments, and the state environmental agency, and has been shown in an area shopping mall as part of a Health and Fitness Show. Locally produced videos are sometimes combined with ones that show successful citizen efforts in other parts of the state and are themselves utilized and modeled by many of the eleven hundred Leagues across the country.

Quite often members of the League who have spearheaded these projects have been appointed to state and local water councils and health committees to establish legislative and administrative agendas for the future, and some have served on federal committees, such as EPA's Effluent Guidelines Task Force. Others have developed their own green businesses, and still others do "environmental shopping tours" with the collaboration of local supermarket managers to educate consumers. The California League has produced educational videos on reducing hazardous waste in households and small businesses and has received funding from IBM, Hewlett Packard, and Norcal Solid Waste Systems to distribute these to schools, libraries, and community groups. In some states, such as Colorado, all local Leagues have collaborated in statewide education on waste options under a grant from EPA. In others they have partnered with state Cooperative Extension Services, and still others have engaged in multiyear, statewide policy dialogues that promote dispute resolution among traditional adversaries in water resources. In many counties they have spearheaded groundwater coalitions, and in some they have helped to establish watershed associations.

While Leagues emphasize cooperation and consensus, they fully recognize the power that comes with their distinct capacity as one of the nation's most respected civic organizations to convene public and private actors, challenge them to action, and generate information that can damage their reputations should they refuse to work together for the larger good of the community. Realtors, for instance, are aware of the negative impact that a League survey of drinking water might have on potential home buyers, and Leagues use this power strategically to achieve industry buy-in to civic and legislative efforts. Nonetheless, as Elizabeth Kraft, the former LWVEF environmental director, says with a wry smile, "We League ladies are always very polite."[26]

The emergence of civic environmental approaches to water quality and conservation over the past several decades has provided much opportunity for mainline civic and sporting associations to reorient themselves. The League of Women Voters is perhaps the most striking example, but it hardly stands alone. Local projects are often able to draw volunteers from Scout troops, Jaycees, and Lions. Local Retired and Senior Volunteer Programs were first enlisted in 1988 in wellhead protection in El Paso by Brad Cross, Texas's Wellhead Protection Coordinator, who modeled his work on the activism of his own retired parents. These programs have been replicated throughout the state and have expanded to include water protection mentoring by seniors in local schools. In collaboration with EPA, they have been diffused through RSVP and other retired volunteer networks to communities across the country. Seniors bring high levels of legitimacy, networks of friends and colleagues, free time, and a historical perspective on the community. Some are highly skilled engineers and chemists with prior experience as managers in major corporate and military organizations. In the words of Bob Green of Allentown, Pennsylvania, who retired from the Navy, where his job was to make potable water "even purer than what we drink" from sea water to operate steam machinery, we seek to "give something back to the community."[27]

Boating, fishing, surfing, and hunting associations as well as garden clubs also provide volunteers, contribute funds, and host public events to support water projects. They use their social networks to convince farmers to work with agencies and watershed alliances to introduce best management practices that reduce the use of specific chemicals or to fence off cows from stream access. Groups such as Trout Unlimited and Ducks Unlimited provide substantial support at the national, state, and local levels. Numerous other sporting associations have progressively incorporated conservation work into their core mission and activities, including national, regional, state, and local organizations of canoe cruisers, kayakers, whitewater rafters, flyfishers and anglers, as well as trade associations such as canoe liveries and outfitters. An increasing number of local farm associations are responding to the mix of regulatory controls, financial incentives, social pressures, and technical assistance, and have joined in educating their members about best farm-management practices and developing voluntary agreements. And national youth groups, such as the YMCA and the National 4-H Council, as well as groups focused specifically on the environment, such as the Student Conservation Associations and Earth Force, sponsor an array of environmental education and restoration projects.[28]

Over the past decade religious organizations have also become increasingly engaged in environmental work. The National Religious Partnership for the Environment (NRPE), established in 1993 as a major interfaith initiative, has documented two thousand model congregational projects, and a study commissioned by Independent Sector estimates that 40 percent of all religious congregations engage in environmental activities of one sort or another. NRPE conducts leadership training and has provided education action kits to more than sixty thousand congregations, including every Catholic parish in the country. Environmental projects, such as the Presbyterian Church U.S.A.'s Restoring Creation program or the Episcopal Church's focus on watersheds like the Connecticut River, are becoming increasingly common, and sermons appeal to parishioners' responsibility to "assist in the work of God's Creation." The National Conference of Catholic Bishops has called for a "new ecological ethic," and the Central Conference of American Rabbis speaks of preventing environmental desecration as "part of the covenant with the Creator." The Evangelical Environmental Network has organized over one thousand Noah Congregations and Creation Awareness Centers and has worked to defeat Republican efforts in Congress to weaken the Endangered Species Act. They are fond of quoting Ezekiel, who decries the waste of God's gifts: "Is it not enough for you to drink clear water? Must you also muddy the rest with your feet?" Local chapters of environmental organizations, such as the Sierra Club, have begun to build partnerships with congregations, and their national leaders have come to recognize the new opportunities this provides. As Carl Pope, executive director of the Sierra Club, noted in November 1998, "The environmental movement for the past quarter of a century has made no more profound error than to misunderstand the mission of religion and the churches in the preservation of Creation."[29]

Mainline civic organizations have increasingly become involved in environmental activities as many of their own members have developed ecological values and have been able to draw upon information resources and action models from conservation groups. Civic approaches are especially prevalent where action models stress concrete work that creates visible things of public value, such as trees and vegetation planted along a river, refuse removed from a stream, or fences constructed to keep cattle from despoiling water sources. Youth raising oysters derive a sense of contributing visibly and directly to restoring the public treasure of an estuary. Those youth who stencil hundreds of storm drains with "Don't Dump: Drains to River" and "Don't Dump: Drains to Drinking Water" create a visible sign of their role as educators and protectors of the community and as full-fledged citizens with the responsibility and authority to reinforce basic civic norms. Such activities provide traditional civic associations and youth groups with relatively noncontroversial opportunities to engage their members, reach across dividing lines in local disputes, and celebrate accomplishments in the community.

Citizen Monitoring

Volunteer citizen monitoring is critical in water resources protection and restoration, and citizen "watches" have proliferated in recent years. They mobilize volunteers locally from a variety of existing environmental, civic, and homeowner groups and increasingly network on an extra-local basis. Statewide "lake watch" programs might include hundreds of lakes, and "river watch networks" may extend along several hundred miles and include dozens of monitoring sites. Student and other youth groups have become key to volunteer water quality monitoring, often as part of science curricula, and national and state support networks provide curricular models, training opportunities, and learning networks to other youth and teachers in their watershed and beyond. Young people who gather in a Student Congress to share their water-monitoring results among other students throughout the watershed and among adult environmental and civic groups and agency professionals derive a sense of the broad impact of their work and often brainstorm to develop an action agenda. For instance, the Deschutes and Nisqually Project GREEN Student Congress in Olympia, Washington, established the goal of educating farmers and other landowners about the damage caused by animals, fertilizers, and herbicides. Students in Fleming County, Kentucky, have gone still further. They began with a project to reduce cow dung runoff into streams and now run a farm to develop and test new ways of farming that reduce pollution yet contain costs. Their work has helped to catalyze a Community Farm Alliance among family-owned farms, and they plan to buy the land so that they can develop a program for young people across the state to learn and work on these issues. As Glenn Tremblay, a science teacher at Boothbay Region High School in Maine, has noted, students know that as their water quality monitoring data go into the computer, "in ten years people will still be using those results. . . . Students are willing to make the effort to perfect their technique because they know that their results matter."[30]

The resources that support the formation of local groups and link them to similar projects beyond their locality have substantially increased over several decades. National conservation groups provide much support. For example, in 1969 the Izaak Walton League of America sponsored David Whitney to travel the country in a Winnebago—the "water wagon"—dispensing equipment and teaching basic biological and water-monitoring skills as part of its new Save Our Streams (SOS) program. SOS now provides a low-cost monitoring toolkit and video, offers training to groups that would "adopt a stream," and maintains a Monitors database of more than five thousand water protection programs, many of which participate in SOS. The River Watch Network forms partnerships with local watchdog groups, but only on condition that they commit themselves to develop a scientifically credible water-monitoring program and a technical support partnership with a local agency, involve at least one high school or college, and agree to work with river users, including polluters, to develop positive solutions. The National Oceanic and Atmospheric Administration, the U.S. Coast Guard, state coastal commissions, and regional water quality control boards now regularly partner with hundreds of citizen "baykeeper," "deltakeeper," and "sanctuary watch" programs that provide complementary, cost-saving monitoring capacities. EPA publishes and widely distributes a variety of methods manuals and the national newsletter for volunteer monitoring, as well as a National Directory of Citizen Volunteer Monitoring Programs. It hosts a biennial National Citizen Volunteer Water Monitoring Conference, provides grants to states to build volunteer capacities as a supplement to other monitoring activity, and through its regional offices holds workshops to build partnerships. EPA estimates that in 1994 approximately 340,000 citizens participated in more than 500 volunteer monitoring programs.[31]

Land Trusts

Land trusts and other public/private partnerships for land conservation began to develop slowly in the mid-1960s, when their number stood at 130.

But as a former vice president of the Nature Conservancy has noted, "In the 1980s, this modest, piecemeal cooperative effort exploded into a nationwide movement involving every major federal landowning agency, every state, [and] hundreds of localities."[32] By 1990 there were 889, and by the end of the decade approximately 1,200. These nonprofit organizations bring a variety of advantages to attempts to save land for public purposes: greater agility than government agencies to purchase land and thus benefit from timely cost savings, networks of personal contacts to private landowners, and volunteer land stewards to help maintain the land. Indeed, half of all land trusts run solely on volunteer labor and on annual budgets that are typically less than ten thousand dollars. They can generate a sense of civic possibility when other options seem closed, and the added resources and savings they can bring help to convince legislators and taxpayers that they are getting a good deal for their money should they earmark funds or pass a bond issue. As land trusts have built their capacity by preserving smaller parcels, they have progressively fostered partnerships with government for oversight of much larger areas, which permits them to protect entire threatened ecosystems, develop sustainable agriculture, and preserve greenway corridors of open space for recreational and scenic purposes. Greater scope allows them to shift from pragmatic to programmatic protection and to work in collaborative planning efforts with state and federal agencies. As the U.S. Fish and Wildlife Service and California's State Coastal Conservancy have learned, the most effective partnerships result when agency officials can rise above the bureaucratic turf and inspire the land conservation community and ordinary citizens with a broad and ambitious vision for their common work. Nonprofits likewise have learned that the slow process of building social trust and forging consensus with agency officials caught in many complex political and bureaucratic webs is more essential to long-term success than just "doing deals."

An example of an innovative international partnership involving land trusts is the North American Waterfowl Management Plan (NAWMP). Drawing upon two decades of experience in forging public/private partnerships that dates back to the 1960s, the U.S. Fish and Wildlife Service developed NAWMP in 1986 to respond to the dramatic decline of duck species to the lowest levels ever recorded. In an attempt to restore them, it signed an agreement first with Canada and then with Mexico to protect an additional six million acres of habitat in thirty-four geographic areas. NAWMP has developed an elaborate set of partnerships with over twenty national organizations, including groups such as the Sierra Club, Ducks Unlimited, the Federation of State Waterfowl Associations, and the National Rifle Association. Twenty joint ventures have also been created in specific habitats involving more than two hundred other conservation groups, many small businesses and large corporations, and hundreds of private landowners. Partners in joint ventures raise money to buy land, which is facilitated by the cost-sharing arrangements of the North American Wetlands Conservation Act of 1989. They mobilize volunteers, often on an extensive scale, such as the five hundred who turn out on "workdays" on the Cosumnes River venture in California to plant trees, or the Boy Scout troops who have collected tons of acorns for a major seeding effort on the Cache River in Illinois. They arrange land swaps with farmers who trade floodplain holdings for land away from the river. And they do extensive outreach and education among their members. Often the strongest joint ventures sponsored by the NAWMP build on previous citizen organizing and partnership efforts dating back to the 1970s.[33]

Watershed Associations and Councils

Watershed strategies combining civic action and government collaboration have become increasingly prevalent in recent years. Some groups were founded in the 1960s and established successful collaborative protection and restoration programs in the 1970s that later served as models for others. But over the past decade, the growth of various kinds of "watershed associations," "watershed councils," "watershed alliances," and kindred "friends" groups for larger rivers and lakes, as well as smaller streams and subwatersheds, has accelerated markedly. Practitioners now refer to the phenomenon as a new "watershed movement." By the late 1990s several hundred watershed associations had emerged, with notably denser concentrations in New England, the mid-Atlantic, the Great Lakes region, Florida, California, and the Pacific Northwest. Leading innovators have come to watershed work via other participatory projects, such as community planning, community health, antitoxics organizing, community development, nuclear weapons freeze, and other forms of grassroots organizing, as well as through civic and sporting associations such as the YMCA and the National Sports Academy, and through the Audubon Society, Sierra Club, and National Wildlife Federation. They see themselves as building a movement around a vision of "watershed democracy."[34]

Watershed associations develop in a variety of ways. Many start out as small wetland or river watch groups, often in a dispute with a private developer or government agency, and only gradually develop trusting relationships with adversaries and other community stakeholders. A good number fail before getting this far, overwhelmed by the relative power of developers, local land speculators, and government officials whose careers are tied to generating ever-increasing revenues from development.[35] Some watershed councils, such as the Yakima River Watershed Council in Washington and the Henry's Fork Watershed Council in Idaho, are established only after years of conflict and stalemate among local commodity interests, government agencies, tribes, and conservation groups. Such watershed councils are often designed to provide representation to the most prominent adversaries, and typically employ consensus decision making and other community-building techniques. Some watershed alliances bring together local civic, boating, religious, and environmental organizations and chapters of national organizations that have been working on some aspect of protection and restoration, such as the Long Island Sound Watershed Alliance, with more than two hundred member groups. Others begin as local partnerships engaged in restoration and develop ambitious sustainable development projects. For instance, in Willapa Bay in southwestern Washington, the Willapa Alliance began with a salmon restoration project involving conservationists, local farmers, oyster growers, and the Weyerhaeuser Corporation, a major timber company. With the support of Ecotrust and the Nature Conservancy, as well as the innovative South Shore Bank in Chicago, which has pioneered community development financing in the inner city, the alliance has created a set of financing institutions for sustainable development projects in salmon fishing and oysters, nontimber forest products, and red alder. These projects serve to compensate for the large job losses in the timber industry in the 1980s. Still other watershed alliances begin with a project that directly improves the watershed through public work and then expand by bringing in stakeholder groups with competing interests and forming complex partnerships with government agencies.[36]

The Mattole watershed in Northern California provides a good example of this trajectory. After several meetings sponsored by the Grange and the Cistercian Sisters at the Redwoods Monastery in the late 1970s, the Mattole Watershed Salmon Support Group was formed, and it soon developed an innovative hatchbox strategy to replenish the almost completely depleted coho salmon spawning on the Mattole river. The Pacific Coast Federation of Fishermen's Associations helped the group establish a Salmon Stamp Program as a voluntary levy to support its work. School children and other volunteers raise the fry and then release them into the river, promoting a restoration ethic among young people and leading recently to an Adopt-a-Watershed K–12 curriculum that engages students in both study and restoration work. The effort has been led by Freeman House, a fisherman and carpenter who traces his key formative experiences, as well as networks that later became critical to his gaining state support for the Mattole projects, to the San Francisco New Left cultural community of the 1960s and the bioregional movement of the 1970s. He now sees himself as part of a broad new environmental movement that is "not a war" but is based on consensus and a search for shared territory by place-based organizations whose practice he calls "community building." Drawing upon the relationships of the salmon support group, as well as its rich lore of "work stories," the Mattole Restoration Council (MRC) formed in 1983, comprising a broad array of member groups, including land trusts, community service groups, local community centers, tributary stewardship groups, and worker coops. With grants from the state and other sources, the MRC produced poster maps and a stunning local geography text filled with historical, cultural, ecological, and geomorphologic detail serving to orient comprehensive restoration work and nurture a watershed identity. MRC's initial meeting raised the guiding question: "What would happen if we saw ourselves as common inhabitants of a naturally defined part of the planet rather than as members of competitive interest groups isolated from each other by property lines?"[37]

When California environmentalists mobilized around Redwood Summer in 1990 during the spotted owl controversy that virtually shut down the state's timber industry, tension between groups rose to a pitch in the Mattole, an area with deep cultural and interest-based differences between new settlers and old. Discord was exacerbated by a local ruling that mandated zero net sediment for logging practices. The previous years of constructive work had progressed too far, however, and leaders from the ranching community, environmentalists, and others who had cross-cutting links through churches, the Mattole Grange, the Farm Bureau, and the Wool Growers and Cattleman's Associations formed the more broadly based Mattole Watershed Alliance (MWA). The MWA then proceeded to develop consensus on a range of issues, including voluntary and mandatory restrictions on salmon fishing. On the tougher issues of logging practices and land use, consensus was much harder, and eventually shifted emphasis back to the Mattole Restoration Council. The Pacific Lumber Company, for instance, refused to be bound by the MWA's wishes. But as Earth First! pursued a more confrontational strategy, focusing on junk bond debt that had driven the company to overharvesting, the MWA tried to remain in dialogue. The alliance also introduced consensus training, which proved especially appealing to ranchers who, though concerned with the watershed, disliked going to public meetings where they were always outnumbered and outshouted.

Between 1980 and 1994, these citizen groups engaged in thirty-four restoration projects, including the release of five hundred thousand coho salmon into the waterways and the planting of sixty thousand trees. Two-thirds of the projects received funding from conservation groups and state agencies, such as the California State Coastal Conservancy. State and federal agencies, indeed, have collaborated with local groups in a much broader California Coordinated Regional Strategy to Conserve Biological Diversity, or the "biodiversity" project, though the foundations for this were laid over a long period by grassroots bioregional groups and by intense conflict over resource management at virtually every level of the political system. Resource agencies in the 1990s, with directors and staff profoundly influenced by the participatory and ecological values of the 1960s and 1970s, have utilized the Mattole experience as a model for their field staff throughout the state. And after eighteen winters of painstaking and meticulous work capturing and incubating the eggs and restoring other parts of the watershed—during which time the coho salmon had come to be listed as a threatened species—the Mattole Restoration Council could finally witness its return.[38]

State agencies, legislatures, and governors devoted increasing attention to collaborative watershed approaches during the 1990s, and in some cases directly spurred the growth of local watershed groups and coherent statewide strategies. The Massachusetts Watershed Initiative (MWI) exemplifies this process. Following the lead of the watershed associations formed in the 1960s and 1970s, similar groups began to proliferate, and in 1991 twenty-five groups formed the Massachusetts Watershed Coalition (MWC) to raise awareness of watershed issues, advocate better public policies, and strengthen the work of its members and collaborating agencies. The MWC found a receptive partner in the Executive Office of Environmental Affairs (EOEA). Governor William Weld had appointed as secretary of EOEA Trudy Coxe, who had served for a decade as executive director of Save The Bay in Rhode Island. During this time, Save The Bay had extended its reach into western Massachusetts as it learned the necessity of a citizens' strategy that reached across the entire watershed, affecting the Narragansett Bay itself. Working with the MWC and the Massachusetts Water Watch Partnership, Coxe helped to catalyze broad collaboration among state agencies as part of the MWI, joined by Region 1 of the EPA and the Natural Resources Conservation Service. The state's Department of Fisheries and Wildlife helped to facilitate adopt-a-stream groups and fishway stewardship teams. The Department of Environmental Protection was reorganized to build upon the watershed approach, and regulatory decisions are increasingly driven by ecosystem impacts rather than narrow media controls.

EOEA formed twenty-seven Watershed Teams composed of state, federal, and community partners to facilitate local problem solving and decision making on each of the state's major watersheds and has begun to help form Watershed Community Councils to ensure representation of the broadest array of interests. The Watershed Teams have also helped to form Stream Teams on dozens of other subwatersheds. MWI provides matching grants on a competitive basis to watershed groups, enabling them to build capacity and leverage local funding sources. Watershed groups take initiative in monitoring, restoration, and public education, and they function as leaders and coordinators of watershed plan development and implementation. As of 1998 there were some thirty watershed associations and councils on the major rivers, forty subwatershed alliances and friends groups, seventy stream teams and monitoring groups, and a total of perhaps one thousand grassroots groups of various sorts, including land trusts and conservation commissions, all exercising some form of citizen stewardship over the state's watersheds. Most watershed groups are all-volunteer organizations, though perhaps half of the associations on the major rivers have developed professional staff capacity. Their vision entails citizen ownership and community stewardship of watershed systems and collaborative problem solving among all stakeholders.[39]

Washington State also shifted to a watershed approach after 1993. There the Department of Ecology has made watershed improvement the organizing principle for much of its work and lends assistance to the formation of citizen groups through its Local Action Teams and field offices. The Puget Sound Water Quality Plan has also fostered voluntary action through action teams on some three dozen small tributaries, with funding provided through the Centennial Clean Water Fund and distributed as Public Involvement and Education matching grants similar to those of the Seattle Department of Neighborhoods (see chapter 2). The Department of Fish and Wildlife has facilitated fishery enhancement projects by local groups engaged in cleanup and hatchbox work. The key nongovernmental catalyst for developing citizen strategies and capacities has been the Rivers Council of Washington, founded in 1984 by whitewater boaters to fight dams, protect instream flows, and promote Wild and Scenic River designations. In 1993, however, when the state's orientation was beginning to shift, the Rivers Council also fundamentally redrafted its mission from legally protecting free-flowing rivers to leading a grassroots effort to restore all rivers and watersheds throughout the state by means of "holistic, community-based, and consensus-building strategies." Its new executive director, Joy Huber, brought a decade of experience working with inner-city neighborhood development projects in New York and helped to set the goal "to reinvent the environmental movement from the ground up." The River Council's "62 Watersheds of Washington Campaign" catalyzed a watershed movement around practical action for lay people and modes of engagement that could "build social capital" and embody a "new form of citizen governance." Its extensive survey of nearly 800 citizen groups across the 62 watersheds found some 370 to be engaged in significant watershed projects, and it has progressively facilitated networks within distinct watersheds and across the state.

As in much of the Northwest, Endangered Species Act fish listings and anticipated listings provide incentives for landowners and other economic interests to collaborate. And the continued degradation of many watersheds over two decades of adversarial legal strategies and command-and-control regulation convinced those in the Rivers Council and affiliate groups that the risks of a collaborative strategy were worth taking. But legislative politics have been much more complicated. Key environmental advocacy groups have resisted the transition to a watershed approach based on collaboration and left the field largely to conservative lawmakers whose 1997 bill was vetoed by Democratic governor Gary Locke—though those portions favored by the Rivers Council and the Department of Ecology remained. Tensions between environmental lobbies and collaborative watershed groups are also evident in California and other states, and they pose a major challenge for developing more coherent policies.[40]

Frameworks for Local Water Action

Local citizen organizing has been the driving force behind the emergence of many collaborative projects to protect water resources, as citizen groups have either begun directly with local improvement efforts or have turned from initial protest strategies to pragmatic solutions that could sustain positive outcomes. But as our discussion has indicated, they have been aided by the development of capacities at three other levels: (1) national environmental organizations; (2) state, local, tribal, and regional agencies; and (3) federal agencies, such as the EPA, the Army Corps of Engineers, and the U.S. Fish and Wildlife Service.

First, various national conservation organizations increasingly combine advocacy with civic partnership approaches. The River Network, founded in 1988, helps to build and maintain independent local organizations but draws upon its experience in teaching advocacy groups how to find unlikely allies, from the Army Corps of Engineers to the United Mine Workers of America, and how to work with businesses and private landowners. The River Network helps its partners fashion a vision of the river with the broadest possible appeal and define the economic advantages that might accrue to many stakeholders by restoring watersheds. And it stresses the need for long-term positive solutions, albeit with ongoing, independent citizen capacity to keep an eye on town councils and agencies, monitoring pollution and mobilizing against inappropriate development. The River Network's strategic vision is to establish vigilant citizen organizations capable of effective collaboration on each of the two thousand major watersheds across the country. Having inventoried over three thousand organizations engaged in some form of watershed activity, the network aims to help build their capacities for long-term restoration work by addressing such issues as pollution runoff and riparian habitat protection. As of 1998, the River Network includes some 280 watershed partner groups and has helped to establish and train leadership teams for twenty-three state organizations and several regional ones, such as the Northeast Watershed Team and the Northwest Watershed Network. Major state groups, such as the Rivers Council of Washington and the Massachusetts Watershed Council, are core partners working to diffuse successful models nationwide.[41]

Several national organizations support the work of land trusts. The Nature Conservancy (TNC), formed in 1951 out of several older ecological societies, significantly expanded its work in the 1970s and now partners with almost every federal landholding entity, with all states, and with hundreds of communities in protecting more than eleven million acres. It has six regional offices, fifty-six state chapters, and local stewardship groups on its 1,600 conservancy-owned preserves. TNC membership has grown steadily from 60,000 in 1980 to 832,000 in 1998. Its volunteers and staff provide long-term stewardship for conservancy-owned preserves and for those owned by its various partners. The American Farmland Trust, founded in 1980, works with individual farmers and government agencies to preserve land for working farms and to help farmers develop sustainable agricultural techniques. It inspired and championed the landmark provisions for conservation and wetland protection and restoration of several recent national farm bills, as well as much state legislation, and has helped to form statewide "sustainable agricultural societies." The Trust for Public Land, founded in 1972, has helped to incorporate or train many of the nation's land trusts and increasingly works with a diverse array of community development and community gardening groups to ensure active grassroots involvement. The Land Trust Alliance serves as a national federation of land trusts and is an important advocate in Washington, DC.[42]

Other national advocacy organizations mix independent organizing with collaborative strategies, and community-based groups today draw upon an increasingly sophisticated set of lessons for combining the two and avoiding the traps inherent in each.[43] Several of the major national organizations active in river and watershed conservation are organized into a three- or four-tier structure: national, regional, state, and local. This structure enables them to learn from each other by sharing experiences and models through formal and informal networks and to take initiative at appropriate levels. The National Audubon Society has 9 regional offices, 40 state groups, and 560 local chapters, many of which engage in river and watershed conservation work directly or in conjunction with broader watershed alliances. The Sierra Club has 11 regional offices, 65 state chapters, and 396 local groups, many of which also involve themselves in such work. Both the Audubon Society and the Sierra Club, founded in 1905 and 1892, respectively, had chapter structures that predated the rise of contemporary environmentalism, but both have invested significantly in their further development in recent decades as new opportunities for place-based and collaborative action have opened up. The National Wildlife Federation, founded in 1936, has 13 regional offices, 46 state affiliates and some 6,500 local groups, including its kids' programs, and increasingly stresses watershed approaches, sustainable communities, and land stewardship. Trout Unlimited, founded in 1959, has 13 regional groups, 32 state groups, and approximately 450 local chapters that work to restore river habitat for fisheries. The Izaak Walton League, founded in 1922, has 21 state groups and approximately 400 local groups that engage in a variety of water-monitoring and conservation activities, as well as an Outdoor Ethics program to educate boaters and other recreationists. And various chapters of the Sierra Club, Audubon Society, Trout Unlimited, and League of Women Voters also work in partnerships with the River Network.[44]

Second, the emergence of civic environmentalism has been made possible by the development of capacities for collaboration among federal, state, local, regional, and tribal agencies. Interagency collaboration has provided the context for sustained and constructive citizen action because it enables citizens to focus their attention and resources, rather than seeing these dissipated in fragmentary and often contradictory regulatory frameworks. Indeed, citizen action has often served as the catalyst for interagency collaboration. States have also come to play a variety of roles that assist citizen groups directly, as with funding the production of education and training materials, convening workshops and public forums, and assisting in dispute resolution. They have collaborated with citizen groups to establish new networks and have worked extensively with nonprofit land trusts, watershed associations, and citizen monitoring groups. Without state assistance and cooperation, many innovative civic projects could never have sustained themselves, and some would never have started. Local governments, often with state assistance, have also built capacities to work with citizen and nonprofit groups around water quality and wetland preservation, as well as energy conservation, greenways, and other environmental issues. In cities such as Seattle and Portland, with robust neighborhood associations and other forms of civic activism, and in Chattanooga, Tennessee, with innovative community visioning and action projects among thousands of citizens since 1984, robust "sustainable city" and "sustainable community" partnerships have emerged. These partnerships now serve as models for others in the sustainable communities movement.[45]

Federal agencies have provided a third and crucial level of support. EPA's experience with the Chesapeake Bay Program and other national estuaries in the 1980s, and its increasing receptivity to both internal agency and scholarly critiques of command-and-control over separate pollution media, have helped to shift more of its focus toward place-based approaches.[46] Under Administrator Carol Browner's tenure during the Clinton presidency, this has further accelerated. The agency developed the so called "Edgewater Consensus for Ecosystem Protection" in 1994, incorporated it into its five-year strategic plan, and systematically began to inventory the more than two hundred existing place-based projects in which it was already involved. This effort led to a Community-Based Environmental Protection (CBEP) strategy with a commitment to shift 20 percent of all media program resources. Stakeholder involvement is included as a central component, guided by the cumulative experiences in local wellhead protection programs, the National Estuary Program management conferences, the Clean Lakes Program management teams, the tributary teams on the Chesapeake Bay, and the watershed alliances formed through conservation districts and various other state and federal programs. Grant programs have supported a broad range of volunteer and civic action projects at the local level. EPA has also helped form a self-styled interagency "watershed training cooperative" known as the Watershed Academy. And while there exist other sources for community-based approaches, the experience with watersheds and water quality in the 1980s and 1990s has been the most critical for EPA learning.[47]

The Army Corps of Engineers has also made significant strides over three decades in developing citizen participation and alternative dispute resolution, although with various fits and starts and many remaining challenges, as has also been the case with other agencies. Pressured by environmentalists in the late 1960s, the Corps developed a series of innovative projects, the most notable being "fishbowl planning" in the Seattle District. The design worked out with the Washington State Department of Ecology convened various sides in a dispute over flood control on the middle fork of the Snoqualmie River. It combined four components: (1) public meetings; (2) workshops convened independently by the Sierra Club and valley farmers, with the Corps providing technical facilitation; (3) a citizens' committee to inform and involve a broader array of citizens; and (4) an iteratively modified study brochure that generated, at the urging of the Puget Sound League of Women Voters, eleven alternative plans with neatly summarized pros and cons, and contact information for further discussion and coalition building. The project achieved final consensus, however, only when the governor engaged the Community Crisis Intervention Center of St. Louis as mediator, thus producing the first case of successful environmental dispute resolution in the country.[48] In another instance, the Wildcat–San Pablo Creeks flood control project built directly upon community activism and the Model Cities Plan of Richmond, California, and developed into a successful collaboration that continues today, as civic groups (Urban Creeks Council, Save the San Francisco Bay Association, Contra Costa Shoreline Parks Committee, Richmond Neighborhoods Coordinating Council) and other government agencies joined the process.[49]

Corps Headquarters in Washington more or less supported public participation for much of the 1970s, and thousands of citizens were drawn into the planning process in most districts, though only the Seattle and San Francisco Districts institutionalized open planning. Experience proved ambiguous, however, as citizen activists generally appreciated the process but often opposed the outcomes, many of which had been set in motion years before by the backlogged construction projects of the 1940s and 1950s. Pork barrel politics also played a continuing role even as citizens became engaged in new ways. When headquarters support declined significantly in the early 1980s under the Reagan administration, participation programs largely proceeded in a decentralized fashion, relying upon staff trained in the 1970s. Such programs have continued to the point where "public involvement is now well integrated as a value and practice within the organizational culture of the Corps," as an extensive evaluation by Stuart Langton has concluded, though it is uneven and requires continued citizen pressure. Participation

programs have melded with alternative dispute resolution and other partnership approaches, as the Corps continues to draw upon lessons of smaller,
informal processes and trust-building strategies and as its responsibilities now
cover Superfund cleanups, military base closings, environmental restoration,
and outdoor recreation. Indeed, only in 1990 did the Water Resources Development Act actually extend the mission of the Corps to include environmental protection, though the Corps had established an Environmental Advisory Board twenty years earlier.[50]

FOREST PLANNING AND ECOSYSTEM RESTORATION

The U.S. Forest Service has had one of the most extensive public participation programs of any federal agency over the past several decades. It first developed ambitious participatory initiatives in 1970 and extended these in
1972 with its Inform and Involve program, which was designed by an innovative team that also helped to establish the Interagency Council on Citizen
Participation. The National Forest Management Act (NFMA) of 1976 built
upon these experiences in its attempt to enfranchise historically neglected
environmental and preservationist interests. The act specified at least ten
points during which public participation would be required in the preparation of its mandated long-term forest plans, which were to be completed
over the following decade. Rupert Cutler, President Carter's assistant secretary for conservation, research, and education in the Department of Agriculture (in which the Forest Service is located), was committed to refining
participatory mandates of NFMA and other laws to ensure genuine two-way
communication and independent citizen capacities to generate analyses and
alternatives.[51]

Through such efforts in the 1970s and early 1980s, some forests developed programs characterized by genuine dialogue and consensus seeking
among various user groups. Staff began to nurture deliberative regulatory
cultures to complement and modify a professional ideology based on the
scientific management of the land. Deliberative techniques included intensive workshops to clarify and classify different user values, weekend retreats
to build trust and empathy among traditional opponents, and Trade-Off Evaluation Processes, in which interdisciplinary management teams questioned
specialists for days before a public audience about the trade-offs entailed by
various policy alternatives and the principles and evidence behind various
choices. Some forest managers encouraged citizen groups to articulate their
own coherent vision of what they wanted the forest to look like for years to
come, and local rangers and engaged citizens carried in their back pockets
dog-eared "public involvement summaries" that sketched an array of alternatives to inform ongoing conversations and everyday interactions. These
techniques of public dialogue sometimes formed the basis of environmen-

tal impact statements (EIS) through which divergent user interests could be reframed, and court rulings on the inadequacy of public comment and considered alternatives in a draft EIS could prompt more intensive local deliberation. Some forest managers in the Northwest facilitated the development of citizen groups where none before existed. They generated lists of contacts and laid some of the essential foundations for the kind of town meeting civic culture that was more common in the national and state forests of the Northeast. They also helped to organize informal networks of communication among groups with different interests in the use of forest resources—timber harvest, mineral extraction, grazing, light and heavy recreation, wilderness preservation, wildlife management, and species protection.[52]

Yet for the great majority of national forests, Cutler's premise that increased participation would reduce litigation was not borne out, and administrators began experimenting with formal dispute-settlement techniques. As Julia Wondolleck argues, the earlier hopes were disappointed because participation had not altered an essentially adversarial paradigm, in which groups with often divergent perspectives and interests competed in a political process that had no objectively correct solution but did so under the guise of perfecting the scientific land management model. Staff were expected to provide information, facilitate and analyze public input from hearings and surveys, and explain the basis for decisions that, after careful analysis of all relevant data, they determined to be in the public interest. Despite all of the participatory opportunities, affected interests did not feel represented adequately by the process unless their substantive concerns were accommodated to their satisfaction. This problem was made no easier by the peculiar combination of regional ecology and national significance of forest disputes and by the resulting complexities and tensions of local and national interest group representation.[53]

The participatory process established for most forests was not based on mutual inquiry among competing groups or attempts to resolve disputes collaboratively. Thus, for instance, the RARE II (Roadless Area Review and Evaluation) process, a participatory showpiece of the late 1970s designed to classify (for congressional approval) which national forest lands should remain roadless and receive wilderness designation, involved 50,000 people in providing input into the scope of the EIS, 17,000 in workshops to structure the review process, and 264,000 additional comments on the draft EIS. And still the document was attacked by timber and mining groups, and by environmentalists and other backcountry users as providing too much or too little wilderness protection. Formal hearings were often highly polarized, with all contending groups projecting their hostilities onto agency staff. The participatory process was not designed to be sufficiently informative or convincing to groups with different interests, and it created incentives for strategic behavior and escalating protest in anticipation of administrative appeal, court review, and congressional intervention. These patterns were evident in other planning efforts during the 1980s as well. As one participant put it, the Forest Service "got the interests all fired up and then ran us head-on into each other."[54]

By the early 1980s, however, the Forest Service began to explore formal dispute resolution as a complement to its participatory programs. As the subsequently released draft forest plans were met with typically hundreds of appeals, a growing number of forests began to employ formal dispute-resolution techniques involving various citizen and interest groups, the Forest Service itself, and the participating states' congressional delegations. In some cases, these elected representatives initially spurred the use of dispute settlement because of the serious political fallout of continued adversarialism on federal lands.

Until recently, the civic learning potential of these participatory innovations has been severely constrained by the fundamental dynamics of forest policy put into place during the postwar boom in housing construction and modified only partially by the rise of the environmental movement. The traditional timber regime operated like a classic "iron triangle" that locked together the Forest Service, the timber industry, and the relevant congressional appropriations subcommittees behind ever-increasing harvests. It received local support in states with heavy concentrations of national forests not only because intensive silviculture produced jobs but also because Congress had earlier set aside 25 percent of timber sale receipts for counties to use for school and road construction. Congressional representatives from these states have dominated the appropriations process. And while the pluralist forest policy regime that emerged with the new environmental movement loosened this triangle, and at times reduced timber harvests, Congress continued to leave huge loopholes that favored intensive harvesting well beyond what was sustainable over the long run. The Reagan administration, in particular, ratcheted up harvests, which set the context in which the first round of national forest plans were formulated under NFMA. The shock to this virtually unstoppable policy dynamic came only with the radical depletion of old-growth forests. This development left a strategic opening for the environmental movement to utilize the Endangered Species Act (ESA) to get unprecedented court injunctions against further timber sales in 1989 and 1990, and it led to open revolt among Forest Service field staff themselves.[55]

The profile of Forest Service staff changed dramatically between the 1960s and the 1990s, elevating a new paradigm that stresses ecosystem management and collaborative decision making. Beginning with the Multiple Use and Sustained Yield Act of 1960, the Forest Service has been compelled to hire a larger proportion of professionals trained in noncommodity disciplines, such as wildlife and fishery biologists and ecologists. It has also been compelled to hire an increasing number of women, whose commitment to noncommodity values is significantly greater than that of men in the service. Over the course of three decades, these employees have risen through the hierarchy, and those hired during the housing boom of the immediate postwar years have retired. Timber professionals have also been required to work in multidisciplinary teams under NFMA and have come to appreciate perspectives previously considered outside their framework. Conservation biology was ascendant in the Forest Service in the 1980s. These changes laid the foundation for a profound shift in values, which became especially evident in response to the Reagan administration's dramatic increase in harvests. Over the 1980s, support for increased timber harvesting among Forest Service employees declined from 62 percent to 7 percent, according to one survey. In another, 70 percent placed primary value on wildlife, fish, water, and recreation, but the same percentage saw the agency as placing primacy on timber. In 1989 the Association of Forest Service Employees for Environmental Ethics was established, representing the ascendance of a new resource management paradigm. Forest supervisors became increasingly vocal in their dissent. Indeed, some openly defied Washington's pressure to increase harvests as being a violation of federal environmental law.[56]

By the end of the Bush administration, Forest Service Chief Dale Robertson began to respond to these value shifts among staff, as well as to political pressure from environmental groups and the emergence of an increasing number of innovative projects where significant participatory learning had occurred. He introduced the New Perspectives initiative and ratified ecosystem management as official policy. President Clinton endorsed this shift with the appointment in 1993 of wildlife research biologist Jack Ward Thomas as the new chief, the first in the history of the service not trained as a forester or engineer. The president's Forest Conference, convened in Portland in April 1993 with a broad array of some sixty stakeholders in the Northwest forest disputes, unfortunately proved to be a lost opportunity for conflict management. The conference rhetoric of collaborative problem solving and joint learning was stunted by a design based on adversarial arbitration, which shifted in the postconference phase to some of the least effective traditional forms of public participation.[57] But ecosystem approaches continued to take hold, and Michael Dombeck, also a biologist, succeeded Thomas in January 1997 and has promoted a philosophy of "collaborative stewardship" within the Forest Service. Reflecting on years of experience with citizen participation, he noted, "The public has told us it wants us to be facilitators and educators. We need to bring people together to work within the limits of the land."[58]

Ecosystem management projects have proliferated during the 1990s and have brought new emphasis on forms of participation and collaboration that cultivate long-term relationships among groups with diverse interests and cultures, and that create forums for public deliberation on common values and a common future. These transcend both adversarial participation and formal dispute settlement, and stress informal, open decision-making processes. They nurture public leadership capacities among forest staff and participants from the relevant communities of interest. Building relationships and establishing trust are increasingly viewed as key to making wise, implementable, and revisable decisions in a complex and uncertain environment where relevant information is widely diffused in governmental and nongovernmental organizations alike and where political support, public knowledge, organizational learning, and additional resources are crucial to everyday work. Indeed, a cumulative body of theory and research, as well as established models in the United States and around the globe, highlight the advantages of self-organizing and polycentric systems of common-pool resource governance of forests and fisheries that are capable of adaptive learning and experimentation.[59] Powerful stakeholders in U.S. forests have incentive to participate in cooperative ecosystem management because of the uncertainty generated by ESA listing and the hammer it hangs over their heads. Collaborative planning, however, is hardly limited to forests with explicit ecosystem projects. A recent comprehensive survey found some form of collaborative planning on more than 90 percent of the 155 national forests, where it appears well integrated into day-to-day management and decision making. But as one forest planner put it, "The indirect benefits—the partnerships, networks, trust, and information sharing—are more beneficial than the actual collaborative planning effort itself."[60]

In county and state forests, as well as urban forestry projects, collaborative planning and volunteer stewardship have also become increasingly evident. The Portland Metropolitan Greenspaces Program in Oregon, one of the most creative greenway projects in the country, was established in the 1980s through collaborative efforts of a local land trust, Audubon chapter, and metropolitan service district. Citizen activists have formed Friends and Advocates of Urban Natural Areas (FAUNA), which does extensive public education and coordinates the work of land stewards through its more than sixty local groups throughout the region. Cooperation has spread among other cities and counties, and between Oregon and neighboring Washington State, and more than twenty-five local jurisdictions have passed resolutions favoring creation of a regional system like the Metropolitan Greenspaces. During the 1990s the U.S. Forest Service, with funding from the 1990 Farm Bill, lent increasing support to urban and community forestry and reported steadily increasing capacity at the local level for sustained work. In fiscal year 1997 more than eight thousand communities were participating in the Urban and Community Forestry Program; some 363,000 volunteers had done planting and related tasks; and nearly 300,000 had received technical or general training. In some cases, urban forestry projects have been linked to community development in inner cities.[61]

The Volunteer Stewardship Network, perhaps the most ambitious and influential volunteer restoration effort, was begun in Chicago's North Branch forest preserves in the late 1970s by Steve Packard. As a college student, Packard marched on Washington for civil rights in 1963 to hear Martin Luther King's "I Have a Dream" speech. He learned his participatory democracy through more than a decade of activism in the antiwar movement and an alternative newsreel collective. But as the energy of these movements waned, he took a job at the Illinois Environmental Council, an advocacy organization, and in his free time he returned to an old childhood love of wildflowers. Wildflowers seemed utterly trivial in comparison to mass demonstrations, though one day it dawned on him that he could utilize his organizing skills to preserve and restore the prairie and savanna ecosystems hidden right in the middle of metropolitan Chicago. The local Sierra Club gave him two and one-half minutes to make his pitch one evening, and thus began a network of volunteers who set out clearing shrubs and debris, collecting and planting seeds, storing them in their garages, and growing them in their kitchens. Volunteers researched historical records, revived old Native American burn techniques, and slowly began to restore the spectacular beauty of prairie grasses and wildflowers, and—even more amazingly—savanna ecosystems thought to have been completely lost. The Sierra Club, Audubon Society, and other local organizations began to insert the North Branchers workday schedules in their newsletters, and every Sunday morning volunteers began to gather. They came from garden clubs and neighborhood associations. They included carpenters, retirees, students, scientists, Girl Scout and Boy Scout troops. Many were attracted by the consensus methods and sought places for environmental commitment beyond what they perceived as the strident and ideological posturing in other groups. Some came just for the sociability. Yet many came to do work of deeply lasting, even eternal value with a larger spiritual purpose, akin to "building cathedrals." As Packard recalls, they saw themselves as building not just constituencies, but "congregations for the prairies," because congregations last from generation to generation. At first there were failures, but interesting failures. Or progress was so slow as to be barely visible. When Packard joined the Illinois Nature Conservancy staff in 1983, he began to extend this approach throughout the state organization. A decade later some 5,000 volunteers labored on more than 200 sites and had restored over 30,000 acres, half of these within metropolitan Chicago.

The Volunteer Stewardship Network has provided increasingly sophisticated training and has built relationships with thousands of homeowners, agency staff, preserve owners, animal rights activists, civic associations, businesses, and ordinary visitors to the restored sites. It has established a model now recognized by the Nature Conservancy nationally and emulated by a variety of state conservancies within and outside TNC, which have begun to see themselves as part of a larger "restoration movement." This step did not come without opposition from some, including Packard's boss in the Illinois Nature Conservancy, who saw TNC's mission as merely buying up land, hiring professional stewards, and avoiding politics. But as others high up in TNC began to realize that they could never buy enough land to preserve bioregions and broader landscapes and could never buy the passionate commitment they got from these volunteer stewards, the organization proved capable of learning from such grassroots efforts. It recognized that its chapters would have to work with public and private owners and build new kinds of political relationships if it was to fulfill its larger mission. As Packard has put it, "There is this mentality in the United States that democracy is wonderful but politics is dirty. You can't have democracy without politics. So we decided our job was to figure out how to do wholesome, ethical, effective environmental politics."[62]

Today the Illinois chapter of TNC supports the work of nearly six thousand "citizen scientists" in the Volunteer Stewardship Network. Packard himself, now with the National Audubon Society, heads the Chicago Wilderness Program, a local partnership of more than ninety civic groups, institutions, and agencies engaged in long-term stewardship and restoration, which is but one of twenty-nine of Illinois' C2000 Ecosystem Partnerships.

TOXICS AND ENVIRONMENTAL JUSTICE

In the mid-1970s local labor and community activists began forming Committees on Occupational Safety and Health (COSH) in cities across the country and documenting the extent of exposure to hazardous chemicals in workplaces. Their efforts had been facilitated by the research and legitimacy provided by the creation in 1970 of the Occupational Safety and Health Administration (OSHA), its affiliated National Institute of Occupational Safety and Health (NIOSH), and its accompanying citizen participation programs. In 1976 Congress passed two laws that set the framework for the overall regulation of toxics: the Toxic Substances Control Act and the Resource Conservation and Recovery Act, both of which also contained ambitious provisions for informing and involving the public. But in the summer of 1978, before EPA was able to set in place the enormously complex technical and administrative procedures for tracking, managing, and disposing of hazardous wastes, the dramatic revelations of homes and children exposed to toxics from the old Hooker chemical plant in Love Canal, New York, appeared in the national media and received widespread publicity for the next several years. President Carter visited Love Canal and declared it a disaster meriting relocation for families near the site. The COSH movement began to forge links between workplace and community in its campaign for "right-to-know" laws at the state and eventually the federal level. Grassroots groups sprang up in increasing numbers, especially in communities being considered for the siting of hazardous waste treatment facilities, or where other contaminated dumpsites were discovered. Indeed, EPA's own campaign in 1979–80 for a Superfund law to support cleanup activities identified dumpsites in congressional districts across the nation, and thus helped spur grassroots mobilization.[63]

Two national networks formed in the 1980s to provide organizing, technical assistance, and overall strategic guidance to the emerging antitoxics movement. The first, the Citizen's Clearinghouse for Hazardous Wastes (CCHW), was formed in Arlington, Virginia, in 1981 by Love Canal mother and housewife Lois Gibbs. CCHW drew inspiration from old-style Alinsky organizing, as well as from Ella Baker, the civil rights leader who influenced the participatory ethos of SNCC and SDS in the 1960s. In stressing the need to "rebuild democracy from community to community," CCHW responded to the voices of the many working-class and minority women who emerged as local grassroots leaders in defense of homes, children, and neighborhoods.[64] The second network, the National Toxics Campaign (NTC), was founded in 1984 by John O'Connor, a community organizer from Massachusetts Fair Share. The training offered by NTC also drew upon old-style Alinsky organizing and stressed a relatively short, eight-week campaign to recruit members. NTC grew rapidly as a national coalition that helped to spearhead the grassroots campaign to reauthorize Superfund in 1986. O'Connor emphasized a conception of "environmental democracy" that includes three rights: the "right to know," the "right to inspect," and the "right to negotiate" directly with responsible parties. The first is embodied in various state laws and the federal Emergency Planning and Community Right-to-Know Act (EPCRA), which established a Toxics Release Inventory (TRI) to provide plant-by-plant data on toxics. The second has taken the form of "citizen inspections" of waste facilities and dump sites, and the third has led to a strategy of "good neighbor agreements" between community groups and local industries.[65]

Over the 1980s both NTC and CCHW responded to the growing evidence of "environmental racism," and increasingly worked with organizers from minority communities. The phenomenon of environmental racism first received public attention during a nonviolent civil disobedience campaign against the siting of a polychlorinated biphenyl (PCB) disposal landfill in a largely poor black county in North Carolina in 1982. Subsequent research by sociologist Robert Bullard, by the United Church of Christ's Commission for Racial Justice (UCC/CRJ), and by various legal scholars, documented what appeared to be clear patterns of racial discrimination in the siting of waste facilities, the creation and enforcement of environmental and land use regulations, and the cleaning up of polluted areas.[66] By the end of the 1980s a self-described "environmental justice" movement emerged, utilizing a civil rights "justice frame" to understand issues of environmental protection. More than five hundred participants from all fifty states and abroad met at the First National People of Color Environmental Leadership Summit in Washington, DC, in October 1991 to formulate principles that would guide the movement in the following years.[67]

EPA and Civic Capacity Building

Beginning in 1990 the movement also began to get its first serious hearing at EPA under William Reilly, and during the Clinton administration the doors were opened wide. Robert Bullard and Benjamin Chavis (then executive director of the UCC/CRJ) were appointed to the newly elected president's Transition Team in Natural Resources and Environment. Carol Browner, who was appointed administrator of EPA, had earlier served as the first Washington lobbyist for NTC and was thoroughly familiar with the issues posed by the grassroots movement.[68] She moved quickly to initiate a variety of environmental justice projects and to strengthen community participation in Superfund. She also changed the name of the Office of Environmental Equity, established under Reilly, to the Office of Environmental Justice (OEJ). In early 1994 President Clinton signed Executive Order 12898 establishing interagency working groups, strategies, and model projects on environmental justice and established the National Environmental Justice Advisory Council (NEJAC), with representatives from environmental justice groups, academics, industry, tribal and state governments, and other nonprofits. As Robert Bullard, who has served on the NEJAC along with other prominent advocates, has noted, a "new paradigm has taken hold" as a result of the collaborative efforts of grassroots activists and agency staff committed to enhancing citizen participation.[69]

With the help of NEJAC, EPA has developed several approaches to build civic capacities. The Office for Environmental Justice has established grant programs to develop the capacities of local community, tribal, ethnic, business, and educational organizations to initiate pollution prevention activities and to carry these out with the involvement of multiple stakeholder groups. These can take various forms. Some community health centers hire medical professionals with community-organizing skills to work with employers and employees in local autobody repair, dry cleaning, and printing shops to educate them about alternative work practices and safe disposal options, and to build relationships among them and their neighbors. The Korean Youth and Community Center in Los Angeles has partnered with UCLA and Clean by Nature, the first 100 percent wet cleaning firm in Southern California, to diffuse clean practices through the extensive network of Korean-owned dry-cleaning firms. Retired engineers and scientists working with the national Environmental Careers Organization serve as mentors to community groups in developing pollution reduction and energy-saving strategies for homes and "good neighbor agreements" with local businesses. The Dudley Street Neighborhood Initiative is one of many community development, Empowerment Zone, and Enterprise Community initiatives to work with local employers and microenterprises on environmental justice and cost-effective pollution reduction strategies, and the National Association of Community Development Loan Funds has been funded by OEJ to diffuse similar small business-financing practices among its forty-six lending institutions nationwide. Denver Urban Gardeners identify and help clean up polluted land parcels that they then turn into community gardens. Elementary and high school groups, citywide ethnic associations, CDCs, and state Head Start associations have developed projects to educate people in poor and minority neighborhoods about environmentally safe homes, emphasizing the prevention of lead poisoning. Historically black colleges and universities, tribal colleges, and other universities serving minority groups have partnered with local community groups and churches to conduct research and develop community-based strategies. Local watershed associations and statewide coalitions have incorporated toxic reduction and cleanup into their mission.

While these various grant programs remain very modest relative both to need and to other kinds of spending on toxics, they have helped to establish and disseminate models for pollution reduction and education that build upon existing civic networks and enable local groups to focus on dangers that are most threatening to their health, homes, and neighborhoods. In many cases, these efforts have entailed a learning process that shifts attention away from inactive hazardous waste sites and facilities, which may present relatively minor risks. As the new forms of representation, such as the NEJAC, have enabled OEJ to learn a great deal from the organized movement, the office also sees its mission as educating local groups about how to focus energies and resources on those risks most threatening to their communities and to avoid the kind of "mysticism about chemicals" that can distract them. As Robert Knox, assistant director of OEJ, put it, "We are not always successful in educating them, but many do come along. And we expect them to learn mutually with us when we support their work."[70]

Through the 1990s the Office of Pollution Prevention and Toxics (OPPT) at EPA also developed a series of initiatives to foster civic capacity to reduce and prevent pollution and to enable community groups to access information and fashion strategies for environmental justice. OPPT funded the Right-to-Know Network, which has served nationally to enable community groups to utilize the Toxics Release Inventory (TRI) data more effectively. OPPT's Community Partnership for Environmental Protection in South Baltimore, the most industrialized part of the city, containing eleven TRI facilities, was developed as a pilot to learn how to build complex partnerships to reduce pollution at the community level in ways not possible through national and state regulations and to link these efforts to broad community development. The Baltimore partnership brought together churches, schools, Johns Hopkins University, the city health department, Sierra Club, Chesapeake Bay Foundation, local activists, businesses, and the chemical industry council to develop shared priorities and strategies based on the most sophisticated community-level study of pollution ever conducted by the EPA or any other state or local agency. Its efforts have yielded significant reductions in air pollution and a variety of community health and environmental restoration projects, and EPA has worked with other regional offices and cities to diffuse its lessons.[71] The OPPT has also conducted a series of Design for the Environment (DfE) projects to enable industry, in collaboration with environmental groups and labor unions, to develop cost-effective toxic reduction strategies. In dry cleaning, for instance, DfE has built upon the work of the Center for Neighborhood Technology (CNT) in Chicago to develop a variety of local networking strategies for sustainable manufacturing among small businesses. CNT borrowed the "wet cleaning" process that reduces the use of perchloroethylene from an innovative shop in England, helped a local dry cleaner introduce it, and then joined the Professional Wet Cleaning Partnership with industry leaders, labor groups, and the Tellus Institute to test and certify the process.[72]

The Design for Environment Printing Project, a voluntary, cooperative effort between the printing industry and the EPA, builds the capacity of printers themselves to make responsible and informed choices about how best to protect the environment of their communities and the health of their workers. The adversarial strategy leaves printers simply reacting to the latest environmental regulations and has been ineffective in addressing what is probably the industry's biggest negative impact on the environment: the effect of many small printers in one area. As OPPT's Henry Topper puts it, the cooperative approach is "designed to put them ahead of the regulatory curve and to provide the information and social networks needed to make continuous improvements that are both responsible and cost effective." In one of the early projects, printers themselves identified a chemical application, blanket washing, that they felt presented serious concerns in the workplace and the environment. Volunteers joined a coordinating group with staff from OPPT and began to mobilize their own assets to develop and test alternatives and to communicate this information throughout the industry. Almost all sectors of the industry have made contributions. Suppliers have donated their products for comparative evaluation, and shops volunteered to use alternative blanket washes and carefully to record their experiences with the help of a consultant. Staff from the printing trade associations, both national and local, have been actively involved, and the Graphic Arts Technical Foundation performed lab tests and screened alternative blanket washes. Printers around the country have met in focus groups to give advice on the direction of the project and to define how best to communicate the results to printers to ensure the most effective and widespread use of the alternatives. EPA staff have helped with the technical review and other aspects of the project and have developed with the printers the kind of information on comparative risks, exposures, performance, and the costs of alternatives that will permit informed and responsible choices. And the trade press has publicized the results to printers across the nation.

The Design for the Environment approach treats printers not as potential lawbreakers, but as citizens capable of collaborating with each other and with government in defining a responsible environmental agenda and carrying it out with the assets that they themselves can mobilize: their knowledge and skill as workers and managers and their commitments to their communities and to their own health and well-being. The process builds trust, as well as the networks capable of continuous learning and improvement as they move to define further areas of environmental concern. The cooperative effort to produce essential environmental information levels the playing field in the industry by making information available to printshops of all sizes, thus allowing small shops to remain competitive while making more environmentally sound choices.[73]

Information, Power, and Neighborliness

Community organizations first began conducting plant inspections and signing "good neighbor agreements" with corporations as part of the Massachusetts Fair Share campaign against toxics in the late 1970s and early 1980s. The National Toxics Campaign (NTC) built directly upon this experience over the next decade, and its coalition with other community and labor groups to pass EPCRA in 1986 led to the creation of the Toxics Release Inventory. The TRI, a computerized national database of toxic chemical releases by individual manufacturing facilities, is available on-line, on CD-ROM, diskettes, in print, and in other forms. The 1990 Pollution Prevention Act, together with a variety of state laws, further mandated that firms required to report data on toxics also report on their pollution prevention activities.

This power of information, an increasingly important tool for communities, has led to the development of interlaced national networks, state and regional projects, and local initiatives to enable citizens to use technical information effectively and to negotiate directly with companies. Both citizen and industry groups agree that the TRI has prompted increased face-to-face meetings and collaborative problem solving, rather than community hysteria or litigation. In one survey, 85 percent of citizen TRI users reported engaging in direct pressure on firms, and 58 percent said the facilities eventually pursued source reduction. Many other firms implement reduction strategies to avoid possible inclusion on a "Who's Who of Toxic Polluters" or a "Toxic 500" list compiled from TRI data by the Natural Resources Defense Council and the National Wildlife Federation in the late 1980s. Such data have also helped catalyze attention by the media, stock markets, regulators, and state legislators. Toxic emissions for the listed chemicals have been reduced substantially over the past decade, making EPCRA one of the most successful environmental laws in the country.[74]

Good neighbor agreements are a form of flexible, community-based environmental protection whose underlying philosophy is the mutual acknowledgment by a business and an independent community organization of the need to build a relationship responsive to the needs of each. Agreements are formally negotiated. Some remain voluntary and without legally binding language; others are attached as a condition of formal permitting processes and can be legally enforced. An agreement might include the community's selection and supervision of an independent expert to conduct a safety audit, paid for by the company, as well as the installation of new testing equipment, safety and notification procedures, and the availability of relevant data in the local library. It also might include a range of measures to upgrade jobs, provide greater opportunities for local residents, and increase financial commitments to vocational programs in local high schools. For example, the Unocal Refinery agreement worked out with community leaders, labor unions, and Communities for a Better Environment in Rodeo, California, in 1995, after two hazardous chemical spills, included many of these elements, as well as specific financial commitments to improve transportation infrastructure and to support other community and economic development projects.

The Good Neighbor Project, which spun off from NTC in the 1980s, provides technical assistance and training to local projects around the country and has helped state and regional groups develop good neighbor strategies and neighbor-labor alliances. Communities for a Better Environment in California has pursued a strategy of seeking legally binding agreements, such as the Unocal agreement, which is part of its permit for continued operation, while Citizens for a Better Environment in Minnesota has pursued a voluntary strategy, though within the framework of the state's Toxic Pollution Prevention Act requiring pollution prevention plans. In Iowa, collaborative work among the Montpelier Endangered Neighborhood Effort, the United Steelworkers of America, and Iowa Citizen Action Network led to the formation of the Coalition for Corporate Responsibility, which succeeded in getting the state's economic development subsidy law to grant extra consideration for those programs that include a good neighbor agreement based on "environmental, economic, labor, or other social and community standards" and to require full repayment if a company does not abide by its agreement.

The Good Neighbor Project itself has favored the development of binding agreements. It has also been a consistent advocate at EPA for strength-ening participatory rules in voluntary pollution prevention programs, such as Project XL, where it sees far too much room for industry to manipulate required "stakeholder participation" by selecting weak community partners without independent organizing capacity. As Sanford Lewis, the director of the Good Neighbor Project, notes, good neighbor agreements are not about "feel-good notions, they are about power."[75]

Another way in which some companies have engaged with communities in a mutual learning process is through Community Advisory Panels (CAPs). The Chemical Manufacturers Association (CMA), under great public pres-sure in the 1980s, developed a Responsible Care Program, whose adoption is mandatory for all of CMA's 190 members. This program recommended, though it did not require, that plants establish CAPs to ensure effective com-munication and trust building with local communities. The innovation has been diffused rapidly as a result of official support. In 1991 there were 56, and by 1997 over 316 CAPs nationwide in the chemical industry. CAPs take a variety of forms and operate with varying degrees of success, but some demonstrate considerable potential to include strong, independent com-munity representation.

The Vulcan Chemicals chlor-alkali manufacturing facility in Wichita, Kansas, exemplifies the kind of extended learning process in a plant that was the focus of much public controversy but was able to generate top man-agement support and participation by local environmentalists and other civic groups. Controversy began in 1986, after thirty years of seemingly good re-lations between the plant and the community, when a group of fifteen neigh-boring families filed suit against the plant for damaging their health. Ten-sions were exacerbated when the plant announced the following year its intention to build an incinerator for hazardous wastes, which it believed was a responsible way to guarantee its customers cradle-to-grave management of pentachlorophenol waste. The Sierra Club and Greenpeace campaigned actively against the company, and Lois Gibbs of CCHW appeared at a local meeting urging civil disobedience. Then in June 1988 a local representative of the Sierra Club met with the plant manager and a public affairs repre-sentative from company headquarters, and they agreed to hire an outside facilitator and to establish a Community Involvement Group (CIG)—another name for CAP—to see if they could resolve the incinerator dispute. The CIG included company officials, the Sierra Club, League of Women Voters, Kansas Natural Resources Council, and Wichita/Sedgwick County Health Depart-ment. Over time others were added: close neighbors and residents of sur-rounding communities, local universities, and industry. Greenpeace chose not to participate in such a collaborative process.

After some initial meetings, the company decided to cancel the inciner-ator, citing escalating cost estimates, though CIG members saw their own continued skepticism as contributing to the decision. Vulcan decided, however, to keep the CIG going, since other environmental conflicts were anticipated, and the economic development community was expressing concern about such controversies dampening the investment climate in Wichita. In addition, the EPA and Kansas Department of Health and Environment let the company know that they preferred some form of ongoing community involvement. In other words, a set of relationships that had evolved within the CIG and within the larger regulatory community was brought to bear and then applied systematically to a series of other problems.

On the next issue, deep-well disposal, the CIG demanded funding to hire an independent team of consultants, whose progress the group reported to regulators and whose final report was made available to the broader public. Although the consultants did not explicitly recommend against the practice and the company was granted the necessary permits, it nonetheless decided to phase out deep-well injections, reducing them by 90 percent over the next seven years. TRI data gave the CIG added leverage when Vulcan turned up on a *USA Today* "Top Polluters" list, and the local plant manager used the CIG as leverage with headquarters to build a plant that will convert the waste into other useful sodium chloride products. As the plant manager explained, the CIG members are "not kids, but adults. . . . We're either going to fight with [the community] for the rest of our natural born lives, or we're going to accommodate [them] in one way, shape or form." After a series of other successful efforts by the CIG to improve the safety design of the proposed new facility, the plant manager agreed to lead a twenty-six-company committee in Wichita to participate in EPA's voluntary Project 33/50, which committed them to reduce emissions of seventeen chemicals by 50 percent by 1995. The committee went beyond this target and included all chemicals they were discharging. As the plant manager explained, "When you get involved in community involvement groups, you suddenly become a source of leadership whether you want to or not."[76]

Superfund, NIMBY, and Public Policy for Democracy

Civic innovations for grappling with the problems of toxics and environmental justice have emerged over the past decade in a context often marked by fierce local mobilization against perceived risks to family and community and by strong claims for rights to information and participation. Yet the development of civic capacities for deliberation about relative risk and effective response has been blocked by features of the antitoxics and environmental justice movements themselves and by some of the very policy designs that have spurred local mobilization. These problems are particularly evident for Superfund.

As Marc Landy and his colleagues have argued, the original policy design for Superfund was driven by EPA institutional interests to build a political base and secure budgets during difficult economic times in the late 1970s, when it was still uncertain whether public support could be sustained for ecological activities that appeared to have few tangible benefits. Administrator Douglas Costle thus chose a public health strategy focused on cancer risks. Media coverage of Love Canal provided a perfect opportunity, and the agency set out to show the public that hundreds of Love Canals existed across the nation. Despite limited evidence of actual health risks at most of these sites, the agency ordered each regional office to compile lists of the worst ten and worked with sympathetic congressional staffers to extend the list to each member's district. The costs of the proposed new program to taxpayers could be disguised through an off-budget chemical feedstock fee and a liability scheme that could hold any potentially responsible party (PRP) liable for the entire cleanup costs, even if it had only the most tangential responsibility for the problem, had observed all existing laws, and had operated within the bounds of contemporary scientific knowledge.

A policy design based on grants to the states had been stalemated in Congress because of an ideologically polarized framing. Liberals wanted a big federal program as the only speedy and effective way to respond to a perceived national crisis; conservatives wanted a program run by the states—*not* to bring cleanup decisions closer to local communities and build capacities for responsible choice, but primarily to reduce the scale of the program. EPA's refusal to consider a policy design based on a fixed budget and state grants meant that every community near a hazardous waste site had an incentive to clamor for the most expensive cleanup possible. Cleanup thus appeared as a free good with no opportunity costs, and communities did not have to deliberate about "How clean is clean?" in view of possible alternative uses of the land or competing claims by other communities for cleanup dollars and other resources that could be used to significantly improve health and environment.[77]

Under the Superfund policy design, for instance, an environmental justice group in the inner city did not have to ask whether it made sense to spend, say, 30 million dollars to clean up an old factory site to meet the "eat dirt" standard for children playing on it or whether much less could be spent on capping and containing the toxics so that another factory might safely take over the site and bring jobs to the neighborhood. It did not have to ask whether spending less might permit several other deserving poor and minority communities to begin cleanup, thus spreading the overall benefits more equitably, or whether some of the available money should be spent on lead abatement programs, which would directly improve the health of many inner-city children. Nothing in the policy design encouraged or required concerned citizens to deliberate about these kinds of relative costs and benefits or to pose issues of environmental equity and justice more fully.

As we noted earlier, EPA's own learning process related to enhancing community participation on toxics started quite propitiously under the Superfund Community Relations team headed by Steven Cohen and informed by the ICF, Inc., report from some twenty participatory water projects. This report anticipated the major contours of the antitoxics movement already in 1980–81. Reagan's initial appointments and budget cuts disrupted this process, though it was renewed slowly but steadily under each subsequent administrator after Ruckelshaus's return. EPA listened to advice on the design of community relations plans by the Environmental Defense Fund, which assembled grassroots groups to develop guidelines, and it progressively expanded its Community Relations office. It thoroughly revised the *Community Relations Handbook* twice to guide local practice and to incorporate lessons from the field on the need for public information repositories, observation decks for monitoring site cleanup, open houses, community interviews, informal meetings, community work groups, and continual communication. And it renewed explicitly its commitment to "participatory democracy."[78]

Flaws in the overall design of Superfund, however, as well as the reauthorization deadlock in Congress in the mid-1980s, led staff to develop highly defensive postures toward communities. Officials sought to avoid causing further alarm, committing unavailable resources, encouraging unrealistic expectations, or creating additional legal liability. Information was often withheld or presented in unnecessarily mystifying technical terms, thus breeding further mistrust, dependence, and rage among local residents. Even as well-meaning Community Relations staff tried to do effective outreach, they remained subordinate to technical staff, who dominated public meetings and sometimes were not even aware of what the Community Relations Plan entailed. Communication was often a one-way affair, and chances for public voice were delayed and discontinuous, lacking links to actual decision making. The initial interviews and the development of the Community Relations Plan often did not occur until three to four years after a site had been placed on the Superfund list, and the next mandated chance for formal public comment came several years after this. It is no wonder that local residents felt that the agency was deliberately keeping them in the dark. Community Relations staff were themselves relatively low in status within EPA, with few chances of mobility or access to real authority, and turnover was high. Thus, despite some substantial learning that served the agency well during the 1990s, the first decade of communities' experience with participation in Superfund was extremely contentious.[79]

During the 1980s it became increasingly scandalous how few sites had been cleaned up, how long the process took, and how great a percentage of the funds spent went to transaction costs, especially legal fees, within the complicated liability schema that encouraged PRP resistance. State and local environmental officials became increasingly cognizant of the opportunity costs and recognized Superfund spending as excessive in relation to other environmental problems,[80] and EPA itself came to similar conclusions. Yet in 1986 Superfund was reauthorized with the same policy design, even with several new features that exacerbated its flaws. It proved resistant to basic changes because, Landy and Hague argue, a "coalition for waste" had formed around the program. National environmental groups had a stake in continued mobilization by local communities that wished to get named to the National Priorities List, and the permanent treatment standard's very unattainability provided an invaluable organizing tool, even though seeking attainment might actually increase the net health risks of abandoned hazardous waste sites by concentrating resources on fewer sites. The waste treatment industry has a major financial stake in the continual proliferation of Superfund sites that merit gold-plated, "Cadillac" treatment solutions. And the legal community generates political support since Superfund is one of the most important sources of new business for major law firms. Indeed, some have called Superfund a "full-employment program for lawyers."[81]

Thus, while antitoxics and environmental justice organizing has helped to catalyze a range of civic innovations, its entanglement in the policy system of Superfund has also limited and distorted civic capacity building for more effective and equitable responses. Profound resistance, sometimes bordering on incomprehension, exists within the environmental justice movement to the notion that responsible civic action involves choices about relative risk, limited funds, and opportunity costs. This view is quite understandable given the nature of toxics and the disproportionate burdens on many poor and minority communities. But toxics movement organizers often encourage individual communities to believe that the immediate and most expensive resolution of a problem is the only acceptable and just one, regardless of the impact this may have on other worthy resource and justice claims for reducing toxic hazards and improving health. They reject the results of collaborative community research that does not validate their preconceptions of where to focus the blame, as they did in the South Baltimore community partnership when industry emissions did not appear as the main culprit, or they condemn partnerships and good neighbor agreements as divide-and-conquer strategies that should be refused outright. They often resist community health strategies that might target factors having demonstrably more impact on minority health, such as indoor air pollution, smoking, and obesity, because these may be interpreted as "blaming the victim." And they reinforce NIMBY tendencies toward every local facility-siting decision, or propagate NIABY ("Not in Anyone's Backyard") as a general stance that will "stop up the toilet" and force massive changes in production techniques to reduce toxics at the source. While the latter goal is certainly worthy, the strategy tends to undermine the search for siting procedures based on extensive public participation and burden sharing, which have advanced significantly in recent years and are the sine qua non of effective toxics policy.

These problems are, to some extent, part of an inevitably messy and con- voluted learning process. At the birth of Superfund, none of the major pol- icy actors within EPA, the two parties in Congress, the interest groups on ei- ther side of the issue, or the conservative or liberal think tanks had a credible approach to enhance civic deliberation or empower communities to deal with the problem of hazardous waste sites. Both the capacities and rights of local communities to participate effectively in a risk-communication process that could progressively distinguish among different kinds and degrees of risk and injustice were poorly developed. A movement-building strategy thus made a great deal of sense and has yielded significant results in both the signals it has sent to institutional actors to reduce toxics production and in the civic innovations it has begun to generate. But a movement-building strategy has had its traps as well. As Christopher Foreman, Jr., has argued, the environ- mental justice movement has been able to maintain its internal harmony as a radically egalitarian, bottom-up coalition only by validating all grievances as equal and all claims of environment-related anxiety by people of color as worthy, thus making it difficult to see the notion of acceptable risk as any- thing but an excuse for further victimization. The coalition strategy has also made it impossible to utilize the NEJAC to set overall policy priorities, such as practical lead abatement or farmworker chemical exposure, for which sci- entific evidence of harm is much greater than for many other hazards. By deflecting attention from serious to lesser hazards, the environmental jus- tice movement may be unwittingly increasing the dangers faced by minority and low-income communities and worsening the inequities they face.[82]

But alongside this movement building, and in response to it, other de- velopments promote civic learning with the potential to move beyond some of the earlier dilemmas. This is especially evident where toxics and envi- ronmental justice organizing have become progressively embedded in broader community development efforts and have been able to achieve voice in corporate and regulatory institutions. As an increasing number of multi- issue community organizations and neighborhood associations take up the problem of toxics, it becomes less possible to elevate it above the range of other community concerns and more likely that communities will deliber- ate about relative risks and costs and alternative strategies to improve the long-term viability of neighborhoods. Empowerment Zones and Enterprise Communities likewise provide incentives and opportunities to link toxics and environmental justice to broad strategies and to preexisting community de- velopment corporations, community land trusts, and other groups. The EPA's Brownfields Initiative, launched in 1995 and partially linked to Empower- ment Zones, also enables communities, developers, and banks to collabo- rate in the redevelopment of sites by streamlining administrative procedures, adjusting Superfund liability regulations, granting Community Reinvestment Act credits, and enabling community groups to participate in the choice of properties to be developed. In some cities, community groups have been left behind or have been unable to formulate their own vision and coalition to make timely negotiation with developers workable. But in others they have established viable partnerships and strong agreements with city authorities on community involvement. To this extent they have been able to avoid what appeared in the early 1990s to be a collision course for environmental justice and community development. The opening of avenues of representation at the local level and through the NEJAC has elicited increasing cooperation in these kinds of efforts within the environmental justice movement, though skepticism remains about the delisting of thousands of sites from Superfund estimated by EPA as not posing serious risks.[83]

To the extent that broader community development strategies continue to expand and other civic capacity-building efforts through the OEJ, OPPT, and state agencies can be strengthened, designing a toxics policy based on greater civic deliberation becomes increasingly possible. As good neighbor strategies become more robust, sustainable communities projects proliferate, and watershed approaches increasingly incorporate environmental justice concerns, these possibilities increase further. Likewise, participatory approaches to comparative risk assessment and facility siting have progressed substantially in recent years.[84] And some of the regional EPA offices have integrated environmental justice with broad, community-based environmental protection (CBEP) strategies. It is not yet clear how all this might alter the political conditions favoring reform of Superfund or loosen the hold of the coalition for waste. But proposals for reform that favor grants to the states and include strong requirements for citizen participation can now rest on a much more substantial foundation of state and local groups capable of making such deliberation feasible and equitable than was the case when Superfund was first passed or last reauthorized. And more local groups are demanding alternative strategies and resisting movement fundamentalism. As Kathy Milberg of the Southwest Detroit Environmental Vision Project, whose own views have shifted significantly, has noted, "There are a lot of environmental groups . . . who say all land must be cleaned up to pristine standards. But they don't live here. They aren't losing their kids to economic death."[85]

CONCLUSION

Civic environmentalism has emerged as part of a complex learning process extending back to the participatory democratic movements of the 1960s and 1970s and to the core participatory norms and procedures established within administrative law and environmental legislation. Many leaders and activists of the environmental movement were socialized in the participatory ethos of the New Left and succeeded in establishing mandates for participation and deliberation within the regulatory arena. In the absence of the kind of organizational infrastructure that, hypothetically, might have yielded civic approaches earlier—state and local government capacities for effective regulation, vibrant local environmental organizations, traditional civic organizations capable of shifting quickly and effectively to environmental work, employer associations predisposed to cooperate with other regulatory actors—the environmental movement responded rationally to the existing political opportunities and to the available regulatory knowledge base. It thereby helped to build a public-lobby regulatory regime with rather narrow parameters for citizen action and rigid tools for regulatory compliance. Because its participatory ethos was wedded to a collective "rights-to-safety" frame, it tended to reinforce some of the worst features of command-and-control regulation and nondeliberative policy design and helped inhibit policy learning in some very distinct ways.[86]

At the same time, however, public participation programs slowly began to yield new skills, relationships, and models oriented toward collaborative and community-based problem solving and further established the power of citizens to impose costs, which has been essential to their acceptance as full partners in dialogue and negotiation. At various levels below that of national policy design, multisided learning emerged among citizen and environmental groups, agency officials, and corporate environmental staff, and progressively became embedded in informal networks and institutional programs capable of pursuing civic strategies for environmental improvement. Such learning was evident already during the Carter administration, which increased support for local participation. But it gathered considerable momentum as federal policy stalled in the early 1980s, states and localities took significant new initiatives, and the capacities for *both* protest and collaboration increased at the grassroots level. From the mid-1980s onwards, civic environmental approaches began to gather significant momentum and today are evident in many arenas.

These take a variety of forms and employ a diverse yet richly civic nomenclature. They include watershed "alliances," "societies," "associations," and "councils." They engage citizens as "stewards" of public lands doing the meticulous public work of preservation and restoration, and challenge them to be "vigilant" on river and lake "watches." They invite citizens to become "friends" of the forest or urban greenspace, and to "adopt" a stream and "raise the young" of a species that has been depleted from its habitat. They develop "good neighbor agreements," "community covenants," "policy dialogues," and "common ground projects" among traditional adversaries and diverse user groups. They donate money and build partnerships to finance "land trusts" and manage local resources collaboratively. They emphasize the moral responsibilities of all individual citizens and households, not just polluting businesses and agencies, and they identify myriad opportunities for public work by ordinary Americans willing to do simple things like removing debris and planting trees along a river, or learning new skills for sophisticated water quality testing and ecosystem restoration. Many groups are novel forms of association that have formed to address new and complex problems whose main features and possible solutions have only gradually become apparent over the last several decades, such as the degradation of entire ecosystems, the loss of key indicator species, or the threat of toxic chemicals. Some, such as watershed associations and estuary programs, have a variety of newer and older conservation, sporting, civic, religious, and school projects nested within them or affiliated with them over a broad geographic area. Many of these associational forms have emerged only after, and as a result of, extensive conflict and advocacy organizing, though some have arisen at the edges of that conflict and have pursued collaborative public work strategies from the beginning.

Here too, however, a learning process is evident. As the environmental movement has been effective in diffusing its values among the broad public and has helped to generate new civic models, it has opened opportunities for environmental engagement by mainstream civic associations and religious congregations uncomfortable with conflict models. Many of these have been searching in recent decades for ways to retain and recruit members and have had to compete with organizations representing new forms of civic activism. They have thus hired staff with previous experience in the environmental movement and have invested in developing environmental programs at the local, state, and national levels. This same trend is evident among the extensive networks of sporting associations that have come to recognize their clear self-interest in conservation and that combine advocacy with moral education of their members in a "stewardship ethic," encourage civic "vigilance" through monitoring, engage in local partnerships, and generate additional revenue for conservation through voluntarily imposed fees or donations at sporting and recreation facilities. In short, there has been a very substantial and sustained process over several decades of building new forms of social capital, as well as mobilizing older forms, to address environmental problems.[87]

The relationship between the development of the environmental movement, as it is usually characterized, and the process of civic environmental innovation is complex, paradoxical, and contentious, to be sure. The movement has generated the moral resources, social identities, and everyday practices that have inspired and sustained involvement in a broad array of contexts. It has nurtured rhetoric and rituals of the "sacredness of the earth" and of personal and collective responsibilities for preserving it, which in turn have enabled the movement to tap the cultural resources of mainstream civic and youth associations, schools, and religious congregations. The movement has also nurtured the arts of open discussion, consensus seeking, and collaborative action in small groups ranging from local chapters of the big national organizations, such as the Audubon Society and Sierra Club, to ad hoc affinity groups, thus providing substantial numbers with experience in the arts of participatory democracy. While the radical Green, ecofeminist, and direct action groups have been highly prone to instability, many activists socialized through them have maintained long-term commitments and—often after repeated bouts of organizational dissolution—have brought their skills to civic environmental settings. In the process, they have simultaneously enriched the collaborative and consensus-building skills available in these settings *and* have refined their own practices so that constructive work could be better sustained and the circle of civic actors broadened. Becoming older and more rooted in a particular geographical area, together with family and job commitments that connect activists to wider crosscutting networks in the community, form the background for many of these choices.[88]

Yet the moral resources generated by the environmental movement have at times produced a kind of fundamentalism that tolerates no compromise between the sacred and the profane, whether this be in the form of collaboration with "evil polluters," the acceptance of any level of environmental risk, or the calculation of any trade-off between environmental and economic values. This stance is especially true in radical environmental groups but is not confined to them.[89] Such fundamentalism can distort policy and opinion making and undermine reasoned deliberation. Good evidence shows, however, that when provided with opportunities for democratic deliberation on complex environmental issues, the public does not invoke fundamentalist beliefs. Rather, it considers reasoned arguments in context, weighs trade-offs, and listens to opposing views. It evaluates the procedures by which decisions are reached and the trustworthiness of those most involved in making them. And it strongly prefers pragmatic solutions.[90] Militant activists at the local level often initiate or join in collaborative projects when the limits of conflict become evident and new opportunities present themselves—though often to the dismay of their more fundamentalist organizational allies, such as CCHW or Greenpeace. Thus, the development of moral resources over the past three decades, which has been so important in anchoring and broadening environmental commitment, has undoubtedly benefited the emergence of civic environmentalism far more than it has threatened it with fundamentalism, though continuing concern with the latter certainly seems appropriate.

The substantial support for civic approaches that has emerged among the broad public, as well as among organized environmentalists at the local level, belies simplistic accounts that neatly divide the movement into a conservative "mainstream" and a radical "grassroots" or that view the past decades as one of missed strategic opportunities for radical mobilization and fundamental value betrayals by increasingly institutionalized national organizations.[91] The role of national organizations has been much more complex. Since the 1960s the professionalization of older conservation groups such as the National Audubon Society, Sierra Club, and National Wildlife Federation has shifted power and resources to their national offices relative to local and state affiliates, and has enabled them to play a stronger role in the evolving public-lobby regulatory regime. It has also enabled them to politicize a membership base that was wedded primarily to birding, fishing, and nature walks, though not without considerable internal struggle. Nonetheless, despite the professionalizing tendencies in its national San Francisco and Washington lobbying offices, the Sierra Club's top leadership has remained relatively weak, and volunteer leadership has taken broad initiative at the local level. A significant amount of this initiative is now civic environmental, and specific programs, such as the Ecoregions Program and the River and Watershed Management Group, support the development of innovative approaches. Regional staff have participated in the Watershed Innovators Workshops sponsored by the River Network. Former leaders, such as Douglas Wheeler, who became Secretary of the California Resources Agency under governor Pete Wilson in the 1990s, have gone on to play prominent roles in catalyzing collaborative approaches to ecosystem restoration and habitat conservation planning, as have many local chapter leaders, activists, lawyers, and wildlife specialists. Chapter meetings and newsletters serve as information and networking sources for civic initiatives that are not formally those of the club. While more radical club members and national leaders have some legitimate concerns about forms of local collaboration where conservationists are at a serious power disadvantage or where interests of broader constituencies are excluded from place-based deliberation, they have not reversed the tendency of local activists to participate in civic environmental projects of all sorts.[92]

The National Audubon Society reinvigorated its chapter structure in the late 1970s and early 1980s and utilized it as a lobbying force. Although this political and adversarial strategy was deemphasized after the overwhelming reelection of Ronald Reagan to a second term in 1984, chapters have retained wide latitude and have received positive signals from the national office to engage in collaborative projects. The National Wildlife Federation (NWF) also made the transition from one of the most conservative of the old organizations, dominated by hunting and fishing interests, to a professionalized environmental organization engaged in national policy. But it has maintained an extensive network of local groups, which engage in many sorts of collaborative community and ecosystem projects. The magazines, journals, and presses of these national organizations, as well as those without local chapters, such as the Natural Resources Defense Council, have helped to publicize innovative civic models throughout the organized movement.[93]

The intense pressure that these national organizations have felt in recent years to devolve more decision-making authority and resources to the grassroots has been less about radicalism versus professionalism than about disillusionment with what can be achieved through the national public lobbies and about building state and local capacities for more effective, innovative, and sustainable approaches. In addition, other national networks have emerged in these years, or have transformed themselves to foster innovative civic approaches. These include such organizations as the Nature Conservancy, River Network, and American Farmland Trust, which have combined advocacy with civic environmental approaches, and have successfully promoted legislation and policy design at the federal and state levels that enhance civic capacity. They include specific programs within national civic and youth organizations, such as the water, solid waste, and recycling projects of the League of Women Voters, or the Earth Service Corps of the YMCA. And the infrastructure to support civic approaches has also been enhanced considerably by the sustained development of national, regional, state, and local centers and networks for dispute resolution, much of whose work focuses on the environment, and much of whose staffing is provided by volunteers.[94]

Furthermore, local, state, and federal agencies have progressively developed capacities for civic environmentalism over several decades. These became manifest especially in the 1980s after basic state regulatory capacities had been established, and stalled federal policy created new opportunities and incentives for local and state government initiative, and for partnerships with private and nonprofit actors. Many of these actors had built horizontal networks and shadow learning communities and came to share perspectives on the need for new approaches to such issues as nonpoint pollution and ecosystem protection. In the 1990s the forms of collaboration have blossomed further, as state and local agencies have learned to work with land trusts, watershed alliances, and citizen monitoring projects and have gained considerable experience in dispute resolution with organized environmental, business, and other competing user groups. Likewise, federal, state, and local agency capacity for civic environmentalism has been complemented by increasing interagency collaboration and by the rising, if still very uneven, support that federal agencies have given to collaborative and place-based approaches. Specific programs exist in the EPA, Forest Service, Fish and Wildlife Service, Army Corps of Engineers, Department of Energy, Bureau of Land Management, and National Park Service. EPA has progressively built capacity through the National Estuary Program and other water programs, the Office of Pollution Prevention and Toxics, and the Office of Environmental Justice, and community-based environmental protection (CBEP) has become important to the work of its regional offices.

The challenges confronting a more coherent and sustained strategy for civic environmentalism nonetheless remain substantial. Within the Army Corps of Engineers and Forest Service there exist powerful bureaucratic forces resistant to increased stakeholder involvement if it threatens traditional management paradigms or favored constituency interests. The paradigm of ecosystem management on watersheds and multiple-use lands labors under significant ambiguity and mixed support in the courts and Congress.[95] Power and budgets at EPA still lie preponderantly with narrow regulatory programs and are buttressed by a highly fragmented committee structure in Congress closely linked to public-lobby and industry constituencies that have heavy investments in fragmentary statutes. The ability of Congress to create a clear statutory mission for the EPA, which it has lacked since its creation in 1970, continues to be hampered by ideological pendulum swings between regulatory relief on the Right and tough enforcement on the Left. The Office of Sustainable Ecosystems and Communities, which was charged with agency-wide coordination of CBEP, has since been dismantled, and its staff returned to various water programs. The main champion of CBEP, deputy administrator Fred Hansen, left the agency in 1998 to return to Oregon, where community-based approaches are thriving. Organizational culture and career opportunities still overwhelmingly favor rule making and enforcement. The reinventing government initiative at EPA has failed to address adequately the role of responsible and productive citizenship in environmental regulation and has thus been unable to raise the themes of civic environmentalism to a new level of public discourse. "Reinventing government" has still not been effectively tied to "reinventing citizenship," though the potential to do so is considerable.[96] And while social learning on industrial ecology within firms and sectoral networks of firms has been substantial, and an emerging concept of corporate environmental citizenship has begun to take hold, industry lobbyists continue to develop legal strategies for greater secrecy of environmental audits, resist guidelines that would specify sufficient resources and power for independent citizen stakeholder groups in voluntary pollution reduction programs at EPA such as Project XL, and campaign for outright rollbacks in Congress that make genuine civic collaborations that much more difficult.[97]

Nonetheless, civic innovation has now proceeded far enough to provide substantial opportunity to alter the public discourse on environmental regulation and perhaps to build the kind of constituency that would enable significant movement within Congress, agencies, and environmental and industry lobbies, though this change will not be easy. The most elaborate proposals for moving further toward civic environmentalism are the National Academy of Public Administration (NAPA) reports to Congress on the EPA, though several other sets of proposals converge in this direction as well and testify to the breadth and depth of policy learning.[98] The NAPA reports propose not only to build upon the substantial successes that top-down regulation has achieved since 1970, especially on point-source pollution, but also to redefine the agency's mission. The new mission would be to provide national leadership in setting goals and priorities, and to enforce some standards itself, while overseeing state enforcement of others. Yet the new mission would use information about environmental risks and trends "to engage the nation, states, tribes, communities, and businesses in a process of anticipating, defining, prioritizing, and addressing problems" and to support problem-solving activities through technical assistance, increased flexibility, and the development of information capacities appropriate to the communications age. It would stress citizen participation and broad stakeholder involvement in the development of any voluntary programs that move "beyond compliance" and would orient priority setting around public values, with attention to cost-effectiveness, equity, and the welfare of future generations. And its model of "accountable devolution" would stress results rather than procedures in EPA's relationship with states. This new mission would provide great scope for continued civic innovation without abandoning essential regulatory functions and would utilize market incentives while recognizing that markets must remain embedded in civic infrastructure and democratic norms.

While significant progress has been made in implementing the recommendations of the NAPA reports, many obstacles impede such a reorientation.[99] Whatever the specific policy turns in the immediate future, however, the substantial civic capacities that have been built over the past several decades, along with the policy learning that has accompanied and informed this process, will provide a focal point for continued innovation. The leadership of a "civic environmental president" at the turn of the century could promote this process considerably and could provide further impetus to civic renewal on a broader scale. If we could add but one element to the mix of innovative strategies that would provide opportunity for presidential leadership and agency reinvention, while building upon and further catalyzing the ecosystem restoration, watershed democracy, and sustainable communities movements, it would be to convene (even mandate) an annual interagency Community and Environment Festival on Earth Day, in collaboration with leading local civic innovators and national networks across the country. This event would be designed to celebrate their efforts, raise the visibility of civic problem-solving models, and honor the deepest democratic and spiritual motives of citizens to protect the "sacredness of the earth" and to carry out the public work of "restoring Creation." It would share lessons broadly through critical discussion, build new networks, and diffuse practical tools and educational resources. It would establish a public context for agency accountability for catalyzing civic efforts. Such a festival would lay claim to the cultural authority of collaborative models to increase the political leverage upon agencies, lawmakers, industry groups, and environmental lobbies themselves for sustained civic innovation.

FOUR

Community Health
and Civic Organizing

The American health care landscape has changed enormously in recent decades. At the end of twentieth century, increasing marketization and commodification of health have defined the dominant trend, and the unhappy fate of the Clinton plan marked the most dramatic of successive failures to achieve universal coverage. This episode represented a major failure to develop a public policy for democracy in which reform elites might have engaged citizens in the kind of civic conversation and public work needed to grapple with the complex challenges of health reform. In the present chapter, we examine efforts over the past four decades to make community participation a key component of health care systems and policy formation, and we consider how it might continue to inform strategies for broader change.

Contrasting with many forms of community development and civic environmentalism previously examined, citizen organizing in the health arena suffers relative disadvantages in its capacities to mobilize independently around the solidarities of place represented by neighborhoods and ecosystems or to utilize protest as leverage for developing innovative collaborations with powerful institutions. Nonetheless, since the early 1960s, when patient empowerment and community involvement were virtually nonexistent, participatory norms have significantly challenged professional dominance in medicine. Innovative democratic and community health approaches that mobilize civic networks and engage citizens in collaborative public work with health professionals and institutions now offer important alternatives to the hegemony of the medical model of acute care for improving the health of populations.

Our analysis focuses on four sets of community-based innovations. Community health centers (CHCs), the first, originally emerged as part of the Community Action Program in the 1960s. Their mission was to extend primary care to underserved populations. The community health center movement generated an ambitious vision of disease prevention and health promotion engaging medical professionals, community health workers, and self-help support networks in collaborative work to improve health and foster broad community development. While the movement's institutional base has evolved considerably in subsequent decades, its innovative vision and practice of community-oriented primary care have narrowed substantially because of various policy constraints. Nonetheless, recent efforts to build healthy communities have continued to refine that vision and practice in other settings. Health Systems Agencies (HSAs), the second major federal effort in the 1970s, institutionalized citizen participation in health planning throughout the country. Although citizen representatives and policy networks demonstrated a noteworthy capacity for learning within a policy design that was deeply flawed from the outset, the HSAs proved much more vulnerable than the community health centers to a hostile federal administration after Reagan's election in 1980.

A third set of innovations, originally incubated within the HSA infrastructure, is the independently organized Health Decisions projects, which introduced citizen deliberation about underlying health values as an essential component of policy formation in a number of states. Oregon Health Decisions organized extensive public discussion in community meetings and health care parliaments throughout the state over a seven-year period leading up to the nationally visible—and initially quite controversial—Oregon Health Plan of 1990. Health Decisions groups in Georgia, California, and other states, as well as the American Health Decisions national network, have also refined the practices of civic conversation and public deliberation on a variety of health reform and bioethics issues throughout the 1980s and 1990s. They offer important lessons for democratic policy design. The healthy communities movement represents a fourth stream of innovation. Launched in the late 1980s as part of an international healthy cities movement, it builds substantially upon the perspectives and networks of the first two streams, as well as upon a range of other community-based and self-help approaches to health and social service reform, HIV/AIDS prevention and care, community and sustainable development, and the women's health, disability, and independent living movements. The healthy communities movement in the United States has continued to generate a growing array of local partnerships throughout the 1990s, as well as state networks and a national Coalition for Healthier Cities and Communities representing a number of key civic, government, and health system actors well positioned to drive innovation in the coming years.

To be sure, rapidly changing health care markets and the lack of a universal system of insurance coverage provide many obstacles to robust healthy community work and civic engagement beyond institutional collaboration and service integration. The progressive commodification of health also re-inforces narrow consumer orientations among the public that make the search for sustainability and equity increasingly difficult. Yet some features of managed care also provide opportunities for innovative community health strategies. And the continued refinement of civic practice in health could lay foundations more solid than those that existed in 1993–94 for a national health reform process that engages citizens, communities, civic organizations, and institutional and policy elites in a more fruitful and collaborative search for workable system reform.

COMMUNITY HEALTH AND DEMOCRATIC PLANNING IN THE 1960S AND 1970S

Two sets of federal initiatives promoted citizen participation in the health arena in the 1960s and 1970s. The first, the Neighborhood Health Center (NHC) program, emerged in 1965 as part of the Community Action Program of the Office of Economic Opportunity (OEO). It was subsequently transferred to the Department of Health, Education and Welfare (HEW) in the early 1970s and then to the reorganized Department of Health and Human Services (HHS) later in the decade. The purpose of NHCs was to provide a system of primary care delivery responsive to poor communities. The second initiative was the system of local Health Systems Agencies (HSAs), established by the National Health Planning and Resources Development Act of 1974 and funded by the federal government largely as nonprofit organizations. The mission of the HSAs was to coordinate existing public and private resources and to develop plans to address issues of cost, access, quality of care, and health education. HSAs were also intended to catalyze the development of multi-institutional systems and to regulate capital expenditures for hospitals and nursing homes. Both the NHCs and the HSAs had explicit mandates for consumer participation, and they helped to mobilize community activism in a variety of forms.

Community Health Centers: Poor People's Medicine

Though health was not initially a mandate of the OEO, medical screenings conducted for Head Start, Job Corps, and other programs revealed glaring health problems among the poor that impeded the OEO's explicit mission of removing barriers to learning and productivity. Some Community Action Agencies began to submit proposals to improve health by purchasing private medical services. In 1965, policy entrepreneurs within the OEO quickly responded with a demonstration program for neighborhood health centers, which was expanded the following year under Senator Edward Kennedy's initiative as Congress revised the Economic Opportunity Act and as the OEO created an Office of Community Health Services within the Community Action Program. Innovators within the OEO were drawn from medical community activists who had developed participatory ideals as part of the civil rights and student movements and who viewed health as a matter of human right and dignity that was systematically violated by the kind of care that the poor received through the typical hospital outpatient department—if they received any care at all. Indeed, during these early years the NHC program was known as the "Healthrights" program. Key local innovators, such as Dr. Jack Geiger, had worked with pioneers in community health on the international scene, particularly Dr. Sidney Kark in South Africa. Others were drawn from the nonmedical reform community, such as Lisbeth Bamberger Schorr, who had helped set up a community health center for the United Auto Workers in Detroit, then served on the AFL-CIO staff to win passage of Medicare, and subsequently came to play the key role at the OEO in developing the NHC program. Other innovators emerged at HEW, especially John Gardner, the secretary, and Dr. Philip Lee, the assistant secretary for health and scientific affairs, who developed an NHC program under section 314(e) of the Comprehensive Health Planning and Public Health Service Act passed by Congress in 1966. Congressional staff, with whom these various innovators built the strong relationships that enabled them to expand the NHC program even as Nixon and Ford later attempted to undo it, also shared participatory ideals through prior engagement in the student and civil rights movements. Local activists drew upon organizing and leadership skills developed in other areas of community action and civil rights work.[1]

The emerging vision of community health that informed the development of NHCs was an ambitious one. It sought the reintegration of personal and public health through disease prevention and health promotion practices of medical staff, newly trained family and community health workers recruited from local neighborhoods, and self-help support networks. It included broad community development to change the social and physical environments that affect health. Employment and training within the NHCs were key components of local community and economic development. Work was to be reconfigured in teams of physicians, nurse practitioners, family health workers, and community organizers in ways that challenged traditional medical hierarchies, solo practice, and passive patient roles. Consumer participation would enable local residents to help set priorities of NHC boards and, as with other community action programs, break the link between poverty and powerlessness. This new health model, though developed for historically disadvantaged communities, was intended to serve as a basis for health reform throughout the country. In the vision of key reformers, indeed, a network of comprehensive community health centers would become the hub of the medical care universe, and together the OEO and HEW planned for 1,150 NHCs to be built within a few years, while the policy moment seemed ripe. Medicare and Medicaid had just been enacted and thus seemed to justify expansive goals.[2]

The first proposal funded by the OEO reflects this ambitious vision, as well as the accomplishments possible under certain circumstances. Dr. Jack Geiger of the Harvard School of Public Health teamed up with Dr. Count Gibson, chair of preventive medicine at Tufts University Medical School, to develop the Tufts Comprehensive Community Action Program. It had two sites, one in Boston and one covering five hundred square miles of the rural Mississippi delta populated by black sharecroppers. The latter, known as the Tufts-Delta Health Center, devised a comprehensive participatory strategy with numerous points of entry into the problems of health and poverty. Multidisciplinary teams provided a broad range of clinical services, home health care and health education, as well as environmental health services that included housing inspections and rehabilitation, well and water supply testing, and sewage system installation—all with major self-help components built into them. A home management program developed classes in home economics, home arts and crafts, and loans of sewing and washing machines. Training and education services included basic literacy, high school equivalency, and college placement at universities such as Brandeis and Tufts, as well as in-service training for nursing, medical records, family planning, day care, and nutritional counseling. Some programs combined in-service, paraprofessional, and professional training.

Community development and organizing skills were also a focus, because the most important entry point of all was seen as the organizing of ten local health associations and centers capable of designing and delivering a broad range of services that included patient transportation, home visitation, Big Brother and Big Sister mentoring, volunteer probation work, and home nutrition. The associations were established long before any services began. They utilized local people as organizers under the guidance of a professional organizer, and conducted scores of meetings in homes, churches, and schools. The local centers they set up also served as focal points for voter registration and civil rights activity. The main health center in Mound Bayou—a modern facility employing more than two hundred people, most of whom were local residents—was owned and governed by the North Bolivar County Health Council representing the ten local associations. The council generated spin-off organizations, such as a six-hundred-acre, irrigated cooperative farm owned and run by one thousand families to grow vegetables and high-protein corn that would extend the council's nutrition programs. Within the first year of its operation it produced one million pounds of food and ended hunger in the area. Critical to all this work was, as Geiger noted early on,

the identification of strengths of the individual, the family, the community, the social order, and the culture, and the use of these strengths as keystones in program design. This means avoiding the common professional bias of focusing on pathology alone and therefore building programs that are oriented only to pathology. Conversely, it means shaping programs to fit strong, existing, local social institutions, even if they do not fit comfortably with the expectations and customs familiar to the professional and the middle class.[3]

A more explicit formulation of the assets-based approach to community empowerment in these early years would be hard to find. It was, without doubt, a seedbed for future thinking.

Not all centers, as we shall see, lived up to this ideal or even aspired to it. But with the critical support of reformers within the federal bureaucracy, a neighborhood health center movement emerged, forged state and regional networks, and established a national association to further its capacity building and policy work. By 1968 the OEO had funded some fifty centers, and by 1971 another fifty. HEW funded fifty NHCs, as well as sixty or so comprehensive health care projects for children in low-income areas under an amendment to Title V of the Social Security Act. Bureaucratic advocacy within the OEO and HEW proved critical to early NHC development. Although President Nixon halted the expansion temporarily in the early 1970s and shifted authority to HEW with the disbanding of the OEO, the Bureau of Community Health Services (BCHS) at HEW developed an effective strategy that extended the program. In 1975, over the veto of President Ford, Congress provided the detailed legislation for a renamed Community Health Center program that permitted it to grow further. BCHS strengthened congressional support with a more broadly distributive Rural Health Initiative, and under President Carter administrative support solidified and funding expanded still further. By 1980 the number of community and migrant health centers reached 876, serving 6 million people. This expansion represented the most extensive effort to provide ambulatory care to poor communities ever undertaken in the United States. Favorable studies of the quality of care delivered, as well as overall cost effectiveness (reductions in hospitalization rates, length of hospital stays, and use of hospital emergency rooms) bolstered the arguments of proponents.[4]

The National Association of Neighborhood Health Centers was founded in 1970 after the first national consumers' health conference and was supported by a training contract from the OEO. Over the next several years Massachusetts and New York and then other state and regional centers in the West, Midwest, and South were formed with similar contracts. After the 1975 legislation, the association changed its name to the National Association of Community Health Centers (NACHC) and expanded its membership to include a variety of other family health centers, migrant health programs, Indian health programs, and maternal and infant care programs. It was successful in the early 1970s in establishing the principle of majority consumer representation on CHC boards, which the OEO and Congressional staff supported, as well as the principle of governing boards rather than advisory ones. Its own delegate assembly at annual meetings was instituted according to a rule of four delegates from each center, two of whom had to represent residents served by the centers. Over the course of the decade, NACHC became increasingly effective at the national policy level. Subsequent grants by the Robert Wood Johnson Foundation have enabled it to build primary care associations representing the majority of CHCs in virtually every state. These have collaborated with state governments and health departments to plan primary care for medically underserved areas. NACHC has also developed the policy and managerial expertise to address a whole range of issues critical to the survival of CHCs in an environment increasingly dominated by managed care and Medicaid reimbursement. By the 1980s it was strong enough to withstand repeated attempts by the Reagan administration to incorporate CHC funding into larger health block grants, though it did have to adjust to budgetary cuts, the narrowing of services, and the complete defunding of some centers, even as it refined its own capacities to support the work of those remaining.[5]

From the beginning, however, success was purchased at a price; the very extension of CHCs narrowed their vision and practice considerably. First of all, legislation supporting CHCs was made possible only by defining CHCs as "poor people's medicine." This label was necessary to allay the opposition of the American Medical Association, as well as local practitioners and medical societies, who feared that CHCs would compete with private providers and suspected their role in national health reform efforts. The 1967 amendments to the Equal Opportunity Act thus shifted the principle of eligibility from residence in low-income communities to income criteria defined by the official poverty line or Medicaid eligibility, with explicit limits subsequently established on the percentage of paying or partially paying nonpoor who could be served by the centers.[6] Such criteria made it considerably more difficult for centers to build upon existing social networks, which typically extended across such bureaucratically constructed boundaries. As a result, the pool of area residents eligible to serve on boards was narrowed, often excluding the very people who had more extensive community ties and organizing skills, such as teachers, preachers, funeral directors, and small business owners. Of course, it was inevitable and often productive that the poor would mobilize and militants would challenge those whom they perceived as community "gatekeepers." These included people initially hand-picked by the hospital and medical school sponsoring institutions, which had received a disproportionate number of the early NHC grants as a way of legitimizing the program and catalyzing change agents within these mainstream institutions. But income eligibility restrictions probably exacerbated these conflicts at a time when the challenges of developing basic administrative and managerial capacities were already substantial. Turnover on boards and among center enrollees was high as a result of people cycling in and out of official poverty status and was compounded by geographical mobility and competition by other market providers.[7]

Likewise, less access to existing social networks and community assets constrained innovative practice. As Geiger argued after more than a decade of experience,

> in recent years there has been a growing recognition that the first locus of primary care decisions is not in health services at all, but in families, social networks, and basic community institutions such as the church. The task can be redefined: It is not simply to involve the community in the programs of a community-oriented practice, but rather to involve the practice in the basic processes and structures within the community. . . . This is the real significance of the development of organized lay referral networks, the training of "health facilitators," and the systematic enlistment of churches and other community-based institutions in health education and case-finding. They have the potential to create "agreed social objectives" in relation to health in specific communities.[8]

Second, the price of securing funds to extend the CHC program was the narrowing of the range of activities supported and the application of efficiency standards that often proved inappropriate. Thus, as the program shifted from the OEO to HEW, funds for training area residents, and for environmental and other nonmedical activities, were curtailed, thus further affecting innovative services and generating much tension with locally hired staff over the future of their jobs. Funding uncertainties, especially during the first decade, when centers depended on yearly appropriations from Congress, led to a relatively high turnover of medical staff, which made the refinement of community practices more difficult and further heightened the contrast of professional and nonprofessional career options. HEW efficiency standards developed for nonpoor clienteles overlooked the complexity of the health problems of the poor, the need for patient education and outreach, and the relative effectiveness of nonmedical activities. Even as the CHC program was extended under President Carter through the Urban Health Initiative, its mandate narrowed to the delivery of basic *medical* care, rather than comprehensive or innovative *health* services, and education and outreach were further de-emphasized. Cost containment gained greater prominence as a goal, and the coordination of existing medical resources in the community was stressed over the creation of new community resources. As the centers, under relentless pressure, learned to recoup more funds from Medicaid and other third-party payers, this predilection for traditional medical care was further exacerbated, and many centers became little more than Medicaid mills focused on reimbursable acute care. Medical staff, often overwhelmed, came to neglect community epidemiology and prevention, not to mention relational organizing through existing social networks. In the absence of the latter, community residents were as likely as not to judge the effectiveness of the centers in terms of the quality and quantity of acute care found in mainstream medical settings.[9]

A third factor constraining community-oriented approaches was the rapid spread of health care markets from the 1970s onwards. Community theorists and practitioners came to see the dilemma clearly as it affected both CHCs and managed-care plans. With many competing providers, relative ease of exit, and the lack of geographical regionalization of primary care, it was not rational for a single provider, even a CHC, to invest in the health of the community through disease prevention, health promotion, and community epidemiology, because a provider had little assurance that it would reap the full benefits of its investment (healthier members, savings that could be applied to other services, measurable public credit). Indeed, a single practice could not accept responsibility for the health of the community, in most instances, even if it wanted to.[10]

Consumer Participation in Health Planning: The Health Systems Agencies

Health planning also became an arena for expanded democratic participation in the wake of the movements of the 1960s, especially with the passage in 1974 of the National Health Planning and Resources Development Act. As James Morone has argued, the reform was perhaps fatally flawed from the beginning, since the state was too weak to institute universal insurance with effective cost controls, as had recently occurred in Canada. And the new Health Systems Agencies (HSAs) in which consumers were represented lacked effective power to counterbalance the variety of suspicious and hostile opponents that mobilized to contain the "democratic wish." In the end, the act may have done less to empower an oppressed group than it did to subordinate a dominant one, namely, doctors.[11] Yet the effort spawned vastly increased organizing by consumer advocates, new claims to democratic representation, and a dynamic of participatory learning with a legacy for subsequent innovations.

The Health Planning Act of 1974 established 205 local HSAs as nonprofit organizations funded by the government yet designed to be independent of direct political control. HSAs were to develop plans for improved quality, equal access, and coordinated utilization of existing resources, while simultaneously tackling medical inflation, which had begun its relentless upward spiral. They were thus granted significant authority to recommend denial of "certificate of need" applications for capital expenditures, though the efforts of liberals, such as Senator Kennedy, to wed strong citizen participation to broader HSA authority were defeated in the final legislation by lobbyists for doctors and hospitals. As the president of the AMA noted in his metaphor for consumer representation at the time, "Passengers who insist on flying the airplane are called hijackers!"[12] A majority (but not more than 60 percent) of seats on the HSA governing boards was to be reserved for health care consumers chosen in a manner "broadly representative of the social, economic, linguistic, and racial populations, geographic areas of the health service area, and major purchasers of health care."[13] Meetings were to be open to the community, with adequate public notice, planning documents on file at public libraries, and opportunities to comment at public hearings.

Some HSAs used these opportunities quite innovatively, especially those which, as Barry Checkoway and others argue, developed community-organizing methods to enhance participation and generate accountability to specific constituencies.[14] The West Bay Health Systems Agency in the San Francisco area, for instance, built its consumer representation strategy upon a network of previously existing civil rights, neighborhood, and women's groups and helped them to form a community coalition to mobilize participation and broaden discussion. Subarea councils were established, and full-time paid staff with activist backgrounds were chosen in consultation with community groups. Staff assumed responsibility for continuous outreach to promote further involvement in the councils and to ensure that minorities, women, and other medically underserved groups would participate in committees and task forces and stand for election to the HSA governing board. Community workshops were held to formulate the first HSA plan, and 3,750 people were involved in several rounds of discussion and revision before the plan was approved by the HSA board. The Western Massachusetts Health Planning Council drew upon a tradition of town meeting democracy and social activism and mobilized several thousand people to participate in a great variety of committees and subarea councils, which in turn elected the consumer representatives to the governing board. Subarea coordinators and staff, hired because of their activist experience and deep commitments to participatory democracy, identified and recruited other concerned citizens and provided leadership training, technical skills, and personal support. Staff organized various educational activities in local communities and schools and took responsibility for weekly health columns in local newspapers, as well as presentations on TV and radio. In the San Diego area, the California Public Interest Research Group obtained a Science for Citizens grant from the National Science Foundation to conduct intensive training workshops for 180 consumer advocates recruited from a variety of community groups, with the aim of enhancing their participation on the HSA board and making the latter accountable to specific consumer constituencies. These workshops not only covered a range of health, environmental, and technological issues, but also provided leadership and problem-solving skills. Many workshop trainees subsequently became involved in HSA committees, and some assumed leadership positions on the subarea councils and the HSA board itself.

Consumers found themselves at a decided disadvantage, however, in HSA representative structures, and empowering designs such as these proved to be the exception, not the rule. Health care providers were far better organized than consumers, had greater resources for participation (e.g., paid time off from work), and could more easily articulate collective interests and mobilize expertise in their favor. In the early years, provider representatives frequently helped designate acceptable consumers for the boards and mobilized their own constituencies of health professionals to vote in choosing them. Suits filed by groups like ACORN, Public Citizen's Health Research Group, and the Center for Law and Social Policy, forced HEW and Congress to broaden consumer representation to minorities, people with disabilities, and others often overlooked, and to limit certain practices like crossover voting and self-perpetuating boards that ensured provider dominance. But the narrow majority status of "consumers" on the board—a category that stretched from the poor, elderly, and people with disabilities to union officials, corporate financial officers, and insurance company representatives—could easily be eroded in the face of multiple disadvantages, namely, diverse interests, dispersed constituencies, and deficient expertise. As a result, many citizen representatives simply failed to show up at board meetings.[15]

Equally problematic, as activist as well as academic critics quickly noted, was that procedures for descriptive representation designed to mirror the demographic characteristics of the consuming public did little to provide for accountability of the chosen representatives to specific consumer constituencies. Having a Latino name, in other words, did not ensure a delegate's accountability to specific Latino neighborhoods or organizations. This problem was compounded by the great diversity of possible claims for distinct representation, and an enormous amount of effort went into creating demographic microcosms that would secure legitimacy on HSA boards but were at best only loosely connected to specific consumer interests and functional tasks.[16]

To its great credit, however, the health reform act not only elicited health organizing and participation to an extent previously unknown but also facilitated learning processes that addressed many of these issues relatively quickly and insightfully, before the Reagan administration's hostility to participatory planning obstructed further progress. By 1981 tens of thousands of citizens had become actively involved within the HSA participatory framework. Grassroots groups proliferated, and a variety of support networks emerged on state and national levels. Health-planning mandates for citizen participation virtually gave birth to these groups, though the mandates themselves represented long-term normative shifts favoring participatory rights. As Morone argued at the time on the basis of field work in six quite diverse HSAs, "There is a widespread sense of learning and improvement among a 'core' of the consumer members. Consumer representatives are developing considerable skill and knowledge. . . . Almost every veteran board member emphasizes how much they have learned." Community members, in short, had become actively and knowledgeably involved in their health care system. This learning manifested itself within a half decade of initial implementation and testified to cumulative participatory learning over a longer period. As Morone notes further, "Many HSAs unwittingly benefited from that political socialization" and "policy making experience" provided by Community Action Programs fifteen years earlier, whose enfranchisement of previously marginalized groups had nurtured a "sophistication" far beyond the former "politics of conflict and the rhetoric of imminent crisis."[17]

Learning was evident in policy circles as well. Congressional committees heard extensive testimony by proponents of public participation, including Georgia Legal Services, which sued HEW over the underrepresentation of women, people with disabilities, and poor people, and the lack of adequate specification of methods of selection that insured accountability to the public. The 1979 amendments to the Health Planning Act incorporated several important changes: at least one HSA staff member had to provide technical assistance to consumer representatives on the board; consumer majorities had to be guaranteed on all subcommittees; some expenses could be reimbursed in advance for participants' travel, meals, and childcare; self-perpetuating boards were proscribed; and consumer participation had to be actively solicited by mechanisms made public to HEW. The Senate committee report explicitly noted that being a member of a group is not sufficient to prove representativeness and that mechanisms had to be developed to ensure that, "to the maximum extent possible, these representatives be fully accountable to these constituencies."[18]

The National Council on Health Planning and Development and the Bureau of Health Planning of HEW took up this mandate in a series of hearings and conferences that featured prominent proponents of community-organizing models of representation and accountability. Along with the American Health Planning Association, the Centers for Health Planning, and other organizations, they began to disseminate "best practices" in the broader planning arena. The National Council's report of February 1981 focused much attention on ways of improving selection and accountability. It urged that HSAs aggressively encourage independent community and consumer organizations to deliberate on key issues in public forums and to select accountable representatives to serve on HSA boards and committees. The report suggested ways in which consumer representatives could organize as caucuses within HSAs to prevent the dilution of their power and to broaden grassroots participation on task forces and local councils. And it recommended further capacity building that would permit the HSAs to develop "innovative and alternative service delivery arrangements, . . . health promotion and disease prevention . . . and the use of epidemiology in health planning,"[19] all goals of the community health center movement and community-oriented primary care as well.

The National Council considered ways to narrow the expertise gap between provider and consumer representatives, particularly to strengthen staff support for the latter, remove jargon from relevant information, and facilitate discussion based on the most important real-life health concerns of their constituents. The council did not go as far as some urged in recommending that consumer representatives have control over their own staff, but it did address ways of strengthening civic competence through leadership training, running meetings, and resolving conflicts. It also urged HHS to recommend that Congress clarify the intent of citizen participation and strengthen the role of consumers in health planning. Equally important, however, was that the council began to validate the everyday competencies that citizens brought to the planning process, and recognized that planning should be guided by the values of ordinary people, not driven primarily by expertise.[20]

While substantial capacities for civic and policy learning manifested themselves in the first half dozen years of the Health Planning Act, they were obstructed by a fundamental flaw in the original design: the HSAs had little real power to alter the overall logic of health care spending. As Bruce Vladek pointed out shortly after the HSA structure was initially put in place, Congress had "not revised the rules of the health care game, but merely added another player." And within the limited HSA authority to approve or disapprove of projects funded under the Public Health Service Act (a mere 10 percent of only the federal piece of the health-spending pie), this new consumer player could be expected to engage in interest group bargaining with strong norms of reciprocity and log-rolling with other established players. Thus, providers and consumers in any given HSA had strong incentives to collude because the effective choice they faced, even amid strong signals from HEW bureaucrats to control costs, was "the choice between accepting 'free money' for their area or allowing it to be spent in another area."[21]

Some community organizations used this leverage to bargain for increased access and innovative services to underserved groups in return for their support of "certificate of need" applications to expand facilities favored by provider groups. But the Health Planning Act provided little authority or incentive for consumer representatives to develop workable alternatives responsive to issues of cost, quality, and access together, as many complained in frustration, or to debate these in terms of a broader public interest rather than the interests of specific consumer interest groups.[22] Moreover, many community and civil rights activists who joined the HSA boards in the hope of developing community-oriented primary care and other alternative health services and expanding local participation were simply outvoted. With the likelihood of national health insurance fading and little chance of Congressional passage of a bill to contain galloping health care inflation in the late 1970s, HEW placed further pressure on HSAs to be stringent. Even community activists tended to reinterpret their mission in terms of cost control.

Many in the public interest and community-based health movements were keenly aware of the tendencies of HSA consumer representatives to constrict their vision in the face of narrowed mandates from Washington and a convoluted system of third-party insurance that insulated general consumers from the causes of spiraling inflation. Some argued for creative educational and media strategies to broaden public discourse and reframe alternatives in such a way as to link issues of quality care, community-oriented practice, equitable access, patient rights, and cost controls. But this dynamic of participatory learning that had developed quickly within the broader public interest and community-based health movements, as well as within some of the planning agencies, was deflected within the formal structures of many HSAs themselves by the twin constraints of official mandate and insurance finance. As a result, the public discussion of equitable and innovative alternatives tended to get displaced to the peripheries of the very institutions of participatory planning that had done so much to foster democratic deliberation about health care—indeed, far more than had ever occurred in the history of health care reform in the United States.[23]

The legacies of these two major efforts during the 1960s and 1970s to introduce citizen participation into health care planning and delivery have been quite mixed. Community health centers narrowed their vision considerably in an effort to survive and expand in an environment dominated by uncertain federal funding, unfriendly reimbursement practices of Medicaid and other third-party payers, a suspicious and politically constraining AMA, and HEW efficiency standards based on traditional medicine. The further spread of health care markets and the tenuous geographical basis for effective community-oriented primary care impeded their efforts on many fronts. Nonetheless, a national network and local infrastructure of CHCs has been built over the course of three decades. By the mid-1990s, 627 federally funded CHCs served more than 5.8 million persons, and another 500 "look-alike" clinics receiving no federal money were funded by state and local agencies or operated by charitable organizations.[24] These centers serve the poor, including highly vulnerable subpopulations of low-income pregnant women, migrant workers, people with HIV, substance abusers, and the homeless. Their administrative and managerial capacities have expanded enormously. The National Association of Community Health Centers has continued to develop as a relatively effective network for policy and capacity building. Some centers—though exactly how many remains uncertain—have fostered continued innovation around a rich vision of community-oriented primary care.[25] The CHC program has helped to stimulate the growth of departments of community medicine, as well as new networks linking hospitals and medical schools to communities. CHCs, in short, provide an important foundation for innovative practice, and some have become involved in broader healthy community projects in recent years.

Health Systems Agencies also helped to foster new collaborative relationships among provider institutions and community groups. They generated new capacities at the state level for health planning, citizen representation, and regulation of the medical profession, and they legitimated federal action at a time when it had few other effective avenues open.[26] As Morone argues, "Regardless of ideology, apparent self-interest, or the bias of organizational design—the HSAs confounded all predictions and became the most forceful regulator in the region."[27] Every subsequent administration has built upon that enhanced authority over the medical profession, even conservative ones such as that of President Reagan. Citizen representatives and support networks demonstrated substantial capacities for learning within a few short years. This was no small achievement given their own great diversity and the enormity of the challenge of engaging on an equal footing with financially well endowed and technically expert representatives from provider, insurance, and employer organizations. Many utilized the skills and networks they had developed through the HSAs in subsequent health initiatives aimed at building community and institutional collaborations, and some state reform efforts, such as the one in Oregon that we consider next, built directly upon the democratic infrastructure set up by the HSAs. The narrowing of goals to cost control among many citizen representatives did not occur within the policy networks most active in facilitating their work. Nor did it happen without persistent efforts to place community-oriented primary care on the HSA agendas. Furthermore, the deep internalization of cost control by HSA citizen representatives can be read, at least in part, as a legacy of responsible civic behavior in spite of incentives to act otherwise, delays and disappointments on issues dear to them, and strident criticisms by local community groups allied with providers to save or expand unnecessary facilities. Citizen representatives, indeed, reasoned quite strategically that any future role for democratically constituted HSAs in a national health reform would depend on their performance in controlling costs.[28]

OREGON AND THE HEALTH DECISIONS MODEL

While the Reagan administration's hostility virtually ended the federal role in promoting grassroots participation after 1981, the momentum of public involvement sustained itself at the local and state level in some areas. States experienced relentless pressures of rising costs, particularly of Medicaid, and some began experiments in the 1980s and early 1990s to institute reforms and provide universal access. One of the most interesting experiments from the perspective of civic innovation is the participatory reform process begun in Oregon in the early 1980s, which helped to develop a "health decisions" approach in other states. The Oregon process built directly upon HSA organizational infrastructure and networks, as well as the community-based and public interest organizing of the preceding years. But it explicitly sought to create broader deliberative forums in the public arena that could articulate fundamental values to guide policy choices and build consensus around a conception of the common good in health care. During the 1980s, the process, fostered by the collaboration of civic professionals in the health care system and advocacy groups for the medically needy, involved thousands of citizens in Oregon in several rounds of broad public discussion at community meetings and two statewide Citizens Health Care Parliaments. The legislature then agreed to establish a policy design for reform that built directly upon the civic learning and trust building that occurred as a result of this work. This design included further community meetings, public hearings, opinion polling, and expert testimony in a process of formal deliberation by an appointed commission intended to limit special interest bargaining. The resulting Oregon Health Plan generated broad public support in the state but also sparked considerable national controversy. Because the model has much relevance to a sustainable national strategy for health reform rooted in responsible civic conversation, and because contentiousness in policy circles has obstructed the potential for learning from it, we develop the case at some length.

The process began in 1981 when Dr. Ralph Crawshaw, the chair of Oregon's Statewide Health Coordinating Council, proposed a Governor's Conference on Health Care for the Medically Poor, partly in response to the economic downturn that had left many unemployed. The Health Coordinating Council was the body mandated by federal law to meld the plans of Oregon's three HSAs into a statewide plan. Crawshaw's initiative galvanized a Coalition for the Medically Needy to lobby successfully to extend an additional ten million dollars of Medicaid funds to pregnant women and children. The panel of ethicists, primarily from the religious community, who convened around this issue proposed a much broader debate about the values of equity and public funding, as well as the ethical and legal issues of high-technology life-support systems. Out of this grew the Oregon Bioethics Conference, which Crawshaw agreed to head, along with bioethicist Michael Garland from Oregon Health Sciences University (OHSU). Initially the board of this group was identical to that of the Health Coordinating Council, and convened immediately after the latter's meetings. Three of its part-time staff were borrowed from the three HSAs, thus ensuring at least minimal organizational resources and well-developed community-based networks through the HSA boards and their subarea councils. One of the three was Lauretta Slaughter of the Black Health Coalition, a group that would continue to lend its support to an innovative civic process. Even as the bioethics conference established its own independent identity as Oregon Health Decisions (OHD) over the next few years, it retained the HSA executive directors on its board and envisioned itself working closely at the grassroots level with the subarea councils.[29]

Community Meetings and Health Care Parliaments

Beginning in September 1983, OHD trained thirty-two volunteers from diverse professions, who were recruited through HSA networks to conduct community meetings on bioethical issues and who received guidance from advisory committees of physicians, nurses, attorneys, and the clergy. The training conference itself was addressed by prominent experts in bioethics, law, economics, and medicine, two of whom had served on the President's Commission on Biomedical Ethics. It was covered by major area newspapers and all four Portland TV stations, some of which supported the ensuing process in their editorial pages. Footage used to produce a videotape for public discussion was also aired on public access cable channels. Over the next months, some three hundred meetings were held in a great range of natural settings, from church and ministerial association gatherings, hospital staff meetings, and senior centers to medical and nursing school classrooms, Rotary Clubs and chambers of commerce—indeed, in any setting that agreed to host such a discussion. Some five thousand people, most from the general public, attended these meetings, which became public spaces for deeply moving individual stories about medical care, bioethics, and existential issues of life and death.

Seventeen communities convened formal town hall meetings. OHD then issued a report based on all the meetings, which stressed issues such as dignity and autonomy of sick and dying patients, increased focus on disease prevention and health promotion, access for all, control of costs, and open and fair allocation decisions. This report stimulated further public discussion and laid the groundwork for the first Citizens Health Care Parliament in October 1984, which viewed itself as beginning to establish a new "health constitution" based on rights and responsibilities of various parties in health care. Some sixty-seven delegates attended from the previous community meetings and from the HSA and OHD networks, and they agreed upon a general set of ethical principles to guide health decision making, including basic rights of access for all, full information, personal choice, and community consensus where rationing may be necessary to control costs. Several thousand copies of the report from the parliament, as well as a videotape, were disseminated through civic networks and into medical and nursing education classrooms and patient waiting rooms. Local media covered the story, as did the *Wall Street Journal* and the *Los Angeles Times*.[30]

From the beginning, OHD was focused on policy implementation, both on individual bioethics policy such as living wills and societal bioethics such as adequate health care. It separated organizationally from the Health Coordinating Council when the latter failed to pick up the ball after the parliament, though OHD still envisioned building local chapters through the HSA subarea council networks. In 1986, however, as the Reagan administration defunded the HSAs, OHD shifted more attention to the legislative arena. It had previously sent every legislator its first report, *Society Must Decide,* which made the case for public input into the hard decisions needed on the way to universal access. Senate President Dr. John Kitzhaber, a liberal Democrat and formerly an emergency room physician, read the report and, through the HSA networks, he became increasingly familiar with OHD thinking. Kitzhaber also participated in a study group within the legislature that read books like Benjamin Barber's *Strong Democracy,* which made a passionate case for face-to-face democracy and public deliberation and which was an OHD favorite as well. In response to continued concern for the uninsured, as well as difficult issues facing the legislature on defunding expensive organ transplants for Medicaid patients, OHD convened another series of nineteen community meetings across the state in 1987 as part of its "Oregon Health Priorities for the 1990s" program, and asked Kitzhaber to chair its steering committee.[31]

These meetings were designed to explore why people value one particular health service over another and to generate a set of principles to guide legislative policy making and health care resource allocation in an age of fiscal limits, high tech options, and deep concerns over equity. The draft of principles that emerged from these meetings was debated intensively and revised at the second Citizens Health Care Parliament on September 23–24, 1988. This parliament was attended by 50 delegates: 24 from the community meetings, 15 appointed by county commissions, and 11 sent by citizen groups with a history of involvement with health issues over the previous years. Among the latter were the Human Rights Coalition, United Seniors, the Black Health Coalition, Oregon Fair Share, the Human Services Coalition, and the Northwest Foundation for Children. The parliament approved a set of fifteen principles, and disseminated them widely over the next months. These included universal access to adequate health care, as well as a recognition that health care should have a claim on government resources only to the extent that no alternative use of those resources would produce a greater increase in the overall quality of people's lives. Thus, while the right of every individual to adequate care was strongly affirmed, there was an important shift away from the rhetoric of substantive health "rights" irrespective of relative costs, benefits, or alternative uses of resources that might improve people's lives, such as education. And while the Citizens Parliament recognized the role of expert judgment, it most clearly affirmed the centrality of an open and participatory process, where citizens themselves deliberate over practical policy choices informed by values—a process it explicitly called "strong democracy."[32]

Making Policy Deliberatively

While Kitzhaber acted as the key policy entrepreneur reframing the issue from one of an uncaring government (the transplant controversy) to one of fair and ethical allocation of scarce resources,[33] the grassroots bioethics work, community meetings, and health care parliaments catalyzed by Oregon Health Decisions enabled his efforts. Kitzhaber took the lead in criticizing the existing system that, in effect, rationed people rather than services and did so out of the public view with no real public accountability. He also commissioned a study of other states that noted similar patterns, such as Illinois, where Medicaid reimbursed for organ transplants up to $200,000 per case, but 60 percent of all black children in inner-city Chicago had not received preventive vaccines, allegedly because of lack of resources. In 1989 the legislature passed a package of three statutes known as the Oregon Basic Health Services Act to expand third-party coverage for those lacking insurance and to build the reform process upon the foundation of focused civic conversation. One statute expanded Medicaid eligibility to 100 percent of the federal poverty guideline, from the current 58 percent, in which a family of three earning $5,500 per year was ineligible for coverage. Another statute created incentives for small business to offer insurance on the road to a scheduled employer mandate, and a third provided funding for a high-risk insurance pool. The goal of the legislation was to extend coverage to 450,000 Oregonians currently lacking insurance, or one-fifth of the state's population, and to another 230,000 who were underinsured. Governor Barbara Roberts, in conjunction with legislators, then established a Health Services Commission (HSC), whose function was to recommend a prioritized list of condition and treatment pairs to the legislature. This list would determine overall Medicaid funding for the following two years and hence determine the cutoff point of publicly funded services, but the legislature would not alter the order of priorities on the list. This basic benefit package would also be required of any private insurance plan offered under the aegis of the small business and high-risk programs, and was intended to serve as a model for defining basic benefits along the way to universal insurance in the state. By establishing funding levels, the legislature would determine where to draw the line on the list that separated funded and nonfunded health care services but could not rearrange items on the list in response to interest group pressure.

The HSC was composed of five physicians, four consumer representatives, one nurse, and one social worker, a mix that reflected previous years of organizing and advocacy, especially for poor women and children. Among the physicians were Tina Castanaras, a Latina doctor at La Clinica del Cariño who defined her professional mission as serving the poor, and Paul Kirk, who served on the boards of the Washington County Head Start program and the Healthy Mothers/Healthy Babies Coalition. Consumer representatives included Amy Klare, the research education director of the Oregon AFL-CIO, and Sharon Gary-Smith, an African American community organizer and health specialist with the National Black Women's Health Project and head of its Oregon network. Gary-Smith also headed a consulting firm specializing in antiracism, diversity training, and alliance building, and previously had served as clinic director of a family medical center in Seattle. These four, along with social worker Yayoe Kuramitsu, comprised the Social Values Subcommittee of the HSC, and all but Kirk helped with outreach, design and facilitation of subsequent community meetings. Also serving as consumer representatives were Ellen Lowe, associate director of Ecumenical Ministries of Oregon, long-time community and environmental activist, member of the Salem City Council and Planning Commission, and representative on the state Hunger Task Force; and Bill Gregory, the owner and president of Gregory Forest Products, a major employer in Douglas County, a leader in providing comprehensive health services for employees and their families, and a board member of OHD. Donalda Dodson, a public health nurse with a county health department, who managed its clinic, family planning, and refugee services, was a member of the Healthy Mothers/Healthy Babies and Early Intervention coalitions, and was active with the Marion County Teen Parent Program.[34]

The HSC was mandated by law to "actively solicit public involvement in a community meeting process to build a consensus on the values to be used to guide health resource allocation decisions."[35] At its first public meeting in the Kaiser Town Hall Auditorium in September 1989, the HSC unanimously chose Oregon Health Decisions to conduct community meetings across the state for this purpose. These were to be complemented by twelve formal public hearings in eleven cities and a public survey, both important indicators of public opinion, but neither particularly deliberative in their methods. The HSC, in turn, would deliberate on the basis of all of these sources of input about health values, and on the basis of testimony by expert panels on relative costs and effectiveness of treatments, and then draw up the actual list and modify it through an iterative learning process.

More than 1,000 people participated in community meetings that were held in January, February and March of 1990. Attendance ranged from a low of 3 to a high of 120, with an average of about 20 people over the 47 meetings. Volunteer coordinators and facilitators, trained by Oregon Health Decisions, conducted the meetings according to a standard format, which began with introductions and a slide show on the crisis in health care, especially how it affects the uninsured and the poor and how their costs of treatment get shifted to other health care consumers. Participants then broke down into smaller tables where necessary and, on the basis of a sample list of health care situations and categories of treatment, began a dialogue on the values underlying the choices they might make. After about an hour of this, the tables prepared highlights of their discussions and then reported back to the whole community meeting, though participants at quite a few meetings continued to engage each other well beyond the scheduled two hours. They discussed the importance of equity in access and how having some people going without care affects everyone. They discussed the importance of care in helping people to be independent and productive members of society, but many expressed concern that this goal not be interpreted in ways that might discriminate against disabled, elderly, poor, and minority groups. Citizens stressed prevention as both cost-effective and empowering and debated how to think about personal responsibility versus victim blaming in regard to drug and alcohol dependency and repeated claims on rehabilitation services. They noted that the quality of life represents a value distinct from the mere length of life but insisted that no medical expert or government agency could replace individual judgment in determining such quality. And they discussed the need for treatments to be cost-effective, though they emphasized that cost should not be the most important measure—a view that helped reorient the basic way that the HSC had begun to think about rankings. Citizens at the meetings did not, however, develop any specific rankings for the final list, contrary to what some prominent critics who neither visited Oregon nor read the primary source materials seemed to believe. Rather, they utilized hypothetical scenarios as a way of clarifying values.

The report of the community meetings to the HSC listed a total of thirteen values, with a summary of the discussions and divergent points of view. It also provided basic demographic data on the participants and included a candidly self-critical evaluation of the community meetings process, with suggestions for improving it as part of ongoing deliberation during periodic reviews of Medicaid priorities and subsequent phases of broader health reform. The most obvious limitation of the community meetings process was that participation was less than hoped for and was skewed towards health professionals and those with above-average incomes and education. (However, 31 percent had combined family incomes of less than $25,000, and only 34 percent had family incomes over $50,000. Among the health professionals, very few were doctors; most were nurses, social workers, and technicians.) Active outreach by the organizers and by those on the steering committee with strong links to medically underserved communities had not succeeded in getting a more representative group. Three of the community meetings were held in low-income housing projects, but only 14 percent of those who attended overall were either uninsured or Medicaid recipients, the initial target population of the reforms. The meetings with much greater proportions from these groups, however, did not seem to discuss basic health values very differently from other meetings. And health professionals who participated in the meetings provided valuable first-hand experience that enriched discussions of common values and did not primarily argue for specific kinds of treatments or self-serving priorities. When such digression occurred, the trained volunteer facilitators brought the discussion back to the question of underlying values. Persons with disabilities and mental health problems were also underrepresented. The OHD evaluations stressed the need for further meetings in natural settings and regular prescheduled meetings of churches and civic groups among the target population. The purpose of the twelve formal public hearings was explicitly to "accept testimony and information from advocates for seniors, handicapped persons, mental health services consumers, low-income Oregonians, and providers of health services." More than 1,500 people attended these.[36]

The commissioners repeatedly returned to the community meetings and public hearings in their discussions of how to rank seventeen broad categories of care, thus making it evident that they felt obliged to act as instructed representatives of the community. The high rankings given to prevention and community compassion (or comfort care) derived directly from the community meetings. This community guidance proved especially important in the revisions of the draft priorities list based on cost-benefit analysis released in May 1990, which had obvious technical problems and was constructed before the commissioners had the time to discuss fully the results of the community meetings released during the previous month. They grouped these seventeen into three broad categories and utilized information on cost and effectiveness of condition-treatment pairs to develop a ranking of 709 items. In 1991 the legislature passed an expanded budget for the new Medicaid program that funded services through line 587 and included 98 percent of services in the "essential components of basic health care" group, 82 percent of services in the "very important elements" group, and only 7 percent of services among the "elements valuable to individuals but of minimal gain or high cost." The latter group included such things as in-vitro fertilization and sigmoidoscopy for persons under forty years of age. The "essential" category included services such as maternity care, preventive care for children, comfort care, preventive dental care, and care for chronic conditions that are fatal and for which treatment improves life span and quality of life. The overall Medicaid budget was increased by 33 million dollars, a considerable achievement during the first year in which the state operated under a property tax limitation that strained budgets and political alliances.[37]

Consensus and Controversy

The Oregon Plan passed the legislature with very broad bipartisan support (19 to 3 in the Senate and 58 to 2 in the House). It was not especially controversial within the state, though some advocacy groups that helped organize the community meetings continued to worry that currently funded services could be eroded over time. Two basic reasons account for the relative consensus. The first is that elected political leaders, especially Kitzhaber, bargained personally with various interest groups and agreed initially to exclude from the priority rankings process those covered by Medicaid programs for the aged, blind, and disabled, which were brought into the program later, and mental health and chemical-dependency services, which were also subject to phased implementation. Specific concerns of doctors, such as higher reimbursement rates and relief from liability for refusing noncovered treatments, were also addressed. Liberal lawmakers liked the expansion of coverage, and conservatives could buy into the rationing elements of the plan.[38]

The second reason concerns civic culture and democratic process. The community meetings, despite their admitted limitations, built upon a legacy of trust and collaboration forged over a decade through prior community meetings and health care parliaments, in which advocacy groups (including those representing the poor), civic professionals in health care, and other citizens deliberated about broad health values to guide the hard decisions about achieving equitable access and responsible allocation of resources. In some cases, their collaboration went as far back as the HSAs in the late 1970s and extended to legislative action to address the needs of the medically needy. These trust-building initiatives around health occurred in the context of a larger political culture in the state, in which both the general public and politicians conceive of politics as a participatory activity centered on some notion of the public good. This political culture, with strong roots extending back to its New England settlers and to its populist progressive reform movement of the turn of the century, has renovated itself in a variety of ways and in numerous other policy arenas since the 1960s, as we have seen in our previous discussions of neighborhood associations, community policing, participatory planning, urban forestry, and watershed associations. In the health reform process, advocates for people with disabilities, poor women and children, and mental health and chemical-dependency services, found the deliberative process to be open to their specific concerns. They recognized the importance of bringing in tens of thousands of currently uninsured, even if it meant low priority for some treatments. And, on balance, they saw the priority list delivering more of the services that they themselves most valued, such as prevention and primary care. The aged, blind, and disabled were included from the beginning in a range of innovative programs for those needing ongoing, long-term care. If anything, services to women and children were ranked higher on the list than a stricter application of treatment effectiveness might have warranted. This ranking occurred because certain commissioners could effectively argue that these were values strongly expressed in the community meetings.[39]

Overall, the policy design was based on a set of what we would call "deliberative democratic complementarities" among various components: an elected legislature; an appointed but broadly representative commission; panels of experts; face-to-face, structured conversations among citizens about underlying values; formal public hearings; individuals polled through representative sampling techniques; and organized collaboration; as well as lobbying by interest groups. These deliberative complementarities operated within a framework designed to limit traditional interest group bargaining in favor of broad public judgment. The process was relatively transparent and designed to generate the appropriate kinds of insight and legitimacy through each component, without compromising core tenets of pluralism and representative democracy.

On the national level, however, Oregon's request for a Medicaid waiver encountered fierce criticism and unrestrained invective, if not utter scorn, from a variety of liberal policy analysts and interest groups, thus helping to filter out civic deliberation from health reform policy frames. The prominent liberal journal, *The American Prospect*, ran only one short article that caricatured the Health Services Commission as simply "dominated by health professionals," ignored completely the community deliberation process, and urged that this "horrifying watershed in the evolution of health politics" deserved no serious attention and respect, but "ought to cause shame and disgust."[40] Referring to the civic culture spawning this democratic experiment, another prominent liberal critic in *Health Affairs* elaborated a grotesque caricature of Oregon as a

> Shangri-La setting where Marlboro people and their above-average kids hike, swim, fish, and hunt in pristine streams and forests primeval; where the poor, the lame, and the sick are snubbed as nasty, brutish and short on self reliance; and where once the two-minute warning sounds on life's little playing field, the good citizen limps stoically off to the sidelines to down a draught of hemlock.[41]

To be sure, there were serious issues at stake. Perhaps the key one was whether a process in which the poor were statistically underrepresented and which initially excluded several programs for groups (such as the aged and disabled) that consumed 70 percent of the Medicaid budget, was fundamentally discriminatory to poor women and children. Some argued that any broad cross-section of the population deciding on policy that affected only one group, especially one as politically vulnerable as poor women and children, was inherently undemocratic. And because the law established no minimal baseline of services, further erosion was possible, even likely, as popular referenda limited tax revenue, and the legislature looked for further budget cuts. Another important argument against the plan was that Oregon had presumably not earned the right to ration, as its Medicaid spending as a percent of state budget was low by national standards and it had not first attacked all the other sources of waste (administrative costs, provider salaries) before focusing on programs for poor women and children. Besides, with a national system of universal coverage most of the questions raised by the Oregon model would disappear, and the Oregon debate might slow progress on this front.

Proponents of the plan responded that Medicaid spending in Oregon was more efficient than in many other states because more people were in managed-care plans and other innovative services for the elderly, and that AFDC cash payments were higher than in most other states. The health of poor women and children could not be measured by the number of dollars spent on health care. Besides, they argued, none of the other strategies for national insurance and rational cost containment had yet proved workable. It was thus necessary to start somewhere and to work within the limits of public support and political feasibility in the state, while making corrections and building political trust through an open process that was accountable on cost containment, so that universal coverage in the interests of the poor and uninsured could go forward. Indeed, progress on universal access was unlikely at the national level as well, they argued, unless lawmakers and the public could be convinced that an accountable process of cost containment had been first set in place. Neither Medicare nor Medicaid had inspired much confidence on this front since they were passed in the 1960s, and representatives of health ministries from countries with universal coverage, ranging from Canada and Australia to Germany and England, were visiting Oregon to learn how to address similar cost pressures besetting their own systems.[42]

American Health Decisions and State Networks

By the mid-1980s, Oregon Health Decisions had helped to spawn American Health Decisions (AHD), which conceived itself as a grassroots movement committed to ethically informed citizen participation in health policy. AHD had groups in ten other states. The Prudential Foundation collaborated with the Hastings Center to offer the first round of community bioethics grants in 1985–87, and some forty nonprofits responded, including numerous Health Systems Agencies seeking to expand their agendas and ways of engaging citizens. Of the original six projects, four (Oregon, Idaho, Iowa, and Washington) built directly upon the HSA infrastructure. The Idaho HSA sponsored 150 meetings across the state, trained 100 volunteer discussion leaders, and held a health care parliament that developed recommendations for the legislature. The Puget Sound HSA in Washington sponsored 211 meetings on issues of access, allocation, and rights and responsibilities in making health care decisions, and a statewide conference produced and distributed a final report to 1,000 community leaders throughout the state. A fifth project, California Health Decisions in Orange County, was autonomous but housed in an HSA office and facilitated hundreds of community meetings and several citizen health care parliaments, partly through HSA networks. It subsequently spun off similar projects in five other major cities. The Office of Health Planning at HHS had begun to lend support to diffuse the Health Decisions model nationally. Thus the Reagan administration's decision in 1986 to defund the

HSAs disrupted the ongoing learning process about broadening and deepening the civic discourse on health care values and public choices.[43]

Some projects continued with private funding and even expanded over the next few years. By the early 1990s, despite the lack of official institutional bases and generally meager funding, projects had spread to twenty states. Some, like Georgia Health Decisions and California Health Decisions, refined the methodology considerably. Georgia Health Decisions (GHD) was founded in 1990 by a well-connected group of health professionals around Dr. Nicholas Davies as a response to decreasing access and rising costs. GHD set out to build a citizens network that could develop a values-based vision for reform, though not a specific plan. With substantial funding from the Whitehead Foundation, the Woodruff Family Foundations, and other foundations and corporations, GHD was able to hire Beverly Tyler as full-time executive director and James Beverly as associate director, and engaged the services of several individuals and organizations with considerable experience in public opinion research and the design of deliberative democratic process. In the initial phase during 1992, GHD held 257 community forums in 104 counties, many of them in conjunction with churches and synagogues, senior centers, League of Women Voters chapters, local chambers of commerce, and professional associations. Special outreach efforts were conducted to recruit local civic, religious, and business leaders in African American, Hispanic, Korean, and Chinese communities, in conjunction with AHD's larger Minorities Outreach Project, funded by the Kellogg Foundation. The project was kicked off with a local media campaign involving six newspapers and five television stations across the state and a reception for state legislators, health care professionals, and advocacy groups hosted by governor Zell Miller, who endorsed the GHD project. It was also timed in conjunction with the national airing of the PBS/WGBH special, *Condition Critical,* a two-hour program in town-hall format hosted by prominent talk-show host Phil Donahue and developed in conjunction with the Public Agenda Foundation, National Issues Forums, and AHD.

The community forums ranked five top priorities, which included basic care for all as number one and environmental protection as number four, and they ranked among the bottom five the right to sue. They also discussed trade-offs they might be willing to make to achieve their goals, such as some limits on choice of doctor and use of high technology. From its early testing, however, GHD recognized that the community forums, while important for public education and network building, often become too unfocused, open to generalized complaining, or dominated by a self-selected minority. It thus contracted with Dr. Alan Dever of the Mercer University School of Medicine to design seventy focus groups to clarify health values and concerns within representative demographic clusters, and employed a medical anthropologist to analyze the 3,500 pages of transcript. Special focus groups were scheduled with the homeless, disabled, migrant farmworkers, and Chinese and Korean immigrants. Dever's final report grouped the twenty previous clusters into four "superclusters," which tended to share a distinct set of common socioeconomic characteristics and value perspectives in their assessment of the health care system. A series of retreats were held during 1993 involving representative groups of local participants, regional board members, and select provider and payer organizations to identify core questions and values in the debate and to build a coalition to take ownership of a vision statement.

GHD also contracted with the Harwood Group, a prominent research and consulting firm specializing in democratic deliberation, to hold a series of focus groups that could validate the supercluster analysis. When this was accomplished, the Harwood Group designed citizen panels that would engage people from the separate supercluster meetings in an intensive, day-and-a-half long discussion. Thus, in citizen panels of sixteen, four participants each from the polite conservatives, transitional hardliners, needy self-reliants, and those highly dependent on public benefits discussed common values and underlying tensions in health care. The Harwood report on these panels was then used to draft and test a vision statement. GHD published and distributed a handsome thirty-six-page brochure, *Georgians Speak Out on Health Care: What They Want and What They Are Willing to Do,* summarizing values and trade-offs in richly contextualized language with quotations drawn from the citizen conversations. Citizens appreciated how much they learned and how they reframed their views through these kinds of conversations, which they saw as essential to ongoing reform efforts.

Ten thousand copies of the executive summary were printed, and media spokespersons were trained from each regional board. This communication strategy built upon the ongoing work of a speakers bureau that addressed some seventy organizations (League of Women Voters, Kiwanis, Rotary, Chambers of Commerce, religious organizations) during the earlier phases, and of the Community Liaison Group, whose quarterly meetings included members of professional associations and advocacy groups, such as AARP, the Atlanta Healthcare Alliance, and the Georgia Hospital Association. The purpose of these periodic meetings was to educate such groups about this kind of civic dialogue, update them on its progress, and begin to build support for later collaboration. GHD also met with state legislators and with the Georgia congressional delegation in Washington, DC. This project led to a Georgia Partnership for Health representing stakeholders from every constituency in the state to develop a state health reform plan.[44]

California Health Decisions (CHD) has engaged in a series of major projects since its founding in 1985. In its first years it involved an estimated fifty thousand people in its community meetings and workshops on advance directives, and trained health professionals and retirees to conduct these. A prominent theme in the workshops was people's desire for control over end-of-life decisions, and CHD not only provided practical tools to assist them but also helped create the context for the passage of the Patient Self-Determination Act at the state level. CHD was the major AHD partner in the PBS/Public Agenda Foundation's Condition Critical project, and over a two-year period facilitated 530 community meetings and a statewide health care parliament in September 1992. It also worked in partnership with newspapers in five cities and held special workshops for reporters seeking to cover health reform as part of what was characterized as a "national civic education project" on health. The community meetings deepened the insights of previous work by Daniel Yankelovich and the Public Agenda Foundation, which showed that, while there was a growing consensus among the American public that health care should be a right for all, there was still deep misunderstanding of the extent to which the aging of the population and the impacts of high-technology medicine contributed to health care inflation. In the meetings, CHD facilitators were careful not to let the typical conversation openers of complaint and victimization or the favorite scapegoats of waste, fraud, and abuse short-circuit fuller discussions of costs, trade-offs, and the expectations and responsibilities of citizens themselves. The civic conversation that would be needed for realistic reform and sophisticated "public judgment" (see chapter 5) had only just begun, CHD concluded.

In other projects, CHD has been instrumental in helping to shift millions of dollars of block grant funds to prenatal care for the poor and in facilitating a process that has given Medicaid recipients a voice in designing the managed-care plans of Medi-Cal. Through its Consumer Feedback Loop, it has helped to facilitate collaborative strategies to improve the delivery of Medi-Cal services among consumers, physician provider groups, health plans, the Community Health Center Network, Children First Health Care Network, and the California Department of Health Services. And CHD has utilized such tools to incorporate consumer and physician voices into improving the service delivery of other major health systems and managed-care plans, in collaboration with the Integrated Healthcare Association, a thirty-two-member, statewide leadership group of health plans, physician groups, and health care systems. It gained access to its first two partners through prior community-based networks, namely, through the former executive director of the Orange County HSA, who had given CHD its first desk and phone in 1985 and had since become a senior vice president at PacifiCare, and through a senior administrator at St. Joseph's Health System, one of CHD's original sponsors within the HSA, who had recently completed healthy communities training.[45]

Other state Health Decisions groups have organized extensive community meetings to discuss health values and have engaged in a variety of other educational activities on bioethics, hospice care, and public decision making. But strong state chapters are the exception, not the rule, and most struggle for stable financing and have experienced limited success in finding a handle for policy intervention.

Nonetheless, AHD has continued to refine its capacity for reflective practice informed by democratic theory in the health arena and has been quick to appreciate the connection of this work to broader projects of civic renewal. Prominent bioethicists, especially several associated with the Hastings Center, have enriched its work and brought these themes to the larger public arena, challenging the Clinton reformers in 1993 and 1994 to incorporate citizen deliberation into the design of the plan and anticipating its failure if they did not. Though members of the Clinton health team consulted with AHD, their strategy excluded a nonpartisan process of civic deliberation and education to grapple with underlying public values and acceptable trade-offs, and they also failed to design for democracy in the administrative infrastructure of the proposed regional health alliances. AHD, for its part, was unwilling to play a partisan advocacy role or to endorse the plan's narrow conception of the citizen implicit in the administration's themes, strategy, and formats for public involvement. If, as Theda Skocpol argues, the Clinton plan collapsed partly because it failed to spark a robust "civic conversation" or treat Americans "like sophisticated citizens,"[46] this failure is in no small measure the result of the policy frames and public invective of leading liberal health reform intellectuals that had blocked their capacity to learn from what were by far the broadest, most nuanced, focused, and responsible face-to-face civic conversations on health care among ordinary Americans that had occurred during the previous decade.[47]

HEALTHY COMMUNITIES

If Health Decisions groups have focused primarily upon public deliberation, the healthy communities movement has sought to mobilize the assets of various community and institutional partners to improve the health of specific populations and to strengthen the civic infrastructure itself. The original language of the "healthy city" was coined by Leonard Duhl in 1984 in a presentation to an international conference in Toronto that subsequently led to the Toronto Healthy City Project, the European Healthy Cities Project of the World Health Organization (WHO), and eventually to an international healthy cities movement that currently includes thousands of partnerships in cities around the world. But Duhl had begun to develop a community-based perspective much earlier. In the 1950s as an assistant health officer in Contra Costa County, California, he had first witnessed the Quakers facilitate active resident participation at Neighborhood House, even as public health programs generally failed in their outreach to the most vulnerable populations. As the chief of planning at the National Institute of Mental Health (NIMH) in the late 1950s and early 1960s, he hosted biannual meetings of a national group of innovative interdisciplinary thinkers in medicine and the social sciences, and he worked closely during the Kennedy and Johnson administrations with leading participatory democratic catalysts, such as Richard Boone and Paul Ylvisaker, as well as with Jack Geiger and Joseph English, who were key actors in the development of the neighborhood health centers program. Duhl's office at NIMH helped to draft the original Model Cities proposal, and he then became a special assistant to the secretary of HUD. He also served with Peter Edelman as an advisor to Robert Kennedy during those years when Kennedy formulated his most expansive vision of community self-government, civic democracy, and the public work of citizens in building this country and participating in "its great public ventures." After Kennedy's death in 1968 Duhl left government to become a professor of urban planning at the University of California at Berkeley.[48]

Duhl's approach drew upon the experiences and networks in community-oriented primary care (COPC) among community health centers in the 1970s and early 1980s, which received renewed emphasis through the World Health Organization and the Institute of Medicine, as well as upon various women's health, self-help, and community development strategies that had also emerged in these years. And through the work of Barry Checkoway, who was also at Berkeley in the late 1970s, Duhl became knowledgeable about the most innovative models of community participation in the HSAs, including the West Bay HSA in San Francisco. Mary Pittman, one of Duhl's graduate students and now a prominent leader in the healthy communities movement nationwide, recognized the need for a community approach most clearly in her work on AIDS in the San Francisco Department of Health in the early 1980s. Only when the people suffering from AIDS and HIV joined the conversation did the medical practitioners begin to understand the community contexts that impeded effective responses, including eviction from apartments and firing from jobs. "Healthy communities is all about relationships," Pittman argues, "and we learned how to build relationships with the business community and the housing folks when the AIDS people and their networks of informal caregivers and lovers showed us what was going on outside the hospital."[49]

More broadly, the healthy cities approach has drawn upon the ferment in public health that challenged the dominance of the acute-care medical model, as well as the overspecialization within public health itself. In the United States, indeed, an Institute of Medicine study had diagnosed the public health sector as suffering from disarray, which was partly related to its failure to build political constituencies for its work. And in both the Canadian and European projects, public health and municipal officials had come to realize that universal health coverage was hardly enough to address many of the persistent issues of health and social justice, as well as the intersection of health and ecological sustainability. For this, a community-based approach to primary care, public involvement, and partnerships among public, private, and voluntary sectors would be needed. The initial American projects in California and Indiana followed the European model of formal partnerships of various health institutions with city government, though they included leadership development, public forums, and vision workshops to widen the circle of community participants engaged in developing consensus on problems and strategies. But only when the National Civic League worked out a collaborative agreement in 1988 for a Healthy Communities Initiative with the U.S. Public Health Service's Office of Disease Prevention and Health Promotion did a broader emphasis on "healthy communities" begin to take hold that included many different institutional and civic partners and did not rely on formal city involvement.[50]

Healthy Boston

Boston, the first major U.S. city to adopt a healthy cities approach, initially began without any knowledge of other Healthy Cities projects. Judith Kurland, commissioner of the city's Department of Health and Hospitals (1988–93), had formed deep commitments to community models of participation during her service in Washington, DC, during the 1960s. She convened a "visioning group" among her staff in 1990 to begin to address the problems of categorical funding and lack of collaboration across programs. A core belief in her vision was that communities themselves are best equipped to identify their health needs and set priorities and that city health and social service agencies should work with them in addressing problems holistically. City department heads signed on to this vision at a retreat later that year, and Kurland's search for models led her to the WHO projects. She came back from a visit to Calí, Colombia, convinced of the potential of health improvement efforts rooted in broad community development strategies driven by local residents. When Boston City Hospital became eligible for enhanced Medicaid funding from HHS because of its disproportionately high number of poor patients, $6 million was set aside for community prevention activities. Mayor Ray Flynn—a prominent champion of neighborhoods and community development throughout the 1980s—redeployed several officials to coordinate the Healthy Boston project under the direction of Ted Landsmark, who also served as director of the Safe Neighborhoods program.

By summer 1993, twenty-one coalitions had formed in various Boston neighborhoods. Each was required to have diverse participation among social and ethnic groups, as well as representatives from five types of actors: health, education, economic development, housing, and human services. The Gay, Lesbian, Bi-Sexual, and Transgender Youth group was the major coalition not identified with a specific neighborhood. Efforts were directed at identifying and developing new leadership through church and other community groups. One recruitment stream that emerged were women at or near retirement, who often had key networks through their employment in city and social service agencies and were seeking ways to bring their experience and skill to their own neighborhoods. The coalitions engaged in a number of citywide projects, such as Kids Can't Fly to increase the use of window guards, and the Speak Easy Program to enhance English skills and develop a health curriculum for English as a Second Language (ESL) providers. They participated in a local partnership with Health Care for All and the Mayor's Health Line to enroll uninsured children in a no- or low-cost plan, and the coalitions worked with the community health centers and other institutional partners to disseminate the latest health statistics available for specific neighborhoods. Local coalitions also collaborated in the strategic planning process of the Boston Police Department, which had launched what was to become a very successful community-policing effort to reduce youth violence. They engaged in a great variety of projects on health education and prevention for domestic violence, smoking, asthma, teen pregnancy, breast cancer, substance abuse, obesity, and AIDS/HIV. They coordinated gun buy-back programs, organized neighborhood crime watches and safe houses, collaborated in immunization programs, and sponsored other efforts such as community gardens, youth centers, teen mediation programs, and job-training fairs. The Allston-Brighton coalition combined its ESL work with the development of community-organizing skills among its increasingly heterogeneous population. In other cases, the coalitions served as the civic infrastructure for related projects funded by prominent national and local foundations, as well as by other state and federal grants. They tended to develop expansive notions about community health that included enhanced social connectedness and leadership development, rather than the narrow delivery of services.

But if the Healthy Boston coalitions succeeded in energizing new participants and diversifying the stakeholders at the table in many neighborhoods, as well as achieving some notable improvements in neighborhood quality of life, they were unable to realize their most ambitious goals of fundamentally altering the ways that city agencies worked with communities and collaborated among themselves. Under the best of circumstances, such a change would present a major challenge requiring sustained work at many levels. Unfortunately, just as the initial grants were being made to local coalitions, Flynn resigned as mayor to become ambassador to the Vatican, and Kurland likewise left her post, along with a number of other key agency staff who shared the broad goals of Healthy Boston. Two years of turmoil and delay in city government bred distrust among the coalitions and damaged the credibility of the Healthy Boston staff. And city agencies, which were under no mandate to work with the coalitions, often met their demands with skepticism and opposition, and found thinking outside the box of categorical programs difficult. Nonetheless, twelve of the coalitions survived the end of funding from the city, and some have deepened their roots within their communities. They have developed important niches among the range of other community development efforts in Boston and provide the civic infrastructure for various community empowerment strategies by agencies and foundations.[51]

State Networks

Healthy communities work began to spread to an increasing number of states during the latter half of the 1990s. One of the more ambitious Healthy Communities initiatives at the state level emerged in South Carolina through a top-level partnership of the South Carolina Hospital Association (SCHA) and the South Carolina Department of Health and Environmental Control (SCDHEC). In a state with generally low health indicators and only a modest presence of managed care, SCHA reasoned that it made both good business and public relations sense to try to improve health with the resources that could be leveraged by hospitals. The key innovator at SCDHEC, and in catalyzing partnerships across the state, was Peter Lee. A former 1960s civil rights and social justice activist, Lee dropped out of college to campaign for voting rights with the NAACP and to utilize his training in parasitology to work with poor communities through the Episcopal church. These early experiences, and his later work on AIDS through the South Carolina Christian Action Council, left him with a "deep belief in people getting control over their health from institutions." Teaming up with Joyce Hallenbach at SCDHEC, Lee conducted a search that led to the National Civic League's Healthy Communities trainings, in which both Kurland and Landsmark from Boston had begun to play an important role. Lee then established relationships with other key leaders from local primary care and prevention coalitions in the state, as well as from United Ways. The hospitals tithed one million dollars to support community visioning work. Other state partners have been added along the way, including the South Carolina Christian Action Council, Department of Health and Human Services, Municipal Association, Downtown Development Association, and Area Health Education Consortium.

The Healthy Communities Initiative in South Carolina has developed an expansive vision. If the health behavior of individuals is greatly influenced by their social, economic, political, and environmental contexts, then systematic improvement requires organizing. In this model, health practitioners identify and develop leaders from the community who can define their own problems and assume ownership of strategies, including coalition-building, policy, and media advocacy. "In many ways the practitioner's function is to produce community organizers." It is *not* to 'do', but to 'enable.' *Health practitioners serve as facilitators while the community does the work,"* according to the official vision statement. The South Carolina partners made a commitment early on that their projects should aim to build capacity for the long term. They sponsored five-person teams from counties across the state to attend NCL trainings in Boston, Denver, and Oakland and then brought the training program home to the state. Each team had to include one person from government, public health, hospitals, education, and one other, often a local citizen activist. They met for two-day trainings four times yearly and learned core concepts of healthy communities, collaborative problem solving, and the use of NCL's Civic Index. Homework included relationship building and asset mapping back in their communities. Over the first three years of the project more than half of the state's counties had teams who completed the training. Since then, the process has been further opened up to provide broader access and initiative for several hundred additional community-based innovators independent of pairing in specific teams.

Safe Kids Coalitions have formed in eleven counties, along with a variety of other local projects. In Aiken, a city of twenty thousand hard hit by defense cuts, healthy communities work built upon the Growing Into Life Task Force representing sixty-two civic associations and government agencies, from the Breastfeeding Association and the Junior Women's League to Head Start and Clemson University Extension, which set out to reduce the high infant mortality rate and then took on teen pregnancy and domestic and child abuse. It was spearheaded by several people active in the women's movement around children's rights and domestic abuse. Healthy communities also built upon a two-year community visioning and strategic planning process in Aiken involving three hundred citizens on various committees and borrowed from NCL's *Civic Index* and McKnight and Kretzmann's asset mapping. Aiken became the first city in the country to utilize its community-policing bicycle teams, trained by public health nurses, to tap neighborhood information networks to reach out to pregnant women not receiving proper prenatal care. The healthy communities team in Hampton County, a predominantly poor African American county of eighteen thousand, has held seven community forums with over two hundred participants at each on issues such as education, economic development, intergroup relations, and healthy lifestyles. Seven hundred attended the well-baby fair, and a countywide training program on diabetes has also been implemented. Residents have collaborated with Clemson University students in designing a state park. They planned bike trails across the county, and in some cases developed neighborhood associations. In other towns the Creating Health in Communities Project worked with school health teams to train more than five thousand children to do their own visioning and decision making. The children's projects have included first aid and CPR training, constructing a playground with safe equipment, building twenty-five picnic tables to host a community picnic, and designing outdoor covered reading spaces. Visioning in all the programs is taught with a high-level philosophical commitment that citizens of all ages must develop their own vision of a healthy community, because—

as they quote from Proverbs, like Save The Bay and COPS—"Where there is no vision, the people perish."[52]

Several other state networks have developed a distinctive presence over the 1990s, especially Colorado, California, Indiana, and Massachusetts, and another twenty or so were in various stages of formation across the country as of 1998. The Colorado Healthy Communities Initiative (CHCI) was established in 1992 by a grant from the Colorado Trust, a conversion foundation set up with the proceeds from the sale of the Presbyterian/St. Luke's Medical Center in Denver. CHCI was directed in its early years by the National Civic League, and has helped to build core groups in twenty-eight communities across the state, ranging from a small, inner-city neighborhood to large, multicounty areas. It has developed a statewide council that works with legislators on policy development based on the community health indicator profiles generated through citizen participation in many of the communities. CHCI also works with local officials in training and facilitating new collaborative projects. Independent funding encouraged community partnerships to define a broad range of projects based on citizens' own conceptions of the most important health issues in their lives, from transportation, land use, and environmentally sustainable business practices to teen centers, school violence programs, and senior support volunteer networks. Many have also undertaken a variety of more narrowly construed health education and prevention programs, though none of the partnerships focuses exclusively on these, nor are any dominated by health care institutions.[53]

The California Healthy Cities Project is managed through a collaboration of the Department of Health Services and the Western Consortium for Public Health, and is funded through the Preventive Health and Health Services Block Grant. Participating cities—thirty-five as of 1996—receive modest seed grants but are able to leverage additional financial and in-kind resources as a result of the legitimacy they receive from official designation, which requires city council commitment to a healthy city plan. Projects range broadly from community visioning and neighborhood revitalization to youth violence, injury prevention, and healthy lifestyle promotion. Many projects focus on immigrant and other special populations, and the statewide coalition worked with the League of California Cities on many of the local tobacco control ordinances that led to the state's clean indoor air law. Through its projects, the statewide network has positioned itself well over the past decade to become a key infrastructure for collaborating with the state's 250 nonprofit hospitals, which are now required by Senate Bill 697 to conduct community needs assessments and develop annual plans for promoting community health.[54]

Healthy Cities Indiana grew out of the work of the Department of Community Health Nursing at the Indiana University School of Nursing in Indianapolis, which was chaired by Beverly Flynn in the 1970s and combined community organizing with local public health efforts and professional training. After being introduced to the Toronto and European model of healthy cities by Trevor Hancock in 1986, Flynn utilized her position as president of the Indiana Public Health Association to develop similar projects for Indianapolis and then five other cities across the state. Though her Institute of Action Research for Community Health, having become a collaborative center of the World Health Organization, now focuses primarily upon the global healthy communities movement, the Indiana network has continued to develop loosely according to a variety of models generated locally or borrowed from prominent national training partners. The initial project in Indianapolis has been able to develop down to the neighborhood level through its partnership with the city's neighborhood associations.[55]

Healthy Communities Massachusetts has built upon the work of Healthy Boston, as well as the Area Health Education Center/Community Partners in Western Massachusetts, directed by Tom Wolff. Wolff brought critical local and national experience from the community mental health centers in the 1970s and helped to develop health and human service coalitions engaged in community problem solving with mayors, police, and other officials in several areas around the state in the 1980s. Healthy Communities Massachusetts has proceeded to build its network by doing a broad inventory of existing projects engaged in collaborative problem solving on health, sustainable development, and related issues and by establishing a training institute modeled partly on that developed in South Carolina by Peter Lee, who directed the Massachusetts effort in the late 1990s. Judith Kurland, in her current role as regional director of HHS, has also facilitated healthy communities partnerships in the state and throughout New England. Collaborating with them have been the Massachusetts Hospital Association and the Massachusetts Municipal Association.[56]

Coalition for Healthier Cities and Communities

At the national level the healthy communities movement became increasingly active and visible during the 1990s, especially with the formation of the Coalition for Healthier Cities and Communities (CHCC) in 1996 and its progressive development as a learning and policy network among local and state projects. Some 450 organizations were affiliated with the coalition as of late 1998.[57] Several have been critical to movement building, particularly the National Civic League, Hospital Research Education Trust, and Healthcare Forum. Each has contributed specific resources and perspectives that complement each other in important ways and has enabled healthy community practices to be diffused widely.

With a modest grant of $70,000 from the U.S. Public Health Service at HHS to develop the original Healthy Communities Initiative, the National Civic League began to leverage in the health arena its community-visioning practice and training of the late 1980s and early 1990s. NCL has worked with local projects, state networks, and national organizations in developing the specifically civic dimensions of healthy community strategies that often begin more narrowly as service integration dominated by public agencies, hospitals, and health and human service professionals. Though this narrower approach still predominates, many of the major national coalition partners, as well as state networks that began with the European municipal model, have been moving toward civic capacity building. In addition to its civic perspectives and training capacities, NCL brings to the movement its extensive networks with local government innovators and with many national nonprofits beginning to adopt community-building models—some of which, like United Way of America and many of its local affiliates, have been applying these to health work. Tyler Norris, director of NCL's Healthy Communities programs from 1990 to 1995, as well as the Colorado initiative, worked extensively with other organizations in forming the Coalition for Healthier Cities and Communities, and subsequently became its executive director. As he argued at a recent national conference, the healthy communities movement will go forward if it can establish that it is not only medical providers but also "we— citizens—who are the producers of health."[58]

Another major partner in the CHCC, the Hospital Research Education Trust (HRET), is the research arm of the American Hospital Association (AHA), representing some 5,400 hospitals nationwide. HRET provides the home offices and other critical staff and leadership resources for the coalition. It is directed by Mary Pittman, the first CHCC chair, who, as noted earlier, refined her own thinking through work with Len Duhl at Berkeley and the San Francisco AIDS community. In conjunction with the Catholic Hospital Association of the United States, VHA, Inc. (formerly the Voluntary Hospital Association), and the AHA, HRET also manages the national demonstration of Community Care Networks (CCN), funded by the Kellogg Foundation. CCN includes twenty-five local and regional partnerships established among hospitals, public agencies, community health centers, educational institutions, managed-care systems, insurers, and community and advocacy groups. The AHA moved decisively in 1991 toward a CCN vision of community health and accountability, with a seamless continuum of care within fixed resources, as the only way for hospitals to control costs and simultaneously help to achieve fundamental change that recognizes basic health benefits and quality care as "rights of citizenship," in the words of Richard Davidson, its new president. In adopting a community network strategy, AHA tapped into the cumulative experience of foundations with community-based approaches to health, substance abuse, and other problems— especially the Kellogg and the Robert Wood Johnson foundations.

CCN partnerships, which have built upon preexisting collaborations, share much in common with Healthy Communities, and their national meetings have recently been jointly planned and sponsored. Some of the partnerships have developed significant civic capacities for community visioning, neighborhood health councils, parish nursing, immigrant and women's support groups, peer health education, and injury and violence prevention. The Solano Coalition for Better Health in Solano County, California, for instance, has worked with county officials, Kaiser Permanente, local hospitals, and medical and nursing societies to develop community-based clinics, neighborhood health councils, and community health outreach worker training through the local community college. Kaiser has deployed Steve Graham, its innovative director of Community Health Partnerships in Solano, to train others throughout the Kaiser system in Healthy Communities and CCN practices. The Genesis Center of Health and Empowerment, a coalition of twenty-five organizations and the Advocate Medical Group (formerly Lutheran Health System), which is part of the Chicago-area CCN, has utilized community-organizing insights from John McKnight and Paolo Freire in developing its clinic and health education programs for the Latino community, and subsequently joined the metropolitan Chicago IAF project. Most CCN projects, however, while they have developed substantial capacities for institutional collaboration around such programs as child immunization, prenatal care for uninsured women, and geriatric and women's health screening, have not yet been able to generate sustained community involvement, nor have they expressed as strong a commitment as healthy communities to citizen empowerment and a broad definition of health.[59]

A third critical partner in forming the CHCC and building the movement nationwide has been the Healthcare Forum, which Kathryn Johnson transformed from the sleepy Association of Western Hospitals into a nationally prominent training and consulting center committed to developing healthy communities. The Healthcare Forum brings to the coalition its extensive networks to health care executives, especially those who have been in the forefront of building new forms of institutional and community collaboration. It provides services for the development of innovative health leadership and resources that have helped the movement grow. These include Healthier Communities Fellowships for change agents engaged in action research projects, a yearly Healthier Communities Award, Healthier Communities Best Practices Forums, and an especially well-designed best practices guide that builds upon a wide range of experience. Its annual Healthier Communities Summit has provided networking opportunities among executives and has introduced them to key concepts and methods for building civic capacity, rather than just institution-based collaboration. Previous summits, for instance, have included workshops on community-oriented primary care, assets mapping, social capital, the Civic Index, parish nurses, and community visioning.[60]

Other major organizations within the coalition bring important networks and experience as well. The Centers for Disease Control and Prevention

(CDC) in Atlanta brings its extensive ties to local and state health departments. CDC first began to utilize community-based approaches in the late 1970s and early 1980s under the leadership of Surgeon General Dr. Julius Richmond, a pediatrician and now professor of public health at Harvard. More than a decade prior, Richmond had served as the first national director of Head Start, which had developed extensive parent participation and self-help in a range of its educational, health, and other activities. Head Start, it should be recalled, was initially part of the Community Action Program but maintained its commitment to "maximum feasible parent participation" long after CAP's demise and in the late 1980s involved more than six hundred thousand volunteers. Dr. David Satcher expanded the participatory community focus of CDC in the 1990s before becoming surgeon general and has remained committed to a vision of healthy communities. The CDC developed an important tool called PATCH (Planned Approach to Community Health) to facilitate local leadership and decision-making capacities. It learned much from its collaboration with community-based organizations engaged in AIDS work, especially through its HIV Prevention Community Planning Process. Its Committee on Community Engagement has widely distributed a useful compendium of principles and practices of assets mobilization, coalition building, and community self-determination to guide the work of agencies in communities. The Public Health Practice Program at CDC has also been working closely with the Interfaith Health Program, initially housed at the Carter Center in Atlanta, and with public health departments around the country, to help all public health agencies explore ways of developing partnerships with faith-based organizations that can build upon their complementary strengths while remaining within Supreme Court guidelines on the separation of church and state.[61]

The Interfaith Health Program (IHP), established in 1992, provides the coalition with loose ties to various health ministries of the major denominations, national and regional parish nurses associations,[62] and the national Health Ministries Association, as well as to the more innovative community health projects within local congregations and religious health systems. While most of these national groups do not employ the terminology of "healthy communities," some have developed emphases on rebuilding civic infrastructure and establishing public health indicators virtually identical to those used in healthy communities work. The IHP provides technical assistance and hosts meetings of national congregations and professional associations, such as the American Academy of Pastoral Counseling, around the theme of faith and health. Its mission is "not just ministries of mercy but ministries of justice," and it seeks to strengthen congregation-based capacities even while holding government accountable for its responsibilities to poor and dependent populations. The Reverend Gary Gunderson, who describes himself as a "classic late sixties activist who dropped out of ROTC at Wake Forest University to organize against the war," has designed the work of IHP on the basis of questions of faith and structural inequalities that he pursued in seminary. But it was the Oakhurst Baptist congregation in Atlanta that first taught him the lessons of building the structural capacity of congregations for addressing long-term issues and to recognize the key question for congregants: "What work were we ourselves willing to do?" That question constituted for Gunderson the congregation's "genius to take people seriously."

In the three "whole communities" collaborations in which IHP is engaged (Dallas–Fort Worth, the San Francisco Bay Area, and South Carolina), it seeks to develop capacities by reorienting the work of church secretaries, youth ministers, and parish nurses within congregations, and by nurturing a network of mutually supportive "boundary leaders" across institutions. The latter include people of faith, especially lay leaders with strategic responsibilities in secular and religious health systems, who often take initiative in developing healthy community partnerships. IHP also serves as partner in five Health and Faith Consortia linking academic institutions to healthy communities work, including schools of medicine, nursing, public health, social work, and seminaries. The five consortia (the San Francisco Bay Area, South Carolina, Pittsburgh, Atlanta, and St. Louis) are developing research, curricula, and interdisciplinary training models for national as well as local use. And IHP has helped to develop a national strategy for aligning the new financial assets of "conversion foundations," created from the sale of religious hospitals and health systems, with the broader panoply of other assets within religious communities. These financial assets, an estimated \$15–30 billion, represent the largest redeployment of charitable assets the country has ever seen. And while this is a relatively small amount in terms of actual health services, especially for underserved communities, it represents a substantial amount to leverage neighborhood health promoters, parish nurses, community health councils, and other forms of civic organizing for a "faith and health movement," as its leaders call it. This movement, which now also finds support through a formally organized Caucus on Public Health and Faith Communities within the American Public Health Association, has considerable potential to bring a strong civic dimension to the healthy communities work of large institutions. It also embodies the promise, perhaps even the preeminent mission, to orient the public conversation on health toward a more existentially profound understanding of the public work of healing and caring within the limits of medicine.[63]

CONCLUSION

Although capacity building and policy learning have been less robust in the health arena than in community development or civic environmentalism, health innovators have nonetheless proceeded from the 1960s onwards to establish important institutional models, test new civic practices, and build organizational networks for further innovation and policy design. The community health center movement elaborated a vision of health promotion, disease prevention, and community-oriented primary care (COPC) to empower poor people and reconfigure important components of professional practice in ways that continue to inform healthy community initiatives thirty years later. It also generated a national network with more than one thousand health centers, as well as state primary care associations and a National Association of Community Health Centers with significant capacities for policy development and technical assistance. Although CHCs, in order to survive, have adjusted to national policy constraints that have narrowed their vision, they continue to serve as an important component of primary care for poor and other disadvantaged communities and have become partners in some of the emerging healthy community collaborations. Health Systems Agencies provided the stimulus and context for the most extensive health organizing ever in the United States, among a broad array of citizen constituencies, and demonstrated the capacity of citizen representatives for participatory learning in a complex technical field, as well as for responsible and strategic cost control efforts, despite the flawed policy design. HSAs provided invaluable experience and networks, as well as regulatory and institutional handles for multiparty collaboration that have led directly in some cases, and indirectly in others, to Health Decisions and healthy community initiatives. They also provided the COPC vision with a bridge to a broader set of constituencies than those represented in the CHCs. Had they not been undermined by the Reagan administration, HSAs could have provided some of the critical elements for democratic representation in the regulatory structures of a national health reform.

The Health Decisions movement has established and refined models for broad civic conversation and structured deliberation on health values and in several cases has linked these to complex policy formation and institutional partnership building at the state and county levels. American Health Decisions, though it lacks comparable institutional capacities of some of the major intermediary associations in health and other arenas of civic organizing, nonetheless serves as a vital network for learning that has posed some of the most critical issues of public deliberation in health care reform. The healthy communities movement has continued to grow throughout the 1990s, with many new local partnerships, a slowly expanding set of statewide networks, and an increasingly rich set of civic practices both within and beyond institutionally driven collaborations. The Coalition for Healthier Cities and Communities has engaged prominent and strategically situated institutional actors with extensive networks throughout the hospital, public health, and local government sectors, as well as a selective group of innovators within managed care. Its organizational membership has been steadily growing, along with its leadership and policy development capacities. The movement's social and technical knowledge base has been expanded and refined significantly, as evidenced in the Institute of Medicine's impressive compendium of performance-monitoring tools to support continuous community health improvement based on a broad definition of health, a comprehensive conceptual model of how health is produced within the community, and accountability among inclusive community coalitions and regulatory and public health actors.[64]

The healthy communities movement also draws upon a broad range of other approaches that have challenged narrow medical models of health over the past several decades. The women's health movement validated the insight and control of women in the face of male professional power and medical hierarchies and provided another critical point of leverage for prevention and self-care. Thousands of women's self-help groups proliferated in the 1970s, and a network of formal women's health clinics and supportive educational and advocacy organizations emerged. While the medical establishment's attempt to incorporate these challenges often dulled their edge, the broader paradigm has significantly influenced a generation of public health advocates and professionals. Women's health centers have also played key roles in some recent innovative health partnerships.[65] The disability rights and independent living movements have also generated a powerful critique of over-reliance on professionals and have spawned an extensive array of self-help groups, as well as independent living centers built around social support networks among people with disabilities. These movements have thematized the problems of disability in social and environmental terms, including the design of the built environment. And they have attempted to universalize the discourse on disability to be broadly relevant, especially to an aging society living increasingly with chronic illness.[66] Models have also emerged for the empowerment of the frail elderly in nursing home settings, and for cost-effective and comprehensive elder services built around the social and volunteer networks of elders aging in place. Elders can serve as a resource on their own behalf and can leverage their purchasing power as part of broader community development to ensure housing rehabilitation, neighborhood preservation, safety, transportation, and security.[67] Grassroots AIDS/HIV groups have generated community-based models, such as volunteer "buddy" systems, for peer counseling and comfort, as well as community organizing for education and prevention. They build upon preexisting networks of gay and lesbian activist organizations, and other neighborhood merchant and civic associations.[68] And many innovative efforts for engaging citizens in local problem solving around substance abuse, crime, and other public health issues have emerged.[69] These models serve as templates for further enriching healthy communities work and testify to the persistence of deep participatory norms over several decades.

A number of factors are driving the renewed emphasis on community-based health and collaboration across medical and public health sectors, and these are likely to open up opportunities for further innovation in the coming years. With states enrolling more Medicaid patients in managed care, mainstream medical practitioners are increasingly faced with managing the health of poorer and less-educated populations with multiple risk factors, such as HIV/AIDS, sexually transmitted diseases, lead toxicity, and multidrug-resistant tuberculosis. Few managed-care organizations and medical practices have the capacity to respond effectively to these challenges without developing new partnerships with public health actors. But the issue of expanded coverage for clinical preventive services (immunizations, mammograms, Pap tests, counseling) goes beyond poor populations. Public and private purchasers are increasingly requiring such services, while options for going "out-of-network" for them are declining. This shift disrupts linkages between clinical and population-based services that had been established through categorical public health programs, and it creates major incentives for public health actors to define new roles for themselves. The managed-care environment is much less forgiving of strategies that rely on simply making services such as immunization available without also ensuring that specific targets have been achieved. In assuming financial risks, managed-care organizations and medical practices must anticipate health service demands accurately and practice cost effectively, which makes them increasingly dependent on population-based data, epidemiological analyses, and public health strategies.[70]

Some HMOs, such as Group Health Cooperative of Puget Sound with more than six hundred thousand members and twenty-eight medical centers, have made substantial progress in systematically incorporating population-based preventive services into core clinical practices and linking these to community coalition campaigns on such issues as children's bike helmet use and smoking cessation. Group Health also legitimates such investments through elected patient boards and medical center advisory councils and assemblies, as well as through organizational practices that "put a face" on clinical prevention results. It thereby raises their visibility relative to personalized curative treatments, which is an absolutely essential ingredient for sustaining and expanding healthy community work. And it has utilized "town meetings" as forums for communal deliberation among general members and task force experts on controversial issues, such as the five forums organized on whether to cover organ transplants, or those on whether to extend care to the uninsured.[71]

The entire population of a geographic area, not just managed-care plan enrollees, becomes the relevant community in health plan calculations to the extent that it forms the pool from which future enrollees are likely to be drawn. This likelihood increases with the turnover of enrolled populations, such as those on Medicaid, as well as consumer shopping among plans. And as Mark Schlesinger and Bradford Gray argue, "If there are a few large plans [in an area], it is more feasible for any one plan to direct programs to the general community, since it has a greater chance of enrolling any given resident in the future. This increases the degree to which a plan benefits from long-term investments in community health."[72] In addition, evidence continues to accumulate that social determinants exert a powerful and independent influence on health. Along with the future prevalence of chronic conditions that result from the very successes of medicine for an aging population, it thus becomes more economically rational for policy makers and plan administrators to invest in prevention and treatment within community settings that can enlist families, neighbors, parishioners, and other networks of informal caregivers as recognized producers and coproducers of health.

The obstacles to civic organizing and healthy community approaches nonetheless remain very formidable. The commodification of American medicine proceeds at an accelerated pace in the wake of the failed Clinton reforms, and investment by market actors in communities often appears to them as unwise and unbusinesslike. While larger, multistate managed-care plans may cover more of local market share, they are also more likely to respond to the narrow interests of shareholders for quarterly profits, and more likely to succumb to standardization pressure from headquarters, which limits responsiveness to particular communities and constricts the measures of community benefit to such things as numbers of subsidized premiums or services to non-enrollees. High member turnover and annual contracts can as easily limit a plan's view of wise investment in community health as they can expand it. Employers with geographically dispersed employees tend not to think in terms of specific communities. And the turbulence of health care markets can prove to be very disruptive to emerging institutional collaborations.[73]

The progressive commodification of health care also reinforces a narrow consumer orientation among the public. Instead of health care viewed as public work shared among professionals, individuals, and social networks producing something of common value, as Bruce Jennings and Mark Hanson argue, patients consume health services as commodities and increasingly demoralized medical professionals supply these commodities by selling their labor to market-driven actors.[74] Citizens orient themselves to managed-care systems as consumers purchasing commodities, asserting consumer rights, and measuring performance through consumer report cards. While substantial numbers of citizens—approximately one-third to one-half, even absent a strategy of civic education on the broader determinants of health—support an empowerment version of community in health care linked to national reforms, they nonetheless tend to be wary and confused when it comes to estimating the value of this approach relative to traditional clinical services. A clear basis exists for broadening their views, especially when issues such as long-term care and substance abuse are included in their calculations. But there is little immediate likelihood of strong consumer pressure emerging within managed care for healthy community approaches.[75] Unrestrained markets, especially in medical devices and pharmaceuticals, stimulate unlimited health aspirations among consumers, making it difficult to forge public consensus around a model of *sustainable medicine* where citizens learn to live with the financial, cultural, and psychological limits of medicine as they engage in the public work of improving health and securing equity. As Daniel Callahan argues, the chimerical quest for perfect health that underlies much of American medicine, especially when combined with our peculiar emphases on markets and rights, is a recipe for continued failure—not least of all in its corrosive effects on responsible civic conversation and action.[76]

The obstacles are further compounded when we consider the relative disadvantages of independent community organizing that the healthy communities movement displays in comparison to the two other arenas analyzed so far. Civic environmentalism draws upon the moral resources, identities, networks, and power of the environmental movement, even when it charts new collaborative approaches. The community development movement has been propelled by tenants' struggles, immigrant organizing, and grassroots protest against discriminatory bank lending and municipal planning practices, even as it also explores new avenues for collaboration. Civic environmentalism and community development can also draw upon the solidarities of place—an ecosystem or neighborhood—and can demonstrate visible improvements in public goods that motivate further participation and generate a sense of common ownership by independent citizen groups. By contrast, improvements in community health status are generally less visible and harder to measure. Protest tactics are less available, since targeting a medical institution may deplete one's support among public constituencies who depend on it for urgent care or alienate institutional elites with whom one needs to build a partnership to deliver services. Solidarities of place are less relevant for individuals and families dispersed among providers and seeking services on an episodic basis.[77] Healthy communities organizing can overcome some of these relative disadvantages by linking up with community development and civic environmental projects, but often at the risk of becoming less able to demonstrate specific health outcomes. None of these disadvantages is insurmountable, but they do seem to make healthy communities work more dependent on the initiative of large actors (hospitals, public health and municipal agencies), whose conceptions of civic organizing, public work, and community assets often appear thin and who tend to see challenges primarily through the lenses of institutional collaboration and service integration. As Chris Gates, president of the National Civic League, has noted, there is still "a struggle for the soul of the healthy communities movement going on," a struggle between a narrower version of sick care and a broader version of health care and genuine community empowerment.[78]

Leading actors of the healthy communities movement have done much to embed civic approaches within institutionally driven collaborations and recognize many of the difficult challenges ahead, including the need to develop state and national policy supports for the work of communities.[79] Both national and state regulations for managed-care plans can serve to strengthen their community benefit programs, and anecdotal reports already suggest that "nonprofit HMOs, larger plans, plans that have a larger market share, and plans located in communities with mature managed-care markets, all appear predisposed to provide more substantial community benefit."[80] National legislation, as Ezekiel Emanuel and Linda Emanuel argue, could also require various components of democratic governance and community accountability, such as elected trustees and policy boards, to receive federal certification, approval for Medicare and Medicaid contracts, or the seal of approval by AARP or the National Committee for Quality Assurance.[81] Indeed, the democratic legitimacy and trust generated by such participatory designs may be the sine qua non for building the capacity of managed-care plans to stem the inexorable rise in medical costs. National health care reform guaranteeing universal coverage would likely accelerate the kinds of functional and clinical integration that are the preconditions for what Stephen Shortell and his colleagues call "community health care management systems," in which the organized delivery system focuses on community-wide health care needs through alliances and partnerships with public health and community and social service agencies.[82] Indeed, it is in some of those countries with well-established systems of universal coverage where community-based innovations have proceeded furthest.[83]

Equally important is a health care reform process that educates citizens as citizens, as well as health care professionals and nonprofessional employees who will have to collaborate in building healthy communities. Without a sustained public conversation about the social determinants of health, the limits of medicine, and the deeper civic, cultural, and religious traditions and assets that can be mobilized through shared public work, citizens are unlikely to shift away from narrow consumer and commodity orientations to medical care. They are unlikely to engage in sustained public work unless they are challenged to see themselves as more than aggrieved victims and entitled consumers, and unless they are provided institutional and regulatory designs in which to participate effectively for broad public purpose. And they are unlikely to supply a reliable constituency for sustainable reform if their leaders deceive them about costs, limits, and hard choices or manipulate them through cheap populist rhetoric.

The Clinton reform strategy of 1993–94 displayed serious deficits along all these dimensions.[84] Citizens were encouraged in prominent speeches of the First Lady to see themselves primarily as victims of villainous insurance and drug companies. Leading reform groups working closely with the

White House built their public campaign around the endless horror stories in their "victim banks." The president engaged citizens in town meetings and local diners as a kind of insurance "salesman-in-chief," in the apt phrase of Thomas Friedman of the *New York Times,* promising higher benefits with lower premiums, exaggerating the amount and timeliness of savings, and downplaying any constraints upon even the most expensive and experimental treatments. Even when public opinion research revealed the "faulty diagnosis" shared by large majorities of citizens—who erroneously believed that fraud, waste, and abuse were the main culprits driving health care costs—and warned even before the 1992 election that the apparent public consensus for reform was "a house of cards that would fall apart with the first gust of reality," the administration's strategists self-consciously opted to endorse exactly what was faulty in the public's diagnosis, because it provided them with an easy us-versus-them populist framing.[85] The proposed health alliances, intended as the core regulatory institutions of managed competition, were shoddily designed and failed to incorporate any of the lessons of the Health Systems Agencies or Health Decisions projects on facilitating meaningful and responsible citizen participation. The compressed time line and synoptic policy design for reforming such a complex system of health care, with so many institutional stakeholders and legitimate concerns about disruption among ordinary citizens, depleted rather than built civic trust and necessitated a strategy of systematic dissimulation to sell the plan to the public.[86]

The obstacles to reforming the U.S. health care system and achieving universal coverage are, of course, formidable. They go to the heart of our fragmented Madisonian political culture and institutions that make it relatively easy to block reform at any number of points along the way. The barriers include an interest group system that focuses pro-reform groups as much on benefiting their particular constituencies as on mobilizing for common purposes and that provides an ever-proliferating array of other interested stakeholder groups with vast resources and media opportunities to mobilize public fears and grassroots opposition.[87] Political elites are deeply divided over the fundamental ethical principles that should govern the distribution of health care, and the routines of the press are poorly suited to covering complex issues in ways that enhance understanding among ordinary citizens. Even if—perhaps *especially* if—the Health Security Act had passed, both the Clinton administration and Americans' trust in government would have remained highly vulnerable, because few of the underlying questions about costs, limits, and equity would have yet been addressed through civic processes that generated sufficient legitimacy and buy-in. Cutting the right deals and mobilizing more effectively to win in 1993–94, had these been possible, would doubtfully have been enough to prevent masses of ordinary citizens from transferring to government their anger at physicians, insurance, and drug companies, and (later) managed-care plans, once the disruptions of any transition to the new system began to be felt and once it became clear that this new system had not solved many problems as easily as they had been led to believe. Furthermore, the inevitably slow process of implementing the plan, as well as court challenges and predictably ferocious ideological and interest-based mobilization that would have followed passage, would have fueled public anger and may very well have resulted in a delegitimation of government's role *even greater* than that which actually occurred as a result of the defeat of the Clinton plan. Indeed, the plan, had it been passed, might well have been repealed, as the Medicare Catastrophic Coverage Act had been a few years earlier.

These kinds of obstacles provide all the more reason why a much richer civic strategy needs to be at the heart of a renewed campaign for universal insurance, and why we will need to build upon the models, networks, and lessons of healthy communities, Health Decisions, and other kinds of community collaborations in the years ahead if we are to establish the organizational infrastructure and public philosophy to sustain such reform.

FIVE

Public Journalism

Public journalism began as a series of experiments in local newspapers in the late 1980s and early 1990s and soon developed into what Michael Schudson has called "the most impressive critique of journalistic practice inside journalism in a generation" and "the best organized social movement inside journalism in the history of the American press."[1] Also known as civic journalism, it arose in response to a perceived failure of the press to constitute a public sphere in which citizens could understand and engage productively with public problems, rather than simply respond to election soundbites, horserace coverage, and polarized framing of issues. As it began to grow, public journalism became increasingly aware of the range of innovative civic efforts already underway in communities across the country and set out to learn from them. It has since generated an impressive array of innovative practices in newsrooms and communities and an extensive network of practitioners, educators, and organizations committed to reshaping professional and institutional norms. By the end of the 1990s, roughly half of the newspapers in America, joined by scores of commercial and public television and radio stations, had conducted experiments in civic journalism. In some cases, entire news organizations have been refashioned as self-described learning organizations committed to continuous reflection and improvement in the interests of a more robust civic democracy.

The philosophy of public journalism, as manifest in the writings of its leading theorists and practitioners, can be summarized in the following terms: Journalists must assume responsibility for helping to constitute vital publics with the usable knowledge that enables them to deliberate about complex issues and to engage in common problem solving. Because journalists invariably narrate the story of our common life in their reporting of the facts, they should frame the news to enable people to see themselves as active citizens, rather than as mere spectators, victims, or consumers of information. While reporters should not compromise their objectivity through advocacy journalism, or by taking the lead in developing solutions to problems, they can play convening and catalytic roles that bring citizens together to deliberate among themselves and with those in positions of power, so that citizens may help fashion problem-solving strategies and policy responses. Journalists can frame their coverage in ways that enable citizens better to map their own assets and build the knowledge base needed for active and productive engagement. They can shine a comparative spotlight on solutions that seem to work reasonably well in other communities in order to expand citizens' knowledge of potentially useful models and generate a sense of efficacy without advocating specific models or succumbing to feel-good news and superficial optimism. Indeed, civic journalists can be tough on those in power by challenging them to respond to citizens' own agendas and real-life concerns, and to engage with integrity in presenting their views and following through on their commitments. And even as civic journalists help to expand the forums and usable knowledge through which citizens can engage with public life, they hold citizens themselves accountable for grappling with the full complexity of issues and acting responsibly to solve common problems. If there exists a bias in civic journalism, it is a bias toward the difficult democratic work of citizens in a self-governing republic. As John Dinges, former editorial director of National Public Radio, has put it, "We must do our job in a way that allows people to do their jobs as citizens."[2]

We begin this chapter by examining the origins of public journalism, especially as it emerged from the long-term readership crisis of newspapers and the convergence of change agents within academia, several foundations, a leading corporate newspaper chain, and local newsrooms. We then present three case studies important in generating innovative practices and transforming newsrooms, and critical to learning within the broader civic journalism movement. These cases—Madison, Wisconsin; Norfolk, Virginia; and Charlotte, North Carolina—involve individual newsrooms as well as multimedia partnerships. They reveal not only the great potential but also the considerable challenges of changing everyday journalistic routines and organizational cultures. We then look at the civic journalism movement more broadly, its networks and diffusion, several of its national projects, and the contributions of other newsrooms and practitioners. We also examine the vigorous debate that arose within the press on the merits of public journalism. We conclude by considering the potential and limits of public journalism within the larger political economy of a rapidly changing media, and in relation to a variety of other forms of civic engagement with new communications.

ORIGINS OF PUBLIC JOURNALISM

Public journalism grew initially as a newspaper movement and then spread to public and commercial television, public radio, and a few commercial radio stations. A long-term crisis in newspapers manifested itself in the 1980s in declines of both readership and profitability. This crisis created a rare historical moment in which a few corporate leaders and senior editors could attempt to change the direction of an industry. Within academic journalism, a few scholars began to recast the debates on the relationship between the public and the press that had long appeared settled. Several foundations also sought new ways of understanding and framing public opinion, rooted in the American tradition of reasoned and pragmatic deliberation. And in Wichita, Kansas, an editor disillusioned with his craft, but hopeful for his country, experimented with new journalistic values and practices.

This path to innovation might have looked different if either the Public Broadcasting Service (PBS), created in 1967, or the grassroots cable television movement that emerged in the 1970s had been able to fulfill its civic promise. At its very core, public broadcasting was a venture with explicit democratic goals that grew out of two linked forces. The first was the educational television movement sponsored by the Ford Foundation. The second was the concern for the role of a diverse media system in contributing to democracy exemplified by the Carnegie Commission Report of 1967. The report called for the public television system to "deepen a sense of community in local life" and render public decision making visible. Public television should provide forums for debate and a voice for those who might otherwise go unheard, and air meetings in which citizens express "their hopes, their protests, their enthusiasms, and their will."[3] But this mission receded in the face of a convoluted and controversial federal funding compromise that left the system open to attack, especially during a period when liberal programming on the Vietnam war collided with the Nixon administration. Local control was difficult to achieve in face of the programming power of the Corporation for Public Broadcasting in Washington and the major eastern stations with substantial resources (WNET in New York, WGBH in Boston, and WETA in Washington). The weakened system became divided between these eastern programmers and the smaller affiliates in the South, Midwest and West.[4]

Grassroots television activists used the "franchise wars" in the cabling of the cities in the 1970s to gain public access channels in the hopes of expanding participatory democracy. Several progressive networks (Alternative Views, Deep Dish Television, and Paper Tiger Television) supplied syndication, and the National Federation of Local Cable Programmers provided an important voice at the federal and state levels to protect newly won access rights. By the 1980s, there were at least three cable groups. The Left activists focused mainly on political criticism and thus appealed to a fairly narrow spectrum of the already converted. A second group focused on grassroots democracy, defined primarily as community participation. They supported the video production of governments, schools, and other local institutions. A third group produced video oriented toward special interests or low-level vanity entertainment. Together, these created an important infrastructure with some notable achievements, but they were not able to develop the broader public space that had been initially envisioned.[5]

By the 1980s, commercial television was the dominant medium of communication, local news was its cash cow, and the downward spiral of market-driven journalism was in full swing.[6] Only newspapers had the mix of close connection to local communities, external motivation to change, intellectual capital needed to rethink their daily practice, and economic resources necessary to conduct ambitious new experiments to reconnect the community to public life.

Crises in the Newspaper Industry

Newspapers became willing to experiment with public journalism for many reasons, but the strongest catalyst was a long-term readership crisis. By the mid-1980s, it became clear that readership, by any measure, had peaked in 1970 and, when measured by households, had been declining since World War II.[7] Newspaper readership was not growing with the population. Younger people were not reading newspapers at the same rates as their parents, and readership was clearly not keeping up with the massive postwar rise in education levels.

The newspaper industry recognized this crisis and began to seek its causes. A series of studies launched by the American Newspaper Publishers Association (ANPA) in 1977 found a cluster of structural reasons for the decline. The migration from the city to the suburbs had eroded readers' sense of place and their loyalty to metropolitan papers. The rise of television put new pressure on the afternoon papers, as did the decline of blue-collar industrial employment. The number of newspapers radically declined, as joint operating agreements led to the combination of newspapers in previously competitive cities and in many cases to outright merger.[8] In addition, as other studies have shown, newspapers systematically failed to reinvest their profits in gathering news and new readers.[9] By the mid-1970s, cable television began to expand from a means of improving television signals in rural areas to a multichannel urban communication system that generated alternatives to the local newspaper.[10] New experiments with electronic technologies like videotex and teletext foreshadowed the possibilities of electronic information exchange that began to be realized twenty years later with the growth of the Internet.[11]

The readership crises spawned three sets of responses. The first was a market-driven approach: find out what readers want and give it to them.[12] Publishers, and even some editors, were moving away from valuing news content in its own right and beginning to stress a new demographic segmentation of markets, making features more prominent and news softer. This softening did not, however, staunch the bleeding in circulation. The second response was from traditionalists who saw the problem as newspapers not remaining traditional enough. In opening the Pandora's box of readership, publishers had cheapened the news without winning new readers, while simultaneously driving away the old. The traditionalists tended to deny the problem, blaming circulation declines on the readership experiments themselves. At most they were willing to tinker with design.

A third response drew from both the market and traditional approaches. A group of newspaper executives deeply rooted in the public service ethic of the newspaper tradition perceived that technological and demographic shifts threatened newspapers' survival. For them, newspapers were important institutions holding a public trust in which newspapers monitor other institutions on behalf of the public. The trusteeship model encouraged the increasing professionalization of newsgathering and the development of local monopolies in comprehensive community news coverage. These monopolies, in turn, guaranteed a historically high rate of profit in the field of local advertising. As television began to challenge that monopoly and readership began to decline after the war, the structural underpinnings of the trusteeship model eroded. These executives attempted to wrestle with the readership problem without market pandering, and they believed that fundamental changes would have to be made in the relationship of newspapers to their audiences, including new forms of research and design.[13] Such changes would undoubtedly also challenge core norms of news gathering and reporting, especially the beat system's overwhelming orientation to institutional leaders.

A Corporate Catalyst for Community Connectedness: James Batten and Knight-Ridder

One industry leader, however, took the initiative to extend the trusteeship model still further. James K. Batten began his career as a reporter covering the civil rights movement in the late 1950s and early 1960s. He became executive editor of the *Charlotte Observer* in 1972 and subsequently became CEO of its parent corporation. Knight-Ridder was one of the most respected chains in the newspaper business, with a core of flagship papers, such as the *Philadelphia Inquirer, Miami Herald,* and *San Jose Mercury News,* as well as a group of excellent small and mid-sized papers such as the *Wichita Eagle* and the *Charlotte Observer.* During the 1980s Batten became deeply preoccupied with the readership issue. His first response was a "customer obsession" campaign. But he soon began to understand the "customer" as citizen and to employ the language of "community connectedness." Jennie Buckner, a Knight-Ridder vice president under Batten from 1989 to 1993, who would become a key innovator at the *Charlotte Observer*, recalls that Batten wanted to address the "big issues that needed addressing, to be strong, and serve communities well."[14]

In 1987, Batten encouraged an experiment in "community connectedness" that was the first concrete step in moving from the readership concerns of the 1970s and early 1980s to the broader issue of the relation of journalism to democracy. The initiative began at the *Ledger-Enquirer*, a small Knight-Ridder paper in Columbus, Georgia. The paper's editor, Jack Swift, had launched a series of special investigations into the city's problems and published a potential agenda for action. When the community did not respond to the series, Swift took the then-extraordinary step of organizing a town meeting to discuss the issues. From this meeting a new citizens' organization emerged. Both the paper and the group worked for the next several years to address issues that had not been on the civic agenda.[15]

Swift also contacted the Kettering Foundation, which helped him to bring to Columbus a young journalism professor from NYU named Jay Rosen, who in turn got his first practical introduction to the new experiments. In his unpublished study of the Columbus experiment, Rosen laid out many of the cornerstones of what would become public journalism. He argues that publishing information is only the first, incomplete step in the formation of the public. For democracy to work, there must also be local public deliberation. The disappointment that Swift and his editors experienced over the failure of the original Columbus series was nothing less than "a moral response rooted in a concern for the particular community in which they were living. Behind this concern was a more general conviction: that it is wrong for communities to drift without direction when the future is closing in on them."[16] As a result, Rosen argues, Swift and his colleagues became advocates for public discussion rather than for particular outcomes.

In 1989–90, Batten made Swift "editor of the year" in the Knight-Ridder chain, sending a clear message to the rest of the company that this was the course that he was setting. While planning for the annual editors' meeting in 1989, Buckner remembers,

> as Jim and I talked, we shared this belief that one of the things that a strong newspaper could do was really be a central place for discussions of things important to the community. . . . So the theme of this meeting was community, and what was happening to the breakdown in community . . . how did that affect newspapers, and what was the newspaper's role in fostering a sense of community.[17]

John Gardner, a special hero for Batten and a major figure in the emerging civic renewal movement, also spoke at the meeting. A short booklet describing the meeting was widely circulated inside and outside the company. What the conference accomplished, says Buckner, was to

> encourage thinking around this bedrock belief that for a newspaper to be strong it needs to have a special kind of a connection with its community. When communities break down, when people withdraw from public life, when people aren't interested in public affairs anymore, or when public affairs withers, that hurts the newspapers. . . . A bunch of those threads began to be explored, and we didn't have any thought-out goal in mind—we just encouraged other editors to pursue it.[18]

Rediscovering Dewey and Democracy: Academic Journalism and Beyond

The intellectual framework for public journalism was set, in part, by a revival of interest in the seemingly long-settled debate between Walter Lippmann and John Dewey on the relationship between the public and the press. No one was more responsible for this revival in communication scholarship than James Carey at Columbia University's School of Journalism. As early as the 1970s, Carey emerged as the central figure in a new school of American cultural studies, appropriating the pragmatist tradition in the sociology of George Herbert Mead and the political philosophy of John Dewey. By the 1980s, Carey had written a series of important essays arguing that the transformation of journalism was central to the revival of democracy.[19]

In "The Press and the Public Discourse," first published in 1987, Carey lays out the challenge to Walter Lippmann's treatise, *Public Opinion*, in which Lippmann concluded that an informed public is impossible, and that the common interest can be managed only by a specialized class. Lippmann argued that citizens were no longer capable of mastering the information necessary to govern. At best, they could choose leaders to govern for them who in turn would communicate the results of their technical deliberations through the newly professionalizing class of journalists. The role of journalism, in Lippmann's view, was to be turned from the public conversation to the transmission of expert opinion.

Carey claimed that Lippmann took the "public out of politics and politics out of public life."[20] For Carey this was anathema, since "the canons of journalism originate in and flow from the relationship of the press to the public." Carey's conception of the public is drawn largely from Dewey, who hoped that communication media might help recreate public life by evoking a community of rational public discourse. Dewey recognized the importance of networks of small-scale groups, but saw communication as first and foremost an ethical principle. The new media of the 1920s "offered an unparalleled opportunity to widen the arena of learning, the capacity to accept but transcend the particular, to join a wider community of citizens."[21] Publics are called into existence by the need to solve the problems generated by the workings of the market that cannot be solved by private actors.[22] Dewey's concept of the public and its role in the creation of the "great community" became the starting point for those who wished to transform the press.

Carey's writings were widely circulated throughout the burgeoning civic journalism movement, beginning in the early 1990s. He became an intellectual touchstone for journalists struggling to rethink the proper role of the press from the standpoint of the practical problems of running a newsroom. His work also influenced Rosen's 1986 dissertation, which devoted substantial attention to the Dewey-Lippmann exchange.[23] Rosen saw himself as a translator between the academically rooted, Deweyan theory, and a group of working newspaper executives, editors, and reporters, starting with Swift and Batten.

Reconnecting Citizens to Politics and Public Judgment: Early Foundation Initiatives

While some newspapers were experimenting with new relations between the public and the press as a way to address the readership crisis, others within the foundation world were attempting to revive the idea of the public itself in a contemporary American context. The Kettering Foundation, under the presidency of David Mathews, was among the most important forces in this. In collaboration with the Public Agenda Foundation, Kettering developed the National Issues Forums (NIF) during the 1980s as an extensive network of deliberative public forums, whose model of civic conversation on key issues of the day became a template for public journalism. An ambitious practical research program also grew out of this partnership between Kettering and Public Agenda, which sought to deepen the understanding of the disconnection between citizens and public life. Two key studies contributed to the intellectual core of the public journalism movement.

Coming to Public Judgment, published by Daniel Yankelovich in 1991, was the product of a decade of practical collaboration and theoretical discussion. Yankelovich argued that the importance of information in shaping responsible public opinion is greatly exaggerated. This assertion challenged a basic belief of journalism that its primary role was to *inform* the public. Yankelovich made a critical distinction between *public opinion,* the constantly fluctuating views of people largely summarized through poll data, and *public judgment,* a more complex form of understanding public issues that all citizens can, in principle, develop. Public judgment, cast as the highest form of public opinion, does not abandon the connective role between journalism and public life, but deepens it. As an ideal, public judgment offers a practical alternative to the continuous piling of facts upon facts that most journalists themselves recognize has done little to improve public understanding of policy issues. In creating a theory of the stages of public judgment,

Yankelovich thus offered the outline of a developmental program for both citizens and the press. If citizens were no longer to be passive recipients of information provided by elites and transmitted through journalism, then journalists, in turn, could no longer abjure the responsibility for the forming of public judgment. The logical conclusion of Yankelovich's work was a process of mutual discovery between the public and the press.[24]

Citizens and Politics: A View from Main Street America, published by the Kettering Foundation in 1991, was the second influential call for a reconstruction of politics and civic life that year. *Main Street,* as it became commonly known, challenged the conventional wisdom that Americans did not care about politics and no longer wanted to participate in public life. The report, written by the Harwood Group under the direction of Richard Harwood, was based on focus groups with citizens in ten cities. It argued that Americans felt pushed out of virtually every area of public life and could no longer envision their proper role. They did engage in public life in their communities and neighborhoods, but only when they believed they could actually bring about change. The report argued that, despite this disconnection, citizens still wanted to participate, but they viewed the political system as a closed network of special interests, lobbyists, and PACs. They did not trust political officials to create the conditions under which they could once again engage. *Main Street* also suggested refocusing news coverage on policy issues and away from scandal coverage, while creating new "public places" for citizens to meet and discuss issues. These ideas directly contributed to the framing of public journalism.[25]

Beyond helping to establish an intellectual framework for the redefinition of public life, the Kettering Foundation was a network builder that brought together virtually all of the key actors who developed public journalism in subsequent years. In 1990, it sponsored a series of meetings in Washington, DC, which focused on the relations between journalism and community, and then conducted similar forums at Harvard University in Cambridge, at the Kettering Foundation in Dayton, and at the Syracuse University Center in New York. David Broder of the *Washington Post,* widely recognized as the dean of political journalism in the United States, was one participant, and he offered a bold challenge in his widely syndicated column: "It is time for those of us in the world's freest press to become activists on behalf of the process of self-government."[26]

An Editor Reinvents Himself: Buzz Merritt and the Wichita Eagle

The 1988 presidential elections are widely regarded as a low point of contemporary political campaigning. Republican ads linked Democratic candidate Michael Dukakis to Willie Horton, a paroled murderer and rapist. According to Thomas Patterson, the press "regretted what was happening—

it accused Bush of conducting a deceptive, mean-spirited campaign—but was caught in its game-centered paradigm."[27] Postelection surveys showed widespread public disgust with news media performance. While some in the press worried openly about the nadir in confidence in the institution, others sought the source of the problem. Among them was Davis "Buzz" Merritt, an editor with a strong ethic of public service who had been among James Batten's cohort at the *Charlotte Observer* and had also covered the transformation of the Old South by the civil rights movement. Since 1985, after the failure of a long *Eagle* series on Wichita's problems to spur change in the city, Merritt had sat for hours on end in his office brooding about the fate of newspapers and democracy. As managing editor Steve Smith later recalled, "public journalism, I've always believed, . . . was the result of Buzz's reinventing himself."[28]

One week after the 1988 election, Merritt wrote a page-one op-ed column excoriating the "shambles of the 1988 presidential race" and criticizing the "mutual bond of expediency" between the campaigns and the media, particularly television.[29] For the 1990 Kansas gubernatorial election, he and Smith fashioned an innovative Your Vote Counts project with intensive issues coverage driven by citizen concerns and relentlessly pinning candidates down to specifics. Looking back, Merritt says the break with tradition was clear from the start:

> We did something very consciously, which was to do the 1990 voter project. And that was a clear, deliberate, announced, intentional effort to change. . . . We weren't even calling it public journalism then. . . . We said, "This is the right thing to do." And we didn't [ask], "Well, what about this journalistic tradition or that journalistic tradition." We just jumped off the cliff.[30]

The overwhelmingly positive response from citizens showed that they appreciated the paper's courage to leap.

Over the next few years, the *Eagle* further refined its election projects. Its in-depth interviews with two hundred citizens, conducted jointly with Professor Sharon Iorio of Wichita State University, uncovered a recurrent theme, however, that went well beyond the familiar political complaints or demands for greater electoral choice. Sherri Dill, then executive editor, says that citizens told the interviewers,

> "Well, I don't know if this is the government's responsibility. Maybe it's really my responsibility. Maybe we have let them, the politicians, fiddle around with this too long. And we need to get involved in this. Maybe we can't blame them anymore." And that became kind of a theme. And it was strange that it became a theme because it was not a question that we were asking anything about or even expecting to hear.[31]

In 1992, the *Eagle* extended its new approach more deeply into areas of public and civic life that were not directly linked to electoral coverage, especially crime, education, and family stress. The People Project, subtitled

"Solving It Ourselves," underscored the relation between problem solving and civic responsibility. It was organized by Ed Arnone, and its chief writer was Jon Roe. Every Sunday for four weeks, a special section on each issue was followed by discussions featuring the voices of citizens and discussions of their core values. The paper published comprehensive lists of organizations and agencies working toward solutions. Community response was again enthusiastic, and nearly overwhelmed the stamina of project organizers. But this time the reporting helped to lead to specific efforts to renew civic life, such as the Neighborhood Initiative and the formation of Wichita Independent Neighborhoods. Even years later, across race, class, and neighborhood, civic activists attribute greater involvement to the People Project.[32]

Transforming Newsrooms, Engaging Communities

It is difficult enough to launch a movement, and harder yet to transform the daily routines embedded in the system of modern American journalism. At the *Wichita Eagle,* the tensions between the two proved too great. Newsroom innovation began to stall as Merritt invested increasing amounts of time in national trainings; Arnone joined the Kettering Foundation as its communications director; and Steve Smith left for Knight-Ridder corporate headquarters. Without a leadership team capable of transforming traditional hierarchies of the newsroom, sustaining innovation becomes very difficult. As Merritt, a charismatic leader presiding over a very hierarchical structure, ruminated later, "If we had known that we were going to be sitting here today talking about stuff going on on five continents, we would have probably been a little more deliberate about some of the things. . . . The resistance to change and the habits and routines of the newsroom are much, much more deeply imbedded than I thought."[33]

Civic journalists approached change in a spirit of pragmatic learning within their own newsrooms, as well as through a national network that began to take shape in 1992. In that year, Batten urged the Knight Foundation to fund the Project on Public Life and the Press, to be headed by Rosen at New York University. The PPLP began to hold four seminars a year at the American Press Institute outside of Washington and served as a place to reflect on the core values of journalism and democracy among movement intellectuals, journalism leaders, editors, and reporters. Shortly thereafter, in 1993, the PPLP was joined by the Pew Center for Civic Journalism, an initiative urged by Pew President Rebecca Rimel and its board, and founded by Ed Fouhy, a nationally known former CBS news producer, along with Jan Schaffer, a Pulitzer Prize–winning editor of the *Philadelphia Inquirer.* The Pew strategy complemented PPLP in emphasizing the development of experimental projects, spreading the word, and sponsoring research about the movement. It held workshops to introduce hundreds of additional editors and reporters (who may not have been in the more tightly drawn circle of PPLP) to the new approaches. But the Pew Center also provided funds to support innovation.

Almost all of the leading actors in our cases participated in PPLP or Pew Center activities—usually both—and became influential movement leaders in turn. These local examples represent some of the best cases of civic journalism. Their lessons provided feedback to movement networks both directly, through PPLP and Pew Center meetings, and indirectly, through the writings of Rosen, Merritt, Fouhy, Schaffer, and others. The We the People project based in Madison, Wisconsin, pioneered multimedia collaboration among public television and radio, as well as commercial television and newspaper organizations, to engage citizens in deliberation on difficult policy issues, thereby changing the local media environment in which political discussion takes place. It has also used television particularly well to invert the symbolic relations between citizens and government by placing citizens at the center of discussion in many of the usual seats of formal power. The *Norfolk Virginian-Pilot* and the *Charlotte Observer* have institutionalized new team structures to drive experimentation and embed new daily routines deeply within newsrooms now capable of continuous learning. At the *Pilot,* regular "public life pages" are designed to build community capacity by generating usable public knowledge. And at the *Observer* and its multimedia partners, the Taking Back Our Neighborhoods project pioneered an innovative way to cover crime, which helped to catalyze further efforts to improve neighborhoods by housing partnerships, city and county agencies, United Way, and churches within and across areas segregated by class and race.

WE THE PEOPLE:
WISCONSIN—A PARTNERSHIP FOR DELIBERATION

In Madison, Wisconsin, a coalition of television, newspaper, and radio partners has been conducting a series of experiments in public journalism since 1991. The "We the People: Wisconsin" project has focused almost exclusively on encouraging citizen discussion and agenda setting. Unlike the Wichita project, where there was a conscious attempt to found a new kind of journalism, We the People has understood itself as an extension of "the public's right to know," using new techniques of media partnerships, town hall meetings, and citizen forums.

The first stirrings of We the People began with senior journalists reflecting on the direction of their craft and the relations between journalism and public life. David Iverson, Director of News and Public Affairs at Wisconsin Public Television, had been thinking for some time about the survival of quality news on public television.[34] When the Gulf War began in 1991, the *Wisconsin Week* magazine was converted into a nightly town hall meeting of the air. Iverson called Tom Still, Associate Editor of the *Wisconsin State Journal* and asked if he wanted to cosponsor the meetings, and a partnership was formed. By this time, the Kettering Foundation's *Main Street* had been published, and both Iverson and Still were familiar with its ideas. When Iverson was approached by public television station KTCA in Minneapolis to coordinate coverage of the April 1992 presidential primary, he invited Still and *Wisconsin State Journal* Editor Frank Denton to join. The two brought in Wood Communications, a Madison public relations firm, as a partner, and together with KTCA and the *St. Paul Pioneer-Press* (a Knight-Ridder paper), they provided citizen-driven coverage of the entire upper-Midwest presidential primary debate. Citizens sent in newspaper coupons and were selected to form panels representing the populations of Wisconsin and Minnesota. The project proved such a success that Still, Iverson, and Denton decided to continue throughout the election. In this way, We the People was born.

In 1994, the partners added the statewide Wisconsin Public Radio network of eleven stations and the Madison CBS affiliate, WISC-TV. We the People is the only coalition in the entire public journalism movement that has sustained a working group of newspapers, public and commercial television stations, and public radio stations over such an extended period. The remarkable power and reach of this civic media coalition has allowed We the People to reshape the symbolic terrain of the relations between citizens and politics in Wisconsin.

Turning the Symbolic Tables

In many We the People projects, citizens and public officials literally reverse places: citizens assume the bench in a courtroom or the floor in a legislative chamber, while officials and candidates present their case before them. This spatial arrangement began as a technique for television production, but it has taken on symbolic meaning of its own over the years. During coverage of the Wisconsin Supreme Court race in 1995, for example, a cross-section of Wisconsinites, from a well-dressed African American woman to a farmer with a "gimme" cap in a sleeveless tee shirt, sat on the justices' bench, looking down at the candidates, who assumed the positions of lawyers pleading before the court. In a project on health care, citizens formed a mock jury while congressional representatives argued the case for four major health plan alternatives—and after extensive deliberation citizens chose the single-payer plan.

Citizens have traded not only places but also roles. During the 1994 gubernatorial debate, a northern Wisconsin man dressed in an American flag shirt stood up and challenged both the Republican governor and his Democratic opponent to commit that night to offer a detailed written plan for either raising revenues or cutting programs to meet a mandated property tax cut. And he asked for the plans at least two weeks before the election. The candidates promised to deliver, and the story appeared on the front pages of Wisconsin newspapers the next day. Eventually, both candidates delivered on their promise. Reflecting on this event, Iverson noted that politicians "can't blow off a voter's question" as easily as they might a reporter's. They can't even phrase their questions in the same way. "What was great," when the man in the flag shirt stood up, "was at that moment there was no escape."[35]

Just as the questions have changed when citizens switch roles with reporters, so have they when citizens take the role of legislators. In 1993, in a town hall meeting on a property tax freeze held in a capitol hearing room, citizens on a raised platform heard witnesses below, including the governor. Later that year three hundred citizens gathered in town halls in Milwaukee and Madison to try to tackle the federal deficit. Congressional representatives lobbied them as they worked through budget choices in smaller groups to discuss specific deficit issues. In a 1995 project, the People's State Budget hearings were held in three cities, leading to a live broadcast in which citizens took to the floor of the assembly to draft their own state budget. While legislators watched from the sidelines, citizens did their work, and reporting teams "eavesdropped" on the deliberating citizen legislators on the floor.

In each of these projects, citizens have taken center stage, using some form of deliberative process to work through complex public issues live and on the air. The programs have always been preceded by more extensive deliberation leading up to the broadcast in cities and towns around the state and have been accompanied by additional material and further discussions in newspapers, on talk shows on Wisconsin Public Radio, and on the local commercial CBS affiliate. Their purpose is not to change formal decision making but to help form public opinion in a deliberative manner, challenge officials to respond to the concerns of citizens, and provide civic education about how to grapple with complex issues. Over the past decade, Wisconsinites, and Madisonians in particular, have come to expect this kind of treatment of serious public issues. Now, project leaders are often approached by others asking them to "we-the-people" an issue, thus turning a public journalism initiative into a common civic verb.

The Public's Right to Know

The We the People partners are comfortable with this role. They believe their task is to inform people about elections and community issues and then to leave it up to citizens to decide what action, if any, they wish to take. Iverson says it is appropriate to play a convening role that goes beyond just observing and reporting. But he does not endorse efforts to convene citizens if the express purpose is to enable them to develop strategies and networks for problem solving. For example, the *Wisconsin State Journal* conducted another series of civic journalism projects, City of Hope and Schools of Hope, which brought civic and political actors together, confronted them with choices, and insisted that they act on them. For Iverson, this effort crosses the line of legitimate journalistic involvement. And, as we shall see, it opens the larger movement to the unfortunate, and largely unfair, charge of violating the boundary between public journalism and civic action.

Because of this self-conscious choice to draw the line at any kind of public engagement, We the People has taken on a serial quality as it moves back and forth from elections to issues. The project has managed to develop a specific form of media-driven, public deliberation. It is less clear, however, whether We the People has led to new forms of deliberation or civic engagement beyond the symbolic redefinition of the relations between citizens and politics. Surveys conducted in 1995 showed that about 40 percent of Madisonians recognized the project.[36] Tangible effects on public deliberation are more difficult to demonstrate. Field work conducted in Madison from 1996 to 1999, however, found that knowledge and support of the program were moderate; about half of the citizens sampled had some recall of the project and were able to relate knowledge of specific issues and elections in some depth.[37]

Some evidence from Madison suggests that programs targeting specific local problems have resonated more deeply. The We the People of July 1995, for example, concentrated on land use in Dane County. All of the partners believed the topic was important, but they also feared that citizens' "eyes would glaze over." They therefore worked to frame the issue through supporting materials and generate community support for the program. The town hall meeting, broadcast live on both WISC-TV and Wisconsin Public Television, garnered a remarkable 25 percent of television viewers during prime time in Madison/Dane County, an unprecedented rating for any kind of news and public affairs in this time slot, much less a program on land use. Some political observers attributed a shift in the composition of the county board during the next election to the project, which led to the adoption of a comprehensive county land use plan.

The We the People partnership has been one of the most successful in public journalism. The project's longevity, made possible by the stability of the partnership, has enabled it to sink roots in that active civic layer of the community that has made "we-the-people" a verb. We the People's ability to convene public officials and elicit their collaboration with innovative designs derives from the credibility and reputation for fairness and nonpartisanship that Iverson and Still had previously built and from the relationships to elected leaders in both parties that Jim Wood (a former Democratic candidate for lieutenant governor) had cultivated. As We the People's nonpartisan deliberative formats became popular with citizens, it became increasingly difficult for elected officials to refuse invitations to participate without appearing to rebuff the people themselves or to cede the field to members of the other party. And while We the People steers clear of community problemsolving forums such as those at the *Wichita Eagle* and the *Charlotte Observer,* Wisconsin Public Television's Outreach department has collaborated to produce Safe Night festivals for youth in Milwaukee and to diffuse the model nationally through media partnerships in other cities. And the station has progressed further than any other public television station in mapping a multimedia strategy to build a "new information commons" for the digital age to support active citizenship and "put the public back in public television."[38]

THE *NORFOLK VIRGINIAN-PILOT:* NEW VALUES, NEW ORGANIZATION

Civic journalism began at the *Norfolk Virginian-Pilot* in 1993 and has been extended and refined in the years since. As in Wichita, a visionary leader and intellectual who studied the literature on democracy and public life spearheaded change. But unlike the leaders in Wichita, he developed a team organization able to sustain innovation even after he left a few years later.

Cole Campbell, who came to the *Pilot* in 1990 as an assistant managing editor, believed in "participatory management," as he had "participatory democracy" during his undergraduate years at the University of North Carolina at Chapel Hill. He had been inspired by *Pilot* publisher Frank Batten, whom Campbell calls "a big part of the picture of public journalism, even though he would probably disavow that." In the early 1970s, Batten had written that the first role of Landmark newspapers was to present a "faithful and accurate picture of the life of their communities" and to "nourish hope." In 1991, Campbell was made managing editor, and Batten, now CEO of *Pilot's* parent corporation, Landmark Communications, initiated a program for regaining readership. Known as continuous improvement (CI), a variant of total quality management, it held that the key to the newspaper's long-term survival was its growth, which in turn was linked to three kinds of improvements: broadening the base of readers, improving profitability through changes in production, and team-based organization in the newsroom. In the hands of an editor deeply committed to core values of democracy, CI was a management strategy that could sustain innovation.[39]

The value shift that led to the rethinking of the core mission in Norfolk extended over several years, starting in 1990, when a series of investigations of the town of Chesapeake forced the mayor from office, even though many in the newspaper felt he had generally been good for the city. A core group of editors and reporters began seriously to reflect on the purposes of investigative journalism, especially when it leaves the community worse off than before.[40] Prodded in part by this rethinking, a new government team was formed in 1992 and was charged with reinvigorating traditional city hall and political reporting. Campbell and Deputy Managing Editor Dennis Hartig had also begun talking about a form of "solutions journalism." They were aware that citizens were angry at what they saw as the endless reporting of "bad news" that pointed to problems without discussing possible solutions. When Campbell assumed the responsibilities of executive editor the following year, a new "public life team" was formally launched.

Community Conversations

In January 1994 the *Pilot* contracted with the Harwood Group to conduct a series of "community conversations" in the Norfolk area. In a community conversation, developed by Richard Harwood at the *Miami Herald*, a group of citizens is recruited, either at random, through an open call in the paper, or through community organizations. The group assembles to talk through a public issue, with a discussion leader to act as facilitator, a recorder to capture the dialogue, and a reporter to observe and write. The community conversation is like a focus group, but it utilizes the discussion for public ends, rather than for marketing or strategic political purposes. It is deliberative in form, actively seeking the tension and ambiguity that surrounds issue discussion, and it treats these as essential to the story. The conversation itself may or may not be written up as news. From the Miami experiment, however, Tom Warhover, the *Pilot's* new public life team leader, had learned that community conversations required another dimension, which he referred to as "public listening," that included all the informal ways in which reporters and editors engage in dialogue with citizens. For Warhover, this process was essential: "A large part of my job was [getting across that] public journalism was public listening."[41]

The *Pilot* held more than a dozen community conversations between early spring and late fall of 1994. The first breakthrough was a series of conversations on crime and punishment, held across Virginia in a joint project covering the gubernatorial race with several large daily newspapers and the Associated Press. In eight community conversations involving more than ninety people, Warhover, reporter Tony Wharton, and others kept hearing that citizens were deeply concerned about juvenile crime. After a community conversation in one high school library, the leader of the education team noted, "The stories we're writing aren't the stories people are talking about." This comment sparked further reflection, as *Pilot* reporters and editors had to figure out how to use the new form to best effect in daily journalism.

As important as community conversations have been at the *Pilot*, editors and reporters have also learned from their problems. First, they are difficult to sustain. Every hour of conversation requires at least four of preparation. Second, it is difficult to find citizens to commit to two or more hours, and to find people who are not the "usual suspects." A third issue is what to do with the conversations. Early on, some were run verbatim in large chunks, but reader feedback convinced editors that this format was much less helpful than utilizing the conversations to identify issues and frame coverage. As editor Kerry Sipe noted, "The meeting itself is not the story." Former public life team leader Tony Germinotta calls community conversations a crutch. "They're a necessary crutch right now [in 1997]. But better than that is to know your community."[42]

The community conversations, however, have led to a new way of listening to the public. Mike Knepler, the reporter perhaps most immersed in civic life, sometimes writes by constructing an imagined community conversation among a number of people, formulating hypotheses about the story, and testing them out with citizens as he goes through his interviews:

> You can almost hold the community conversation in your head. If you talk to enough people and push them and test them on what they say, and try to get at the values that are salient underneath, you can bounce that off in your head. . . . [In one project] I ended up with interviews from eighteen women on welfare. Each time I learned something, I tested it out on the next one. It's not like having a roomful of people all of a sudden reaching an epiphany to get a public voice. But I'm not sure journalistically what the difference would be.[43]

Knepler is describing the development of a new *public internal voice*. Rather than simply reacting to a story from his own knowledge or a set of professional routines, he is trying continually to reconstruct the public dialogue in the process of reporting.

"Putting Our Street Clothes On"

Cole Campbell left the *Norfolk Virginian-Pilot* in late 1995 to become editor of the *St. Louis Post-Dispatch*. Many of those who had observed the *Pilot* from the outside—advocates as well as critics of public journalism—felt that his departure would be the beginning of the end of the *Pilot* experiment. In fact, Campbell's absence provided a new test for public journalism. Could it survive without a strong leader at the top? Would it be subordinated to marketing?

Campbell was succeeded by Kay Tucker Addis, who was not committed to public journalism in any larger sense. In naming Hartig as managing editor and Warhover as deputy managing editor, however, she showed that she was trying not to unravel the new practices. The public journalism leadership team had sought to build an organization to sustain good work every day. Key to this was integrating the values of public journalism into all teams in a reorganized system of production and accountability. But the CI management philosophy also posed dangers, as its explicit aim was "delighting our customers," a phrase that could be interpreted as almost anything that expanded circulation. Campbell and Hartig had managed to wed this rubric to the goal of being a public newspaper that helped to sustain civic life in the community, much as Jim Batten's "customer obsession" rhetoric had done at Knight-Ridder. But if this coupling of customer and public rhetoric fell apart, the public side would likely be the first to go, especially in the absence of a strong supporter at the very top of the organization.

In a closing remark to his staff, Campbell had said, "Well, you're just going to have to put on your street clothes now." If public journalism was going to survive, it would have to be through the various pathways of daily routine that the teams had begun to create.

Public Life Pages

The most important innovation in this regard has been the set of "public life pages" titled "Public Life," "Public Safety," and "Education." These three special pages appear once a week each on page three of the metro section, renamed "Hampton Roads" to emphasize the community-wide identity of the five major cities that make up the *Pilot's* coverage area. The goal of each page is to enhance "usable public knowledge" and thereby build civic capacity. If citizens themselves are to do public work, as *Pilot* editors discussed at a 1995 meeting at the American Press Institute, then we need to be "doing public work on the public life page," Hartig argues. The central question Hartig posed in designing the pages was this:

> How can we become increasingly seen as a public resource? . . . And to the degree that we can become associated with more public work, we will be increasingly more valuable, our future will be rosier, we will become more linked in parts of the community.[44]

The key to public work for Hartig is *building capacity* within the community:

> Capacity—public knowledge—will come about from routines and disciplines driven by very simple questions. "What is political knowledge? What is the political information that people need day-in and day-out to function effectively in their communities and with their neighbors?" That question has got to be asked every day, and it's just like the grass growing. It's not dramatic, but we've got to build journalistic practices and routines that answer that question.[45]

The pages are designed to highlight usable knowledge, frame choices, and serve time-starved readers efficiently, but in a *public* way "that gives them a lot of information about their own city, but also other cities, so that they can see the wholeness of the place politically."[46] Although the pages vary, each follows a basic format structured with an eye toward citizen use. The pages are designed around the "left rail" (or column), the "right rail," and the three columns "between the rails." On the upper left rail of each page is generally a "how to" section that tells citizens how they can accomplish a task or learn something in particular. On the "Public Life" pages, for example, the upper left rail may contain a story on finding and making sense of city budgets or on appealing an assessment. On the "Public Safety" page, the upper left gives the crime-line telephone numbers of every city and a brief report on results from the line. On the "Education" page, the upper left rail is headed "Making A Difference" and features ways in which citizens are actively working to improve schools. On the lower left rail, the pages generally feature a quick tip or citizen question, such as how to teach reading to your child (in "Education"), or how remain alert to street crime (in "Public Safety").[47]

The upper right rail varies. In the "Public Life" pages on Wednesday, the upper right is always a brief roundup of actions taken at the regular Tuesday night sessions of each of the five major city councils (Norfolk, Virginia Beach, Portsmouth, Chesapeake, and Suffolk). This information is designed to meet citizen complaints that the paper divides the community up and does not let some parts see themselves in relation to others. In "Public Safety," the upper right might feature a success story of law enforcement or citizens taking action at the neighborhood level. "Education" might present a school board roundup or update. Often the lower right will feature some other tool of assessment, such as "Hampton Roads by the Numbers," a graphics box that gives citizens a quick way to compare themselves to others.

The heart of the pages is the three columns "between the rails," which vary from page to page and week to week. The stories are driven by the central principles that Hartig articulates, "choices and consequences," and they are linked to the central function of assessment. The pages are designed to be working tools for citizens, quick and effective ways for them to locate themselves in public life, so that they can see how they are doing, what kinds of problems need to be solved, and what they can do to address them.

The main between-the-rails stories on the "Public Life" pages during spring 1997, for instance, revealed a pattern of useful stories, neither major nor small, that employ standards for comparison that citizens can use. One of the earliest pages was headed "Virginia Beach's To-Do List." Rather than focusing on a single issue, or immediate news, the to-do list goes back six months to revisit the status of the high-priority items that the Virginia Beach city council had set for itself during this period. In a very tight space, writer Karen Weintraub manages to update citizens on the status of eleven major projects, many of which were big news when they were first debated. In the lower right four inches, she has given updates on thirteen additional issues of interest to citizens in Virginia Beach. The writing itself is exemplary for this comparative form. For example, in six short sentences in the item subheadlined "Project: Library Referendum," Weintraub identifies the claimed need for expansion and the reason for its halt: fiscal problems. She discusses the areas of need by specific neighborhood and with reference to general infrastructure. She names what the proposed solution is: more funding. And she tells about a proposed upcoming referendum to solve it. Finally, she describes what the council itself proposes to do. Anyone interested in the library issue in Virginia Beach can immediately get a brief history of the entire issue. Virginia Beach citizens, some of whom may not have thought about the issue, now have some basic information to consider. And other area citizens can see what Virginia Beach is doing and compare it to their own cities.

Other early "Public Life" between-the-rails stories included "Erasing the Eyesores" in Portsmouth, which discusses efforts to improve neighborhood appearance; "Stiffer Fines Pay Off Big" in Norfolk, on how increased parking fines are being used; and "Jobs a Portsmouth Priority" on economic development efforts. Each story focuses on a specific problem and an actual or proposed solution in progress. They are rarely major stories in their own right, but each contributes to the larger comparative picture of public and metropolitan community life.

The second major between-the-rails feature is the "Neighborhood Exchange," written by veteran urban affairs reporter Mike Knepler, whose purpose is to demonstrate a wide range of productive activities available to the citizen. For Hartig, this information is necessary because so much of public life reporting focuses on the official community institutions to solve problems, which "puts a moral weight on our structures and institutions to solve our problems and inadvertently turns us into clients." The "Neighborhood Exchange" attempts to say that, while public officials and institutions are "incredibly important, there's another resource out there. It's the spirit of people who want to make a difference in the community. And we need to see the importance of that and validate it, frankly, as important and legitimate work." The "Neighborhood Exchange" attempts to validate the public work of citizens and help to create some new connections, says Hartig. "So, what we find is that people are so isolated that ideas aren't shared, and because they're not shared, people don't benefit from any exchanges; they don't build a sense of community; they stay in isolation." Knepler himself goes still further in linking his readers to models of civic activism in other communities around the country and providing them with places on the World Wide Web where they can find out more. Because people in local and distant communities alike are acting in ways that model behaviors, Hartig hopes that such stories "might inspire, motivate, guide, and lead others to do the same thing."[48]

From the Pages to the Front Page

Building civic capacity through the public life pages is intended to set a standard for daily coverage of other issues, not to remain isolated in a separate section of the paper. Long and complex stories on political institutions or breaking news from city hall require asking what information people really need to understand the issue. Reporter Karen Weintraub calls this a "literacy approach" to major stories. She defines literacy as the basic information that people need to enter a story they know nothing about. She assumes that most people do not, in fact, know anything about a given issue, or that they might have known but have since forgotten.[49] This approach to stories begins to shift the definition of news. And by asking "What's the problem that this is designed to solve, and how does it link to the community," rather than "What's new," public journalists can offer citizens a handle that allows them to grasp problems much better. If there is a policy issue at hand, for example, a discussion at city hall, Hartig pushes reporters to begin with the problem and to write about it in terms that are relevant to people's lives as citizens. This approach is not inconsistent with what is traditionally called "humanizing" a story. But Hartig says it brings a human scale to stories differently, in a civic and public way. At the beginning when he would ask reporters "What's the problem?" they would often ask with incomprehension what he meant. Hartig might respond, "There's a debate going on here. They're trying to create some knowledge and some actions. What's the problem that this is designed to deal with—not the issue, not the current hot icon. What's the problem? Trace the problem back to the community." This idea of asking first for the civic problem is seen by Hartig as a break from the idea of "the news."[50]

The story of Julian Acken exemplifies what the *Pilot* is trying to accomplish. A computer programmer in his mid-thirties living in Virginia Beach, Acken volunteers for a program for African American boys at the local YMCA, where his own son is involved. He became active in his neighborhood after going through training at the Virginia Beach Neighborhood Leadership Institute, which taught him about city government, how to identify public problems, collect data, run meetings, and organize a civic league. Before he attended the institute, Acken read the *Pilot,* but mostly the sports.

> I read the paper all the time, but I didn't pay attention to the articles pertaining to citizens like me. . . . I pay attention to those articles now, where before I didn't because I really didn't know how it impacted me. I really didn't know how much of an impact I can make by attending these meetings and by voicing my opinion. I didn't know that my voice would be heard.

Now when Acken reads the public life pages, he often clips relevant material to post in his neighborhood. "I can blow that announcement up and post it in my community so that everyone sees it, even those that don't get a chance to read it." He also encourages his neighbors to read the *Pilot* now because it is a useful tool for citizenship. Acken says that a lot of meetings that are important to the community are publicized in the paper in advance: "So I don't want anybody telling me anymore, 'Well, they never tell us about it.' All you have to do is pick up the newspaper—and we will direct you to which newspaper to pick up—and you'll find out what you need to know."[51]

THE *CHARLOTTE OBSERVER:* WEAVING A WHOLE FABRIC

The *Charlotte Observer* has sustained its civic journalism for almost a decade. Like the *Pilot*, it has succeeded through a combination of self-conscious organizational change and an explicit focus on the values and routines of daily journalism. *Observer* editors and reporters no longer see the need for talking so explicitly about civic journalism per se; they believe that their daily practice speaks for itself. Editor Jennie Buckner, however, provides strong and consistent leadership on its core values. As noted earlier, she was with James Batten from the beginning of the Knight-Ridder initiatives and in 1993 returned to running a daily newspaper to put the ideas they developed together into practice. Among the ten sets of news organizations we have examined across the country, the *Observer* has developed the most systematic, deep, and ongoing dialogue with the community. It has evolved to a point where change is driven from the inside, at every level of the newsroom, and from the outside, in the firmly rooted expectations of a broad civic sector that the newspaper has made a promise to the community that it must keep.

Your Voice, Your Vote

Public journalism at the *Observer* began simply enough when in 1991 editor Rich Oppel asked lead political reporter Jim Morrill to find out what issues were on people's minds for the upcoming city council election. It was all "shoe-leather stuff," in Morrill's words, "driving on the west side, stopping at garages, at a barbecue restaurant, talking to folks." Morrill and his colleagues heard that citizens had become disenchanted with "big-ticket, world-class city projects," and wanted to go back to community basics.[52]

In 1992, the Poynter Institute, a journalism-teaching foundation in St. Petersburg, Florida, asked the *Observer* to participate in an election experiment similar to Wichita's, because the paper could attract and withstand serious national attention, and yet the city and paper were small enough for the project to have some visible impact.[53] The *Observer*'s Your Voice, Your Vote project polled one thousand residents to help develop a citizen's agenda focused on the economy and taxes, crime and drugs, health care, education, environment, and family and community life. Five hundred citizens agreed to serve on a panel that would be consulted throughout the election. The paper solicited queries from readers for the candidates and helped to spearhead a voter registration drive, as Morrill and others continued the conversations that had begun in 1991.

The community responded well, and the experiment continued through subsequent election cycles. In 1993 government editor John Drescher extended the new approach to coverage of the state in Your Voice in North Carolina, which involved the *Observer*'s capitol bureau.[54] That same year deputy metro editor Trisha Greene put together a series on education that began with a citizen poll on priorities in public schools and continued for several years thereafter.[55] Probably the most important advance beyond elections was the series of reports on the Freedom Park Standoff, which also began in 1993 and continued in various forms for at least five years. Freedom Park was in a predominantly white, affluent neighborhood that was being used as a center for automobile cruising by mostly African American young people simply looking for a place to hang out, but tying up traffic around the park nearly every weekend. When racial tensions in the park threatened to erupt in 1993, the paper made a conscious decision to apply the new civic approach to its reporting. Rather than simply reporting on the tension, it moved to develop solutions-oriented op-ed pieces from all parties involved. The printed public conversations were widely credited with averting a prolonged confrontation that could have led to violence.

When Oppel left in 1993 to become chief of Knight-Ridder's Washington Bureau, he was succeeded by Buckner. Her style of leadership as a teacher and team leader was particularly suited to catalyzing innovative practice within the organization. Her first major reporting project was Taking Back Our Neighborhoods, which would test these concepts in a new way and institutionalize them more deeply in decentralized team structures than ever before.

Taking Back Our Neighborhoods

"Nobody had ever properly reported on the causes of crime in Charlotte, certainly not through talking with citizens in the neighborhoods most affected,"[56] Buckner later recalled. Her intention was to do it differently this time. The paper received a grant from the Pew Center for Civic Journalism, and public life editor Rick Thames was charged with putting the project together. The story originated, in part, from a series of Freedom of Information requests made earlier to the Charlotte-Mecklenburg police department, which initially refused to release crime data in a usable form. Once the *Observer* won the right to the data, however, it had to decide what to do with it. The team had a choice. It could focus on those neighborhoods with the highest crime rates, which would be predominantly poor and African American, or it could choose a broader range of neighborhoods. In the belief that statistics alone should not drive the decision making, the team chose the latter course. It wanted to provide a grassroots-up look at crime but avoid easy racial stereotyping and further polarization. And it was determined to focus on potential solutions.[57]

The first reporting team consisted of four reporters: Liz Chandler, a nononsense, experienced, general assignment reporter; Gary Wright, the lead crime reporter; Ames Alexander, investigative reporter; and Ted Mellnik, computer assisted reporting specialist. The paper also used part of its Pew

Center grant to hire Charlayne Price-Patterson as community coordinator for the project. While she was hired primarily to coordinate the paper's liaison with the United Way and other community organizations, she took an active role in connecting reporters with neighborhood residents. No one on the initial reporting team was African American, but Price-Patterson, a black woman who grew up in inner-city Buffalo, New York, had extensive connections with the African American community in Charlotte.[58]

The overall design of Taking Back Our Neighborhoods was ambitious from the beginning and added innovations along the way as new media partners joined. The enthusiasm in the newsroom and community extended the project beyond the initially scheduled six months into a second year. In each of the ten neighborhoods eventually designated for coverage, a core advisory panel was established with the assistance of Price-Patterson, which included long-time residents and community leaders, as well as others with a direct stake in the area, such as local businesses and institutions. Together they organized a town meeting in a church or school in each neighborhood and worked with United Way to publicize a "resource fair," where citizens could link up with various local organizations, such as crime watches and legal services. A larger "citizens' panel" was formed from those polled in the neighborhoods about the impact of crime on their lives. High-crime neighborhoods were paired in coverage with others that had developed relatively effective ways of fighting crime.

The *Observer*'s commercial television partner, WSOC-TV, which called its project Carolina Crime Solutions/Taking Back Our Neighborhoods, produced stories on individuals, organizations, and neighborhoods actively engaged in fighting crime and transforming their neighborhoods in other ways. These aired several times each week during the 5:30 P.M. newscast.[59] The media partners, which also included WPEG-FM and WBAV-AM/FM with the largest market of black listeners, coordinated their coverage and urged their audiences to follow the stories in the other media as well. Thus, each neighborhood profile was launched with a special Sunday section of four to seven pages in the *Observer*, followed by a Sunday evening TV special at 6:30 focusing on solutions, with a panel of local residents, police officials, and civic leaders or with coverage of the town meeting. WPEG's *Community Focus* and WBAV's *Straight Talk* discussion shows also aired on the same day. Editor Jennie Buckner put her reputation fully behind the project with a front page photo and editorial. And the paper made it clear from the beginning in its stories and editorials that those who lived outside the neighborhoods covered also had a profound economic, psychological, and civic stake in reducing crime.[60]

Why the paper did what it did and how the project affected the city are closely linked to the *Observer*'s historical legacy. The *Observer* had previously played a range of roles in Charlotte: liberal advocate of racial integration, sometime civic booster and sometime critic of boosterism, mediating voice among competing civic factions. Although the paper has certainly not been hostile toward the poor, predominantly African American sections of Charlotte, these have also not been part of its core readership base. The *Observer* is read by Charlotte's elite, concentrated in and around the banking sector, and by its middle class, which includes both blacks and whites. During the 1970s, civil rights and neighborhood activists challenged the elite to open its ranks and decentralize some power to the neighborhoods through district elections to city council. In the 1980s, the Charlotte-Mecklenburg Citizens Forum was established, and in 1988 it conducted an ambitious project to evaluate the effectiveness of its civic infrastructure by utilizing the National Civic League's Civic Index in a much more inclusive network-building process than ever before, which was facilitated by NCL's Chris Gates. Out of this grew several specific projects, including Carolina Gives and the Charlotte-Mecklenburg Housing Partnership, as well as Central Carolina's Choices, an ongoing regional visioning network. The government set up a City Within a City program to address the needs of those mostly poor neighborhoods within the central core, and established leadership training for residents, as did several colleges and community-organizing groups. Led by Hugh Mc-Coll, chairman of NationsBank, Charlotte's elite also began to mobilize in the early 1990s to avoid the deepening division of the city into rich and poor, outer ring and inner core. It saw Atlanta, where business growth had outstripped the capacities of the city to deal with its own problems, as the example to avoid. Civic leaders from the middle and upper middle class wanted to preserve their own sense of Charlotte as a city where blacks and whites could live together and work out their problems in a civil manner, if not in total harmony. The African American middle class had as strong a stake in avoiding the widening of the race and class fissures as did whites.[61]

Taking Back Seversville

The neighborhood of Seversville is one of Charlotte's poorest. It had suffered from years of neglect by city and county government, school and park districts, and even by the Leland C. Johnson College, a historically black college separated from the neighborhood by a major street. It is not the most representative of the nine neighborhoods that were eventually covered, but it demonstrates the catalytic role that public journalism can play in a community.

As the project got under way, Seversville had an active neighborhood organization led by lifetime resident Wallace Pruitt, some commitment on the part of local churches, and investment by the Charlotte-Mecklenburg Housing Partnership. But other major problems had gone unaddressed. There were no gutters in the area, and flooding occurred during severe rains. A

German immersion school in Seversville did not serve the neighborhood; its facilities were closed to residents after school hours, and the neighborhood had no other recreational or meeting facilities. Because of drug dealing, the area was also one of the highest-crime areas in Charlotte. Citizens linked drug dealing to housing problems, particularly code enforcement, which allowed pockets of neglected housing to bring down the entire neighborhood. And housing was neglected because of a pattern of absentee ownership that had developed over more than forty years, as local cotton mills closed and sold off company-owned housing. Police Chief Dennis Nowicki, who had been hired from Chicago to implement community policing and had focused on Seversville as one of his first target areas, had achieved closer relations between citizens and the police, which led to more active cooperation in fighting the effects of crime. But there was little progress in getting rid of the drug dealing itself.

The first Taking Back Our Neighborhoods reports on Seversville were launched in January 1995. The kickoff began with a televised town meeting by the *Observer*'s key partner, WSOC-TV, which proved to be rather rancorous. Television hosts, whose involvement with the actual reporting and planning was limited, encouraged citizens to confront public officials, who not surprisingly were defensive and felt that the project was out to get them. In the process, the fine reporting by the *Observer* team was overshadowed by the televised public tent show. Some of the most flamboyant results of the meeting, such as the mayor's commitment to fund a new community center, got attention. Residents welcomed this news, but other city officials felt that this was decision making by publicity and that it disrupted hard groundwork and planning that had been done on behalf of all city neighborhoods.

Nonetheless, *Observer* reporting soldiered on for six weeks after the town meeting, and this is where the most important work was done. By listening closely to residents and providing them with public space to formulate what they felt were central problems, the paper and the follow-up reporting on television enabled several issues to come to the fore. By far the most important was the focus on absentee housing that had been lost in the early meetings. Citizens pointed out that community policing was fine but that without housing code enforcement, the roots of the problem would not be addressed. Police came to understand this concern but argued that only housing inspectors could write up violations. In response, community police officers, citizens, and the housing department began to work together more closely, identifying major problem areas and citing landlords for code violations.

The public attention to housing also helped to expand other housing efforts. The local Habitat for Humanity, the largest in the country after Atlanta, was already working in Seversville before the series began. After the first Taking Back Our Neighborhoods reports, more volunteers streamed in, and more homes were started. Executive Director Burt Green says that many new civic connections grew from the series, including a closer working relationship between Habitat, a Christian ministry, and the Charlotte-Mecklenburg Housing Partnership. Habitat serves people who make 40–50 percent of the median income, whereas the Partnership is a public-private venture funded by city and federal money and serves those whose incomes are above this line. Together they were able to coordinate their efforts to provide substantial new housing in Seversville.[62]

The policing and housing activities rippled outward in a virtuous cycle of civic problem solving. The German immersion school was opened up to neighborhood children after school, turning a potential community asset into an actual one. New street gutters were put in, further encouraging new home ownership and renovation. A local bank donated a double-wide trailer as a temporary community center. Citizens from all over Charlotte responded through the United Way with smaller donations of recreation equipment, computers, and other needs noted by neighborhood residents and published in the paper. And eighteen local law firms working pro bono filed public nuisance suits around the city to shut down local crack houses.

By 1996, crime had dropped significantly in Seversville, and murder rates plummeted in the broader area covered by the project. The response of citizens was clear and nearly unequivocal. Wallace Pruitt and his wife Louise consider the project pivotal to the neighborhood's turnaround. At a community meeting that we observed, Pruitt constantly referred to city and nonprofit officials with whom he stayed in touch on issues from schools and parks to lighting and water. A neighborhood street fair had drawn out AmeriCorps volunteers, who painted addresses on the new curbs. Urban League officials discussed GED programs. When two community police officers showed up, they were heartily welcomed and thanked. Neighborhood residents said they felt the coverage had been, in the words of one, "truthful to the neighborhood and its problems." This woman felt that there was more participation and neighborhood involvement after the project and that "kids in the area feel better about the police."[63]

In a focus group after the meeting, Pruitt pointed out that "we've been organized for a long time." He traced the origin of the community's action to the killing of a five-year-old a few years earlier. "Everyone decided it was time for a change," but he says that Taking Back Our Neighborhoods "jumpstarted our organizing." The community learned that

> together you can make a difference. Don't be afraid to speak out. . . . We came together as a community. People were afraid, but now they're more friendly and there's more cooperation. We all wanted the same thing: for the school, the community, and church to work together. The *Observer* played a part. . . . The news people called the shots as they saw it, and that got the city's attention. Now it's spread throughout the whole city, not just Seversville. But we started it. It don't take an army.

Maggie Morrow, a woman in her late fifties, said that after the project, "There are not as many dealers on the street. If people have any suspicions, they call the police. Now the police are harder on drug houses." Her neighbor, Lorraine Massey, in her forties, said, "It's definitely a safer place now. Neighbors know each other. And now the communication lines are open." She spoke of the new complex of forty apartments, the cleaned-up neighborhood, "the barren land turned into the community center. . . . A lot of dreams have been fulfilled because of the program. And the media helped; they covered us, and were there at every church meeting."[64]

Other civic actors echo these sentiments. Burt Green of Habitat told us that Taking Back Our Neighborhoods was "wonderful. It kept a focus on how important it is that we stay connected with our neighbors in the city within a city area." In fact, he was not able to keep track of the effects of the project on Habitat after the first fifty calls. He "just hung in" and when opportunities presented themselves, he tried to connect people.[65] Pat Garrett of the Charlotte-Mecklenburg Housing Partnership also had strong praise for Taking Back Our Neighborhoods. She cautioned, however, that some people in the community "had expectations that there would be immediate results. That's always dangerous." But she says that the project "made a lot of people pay attention. People talk that talk, but when you actually get turnout [at neighborhood meetings] and manage it, that's something." Still she warns that empowerment is "long, slow, and arduous. This was a piece that everybody contributed to, and it will take a long time."[66] Housing activist Jane Burts of the Charlotte Housing Organizing Project was somewhat more critical. She says the series got out a "lot of volunteers who gave time and money to assist the neighborhoods. But it was charitable rather than empowering activity. Still, food, clothing, and housing, as well as many other things were improved for the residents." Burts, however, also refers to the training that neighborhood leaders received. All of the leaders were brought together and "made more aware of what they could do for themselves as a community." Leaders met with people that they could call on in the future. Especially in the poorest neighborhoods, new connections that leaders could draw upon were forged.[67]

Even some city officials who at times felt under siege were positive. Police Chief Nowicki praised the project, even as he felt a bit bruised by it: "The *Charlotte Observer* didn't just give it a couple of seconds. It pointed out problems, and explored solutions with all the stakeholders: business, community, volunteers outside and in" the neighborhood.[68] Isaac Applewhite, assistant director of the Parks and Recreation Department and a prominent African American official, said of the project,

> In the beginning I was awestruck. It is not often you see media organizations, newspapers and TV, get together for the public good. They brought together

leaders in the community that had to respond to the people . . . [The project] put slumlords on notice; it informed people of their true right to assemble and formed an outlet for the general community to come together, communicate, and do something about their communities.

Applewhite's main concern was that "we absolutely must push back attempts to use this as a vehicle for selling more newspapers, getting people to watch programs. It must make a difference in the neighborhoods." He says that the timing of the project helped push the entire county park system to look at equity issues in the distribution of the parks' recreation equipment; many areas in the City Within A City still had playground equipment left over from the 1950s. Taking Back Our Neighborhoods also brought in volunteers and "opened the eyes of people who have good hearts and great minds, but sometimes they need glasses. It was an opportunity to clean their glasses off and look at it a little differently. Churches started to come through. Individuals' volunteer efforts are tremendous."[69]

But were affluent Charlotteans outside the City Within A City moved to think differently about their community or to take new kinds of civic action? About 175 members typically come to the weekly "uptown" meeting of the Charlotte Rotary Club. At the meeting we attended in May 1996, almost all were white, and most were middle-aged men. We spoke with twenty members. Fifteen were aware of Taking Back Our Neighborhoods. Jim Applebee, the Rotary's president-elect, said that Taking Back Our Neighborhoods had prompted his church, the prominent First Presbyterian, to take on a project in the Lakewood neighborhood, with two other churches, Christ Episcopal and Myers Park Presbyterian. The three are building a 3,200-square-foot preschool together, after residents said in the coverage that this was a more important need than additional private housing. Applebee said that there is no question that this involvement is a direct result of Taking Back Our Neighborhoods. Another Rotarian, in his seventies, urged residents to take more responsibility to fight crime in their neighborhoods, and noted that his church, largely white and upper class, has partnered with the African American Wesley Heights neighborhood as a result of Taking Back Our Neighborhoods. A white businessman in his fifties explained that he had held a number of discussions with friends, neighbors, and business associates as a result of the series and that it was a step toward restoring the neighborhoods. Henry Bostick, a marketing consultant, thought that the *Observer* "should be involved in focusing on problems and how neighborhoods can work together to take the neighborhoods back." He had discussed the project with his wife and friends. We heard similar comments from others. The only remotely critical questions concerned whether the paper would keep up its focus.[70]

Public life editor Fannie Flono, one of the *Observer*'s leading African American editors, offered another perspective on Charlotte's "substantial underclass," whom she describes as people who "never rise out of it." People would come

> to these town meetings and talk about one person in the community who graduated from high school. A lot of white people in this community didn't know that those kinds of communities existed in Charlotte. They were just shocked. They were amazed that there would be communities of folks, you know, thousands of people who would live in communities where one person in 1978 graduated from high school.[71]

This simple act of publicly recognizing the radical difference in life circumstances was the beginning of a larger attempt to grapple with the causes of these differences and what citizens together could begin to do about them. And it was part of a conscious strategy by the *Observer* to give residents living outside the high-crime areas a stake in revitalizing them. We found little naiveté among any of the parties—residents of the poorest communities, neighborhood leaders, civic leaders from black and white communities, city officials, or the paper itself—about what a long, slow process they were engaged in. No one treated the series as a magical beginning that would bring deep transformation quickly. But almost everyone spoke of it as a *necessary* beginning that had sparked a civic dialogue that might otherwise never have taken place, certainly not across such wide-ranging racial and class boundaries. And, as Wallace Pruitt of Seversville put it, "Our work with Taking Back Our Neighborhoods enabled us to affirm that we're first-class citizens, and that's how we want to live."[72]

Teams in a Learning Organization: Creating New Reflexes

Taking Back Our Neighborhoods unleashed a process of change that reverberated throughout the newsroom at the *Observer*. For the core group of reporters working on the project, their identities became distinctly wedded to doing public journalism as an essential, if now matter-of-fact, part of being good journalists, and they have incorporated elements of the project into their daily work.[73] The newsroom itself developed into a learning organization, and the teams modified traditional journalistic practices and routines in profound ways that, in turn, subtly transformed relationships among reporters and editors to each other and to the community.

The reorganization of the newsroom into teams was among the most important structural changes, one that served as the underpinning for many of the others. As in Norfolk, this reorganization was driven by a number of factors, including a corporate-wide strategy, for which Buckner herself, as vice president of Knight-Ridder, had been partly responsible. From the beginning, team reorganization was interwoven with Taking Back Our Neighborhoods. It flattened the hierarchy and diffused initiative and ownership of innovation among middle managers and reporters. It created a learning environment, in which teams could democratically set goals and team leaders could function as coaches. The teams themselves reflected a desire to make the entire news organization more civic. The most direct change linked to Taking Back Our Neighborhoods was the creation of a poverty beat, which cut across the teams working on public safety, education, children, and other areas. The reporters on Taking Back Our Neighborhoods were eventually assigned to many different teams, and thus the experience they gained during the project was distributed throughout the newsroom and carried into daily practice.

Buckner summarizes the lessons learned about the relation between public journalism and newsroom organization in this way:

> Well, you can certainly be a learning organization and not do public journalism. But if you're going to do public journalism, I think you have to be a learning organization, because the whole tenet of public journalism is you're listening a lot more and your coverage is informed more by what's happening in your community.[74]

The learning organization laid the foundation for a series of new routines and reflexes that included ways of listening and learning from the community, making time in the face of deadlines, reporting as problem solving, and achieving accuracy amidst complexity. In fact, every reporter we interviewed who had extensive public journalism experience said that she no longer even thought about whether she was "doing public journalism," because it had become a basic reflex.

LISTENING AND LEARNING

The heart of culture change at the *Observer* is learning new ways of listening. As Buckner says,

> You make it [listening] a value. You just say part of what you get paid to do, and part of what will make you successful, is being a really great listener. . . . [T]he really great reporters, I think, it spills out into their lives. That's why they're great. They immerse themselves in the world they're supposed to be covering.[75]

New forms of listening are created to be able to *learn from* the community, not just to *learn about* it. By reframing the listening process in this way, the organization makes a subtle but important shift away from fact finding and toward dialogue as the heart of news gathering. For Buckner, learning from the community is the most important function of the newspaper. Newspapers have to establish the basic facts, of course. But beyond that,

> you also need to understand who you're talking to, what are they worried about, how do you talk to them, where are the connection points, how are they seeing the issues? It might be very different from the way you're coming at it. If

you're upper middle class, you just might not see it the same way. So how are you going to make sure you're getting at it? A lot more discussion about those kinds of issues has to take place [in the newsroom].[76]

Creating this kind of listening involves a more decentralized organization in which individuals share ideas with others and take more direct responsibility for their jobs. Assistant Managing Editor Cheryl Carpenter says different reflexes begin to emerge from these new kinds of conversation:

> If the only conversation about the quality of the idea or how to go with it is a reporter talking to himself or herself, then what you get is probably traditional reflexes. If you get a bunch of people sitting around talking about it, you've got an eight-sided idea, . . . and I think that's when you start moving away from the black and white and moving toward gray.[77]

Assistant Managing Editor Jim Walser says the primary aim of the team structure developed in 1996 was to push responsibility for listening to the community further down. "We had a long debate about whether you need a public editor. . . . I think we have fifty-seven newsroom reporting jobs, not counting sports. . . . And in some ways, you need fifty-seven public editors."[78]

MAKING TIME

To create new ways of listening requires *making time* to listen. The idea of "surplus time" in a newsroom is an oxymoron. It is in the nature of a newsroom to beat deadlines in a race against time. Yet it is precisely surplus time, defined as time to think beyond the immediate facts, that is a central condition of doing public listening. This is why listening, conversation, and changes in ways of thinking about the public are so intertwined with new ways of organizing the newsroom.

Creating surplus time has to begin at the top of the news organization. The editor must be committed to making the time for reporters to think daily, as well as on special projects. In 1996, when Thames was still public life editor, Buckner defined *making time* as his central role:

> Rick's job is to work with all of our teams to help them think about finding the time, listening more, pulling reader groups in, whatever it is, and get a lot of things going. . . . It's the editor and reporter, the team leader and the team, talking about how we're going to find a way to cover for Joe so he can go out for two days and really live with the family that's dealing with whatever the issue is.[79]

Another aspect of making time to think differently is *slowing down* the newsgathering process in the middle of it. This demand flies in the face of common sense for most working journalists, but in fact, it is at the heart of creating a dialogic mode of newsgathering. It is necessary for breaking the old frames of reference in the process of everyday reporting. Carpenter sums up this process well:

> In journalism . . . you have to make decisions very quickly about what the story is: "It's a murder. We know what murderers do". . . . We go into hyper-mode. And those are the moments of glory. And so when we say, "Slow down. Think about it. Let's talk about what the story is about," it goes against everything that is valued from which newspapers operate . . . which is, "Get it, get it fast, and get it right". . . . You don't get awards for thinking in the newsroom.[80]

This idea that to "get it right" you have to slow down is one of the most important new routines to emerge from public journalism practices. Summing up everything else, it says that to listen well you have to stop and think, to slow down, to take the time to hear the public conversation without forcing it into a fixed set of habits or reflexes defined by traditional news gathering. This requirement foreshadows a new core value of public journalism: make the public conversation a starting point for everyday work.

REPORTING AS PROBLEM-SOLVING: SEARCHING FOR COMMON GROUND

Once listening to the public conversation becomes better established, other reflexes emerge. One of the most important is to *frame reporting as public problem solving*. This effort starts with listening for common ground. Carpenter describes this as asking,

> "What do these two sides have in common?" rather than "So and so says this and then you say this." "Where is there common ground between these two factions?" is a question that no journalism school, at least in my day, ever encouraged you to ask. To ask the point of intersection, . . . "Who might be able to solve this problem? Who do you need to talk to to solve this problem?" . . . It almost asks for better thinking and better definition of the problem by asking who's going to solve it.[81]

Carpenter links these kinds of questions to "down-the-road sort of thinking." Traditional reporting begins with the headline or lead, which then shapes the story and pushes it forward. This often results in assuming that no common ground exists. By not asking interview subjects to think counterfactually about what common ground might look like, the story stops short at the appearance of an impasse. Asking these kinds of questions makes a final story more interesting for readers. This is what Taking Back Our Neighborhoods did for Carpenter:

> When the project started, there was a tendency to oversimplify the community's problems. When we went into the neighborhoods, we thought it was going to be a story about bad people. And then we realized it's a story about volunteer organizations and law enforcement and citizen groups and churches and landlords. And suddenly it becomes this six-headed monster.[82]

Recognizing complexity, the "six-headed monster," begins to change the standards of accuracy. Rather than looking for the simple "quote" that can be assembled in a series of points and counterpoints, the simple answer itself becomes the starting point for interrogation. Carpenter calls oversimplification a challenge to accuracy:

> I am always on alert if I hear a very simple problem, because I hardly think they exist. And they sure don't exist in the way people think about their community. I mean, most of the regular folks out there know that everything is connected to everything else. And that's why we [journalists in general] don't ring true to them. . . . And that is the big way we've underestimated how readers think about the community. They hook it all up. We're the ones who don't.[83]

In this framing, accuracy is related to *recognizing and reporting complexity and connection,* so that a more holistic conception of the community and a more complex map of civic life become the baseline for measuring how accurate a story is. The traditional measure of accuracy—repeating or paraphrasing what an interview subject says faithfully—does not fall by the wayside. It is still a precondition for this more complex, and much more demanding, kind of accuracy. But these new forms of accuracy, which are linked to the representation of greater complexity, generate additional demands on both ethics and presentation. For Carpenter, this kind of problem is summed up in the phrase "'This is accurate, but is it true?' And sometimes I think the way to do a daily story is just to present the questions that we don't know the answers to." This kind of reporting moves beyond traditional ethics in *requiring that one's ignorance or doubt be publicly acknowledged* as a condition of conducting a dialogue. Journalists must say not only, "Here is what we know, presented faithfully," but also "Here is what we don't know."[84] Doubt becomes a part of the story, which, in turn, opens up the public space, or at least the narrative space, for genuine dialogue.

MOVEMENT NETWORKS AND DIFFUSION

If teams such as those at the *Charlotte Observer* and the *Norfolk Virginian-Pilot* were essential to transforming their newsrooms into learning organizations, they were no less critical to learning and diffusion within broader movement networks. Indeed, many of the key editors and reporters in our cases and others served as core faculty at the meetings conducted by Project on Public Life and the Press and the Pew Center for Civic Journalism. Each of these organizations, along with the Harwood Group, which provided critical consulting and research, expanded and deepened movement networks in largely complementary ways.

The PPLP seminars at the American Press Institute, which ran from late

1993 through 1997, combined theoretical discussion with intensive reflection on practice. Rosen was joined by Merritt at every session, and Carey participated on a regular basis. Lisa Austin played a critical role in developing and sustaining the network, both as an organizer who actively kept in touch with network members, and by reporting on their activities through a series of important reports that were made available to both public journalism practitioners and to the public at large. By the time PPLP disbanded, it had managed to convene what was probably the most systematic reappraisal of the foundations of the profession ever to occur among practicing journalists, which served to form the identity of the movement as a whole. Seminar participants ranged from a solid core, who would provide the cutting edge of innovation in their newsrooms, to a more diffuse circle of practitioners who received their first introduction to the ideas of public journalism and, in a good number of cases, went on to develop their own projects.[85]

The approach of the Pew Center was more pragmatic than that of PPLP. Beginning in 1994, it organized an ongoing series of workshops that asked practitioners to reflect on a range of reasons for doing civic journalism, problems and obstacles encountered along the way, and actual and potential solutions. Principal presenters and faculty at the workshops almost all attended PPLP seminars, ensuring continual theoretical reflection and cross-fertilization as they moved back and forth. The Pew Center was also the major funder of experiments, with grants ranging from approximately twenty-five thousand to fifty thousand dollars. These were distributed with the goal of encouraging multimedia ventures, community-media coalitions, civic problem-solving projects, and new forms of reporting and editing. From four projects in 1994, the program expanded to fund twelve in 1995 and seventeen in 1996. In the words of Ed Fouhy, Pew Center founder, the strategy was to let a "hundred flowers bloom" to see what worked. To encourage the practice of civic journalism at the highest level, the Pew Center created the James K. Batten Award to recognize the most successful civic journalism initiatives in the nation.[86]

By targeting many different groups of journalists through its workshops and reaching out to anyone, from the simply curious to the accomplished civic journalist, the Pew Center has self-consciously sought to build a broad movement. By the end of 1999 the center had held 31 workshops for 1,800 journalists and had supported 77 civic journalism initiatives involving 148 news organizations. Some 6,000 journalists and civic leaders receive the center's quarterly *Civic Catalyst*.[87] Fouhy and Schaffer's prestigious credentials as mainstream practitioners opened up possibilities for network building considerably beyond those available to PPLP. For instance, whereas PPLP tended to shy away from television journalists, Fouhy and Schaffer almost immediately established a working relationship with the Radio Television News Directors Foundation through Cy Porter, director of its Community Journalism Project, who did more than anyone else to build networks of public journalism practitioners within commercial television. By 1999, the two groups had conducted ten workshops together, involving hundreds of television reporters, producers, and news directors. The Pew Center also actively cultivated relationships with PBS through workshops for PBS reporters, producers, and news directors, both directly and under the auspices of the PBS Democracy Project, starting in 1996. It also funded a workshop to train National Public Radio news directors in 1995, along with an ambitious election project for NPR stations in 1996, discussed below.

The Pew Center has been active in other areas as well. In education it was a key early supporter of the Civic Journalism Interest Group within the Association for Educators in Journalism and Mass Communication (AEJMC), and it formed major partnerships with the University of Maryland and Northwestern University schools of journalism, as well as with the Harvard Nieman Center. It actively maintained contacts with the Society for Professional Journalists, and Schaffer has written for its newsletter, the *Quill.* In 1995, the Pew Center established a partnership with the Poynter Institute for Media Studies, one of the largest and most influential institutes for continuing education and reflection in journalism among both broadcast and print journalists. The Pew Center has also built relationships with minority journalists by cosponsoring events with the National Association of Black Journalists and the Maynard Institute, a leading think tank on issues concerning diversity in journalism. By 1999, the Pew Center managed to reach across one of the major barriers of resistance to civic journalism when it cosponsored a workshop with the Investigative Reporters and Editors on the role of investigation in strengthening community. By 2000, more than 550 civic journalism projects had been submitted to the Pew Center. The networks established by the Pew Center have been essential to diffusing the movement, to deepening the process of innovation in specific newsrooms, and to evaluating practice critically in the interests of further refinement.[88]

The Harwood Group has also played a central role in the development of public journalism theory and practice and has provided direct consulting services to help with organizational transformation. As we have seen, Harwood's *Main Street* study helped to establish the frame through which civic journalists began to understand citizen disconnection and possible reengagement. Harwood pioneered the techniques of community conversation at the *Miami Herald,* which later proved critical to the learning process at the *Norfolk Virginian-Pilot,* where he also helped to institutionalize the public life team before following Cole Campbell to help reorganize the *St. Louis Post-Dispatch.* Harwood developed civic mapping techniques at the *Wichita Eagle,* which were then diffused through the Pew Center publication, "Tapping Civic Life." Harwood also served as a consultant to N. Christian Anderson III at the *Orange County Register,* a resolutely libertarian newspaper that seemed an unlikely candidate for civic journalism. Harwood also worked with Anderson to develop *Timeless Values,* a report of the American Society of Newspaper Editors (ASNE), which paralleled the emerging values of public journalism, but in less threatening language, and provided yet another network for diffusion. To all of this work, the Harwood Group brought a peculiar combination of organizational consulting, sophisticated research, informed democratic theory, and linkages to projects beyond journalism itself.[89]

As the civic journalism movement has grown, innovative practices have diversified further. The *Colorado Springs Gazette* reorganized public life, business, and sports writing teams around a civic mission under the leadership of editor Steve Smith, formerly of the *Wichita Eagle* and Knight-Ridder. The *Gazette's* teams have pioneered such innovations as multistakeholder reporting on issues like school bonds, so that the perspectives of students, teachers, parents, and taxpayers are represented with the complexity they deserve, rather than the usual "on the one hand, on the other hand" reflex. A *Gazette* Training University has provided continuing education for staff. By the end of the 1990s, Smith had built what many regarded as one of the best civic papers in the country.[90] The *Orange County Register* has reorganized the beat system away from its predominantly institutional focus and has introduced a new management system with technology designed to get reporters out into neighborhoods. It has held hundreds of meetings with citizens from what it refers to as the "deeper layers" of political, ethnic, business, and other communities, and it has brought citizens, journalists, and public officials together, under the auspices of *Register* ombudsman Dennis Foley and the Kettering Foundation, to develop a publicly shared understanding of the relationship of media to the community.[91] At the *St. Louis Post-Dispatch,* Cole Campbell conducted an experiment in regional public deliberation, in which the extension services of Illinois and Missouri convene citizens on both sides of the Mississippi in a public visioning process, which was then extensively covered in the newspaper.[92] And at the *Spokane Spokesman-Review,* editor Chris Peck has undertaken a civic mapping project designed to create a community network database that the newspaper can draw upon to improve its coverage of all aspects of the community, while engaging in a collaborative data-gathering and data-sharing relationship with the community. The paper's Key Moments project seeks to reconstruct the critical points in the life cycle of youth in crisis to map community resources that might lead to positive outcomes. The *Spokane Spokesman-Review* was also the first paper to do civic environmental journalism on watersheds in 1992.[93]

As our discussion indicates, the diffusion of public journalism practice has proceeded along a number of tracks within and across larger newspaper corporations, within independent local newspapers and smaller regional groups, across types of media through local multimedia partnerships, and through an array of professional associations, educational institutions, consulting groups, and foundation-sponsored centers.

While public journalism has spread throughout the mid-1990s, its extent remains difficult to measure precisely in the absence of comprehensive surveys. The Project on Public Life and the Press found that at least two hundred of the almost fifteen hundred daily newspapers in the United States had tried some form of public journalism experiment by 1995. The number has grown since then, but the evidence is indirect, and some of it may reveal the basis for potential growth as much as actual practice. One survey by Paul Voakes published in 1997 by ASNE drew a random stratified sample of 1,037 journalists at sixty-one newspapers, who were asked to estimate four civic journalism approaches without the term itself being used to characterize them. This survey found that 96 percent of those surveyed support reporting on alternative solutions to community problems and trade-offs that may be involved; 88 percent support developing enterprise stories, backed up with editorials, to focus public attention on a problem in order to help the community move toward a solution; 71 percent approve of polling the public on pressing community issues and getting candidates to focus on them; and a strong 68 percent approve of conducting town meetings to discover key issues in the community and follow up with reporting on possible solutions. In a 1997 survey by Walter Lindenmann of 554 media executives that asked explicit questions about civic journalism, 56.1 percent of those surveyed agreed that "'civic journalism' has become an important means of enabling them to reconnect with their alienated communities by paying much more attention than they have in the past to what people think." And 51.1 percent agreed that sponsoring citizen forums usually results in better reporting of community issues.[94]

NATIONAL PROJECTS

Although civic journalism has been primarily a local phenomenon embedded in a larger national network of practitioners and institutions, there have been several attempts to develop projects of national scope. In contrast to most local civic journalism, however, the national projects have been led by public television and radio stations, rather than newspapers. Broadcast media enjoy inherent advantages for projects of national scope, and there is a good potential fit between the democratic mission of the public broadcast networks and civic journalism. Both National Public Radio (NPR) and the Public Broadcasting Service (PBS) have engaged in a series of projects, usually anchored in one or several innovative local stations.

The NPR Election Project of 1994 placed the concerns of citizens in five communities (Boston, San Francisco, Seattle, Dallas, and Wichita) at the center of national election coverage. It was developed and led by John Dinges,

NPR editorial director, and the Poynter Institute of St. Petersburg, Florida, and was supported by the Pew Center for Civic Journalism. It encouraged the development of media partnerships among local NPR stations, newspapers, and television stations, both public and commercial, and it built directly upon the experience of those previous media partnerships whose goal was to facilitate citizen deliberation in election years. By 1994, however, some of the lessons of the early 1990s had been absorbed, and the coverage itself was generally more creative. The partnerships were substantial, in Boston involving the *Boston Globe* and WBZ, the NBC television affiliate; in San Francisco, the *Chronicle* and KRON, the NBC affiliate; and in Seattle, the *Times-Intelligencer*. The commitment of NPR lent national legitimacy to the entire public journalism movement.[95]

The 1994 NPR election project gave rise to a spring 1995 meeting at the Harvard Nieman Foundation to develop a civic strategy for the presidential primaries of 1996, which Ed Fouhy predicted would be dominated by "the thirty-second spot, the HIV virus of American politics." The Citizens Election Project, as it came to be called, was sponsored by the Pew Center for Civic Journalism and the University of Maryland College of Journalism, and was headed by former *Time* Washington bureau chief Stan Cloud. Its chief goal was to demonstrate how modern political journalism might be done differently. Its focus was on Iowa, Florida, New Hampshire, and California, where it developed multimedia partnerships and extended the NPR group of participating stations to a total of ten cities. The Citizens Election Project also made the services of the Harwood Group and pollster Andrew Kohut of the Pew Center for People and the Press available to participating partners. The actual impact on Super Tuesday is difficult to determine, but the project did introduce citizen-driven presidential primary coverage for the first time on a statewide basis and helped spur a variety of partnerships that, for the most part, continue in some form up to the present. These include the San Francisco Voice of the Voter project; a Florida network of six newspapers and eleven television stations that focused on the issue of immigration; televised citizen forums in New Hampshire; and a series of town hall meetings in Iowa in conjunction with a national civic journalism project at PBS.[96]

In June of 1994, PBS president Earvin Duggan announced the formation of the Democracy Project, an ambitious attempt to place PBS at the center of the public debate over democracy. Addressing the PBS Convention that year, Duggan called for new cooperative ventures, improved national performance, and "experiments in how the system can think together, have ideas together. Democracy is messy, slow, and disorganized. By thinking out loud together, we can retake the high ground." Duggan offered four ideas for consideration. First, the system should embrace civic journalism. Public television could become a venue for reinventing journalism, helping to redefine the relations of leaders to the people. Second, public television should employ electronic town meetings at local and national levels. Third, coverage of politics should include deliberative polls of the sort that were being proposed by Professor James Fishkin of the University of Texas, to which we return shortly. And fourth, public television should extend joint coverage of politics in partnership with the commercial networks, as it did with NBC during the 1992 elections, both to improve the quality of public dialogue and to get the message of civic journalism to a wider public. With this vision established, Ellen Hume, a prominent media analyst from the Annenberg Center and former *Wall Street Journal* reporter, became director of the Democracy Project and sought to catalyze initiatives throughout the PBS system.[97]

Wisconsin Public Television assumed leadership of several such projects, beginning with Citizens '96, a national series of broadcasts focused on developing a citizen voice during the presidential campaign that was similar to the NPR initiatives. Building upon its experience with We the People in its home state and the Wisconsin Collaborative Project, which linked smaller PBS stations around the country in high-quality public affairs and cultural programming, Wisconsin Public Television formed a partnership with ten stations, each of which, in turn, developed local partnerships with newspapers and radio stations. The partners collaborated in producing a series of national broadcasts and in hosting local citizen forums that would inform topic choices and generate public interest. National and local civic groups helped in this and insisted on stressing a theme that continually reappeared in the local conversations in the coffee shops, homes, and workplaces that were taped for broadcast: citizen responsibility to tackle the problems of their communities. Citizens in the broadcasts spoke of the job insecurity and long working hours that had led some to spend less time with their kids, but they also recognized that they too had often shirked their responsibilities to spend time or had used money to buy their kids off. Senior citizens acknowledged the great strides many of them have made as a result of federal entitlements to Social Security and Medicare, but voiced their sense of responsibility not to shortchange the grandchildren and perhaps to shift some of these resources to earlier stages in the life course. Wisconsin Public Television led a similar partnership the following year called State of the Union, which aired its broadcasts around major national holidays, such as Mother's Day, Labor Day, and the Fourth of July.[98]

The National Issues Convention (NIC), which was aired on PBS in January 1996, represented another initiative within the Democracy Project. It was designed by James Fishkin, professor of government at the University of Texas, as a way to lend a deliberative citizen framing to the presidential primary season. The NIC brought 459 citizens, chosen through representative sampling techniques, to Austin for three days to deliberate about key issues in the U.S. economy, family life, and foreign policy. Their face-to-face discussions in small groups and a large assembly were preceded by the chance to read and study issue booklets presenting information and options in a balanced fashion. These were prepared by the Kettering and Public Agenda foundations according to a model refined through the National Issues Forums over the preceding decade (see chapter 6). Participants' views were surveyed before the process began and again after they had had a chance to discuss the issues with each other, with a panel of experts, and with Vice President Gore and a group of Republican presidential candidates. The *McNeil-Lehrer News Hour* aired thirteen hours of these deliberations, as well as a discussion among other public opinion experts on the significance of the polling. Approximately seventy journalists, many from public journalism news organizations, also came to Texas to report on the citizen deliberations.

While the NIC did successfully portray the desire and capacity of citizens to engage real issues beyond stereotypical public postures and labels and to revise their views through deliberation, it proved to be a very limited (and inordinately expensive) tool for shaping the discourse of presidential candidates, who engaged with it selectively and strategically. And its single-minded focus on a single design for deliberation, as useful as this design might be in some venues, squandered the opportunity to present the national television audience with a richer portrait of the available forms of citizen problem solving, which might have helped set a different tone for the 1996 campaign.[99]

TRADITIONAL JOURNALISM RESPONDS

Almost from the beginning, the public journalism movement struck a deep nerve in the journalism establishment. The strongest reaction came from editors and press critics on the East Coast, especially from New York. In a 1995 *Times Magazine* column, Max Frankel, former executive editor of the *New York Times,* condemned the movement as "fix-it journalism" because of its desire to refashion the news "into a more deliberate act of citizenship, dedicated to the solution and not just description of social problems."[100] Frankel said, in essence, that what was useful was not new, and what was new, the idea of "connections," would distort the news agenda and compromise newspapers. Among the other movement critics was Leonard Downie, Jr., executive editor of the *Washington Post,* who not only denounced public journalism but also proudly claimed that he had given up his right to vote in order to eliminate any appearance of bias in political news coverage. Other critics reacted to specific projects. David Remnick wrote in the *New Yorker* that he wanted to "run screaming from the room" after reading the statement of the *Norfolk Virginian-Pilot's* public life team. And Michael Kelley of the *New Yorker* reproached the *Charlotte Observer's* 1996 Your Voice, Your Vote project as antidemocratic because of its partnership among sixteen North Carolina news organizations to conduct a joint poll and citizens coverage of the 1996 elections.[101]

The response of the critics was remarkable for its hostility. Their criticism encompasses several interrelated categories, though these are sometimes mutually contradictory: civic journalism is nothing new; it is little more than a marketing ploy; it abandons the watchdog role of the press and even sides with specific groups in the community; and it abdicates responsibility when clear moral issues are at stake.[102]

The first criticism is that public journalism is "nothing new." It is what good reporters and editors have always done, "just good traditional journalism." Here critics claim at least some of public journalism's aims and practices: getting away from the desk, talking to citizens, and putting their voices in the paper. Critics acknowledge that public journalism might be calling attention to practices that "good newspapers" follow but that the industry in general had come to neglect. This effort hardly seems to justify a new name or movement. But this line of argument misses the larger question of framing issues through citizen deliberation and listening in ways that reveal the full complexity of problems. Providing a citizens' frame does, in fact, challenge journalistic tradition. And the fact that the challengers came from outside elite circles has threatened their legitimacy.

A second critique is that public journalism is just a marketing ploy, a way for panicked newspaper chains like Knight-Ridder or Gannett to boost profits. As these critics themselves acknowledge, however, public journalism requires more, not less, reporting. Public listening, citizen polls, special projects, and public life pages, whether one likes them or not, are expensive. They take more, not fewer resources.[103] While corporations such as Knight-Ridder under James Batten emphasized the reinvestment in community to increase readership, this was a long-term investment that was unlikely to show short-term gains in profitability. And expanding readership could be credibly linked to enhancing democracy, not just securing the bottom line.

A third line of criticism claims that public journalism leads to community boosterism by editors who want to be loved by the public and who are willing to abandon journalism's essential watchdog role, with its emphasis on misconduct and malfeasance. The deeper issue concerns the abandonment of the conflict frame as the primary lens for local public life. Here public journalism and its critics do at least partly understand each other and clearly disagree. Public journalists hold that they recognize conflict and engage in good investigative reporting as watchdogs.[104] But they also develop frames based on citizens' perceptions that problems can be complex "six-headed monsters" that require strategies for achieving common ground and mobilizing untapped community assets across group dividing lines. A variant of this criticism is that public journalists become advocates in their news pages for specific groups or strategies within the community. While a handful of cases do give some credence to this claim, critics systematically confuse advocating for democracy and advocating the interests of one side or another in a community conflict. This is a distinction that they have seemed uniformly unable to make.

A fourth set of criticisms, which stand in ironic contrast to the charge of advocacy, is that public journalists abdicate both their judgment and responsibility to point out moral violations where they occur. This criticism implicitly recognizes a central idea of public journalism, namely, that editors and publishers have had interests and agendas that they have pursued. Although one strand of modern journalism's mythology holds that the only proper place for moral opinion is the editorial pages, another equally important one holds that timely news coverage of morally significant events can and *should* affect their outcomes.

The case repeatedly offered by critics was the civil rights movement. They asked what would have happened if the editors in the South had been public journalists. Would they have gone to their (white) citizens, listened to their communities, and when they heard that the community wanted segregation, would they have simply reported on the community's will? This example ignores at least three central historical issues. First, the implicit definition of community used by the critics is the white southern community. A hypothetical argument could be made that were southern editors committed to talking to *all* of their citizens, engaging in community-wide deliberation according to inclusive democratic principles, the voices of African Americans might have been represented more clearly and earlier than they were. Second, most southern editors did *not* cover the civil rights movement, or did so reluctantly. It was only the African American movement of civil disobedience that forced the issue on both the media and the government. Third, among those editors who did show moral courage, their connections with their communities often allowed them to take the stands that they did. This was true of the Greenville, Mississippi, *Delta Democrat-Times*, run by the family of Hodding Carter, III, a prominent contemporary supporter of civic journalism. As Carter notes, "We debate as though we honestly believe that we can't chew gum and walk down the steps at the same time, that we cannot involve people in the process and at the same time speak the truth to power."[105]

The debate between public journalists and their critics has never been wholly engaged. While public journalists have directed their criticism to the heart of contemporary journalism, more often than not the critics of public journalism have fought against a straw man. Nonetheless, some of the critics' concerns remain valid for any advanced practice of public journalism, as its best practitioners fully realize. The watchdog function remains central for American journalism and should not be diluted in the interests of common ground. Even as journalists work to bring citizens and civic associations into new forms of deliberation on problems and solutions, they must continue to hold citizens themselves accountable and report critically on nonprofits. And civic journalism needs to remain alert to any tendencies to dilute its practices in the interests of simply boosting circulation.

By the end of the 1990s, public journalism's values and practices were beginning to be absorbed even by some of its severest critics, as the *New York Times, Washington Post,* and *Philadelphia Inquirer* incorporated various techniques, especially in political reporting. Although Max Frankel has never changed his mind about the movement, he addressed its central concerns in a November 1998 column on the role of television in the election just past:

> I get ninety-three channels on my TV screen and not one treats me as a caring citizen. Not even the half-dozen stations that pretend an interest in local news showed any interest in helping me cast an intelligent vote last Tuesday. . . . Nonetheless, having neglected to cover the campaign, the hypocrites on my screen piously urged me on Election Day not to neglect my duty to vote. They seemed wholly indifferent to their failure to help me.[106]

CONCLUSION

Public journalism has emerged as a response to the readership crisis of newspapers and concerns about the role of media in a democracy. Within the span of a decade it has developed from a few small experiments to a national movement that rivals any in the previous history of the American press. The leading intellectual proponents of public journalism have renovated the philosophical legacy of Dewey and generated a new journalistic paradigm to grapple with the more complex problems and publics existing at the turn of the twenty-first century. Working journalists and editors have devised a panoply of new models and practices for helping citizens to set public agendas, hold officials accountable, and elicit civic initiative. They have refined new methods of listening to ordinary citizens, framing issues, generating usable knowledge, and enabling common problem solving. Public journalists have confronted difficult and divisive issues of race, poverty, crime, and economic development in ways that give fresh voice to groups often marginalized by elite debates and that prompt new civic partnerships across neighborhood and institutional boundaries. Beginning with small and medium-size cities in the Midwest, South, and Pacific Northwest, innovative reporting models have been diffused throughout the newspaper world and to a lesser extent in public broadcasting and commercial television. Models of sustainable participative management, organizational learning, and multimedia partnership have also been established. Through the initiative of the Pew Center for Civic Journalism, Kettering Foundation, and Project on Public Life and the Press, a robust national learning network has emerged and has broadened and deepened through partnerships with professional and academic associations and institutions. While reorienting the public values and commitments of journalists to the democratic enterprise, civic journalism has seldom compromised core professional norms of objectivity through direct advocacy or partisanship. It has thus largely been able to weather the storm of criticism from traditional journalism and has established that good professional journalists can be strong partisans of civic democracy.

The emergence and growth of civic journalism represents a strategic response to available opportunities for democratizing the public sphere in the United States in the last decade of the twentieth century, though by no means one that alone will be adequate to the challenges of rapidly changing media environments. Civic journalism responded to the long-term crisis of newspaper readership by mobilizing resources and networks within the corporate world and by renovating the ideals of public trusteeship that were shared by strategically situated innovators. It also leveraged institutional resources and networks within public broadcasting in ways that have enabled innovators partially to redeem the system's original public mission of nurturing local democracy. At a time when new community-building initiatives were emerging in various arenas, but there existed neither an effective citizen movement to democratize mainstream media nor a sustainable model of citizen oversight, such as news councils, civic journalists created a professional, nonadvocacy, community-wide model for reconstructing local and regional public spheres.

A democratic public sphere, to be sure, contains many other necessary forms of deliberation and contestation, including those linked to interest group advocacy and social movement organizing. The latter can spawn alternative media for specific groups and causes or work with mainstream journalists to create alternative news frames for covering issues and movements. Citizens and public interest groups can organize to create direct forms of accountability of news institutions to the public, such as local and national news councils, ombudspersons, and greater public ownership.[107]

Civic journalism may clearly not represent the full array of media strategies needed to democratize the public sphere. But it has responded strategically and relatively effectively to existing opportunities and has developed an invaluable model of community-wide deliberation that elicits democratic agenda setting and complex problem solving among civic and government actors. Amid powerful tendencies to segment audiences and fragment publics through new communications media, as well as through many new social movements, public journalism offers a countervailing terrain of common deliberation, problem solving, and civic identity formation. In our view, it is an indispensable model that provides critical components for a democratized public sphere that neither traditional journalism nor advocacy journalism can provide. Its contribution is essential, even if the media system were to generate new forms of direct public accountability and democratized ownership in the coming years.

Increasing corporate concentration in all of the communications media undoubtedly changes the environment in which civic practices can continue to develop. The emergence of the public journalism movement depended, in part, on the strong support of James Batten at Knight-Ridder and several other CEOs. Corporate headquarters authorized the experiments, or at least created an atmosphere of benign neglect in which they could be nurtured by local editors. But the frenzy of consolidation generated by the growth of the Internet is leading many of those same headquarters to shift attention away from community life and toward cyberspace. Knight-Ridder is only one example, if the most important one, in which corporate strategy has swung away from its earlier public concerns. While civic journalism has managed to grow and refine its work in many settings, it thus remains a fragile achievement.

Creating a democratic public sphere and "information commons" within the new communications environment will require many complementary efforts at the local and state level and in national policy making. Some are already evident, especially at the local level. For instance, there are now more than three hundred community technology centers in the Community Technology Centers Network, which grew initially from neighborhood centers, settlement houses, and public libraries and were supported by government programs, such as HUD's Neighborhood Networks, the Department of Commerce's National Telecommunication and Information Administration (NTIA) grants, and the Corporation for Public Broadcasting's Community-Wide Education and Information Service (CWEIS) grants. The primary mission of community technology centers is to provide access and teach computer literacy to citizens in low-income communities, and they often work closely with civic organizations, churches, and nonprofits in the surrounding community. The Association for Community Networking counts some one hundred fifty community or civic networks as members. These electronic groups sprang from the "free nets" and the community networking movement beginning in the 1980s, and they offer community information resources and training for local groups. Libraries for the Future is the leading national organization working with professional associations and local civic groups to develop new models of libraries as spaces for public problem solving. Local projects range broadly from environmental justice and sustainable development information initiatives in Harlem, New York, and Cambridge, Massachusetts, to training youth as community reporters and editors in Oakland, California, and Newark, New Jersey. More than one thousand public, educational, and governmental (PEG) access cable channels are members of the Alliance for Community Media, which supports local public access organizing and increasingly provides Internet and web training at its centers. The Civil Rights Project is currently working with America Online to develop "circuit riders" to teach low-income and minority communities how to access and best utilize the information resources that are available.[108]

These networks and projects play an important role in developing local civic information infrastructure accessible to everyone and enabling community problem solving to draw upon the full power of the communications revolution. Public policy for democracy in communications will need to build upon these civic efforts and fashion law and regulation around a new concept of the public good in a post-scarcity information age. It will require national policy to ensure that the rapidly commercializing Internet does not crowd out this emerging civic information space. Unfortunately, the passage of the Telecommunications Act of 1996 lifted many of the barriers to corporate concentration that still existed. Since the mid-70s, a loosely coordinated network of organizations representing the public interest has been fighting a series of rear-guard actions before the Executive, the courts, and Congress to prevent the erosion of hard-won gains. Success of this effort will require further bridging of the gap between community information efforts oriented toward local needs and public interest advocacy in Washington.[109]

Public journalism has generated capacities and networks roughly comparable to those in our other three arenas of civic innovation during their first decade of existence, and the movement now faces environmental uncertainties probably not much greater than they did at similar points in their development. Nonetheless, without increased civic action that strengthens the demand side for what professional journalists working in commercial and public news organizations can supply, public journalism will confront serious limits. The most sustainable changes seem to occur where at least moderately vibrant civic life thrives outside the newsroom, and specific institutions and projects—such as the Neighborhood Leadership Institute in Virginia Beach and community visioning projects in Charlotte—support the efforts of citizens. Just as the public journalism movement has developed by learning from civic innovation in other arenas, its future is clearly linked to civic renewal on a broad scale.

SIX

The Civic Renewal Movement

Over the past decade a civic renewal movement has begun to emerge in the United States. It draws directly upon the themes and models of innovation in community organizing and development, civic environmentalism, healthy communities, public journalism, and other forms of collaborative engagement. But it also attempts to raise these to greater prominence in American politics and to define the contours of a much grander mission: revitalizing American democracy for the twenty-first century. The civic renewal movement seeks to build relationships *across* associational networks and policy arenas and to further cultivate common language and action frames. It also seeks to build bridges across some familiar ideological divides of Left and Right. It increasingly calls itself a movement and is beginning to be recognized by others as such, even if its exact contours and purposes are still being defined. In 1994, after the launching of several projects for a "new citizenship" and "national renewal," David Broder of the *Washington Post* referred to the emergence of a new "citizenship movement," as did William Raspberry in the same publication, as well as a variety of local journalists and editors thereafter. In 1998, after key actors in these and similar initiatives had worked for more than a year as part of the National Commission on Civic Renewal, the phrase "civic renewal movement" started to become more common, and it is the one that we ourselves prefer.[1]

In this concluding chapter we set several tasks. First, we develop a preliminary empirical understanding of this nascent movement. We begin by examining some of its core texts to see how the movement attempts to rethink what it means to be a citizen and how citizens act in the world. This constitutes what social movement theorists refer to as the fundamental symbolic work of all movements in reconstructing identities and reframing the scope and meaning of civic action. We then examine in greater depth the organizations and networks at the core of the movement and the role of key movement entrepreneurs in building it. In particular, we focus on three organizations that have been especially critical in developing and refining the themes of civic renewal—the National Civic League, the Kettering Foundation, and the Center for Democracy and Citizenship. These three have also served as important nodes linking a broad range of other important movement actors and networks. Our analysis draws upon extensive interviews and field observations of meetings and other activities that have had movement building as either their primary task or at least an important secondary one. We also draw upon our insights as engaged practitioners in some of these activities, even as we step back to examine them through the lens of relevant social science frameworks, such as social movement theory.

Second, we argue that a nonpartisan movement for civic renewal is needed for the work of innovation to progress much further and to help revitalize American democracy. Without a movement, much civic innovation will remain invisible and segmented, unable to inspire broad and vigorous commitment or to redefine the underlying dynamics of policy and politics as usual. But if movement networks are to extend to the broadest range of civic groups engaged in vital public work, as well as into the heart of institutions where diverse stakeholders work to transform mission and practice, then the movement will need to maintain a principled, nonpartisan stance in relation to political parties and candidates. This position does not exclude public accountability procedures similar to those employed by IAF groups vis-à-vis candidates and elected officials—indeed, it invites even more extensive uses of such efforts to make electoral politics more responsive to civic initiative. Nor does principled nonpartisanship exclude relationships with activists who also strive to revitalize parties as civic institutions in their own right. But it does not link civic renewal *directly* to party renewal.

Third, we examine whether it is possible for this nascent civic renewal movement to flourish in the coming years, and we discuss a number of movement-building challenges it must confront. Though the movement has learned much from civic innovation in various arenas, it still has not established robust relationships with many key networks and intermediary organizations operating within them. And even where there are established relationships, they often do not extend very deeply within organizations. Nor has the movement yet elaborated a set of common tasks around which these networks might build relationships based on mutual self-interests. In other words, the movement has not yet developed a compelling enough set of rationales, incentives, and activities that would respond to the concern that civic organizing networks invariably have, namely, how will a broader movement for civic renewal help in the work that we already do, and why should we commit scarce time and resources to building it?

To be sure, the civic renewal movement seems an unlikely movement. It diverges in important ways from recent democratic movements for civil rights and social justice, and thus does not have available some of the symbolic resources and tactical repertoires that have enabled these movements to develop. The civic renewal movement will have to manage the difficult tasks of drawing upon the energies and insights of other democratic movements, even as it challenges key aspects of the rights and justice frames through which they define problems and orient action. And it will have to develop a more elaborate conception of the political economy of citizenship that will be able to address the productive roles of democratic citizens in creating public and private wealth in dynamic and global marketplaces and enjoying the fruits of their labor in a fair and just manner. But if the civic renewal movement is an unlikely movement, it also builds upon some of the deepest democratic traditions in America and can leverage many important institutional and cultural resources for the tasks ahead. While its future is still uncertain, a range of movement-building strategies exists that can be tested in the coming years. We conclude with one specific proposal that can build strategically upon existing networks and repertoires yet can make a dramatic claim to cultural authority and visibility for the ongoing public work of citizens in building the commonwealth and renewing the legacy of self-government. We call this a National Civic Congress, which would convene annually or bi-annually on the Fourth of July.

RECONSTRUCTING CITIZEN IDENTITIES

Constructing a collective identity and defining an operative "we" that acts in the public arena are among the most critical tasks of any social movement, as much recent theorizing and empirical work have shown.[2] For the civic renewal movement this challenge occurs on at least three levels: (1) reconstructing the identity of "citizens" as competent and responsible actors authorized to do the ongoing public work of building community and democracy and distinguishing it from other common identity constructs through which people tend to view their civic and political roles; (2) developing an "elaborated master frame" that establishes credible commonalties and complementarities among the various kinds of civic innovation and linking these to the broader task of revitalizing civil society and democratic institutions;[3] and (3) articulating an identity for itself as a "movement" that builds upon the accomplishments of other social movements that have been critical to achieving rights of democratic inclusion and participation, while simultaneously distinguishing itself from these movements and providing critical reflection on their limits.

We begin by examining some of the core texts produced by key movement thinkers and organizations, and we later return to a fuller analysis of the historical trajectories and networked relationships that have shaped their production. These documents have circulated widely in circles concerned with civic renewal and have been used to fashion other derivative statements with wide dissemination through a variety of organizational and media networks. We stress texts that have been fashioned collaboratively so as to accommodate—if not always reconcile—a variety of organizational and intellectual perspectives within the movement and to appeal to a broad spectrum of actors through their simplifying of complex themes. Of course, these texts draw not only upon civic practice but also upon a larger scholarly literature, in which lively debate and disagreement occur over virtually every important term, including core concepts such as "civil society," "deliberative democracy" and "community."[4]

The central motif of the civic renewal movement is that "we as citizens must reclaim responsibility for and power over our nation's public affairs."[5] *Responsibility* entails at least several things beyond the usual list of duties to obey laws, pay taxes, vote for representatives, or protest injustice. It involves responsibility for engaging in the shared tasks that build communities and create the commonwealth on an everyday basis or, in the words of Jane Addams, for doing the "civic housekeeping" needed to reproduce the republic. It includes finding ways to collaborate across all kinds of professional and organizational boundaries and to define the civic dimension of every occupational identity. Democracy is fundamentally the shared work of citizens of modest virtue acting pragmatically to solve problems, build productive relationships, and produce things of value. Democratic work is what school children do when they raise baby oysters, plant acorns, and gather water quality data to restore the commonwealth of our ecosystems—and in the process build productive relationships with adult mentors and agency officials based on respect for the contributions that each set of partners is able to make. Democratic work is what COPS and Metro Alliance members do when they spend thousands of hours with their fellow parishioners encouraging them to apply for—and expecting them to succeed in—Project QUEST, a program that they themselves helped to design. Democratic work is what nurses do when they come to public forums to help fashion a deliberative values framework for state health reform, and it is what civic journalists do when they craft new ways to foster responsible and informed public debate that guides policy makers and elicits further democratic work by citizens themselves.

Responsibility means working on common tasks even with people who may share little in common with us and, indeed, may have fundamentally different values on some issues. Thus, the movement enlarges the imagination of what is possible and necessary by highlighting "difficult cases" of common work, such as the work of pro-life and pro-choice activists who collaborate to expand adoption and maternal health services or the work of the militant, gay ACT-UP and Christian fundamentalist activists who spontaneously clasp hands in a great cheer after fashioning a bill for the Colorado state legislature on a mutually acceptable AIDS education program for the schools. Each set of activists accomplished productive work of value to their communities and to a larger polity torn by divisions, even though they disagreed deeply on important values and would continue in other contexts to mobilize around them, as is fully appropriate in a pluralist society.[6]

For most citizens most of the time, collaborative work will not require such a test of values, though it may require understanding and negotiating varied interests in a difficult search for common ground. There are many everyday opportunities to reframe the meaning of the work that we do and to uncover new sources of civic vitality that can improve our communities and transform our institutions. But "how 'the people' might become a responsible public," is a central challenge that demands that we be alert to the "danger of being soft on citizens," as David Mathews argues.[7] Citizen politics thus also means citizens taking responsibility to "own their problems" and not simply to project the causes of these problems onto other social actors. It means a responsibility to deliberate about complex issues and causes, to consider various costs and possible trade-offs, and to struggle to reframe issues in ways that might build upon some set of shared values and lead to mutual gain. Strong democracy requires responsible and informed public deliberation among citizens, complementing and catalyzing deliberation among elected and appointed officials. It is strong talk, sometimes harsh talk, but never simply talk, as it seeks to define ways that citizens can continue to carve out productive roles for themselves beyond decision making. "Democracy means not only discussing our differences, but also undertaking concrete projects with our fellow citizens" and having "real work to do."

The civic renewal movement contrasts this identity of "we as citizens" to other pervasive views. Responsibility for ongoing public work is much more demanding and multifaceted than that required of mere "voters" or "taxpayers," two of the most typical designations in everyday public discourse. "Voters" exercise their rights and fulfill their obligations once every couple of years and perhaps make serious efforts to stay informed in the interim. Yet their engagement does not necessarily extend further, as they wait to give thumbs up or thumbs down to candidates and referenda that offer them consumer choice in the political marketplace. "Taxpayers" provide resources for public programs through their hard-earned income, but the connection of their work to producing public goods ends there, as they wait in judgment on officials who put those resources to good or bad, efficient or inefficient uses. "We as citizens" are also not primarily "consumers" of government services without concomitant responsibilities to make those services work. Thus reinventing government by simply making it more consumer friendly, without at the same time reinventing citizenship, will not ultimately be able to deliver on its promises. "We as citizens" are also not primarily passive "victims," even in those instances when we have been genuinely victimized. And the renewal movement cautions against popular discourses and program designs that develop further vested interests in the kinds of victim identities that have proliferated in recent years. Related to this is the movement's attempt to transform "client" identities, rooted in asymmetrical relations of dependence on professionals and one-way claims to program entitlements, into the identity of citizen as "coproducer" of services and "community-builder" responsible for nurturing productive relationships and mobilizing their individual and community assets as well.

"Advocate" and "protester" identities have been crucial to winning essential rights of recognition and participation in social and political life for groups previously excluded, and they help to reframe public problems in critical ways. But for the civic renewal movement, such identities often become so moralized that they tend to locate righteous action on only one side of a polarized divide, project all blame onto evil oppressors, and leave too little room to work pragmatically across stylized boundaries. And advocate identities embedded in discourses of the "rights revolution" tend to become stripped of responsibilities to consider the full complexity of problems and the relative costs of various solutions or to weigh other worthy claims on social resources. The "we as citizens" of the civic renewal movement recognizes the full dignity of diverse groups within a multicultural polity and validates the struggle for inclusion of those previously marginalized. It regards "our diversity as a strength for practical problem solving." But it insists on "citizenship as a unifying creed" and community building as a way of engaging all groups in common tasks, and thus resists strong versions of identity politics that highlight group differences and classify special oppressions.[8]

For "we as citizens" to reclaim responsibility requires *power* and *skills*, two other key identity-forming components in movement thinking. While power has many institutional and cultural sources, and is distributed very unevenly, developing efficacious identities as citizens requires greater emphasis on enlarging power as the capacity to act and to build public relationships. It is "power with" and not "power over," interactive rather than unidirectional, multiplicative rather than zero-sum. It is power modeled, at least partly, upon women's roles as nurturers of community in everyday life and on themes and practices raised to prominence by the women's movement and congregational organizing.[9] Such power is manifest when the congregations of COPS and Metro Alliance leverage their social capital, protest capacity, and public relationships to bring business, political, and educational leaders in San Antonio to the table to develop a collaborative strategy on job training and placement at livable wages, rather than succumb to the unilateral power of corporate capital to shut down the Levi Strauss plant or adopt the power-resistance strategy of another local group that simply attempted to prevent the closure. Expanding power means developing citizen leadership on a systematic basis throughout society. This requires significant investments in skill building and the arts of democracy, because the pragmatic work of citizens increasingly involves a complex interplay of interests, problems, and relationships, and because holding all power accountable presents a permanent challenge. As complexity increases the challenges of securing civic trust and devalues some older forms of social capital, so must we increase our investments in developing civic leadership skills and models appropriate to the tasks at hand. The movement thus places great emphasis on learning from "best practices" ("civic practices" or "community-building practices") and on providing ordinary narratives that can serve as templates for successful problem solving.[10]

REFRAMING CIVIC ACTION

Reconstructing citizen identities is but one part of a larger challenge to reframe the meaning and scope of civic action and democratic politics. As David Snow and Robert Benford define them, "collective action frames" are "emergent, action-oriented sets of beliefs and meanings that inspire and legitimate social movement activities and campaigns."[11] Frames organize experience, identify problems, attribute blame, regulate relationships, and guide action. Some collective action frames are relatively restricted to specific domains, while others can be elaborated to address a broader range of problems. The civil rights master frame exemplifies an elaborated frame, as its core principles of equal rights and opportunities regardless of ascribed characteristics could be extended from African American struggles to the women's, elder, disability, Native American, student, gay and lesbian, and other rights movements.

The civic renewal movement has begun to develop an elaborated master frame with expansive potential similar to that of the civil rights movement, yet without being primarily a rights or justice frame. The reframing activity of the civic renewal movement is of two kinds, perhaps best viewed as primary and secondary reframing. On the primary level, congregation-based community organizing, the community development and healthy communities movements, civic environmentalism, and public journalism are each engaged in reframing within particular domains. Each competes in significant ways with rival frames of both elite and other social movement actors. Community development and community building thus challenge the frames of various poverty policy and social welfare elites, as well as antipoverty and social justice movements that focus primarily on income transfers and social service entitlements. Watershed, ecosystem, and restoration movements challenge both expert-based and environmental movement frames that are overreliant on command-and-control regulation or adversarialism, even though they locate themselves within the broader environmental movement. The healthy communities movement challenges the dominance of the acute-care model of medicine, as well as advocacy frames focused primarily on the distribution of health as a commodity. The civic journalism movement challenges core professional frames and practices of disinterested objectivity, as well as social movement versions of advocacy journalism. Similar reframing processes are taking place in the community justice movement, new urbanism in architecture, community-based approaches within the social services, community youth development, libraries as public spaces and information commons, the civic engagement movement within higher education, and elsewhere.

For its part, the civic renewal movement recognizes these primary reframings within specific arenas as the foundation of its work and seeks to build upon them. On a secondary level, however, its own reframing takes the form of discovering, validating, and enhancing the commonalties and complementarities among various forms of civic innovation and community building. It stresses that these are of a piece, that they employ many common practices and share many elements of a common discourse. To be sure, key actors within each of these arenas have already been making such connections. They have been learning on both parallel and intersecting tracks over the past several decades, in some cases borrowing ideas and models from each other or transposing them directly as their own career paths cross arena boundaries. For many, this has been facilitated by shared networks and formative experiences in the participatory democratic movements of the 1960s and 1970s. Thus secondary reframing by an emergent civic renewal movement appears as a logical next step to raise this learning to a higher level within the broader polity and to "amplify and extend the master frame in imaginative and yet resonant ways."[12]

The movement also provides an overarching narrative of how the practice of citizenship has eroded over time and attributes blame to a variety of historical forces. And it seeks to embed these within a master frame that reconfigures the relationships among key societal sectors to enable collaborative problem solving and productive public work to assume center stage. In particular, its master frame highlights a threefold ideal of society as composed of robust civil society, catalytic government, and embedded markets.

Civil society consists of a broad range of voluntary civic associations, churches, mutual aid societies, and other groups that mediate between government and the market and provide opportunities for developing civic leadership and nurturing the values of responsibility and self-government. Civil society provided the key to early America's democratic vitality, but according to the civic renewal frame, it has eroded and contracted over a long period of time as a result of the enormous growth of corporate and government actors and the spread of narrow professional ideologies and practices in these two sectors, as well as among nonprofit organizations within the third sector itself. This erosion of civil society has constricted the space in which citizens learn the arts of self-reliance, common problem solving, and democratic self-government and has provided the soil in which narrower identities of the citizen as client, consumer, and claimant have flourished.[13]

A central component of renewing civil society, of course, is "community building." While this term has varied meanings, it decidedly does not imply the restoration of traditional, self-enclosed, or racially exclusive communities of the past. The master frame of the civic renewal movement recognizes a "pluralistic web of communities" connected externally through links to the city, region, nation, global economy, and biosphere, and internally through relationships among families, neighbors, associations, local institutions, and businesses. Community building requires an emphasis on the community's own strengths, rather than its deficits, and on "mobilizing assets" of individuals, associations, and institutions. This way of framing community action is borrowed from McKnight and Kretzmann, who culled it from the practice of effective community development groups in the 1980s. It has since been diffused widely among community foundations, CDCs, settlement houses, United Ways, youth service projects, neighborhood associations, healthy community coalitions, and community-based environmental projects. And while virtually all community-building practitioners in poor neighborhoods recognize a continuing need for outside public and private resources as well as connections to mainstream institutions and labor markets, the feature that "most starkly contrasts" community building from other approaches to poverty alleviation typical in the United States is that its primary aim is not simply giving more money and services to the poor. Rather, it seeks to "obliterate feelings of dependency and to replace them with attitudes of self-reliance, self-confidence, and responsibility."[14] "Reweaving the fabric of communities" and networks of interdependence, especially at the face-to-face, grassroots level where people raise children, create safe streets, and learn the virtues of civility and mutual aid, is one of the central tasks of civic renewal. It provides a foundation for the kinds of community economic development that can help secure the material premises of independent citizenship.

The master frame of the civic renewal movement stresses the potential role of government as a "catalyst" for citizen problem solving and a "partner" in multisided collaborative efforts. It recognizes government as an important provider of tools and resources to aid citizens in their work. It seeks to "put the 'civil' back in civil service,"[15] that is, to rethink the role of public administrators as strengthening the capacities and responsibilities of citizens and dispersing initiative downward and outward, wherever possible, while establishing inclusive democratic criteria for participation. Although the movement is decidedly shaped by critiques of social service bureaucracies that foster one-way dependence and ensnare citizens in a maze of categorical programs, as well as by critiques of regulatory bureaucracies that rely disproportionately on command-and-control, its master frame is not defined by an intense antagonism to the federal government as either service provider or regulator. As John Gardner puts it, those who talk of dismantling Washington "are living in an ideological stupor" that undermines the capacities of citizens to work in appropriate forms of partnership with each level of government. Volunteer and philanthropic efforts to reweave the fabric of community life are vital, but it would be profoundly mistaken to imagine that these efforts could take over the social programs and responsibilities of government.[16] The National Commission on Civic Renewal, representing a broad spectrum of civic conservatism as well as liberalism, is no less pointed in its criticism of those who believe that renewed emphasis on civil society entails less activist government or that reinvigorated localities can substitute for effective national institutions. While healthy skepticism toward national government is an essential part of the American political tradition, the commission argues, "The current level of mistrust is inconsistent with civic health. Americans cannot love their country if they have contempt for its government. Restoring trust in our national public institutions is an essential component of civic renewal."[17]

Market actors constitute the third pole in the master frame's triad. They bring great dynamism and a spirit of enterprise to an open and free society. At their best, business leaders provide essential ingredients of civic leadership in communities and can spur new forms of collaboration. But "unfettered markets" can be corrosive to civil society, to local economies and institutions, and to the capacity of families to resist the onslaught of crass consumer culture and violent media images. They can undermine unions as civic associations vital to the democratic culture of communities and workplaces. Indeed, the command-and-control hierarchies of big business can erode democratic spirit and skill as much as big government. And corporations focused on national and global opportunities for their managers can reduce incentives to become engaged in local civic affairs. The civic renewal master frame eschews both the anticorporate rhetoric of the Left and the antiregulatory rhetoric of the Right and seeks to embed markets more fully in deliberative regulatory cultures and civic networks of responsibility and accountability. It views private employment and corporate culture as legitimate and indispensable venues for public work and the cultivation of citizens.

The dominant metaphors and themes of the civic renewal master frame distinguish it significantly from those movements that construct "injustice frames" as their basic way of attributing blame and reconfiguring the possibilities of social action. The civic renewal frame attempts to constitute not an adversarial but a collaborative "we," even if righteous anger and pointed adversarialism may define the formative stages as well as subsequent episodes through which some parties come into more productive relationship with each other based on mutual respect and recognition. "Cold anger" is anger refined through an organizing and learning process in which citizens develop the capacity to enter into strategic relationships based on mutual self-interests, in which there are "no permanent friends and no permanent enemies," in a favorite phrase of the IAF. "Encounters with unjust authorities," in the terminology of social movement theorists, include *both* the abrasive, if disciplined, initial confrontation in San Antonio with Tom Frost over his bank's discriminatory lending practices in the 1970s *and* Virginia Ramirez's calling to order and accountability the meeting with Tom Frost and his industry colleagues to initiate a collaborative Project QUEST fifteen years later. "Micromobilization" is less about the "practice of rebellion" per se than it is about learning the arts of productive engagement.

The civic renewal frame does not attribute blame to a clearly delineated set of external oppressors and unjust authorities but attempts to hold *all* authority accountable and to distribute blame among all those whose actions may contribute to public problems. Citizens themselves must be held accountable to the extent that their behavior as narrow advocates, self-righteous claimants, and entitled consumers of services may contribute to the systemic problems of democratic governance. To be sure, this way of framing accountability does not mean that all citizens are equally to blame for every problem or that there are not unjust distributions of power and resources that they need to confront. But in doing so, citizens must also ask themselves how they can utilize their enhanced power and resources to build capacities for complex collaborative work and democratic deliberation for which they themselves are accountable, rather than merely to sharpen adversarial identities and the boundaries of righteous action. Metaphors such as "reweaving the social fabric," "building community," "sharing power," "finding common ground," "forging consensus," "building relationships," and "doing public work" predominate.[18]

ENTREPRENEURS OF CIVIC RENEWAL

Several organizations have been particularly critical in developing and refining the civic renewal master frame and in sponsoring activities to build a broad movement. They have served as social movement entrepreneurs and possess a high degree of prominence as "nodes" that have linked individuals and organizations since the mid-1980s. The three core organizations that we examine here are the Center for Democracy and Citizenship, the National Civic League, and the Kettering Foundation. Each has assumed important leadership roles in the movement, sometimes with one or both of the others, although—as in other social movements—there exists not only cooperation but also some degree of competition for leadership and influence over themes and strategies. Examining these three organizations in terms of their developmental learning, network linkages, and movement-building projects also provides us with a window upon a variety of other important organizational networks within the movement, though our narrative style of presentation here is in no way meant to imply that other groups are not important independent actors in their own right. Indeed, in some areas of activity these other groups are even more important than the three upon which we focus, and our analysis here can hardly do justice to their work. As will become clearer in our discussion of continuing challenges, the network building of the past years is only a small part of what will be needed to bring into the movement still other key intermediary associations operating within specific arenas, which in turn will be essential to developing strong linkages to grassroots groups and local institutions. But the movement networks that have been established and strengthened over the course of the past decade represent a substantial foundation upon which to build.[19]

Center for Democracy and Citizenship

One of the most important centers for elaborating the civic renewal frame and linking various networks of practitioners has been the Center for Democracy and Citizenship at the Hubert Humphrey Institute, University of Minnesota. Its codirector, Harry Boyte, has been a key theorist and central player in the movement since its beginning, and his earlier biography encompasses several streams of civil rights, populist, and community activism between the 1960s and 1980s that have helped to define it. Boyte's political engagement goes back to the civil rights movement in the early 1960s, and his father served as an advisor to Martin Luther King, Jr. The most formative experience for Boyte within the civil rights movement was provided by the "citizenship schools," which had been inspired by Ella Baker and refined by local activists, such as Septima Clark and Bernice Robinson, who worked in collaboration with the Highlander Folk Center. The model was then adopted across the South in the early 1960s by the Southern Christian Leadership Conference (SCLC), for which Boyte was a field secretary.

Citizenship schools were at the center of the movement and taught new conceptions of grassroots democracy, the obligations of responsible citizenship, and the essential skills of public life as part of the crusade to enlist blacks to register to vote. They taught the "big ideas" of what it meant to become "full citizens" and provided what many local activists and some leaders, such as Ella Baker and Andrew Young, considered to be the most important organizing infrastructure of the entire movement—the less militant "quiet structures" behind the more visible actions.[20] While the civil rights movement did not develop a way to sustain this work beyond the mediagenic events and mass protests, the model has remained important for Boyte and others. Dorothy Cotton, a director of the Citizenship Education Program of SCLC who was in charge of recruiting students, who helped to train hundreds of indigenous teachers for the citizenship schools, and who was the individual perhaps most influential in getting King himself to recognize the deeply populist dimensions of such work, has remained an important ally of Boyte in recent efforts to develop a civic renewal frame and to legitimate it as part of the true heritage of the civil rights movement.[21]

In the 1970s Boyte emerged as one of the key proponents of a New Populism in the United States, and his 1980 book, *The Backyard Revolution: Understanding the New Citizen Movement,* represented the most influential interpretation of recent trends in citizen action in both activist and scholarly circles alike. He recognized already in 1977 the significance of IAF's attempts to develop a new model of community organizing. And he also critically incorporated insights from conservative circles on the importance of "mediating structures," which were articulated by Peter Berger and Richard Neuhaus in their influential book *To Empower People* and then developed by others as part of a research project at the American Enterprise Institute. Boyte's aim here, and even more clearly in the Reagan years, was to prevent the Right from gaining an exclusive purchase on the theme of community. He called attention to the extensive self-help, mutual aid, and "community-building" projects emerging around the country, including those arising within the women's movement, and joined those, such as John McKnight, Barton Bledstein, and Christopher Lasch, who identified the culture of professionalism as one of the key factors that had led to the "clientelization of the citizenry." Boyte was involved in various Left-populist networks through the Fred Harris presidential primary campaign in 1976 and the National Conference for a New Politics, which included progressive, local elected officials. He held leadership positions in a number of Left-wing organizations, most notably the New American Movement and the Democratic Socialist Organizing Committee, which later merged to form the Democratic Socialists of America (DSA). But until his eventual resignation in 1981, he remained embattled with other DSA leaders, especially Michael Harrington, over the extent to which—in his view—they failed to appreciate how citizen action remained embedded in local communities and cultures and how much the Left itself had become part of a deracinated professional culture.

While Boyte spoke a militant language of "citizen revolt" in *The Backyard Revolution* and worked closely through the first half of the 1980s with key leaders of Citizen Action, such as Heather Booth and Steve Max, to define a new American populism, his thinking began to shift significantly during these years. The Field Foundation, which had funded SCLC's citizenship schools in the early 1960s, and whose current program officer, Richard Boone, had coined the "maximum feasible participation" theme for the Community Action Program, provided Boyte with the resources to develop a Citizens Heritage Center and to hold a major conference and festival in 1982 commemorating the one hundred and fiftieth anniversary of Tocqueville's travels in America. This historical work resulted in the publication of *Free*

Spaces: The Sources of Democratic Change in America, coauthored with feminist historian Sara Evans. Along with his reading of communitarian theorists such as Michael Sandel, Robert Bellah, and William Sullivan, it further enriched Boyte's sense of the power and responsibility of citizenship and the role of movements in developing a public vision and sense of the common good.

Boyte soon found himself, however, on one side of a rather sharp divide among progressive new populists that became manifest at a 1985 conference sponsored by *Social Policy* magazine. On the same side as Boyte stood those who would develop the frame and cultivate the networks of the civic renewal movement over the coming years, such as John Parr of the National Civic League; Ben Barber, political theorist of "strong democracy" and director of the Walt Whitman Center at Rutgers University; and Frances Moore Lappé, director of the Institute for Food and Development. On the other side stood those who, in Boyte's words, remained "stuck in the admittedly necessary fight to prevent Reagan from dismantling progressive gains" but in doing so had cut their ties with local communities, focused their efforts on all the latest mass media and polling techniques, and had become "no longer willing to have a long discussion of the meaning of democracy. For them such a discussion became, at best, something we might do only on a Sunday afternoon."[22]

In the late 1980s, the Kettering Foundation supported the work of Boyte and convened a Commonwealth Seminar with others who have contributed substantially to developing the civic renewal master frame, such as John Gardner of the National Civic League and David Mathews, the president of Kettering. Important democratic thinkers from academia, such as Jane Mansbridge and Robert Bellah, also participated, as did COPS leader Beatriz Cortez. This seminar led to the publication of Boyte's influential book, *Commonwealth: A Return to Citizen Politics,* and then to the development of a partner network for Project Public Life that included a range of people from various organizing circles. Among them were Anthony Massengale, an organizer from south-central Los Angeles who had recently left the IAF to broaden its approach still further; Miaisha Mitchell, a civil rights and community health organizer from St. Louis and later director of the Florida Commission on Minority Health; Dorothy Cotton from the SCLC; Peg Michels, who had been engaged in rural organizing and development work in Minnesota; Patrick Borich, dean of the University of Minnesota Extension Services; Nancy Kari of the College of St. Catherine, who had done professional organizing within occupational therapy; Deborah Meier, leading school innovator from Central Park East schools and the Coalition for Essential Schools; Nan Skelton, who was engaged in youth development work; and Frances Moore Lappé.

For a variety of strategic and resource reasons, Project Public Life focused on developing local demonstration projects of citizen politics in several institutional settings. The most important of these has been Public Achievement, a 1990s model of citizenship schools for young people, which operates within school settings and has now spread to seven cities beyond the Twin Cities. Public Achievement is headed by Dennis Donovan, a former Gamaliel-trained community organizer and principal of St. Bernard's school in St. Paul. This model helped the Center for Democracy and Citizenship develop the citizenship curriculum for AmeriCorps at the national level during the Clinton administration and has had important impacts in other civic education and youth development projects. Melissa Bass, a key trainer and curriculum developer who has brought the lessons of citizen politics from Public Achievement and AmeriCorps to University Extension/4-H curricula, sees this kind of citizenship schooling as a core element in shaping the identity of "we as citizens" in the everyday problem solving and public work of young people.[23]

Building a new citizenship movement had been the goal of Boyte and Lappé when they first joined together in the late 1980s, and they convened two meetings, in 1990 and 1991, to explore these possibilities further. Ernie Cortés and Ed Chambers of the IAF were present at the first meeting, though they were quite skeptical of an effort they saw as lacking depth and too vulnerable to being captured by the media. John Parr of the National Civic League also attended, as did staff from Kettering and more sympathetic IAF organizers, Tony Massengale and Gerald Taylor, at the second meeting. When Project Public Life, however, decided to focus on demonstration projects for the time being, to deepen its own models and to work within realistic resource constraints, Lappé left. She had wanted to develop national training for a larger movement, and when this goal could no longer be accommodated within Project Public Life, she set off to establish the Center for Living Democracy in Brattleboro with Paul DuBois. Together they published in 1994 *The Quickening of America: Rebuilding Our Nation, Remaking Our Lives*, a widely utilized book of civic stories, concepts, and skill-building exercises that incorporated Lappé's previous work with Project Public Life and core insights of community organizing from the IAF. And in 1995 they founded the American News Service, which has brought "stories of renewal" to a broad readership in American newspapers.[24]

The 1992 Clinton presidential campaign provided new opportunities for Project Public Life to expand its horizons, as campaign advisor Derek Shearer, long-time proponent of new models of community and economic democracy, and political ally of Boyte from the 1970s, shared his work with the candidate and invited Boyte to write theme memos for the campaign. After the election, Boyte teamed to write a "White Paper for a New Citizenship" with various colleagues, including Harold Saunders of Kettering, and Suzanne Morse, who had just left Kettering after nine years to head an ambitious new project, the Pew Partnership for Civic Change, which helped bring these themes to several projects of the Pew Charitable Trusts in ensuing years.[25] They also brought people together in Washington for a Citizens Inaugural in January 1993. In addition, the Clinton campaign had received essential help in developing themes of community and responsibility from the Communitarian Network, founded by Amitai Etzioni, which in 1991 had called for "*a major social movement,* akin to the Progressive movement of the beginning of the century."[26] William Galston, one of the main authors of the communitarian platform and a long-time Democratic party issues advisor, became deputy assistant for domestic policy at the White House and was determined to make the themes of the new citizenship central for the administration. He did so first through his work with national Extension Services and AmeriCorps. Then in 1993 Galston helped to secure a grant from the Ford Foundation, under Michael Lipsky's auspices, for the Reinventing Citizenship Project, whose core theme was that it is not possible to "reinvent government," a key administration initiative, without simultaneously reinventing citizenship.

The Reinventing Citizenship Project, directed by Boyte in conjunction with Ben Barber and under the research direction of Sirianni, brought together agency officials whose own thinking had been moving in this direction. These included Peter Edelman, assistant secretary at HHS, and George Latimer, director of special projects in the Office of the Secretary at HUD, as well as representatives from the offices of the vice president and the first lady, and other officials from the Departments of Education, Agriculture, the Army Corps of Engineers, and the Corporation for National and Community Service. The partner network of Project Public Life played a key role in presenting case studies to educate officials about the ways in which government could serve as a catalyst in developing more robust civic capacities for problem solving, instead of undermining capacities, as is much more typical of government programs. And Ernie Cortés drew out the general lessons of IAF organizing for broader efforts to reinvent citizenship. The initial meeting took place with due symbolic note on Martin Luther King, Jr.'s, birthday in the Roosevelt Room of the White House.

Several complementary proposals emerged from the work of the Reinventing Citizenship Project during the first six months of 1994. The first was to establish a Civic Partnership Council, composed of both agency officials and community-building leaders, to promote new participatory models and training within the federal government. The core function of the council, to be chaired by the vice president, would be to catalyze further various "learning communities" of civic practitioners within and outside of government, based on an inventory of best practices. This effort would revive and expand the mission of the Interagency Council on Citizen Participation of the 1970s, but this time through full partnership with nongovernmental actors. It would inventory agency regulations and behaviors toward citizen participation and assess their impact on civic culture, organizational capacity, and productive problem solving. The council's mission would be to develop a comprehensive strategy to redefine and reinvigorate the civil service in order to "make government fundamentally citizenship-promoting in the way that it conducts its basic activities and designs its key programs." The council's work would be part of a strategy to engage the public in a conversation about renewing citizenship in all institutions and to develop further the tools for practical civic education initiatives.

This proposal for a Civic Partnership Council was subsequently drafted as a presidential memorandum by the White House legal office. The administration, however, proved unable to focus on this and other related initiatives once the congressional elections of 1994 took center stage. The president continued to solicit advice from participants of the Reinventing Citizenship Project in fashioning active citizenship themes, which were prominent in his 1995 State of the Union Address. A *Newsweek* headline perhaps captured the potential realistically: "Clinton's State of the Union could be a blueprint for the next big theme of politics—reinventing citizenship—if he can follow it." But he didn't. The Republican takeover of Congress, which might have provided incentives to develop the theme further, also distracted the administration from pursuing specific efforts. And some high in the administration, whose activist networks were primarily among citizen action groups of the type Boyte and others had distanced themselves from in the 1980s, simply calculated that few immediate political gains were to be had from emphasizing the theme of a renewed citizenship.[27]

A second initiative that emerged from the Reinventing Citizenship Project was to establish a parallel civic forum that would build upon the networks that had been strengthened over the previous months. Boyte again led this effort, called the American Civic Forum, and began the process of drafting, circulating, and redrafting the *Civic Declaration: A Call to a New Citizenship*. New partners joined in exploring the possibilities, including the Pew Center for Civic Journalism, the League of Women Voters, the AARP, American Health Decisions, Computer Professionals for Social Responsibility, and Project on Public Life and the Press. Teams of practitioners and academics formed to develop working papers and inventories of best practices in specific arenas, which later formed the basis of the Civic Practices Network and a related set of World Wide Web projects intended as "citizenship schools for the information age." A number of participants and informal advisors spoke of the need to be part of a larger "movement" for civic renewal, including John Dinges, editorial director of National Public Radio, and Dan Kemmis, mayor of Missoula, Montana, and outgoing director of the Leadership Training Institute of the National League of Cities. But as a result of an inaugural meeting in Washington in December 1994, which was ill-designed to accommodate the energy and initiative of those who attended, as well as the reluctance of foundations to fund movement-building at this time, the

American Civic Forum could not sustain itself. Selective networks, however, were strengthened and carried over into other projects.[28]

A third initiative that emerged from the Reinventing Citizenship Project was the National Commission on Civic Renewal. At Peter Edelman's urging, Boyte and Barber drafted a proposal for a Presidential Commission on Reinventing Citizenship, bipartisan in character, which would highlight best-case examples and engage the nation in a broad conversation. But this proposal stalled out in the White House for reasons similar to those that stalled the Civic Partnership Council, which was viewed as its complement. Yet when Galston left the White House to return to the University of Maryland, and Paul Light—also a key participant in the Reinventing Citizenship Project—left the Humphrey Institute and the Center for Citizenship and Democracy to become director of the Public Policy Program at the Pew Charitable Trusts, the proposal was funded by Pew as an independent commission, and Galston became its executive director.

The commission, which began its work in January 1997, was co-chaired by two prominent political figures, Sam Nunn, former Democratic senator from Georgia, and William Bennett, former secretary of education under President Reagan and author of the best-selling *Book of Virtues*. Its work expanded the collaboration among civic conservatives and liberals well beyond any of the previous projects for a new citizenship. Despite many spirited disagreements, especially on the moral crisis in America, commissioners committed themselves to a norm of civility, by which they meant "disagreeing with others without demonizing them. It means respecting them as sincere patriots and partners in a shared quest for civic answers that are both practically effective and morally compelling." The senior advisory council included a dozen individuals who had been prominent in building the civic renewal movement, as well as various academics whose work had focused on deliberative democracy and civil society. While the commission heard from thinkers as diverse as Theda Skocpol on the Left and William Schambra on the Right concerning the relationship between the federal government and civil society, it sent a clear rebuke to those on the Right whose rhetoric urged citizens to view their government as villain and the market as savior. Indeed, it was Bennett—"with the best Republican credentials in the world," as he put it—who was most pointed in the deliberations when he said, "Stop worshipping the market. . . . To worship the market is idolatry." Harry Boyte played an especially important role in bringing the perspective of public work to the commission's deliberations and final report. And the commission heard testimony from a variety of groups engaged in community development, civic journalism, youth service, and civic education. But it was two girls from Public Achievement at St. Bernard's School in inner-city St. Paul, thirteen-year-old Becky Wichlacz and eleven-year-old Tamisha Anderson, who gave the most profound and riveting testimony of all the sessions. They engaged the commissioners directly in a pointed yet thoroughly composed and dignified series of exchanges on the efficacy of public work in their own lives, despite coming from fatherless families that a few on the commission might have blamed for most of our civic problems.[29]

National Civic League

A second organization critical to the development of the civic renewal movement has been the National Civic League. The National Municipal League, as it was called throughout most of its history, was founded in 1894 by Theodore Roosevelt, Louis Brandeis, and other Progressives to reform city government. While Roosevelt was sometimes eloquent on the need for "self-government" and not just representative government at the local level, the league's mission focused primarily on diffusing the city manager form as a way to professionalize local government. By the early 1980s, the league found itself adrift and faced financial crisis, which provided the occasion for serious soul-searching. Civic leaders on the national scene, such as John Gardner, told the league bluntly that "you guys are part of the problem in this country, because you have professionalized management to the exclusion of citizens."[30] John Parr, the only candidate for league president willing to tell them that they would have to redefine their mission radically or finally close their doors, was hired in 1985 to lead it forward. Declaring victory on its original goals and moving its offices from New York to Denver, the renamed National Civic League reoriented its mission from promoting good government to fostering good communities with vibrant civic associations and partnerships capable of sustaining self-government in a period of increasingly complex problems and dynamic change.

Parr had come to these conclusions through a complex learning process over a period of nearly two decades of activism. In the late 1960s, he became a participatory democrat and a student leader in the Vietnam Moratorium at Purdue University, a conservative campus that, along with his small-town, conservative Republican father, had helped him learn to speak a broader language than was common in antiwar politics. In Colorado in the early 1970s, he worked with Common Cause, the citizens lobby founded in 1970 by John Gardner, and he ran Fred Harris's populist campaign for the Democratic party presidential nomination in Colorado in 1976. He also ran Richard Lamm's first election campaign for governor in 1974, which was waged around heavily populist themes and environmentalist antigrowth rhetoric. Though Lamm was elected and then reelected four years later, their long 1978 postelection dinner conversation convinced them both that their strident populism and adversarial approach to growth management had failed and that a new strategy was needed.

Parr then began a series of one-on-ones around the state with developers to identify their own commitments to preserving the environment. These conversations led to a reframing of the problem as one of the quality of growth. Together Parr and Lamm formed the Colorado Front Range Project as a partnership of environmentalists, developers, and city officials. Chris Gates, fresh out of college at the University of Colorado, took his first job with the Front Range Project and became an important strategic thinker and consultant on community-based approaches in the years leading up to the key retreats at the National Municipal League. Gates had years of Democratic party activism extending back to his childhood; at twelve years old he was handing out literature for Eugene McCarthy at the 1968 Democratic Convention in Chicago, which his aunt, the first woman to head the Democratic National Committee (DNC), managed, and he himself has served as a representative from Colorado to the DNC. Gates became vice president of NCL and then succeeded Parr as president in 1995.

Several board members provided critical intellectual leadership to reinvent the league. These included Neal Peirce, the influential syndicated columnist and author on urban and regional issues, and Scott Fosler, president of the National Academy of Public Administration (NAPA) and author (with Renee Berger) of the influential report, *Public-Private Partnerships: An Opportunity for Urban Community*. Henry Cisneros, who had been schooled in the challenges of community empowerment by COPS during his tenure as mayor of San Antonio in the 1980s, brought these lessons to the NCL board. John Gardner himself later became chair and was succeeded by Bill Bradley, three-term senator from New Jersey, who had decided not to seek reelection in 1996. Bradley had become disillusioned with the state of American politics and had begun speaking the language of "civil society" and "civic renewal," partly as a result of the influence of the Reinventing Citizenship Project, in which an aide and former aide were involved.[31]

The National Civic League has played an especially important role in diffusing the themes of civic renewal throughout various networks, refining best practices in collaborative problem solving, and linking networks of leading practitioners as part of a broader movement. Through its Civic Assistance Program and its Program in Community Problem Solving, it has provided training and facilitation for scores of communities engaged in collaborative projects or ambitious community visioning, and its Civic Index has served as an important learning tool for the hundreds of communities applying for the All-America City Awards. Having borrowed the language of "healthy cities" from Leonard Duhl and the World Health Organization in the 1980s, NCL developed its own Healthy Communities Action Project to provide intensive training to health care and social service professionals, corporate and city officials, and religious and community leaders, and it remains a key force in the healthy communities movement. Each year NCL also hosts the Conference on Governance, which brings many organizations together around specific themes, each of which now has a strong component of civic democracy. Its quarterly journal, the *National Civic Review,* provides analysis of innovative thinking and practice and is widely read in local government and nonprofit circles, as are its regular inserts in *Governing* magazine.

In many ways NCL has become the critical hub in a network of professional organizations of public administrators who have incorporated civic renewal themes into their activities in the 1990s, including the National League of Cities, International City/County Management Association, National Association of Counties, National Association of Regional Councils, and National Academy of Public Administration, all of which have been cosponsors of the National Conference on Governance. Former NCL Vice President Gloria Rubio-Cortés, who came to the league after years of working on Mexican American rights issues with La Raza, has overseen its impressive organizational development in recent years. And Chris Gates, NCL's dynamic president, who serves on the boards of many other organizations and civic renewal projects, has done as much as any civic leader in America today to thicken the networks among those who see civic renewal as an important part of their professional and organizational missions.[32]

An important step in this process has been the formation of the Alliance for National Renewal (ANR). As NCL approached its one hundredth anniversary, it began a strategic planning process on how to develop a much broader "community renewal initiative" and to build a "nationwide movement" uniting different sectors to cooperate in addressing "the root causes of problems." In May 1994, 130 individuals representing forty organizations met to go forward; ANR was officially launched in November at the centennial. John Gardner, chair of the NCL board at the time, was the primary catalyst for this effort. He has held an endowed chair in public service at Stanford University and is an influential author, with such titles as *Self-Renewal: The Individual and the Innovative Society, Excellence,* and *On Leadership.* Gardner had served as the president of the Carnegie Corporation and the Carnegie Endowment for the Advancement of Teaching and, as a member of various corporate boards, had drawn the now familiar lessons on the need to spread responsibility outward and downward to motivate employees and drive innovation. He had also been secretary of Health, Education, and Welfare under Lyndon Johnson, where he lent critical support to the development of community health centers. He served as the first full-time chair of the National Urban Coalition, which had brought together business, labor, civil rights, religious, and political leaders in response to the urban riots of the 1960s. In 1992 Gardner spent practically the entire year looking at community problem-solving efforts around the country and was "astonished at the amount of good work that was going on. It reminded me of some of the efforts that were in place back in the 1960s— before the riots hit and left everyone so discouraged."[33]

As already noted, Gardner was also the founding chair of Common Cause

(1970–77), as well as Independent Sector, a nonprofit coalition of some eight hundred voluntary organizations, foundations, and corporations involved in philanthropic and voluntary action. But his thinking had evolved over the following two decades, and he had come to believe that American democracy was much less in need of the usual citizen lobbies and philanthropic activities and much more in need of collaborative efforts to rebuild communities and the fabric of civic life. Nonetheless, given his own networks extending back several decades, he and others at NCL were able to get some of the key national groups, such as the AARP, the United Way of America, the League of Women Voters, and the National Urban League, in addition to Independent Sector and Common Cause, to join in the effort to launch the new Alliance, which has now grown to a membership of 230 organizations.

In its first five years, ANR has further defined the challenges of civic renewal and has linked many individuals among its partner organizations. It has clearly helped to deepen the thinking of selected leaders within these organizations, some of whom have led various community-building initiatives and have even rethought key aspects of their organizational missions. And ANR has helped to diffuse the themes of civic renewal and community building among a broader membership. Gardner's booklet, *National Renewal,* for instance, has sold more than one hundred thousand copies, mostly through ANR member networks. The National Association for Community Leadership, an ANR member organization, incorporated the guide to the Civic Practices Network, another member, into the training for all of its own nearly five hundred member chapters around the country in 1996. ANR has also produced a number of useful tools, such as *The Community Visioning and Strategic Planning Handbook,* and has catalyzed "Good Community Fairs" in cities like Tampa, Florida, and Springfield, Missouri. It has served as a central link in the network of organizations that have helped to disseminate stories of renewal through local newspapers and nationally syndicated broadcast programs. And its own meetings have increasingly focused on the original mission set out by Gardner to "shine the spotlight on community solutions that work" by giving a national forum for innovations to its partner organizations.

ANR's member organizations are diverse and provide networks into local organizations. The Study Circles Resources Center, for instance, has developed extensive, community-wide study circle programs and deliberative democratic forums on issues such as racism, education, jobs, youth, and violence in some eighty cities, in partnership with local councils of churches, school boards, YWCAs, Leagues of Women Voters, and various municipal and state agencies. Professional associations, such as the American Library Association, American Planning Association, National Institute of Dispute Resolution, and International City/County Management Association, provide networks to practitioners across the country, as do member groups such as the National Association of Counties, National Association of Regional Councils, and National League of Cities. In addition, the National Academy of Public Administration, Alliance for Redesigning Government, and Council on Excellence in Government provide networks to many of the leading innovators in the public sector. Nonetheless, ANR is still grappling with the challenges of working more effectively with the larger national associations among its members, whose predominant style of operation is still far from that of community building, and defining a set of movement-building tasks beyond those of loose networking. We discuss some of these challenges further below.[34]

The Kettering Foundation

The Kettering Foundation is a third organization whose work over the past two decades has been vital in building a broad movement. As a relatively small operating foundation spun off from General Motors by inventor Charles Kettering, it positioned itself to lead a national effort at citizen policy dialogues when David Mathews took over as president in 1981. Mathews developed his political interests from childhood stories of distant relatives in colonial Virginia and more recent ones in populist Alabama. After completing a doctorate in the history of education at Columbia University in the 1960s, he became president of the University of Alabama at age thirty-three, where he oversaw its substantial growth during the period of desegregation and then affirmative action. He encouraged a number of partnerships with religious, civic, and educational organizations to address problems ranging from infant mortality to lack of access to health care. Mathews's political philosophy held that institutions of higher learning, from community colleges to the great universities, had no higher mission than to educate adults to "execute the office of citizen." He chaired the Commission on the Future of the South, which stressed the roles of economic development, local government reform, and voluntary civic action, and he served on the Bicentennial Commission before taking a leave from the university to become President Ford's Secretary of Health, Education, and Welfare. While at HEW, he deepened his understanding of the need for citizen participation in the development of regulations, as well as the restorative role of communities in social reform. In his bicentennial address to the United Chapters of Phi Beta Kappa, he emphasized the founding vision of a self-educating republic based on public deliberation and participatory decision making to grapple with the complex policy issues of the day.

In the late 1970s, Mathews convened a circle of scholars, public officials, activists, foundation officers, and civic leaders who shared this vision. Together they established the Domestic Policy Association to develop innovative forms of policy dialogue among citizens. In particular, Mathews worked closely with

Daniel Yankelovich, founder of Public Agenda Foundation, who devised the concept of "public judgment" as critical to such dialogues. Mathews also tapped the wisdom of public participation professionals active at the federal level in the Interagency Council on Citizen Participation. After resigning his position at the university to pursue this work full time and then to become president of Kettering, Mathews developed citizen dialogue as a core mission of the foundation.

The result was the National Issues Forums (NIF). Initially, in the early 1980s, Kettering built upon networks in colleges, and then at presidential libraries, to host NIF, and he achieved a boost of visibility for NIF through joint appearances by Presidents Ford and Carter at its national events, and extensive coverage on C-Span and National Public Radio. Ford and Carter, indeed, both spoke of the need for citizen deliberation about common interests, which in their experience was often drowned out by the strident voices of special interests. Alan Greenspan, then head of the commission to reform Social Security, shared staff and information to help NIF focus on this issue as one of the first three national issues. Several members of Congress, most notably Representative Albert Gore, Jr., of Tennessee, formed a group to meet with NIF citizens in their Washington Week annual briefings. But it soon became clear that the real interest in NIF was not primarily located in any of these institutions, but in schools, churches, literacy programs, and civic associations, which began providing a steadily increasing flow of participants and convenors. As Mathews notes, "We misdiagnosed where the interest would be."[35]

Kettering thus redirected its efforts further toward the grassroots. This move led to the expansion of NIF over the next decade from 30 at the first Wingspread training conference in 1981 to more than 1,300 potential convenors and moderators at the 1993 annual summer Public Policy Institute, 900 others at regional training institutes at 13 sites around the country, and forums conducted over the previous year in approximately 1,440 adult literacy programs, 2,600 high schools, and 1,300 other civic organizations. The Learning Channel and PBS had specials on NIF and included leading members of the press, public interest groups, and Congress. By 1986, annual participation in the forums and study circles stood at nearly 100,000, and many participated in an annual national television program, "Public Voice." By 1999 there were 22 regional Public Policy Institutes training convenors and facilitators. During this period the diversity of participants increased enormously in race, class, age, gender, and region, as NIF programs were developed for corrections facilities, women's groups, 4-H clubs, senior citizen programs, youth organizations, university extension services, literacy programs, libraries, environmental groups, neighborhood associations, colleges, and Catholic parishes.

Many groups utilize the issues books and starter videos developed each year by the Public Agenda Foundation on important national issues, such as preparing the workforce for the twenty-first century, dealing with stagnating wages, controlling alcoholism, protecting the environment, and responding to the problems of youth in our society. These materials provide a nonpartisan presentation of information and a cluster of choice frameworks that typically guide policy discussions. But groups also use the NIF methodology and materials to help them grapple with issues specific to their local communities and institutions, and they often link these to public forums with local and state lawmakers. This process, not surprisingly, has led in many settings to a shift from discussion to concrete community action. As important as its wrestling with specific issues, however, is NIF's role in cultivating a culture of deliberation that enables participants to consider alternatives, to understand why some issues are so hard, and to become predisposed to try to understand the reasons underlying positions very different from their own. While NIF methodology undoubtedly has its limits, it has had important educative impacts among participants on many issues and in quite diverse settings. And it has provided the single largest source of experiential insight into everyday public deliberation among ordinary citizens, which the Kettering Foundation has mined and refined over two decades for the further development of deliberative democratic theory and practice.[36]

Kettering has complemented its NIF work with several other strategies for building civic capacity. The first is the popular translation and diffusion of democratic thought to an audience of civic educators, government innovators, and community activists. The major vehicle for this, the *Kettering Review*, published several times a year since its inaugural issue in the winter of 1983, contains an array of essays and excerpts from the classics of American democratic thought, civic republican history, and contemporary democratic theory. The public opinion analyses of the Public Agenda Foundation/Daniel Yankelovich Group, Doble Associates, and the Harwood Group have also been staples in the review. Each has partnered on various projects with Kettering in developing a more refined way of interpreting citizen dissatisfaction and articulating an authentic public voice. For example, during the months after its initial publication in 1991, the Harwood Group's *Main Street* study of citizens and politics (see chapter 5) was the subject of more than one thousand newspaper stories and editorials, including a lead editorial in the *New York Times*, David Broder's syndicated column in 140 newspapers, and Associated Press articles in at least 262.[37]

A second complementary strategy has been the incubation of projects and the development of networks among intellectuals and innovators. As we noted above, Kettering supported the work of Harry Boyte in the 1980s in the Commonwealth Seminar, and it convened other theorists and organizers around this theme. Boyte's work helped legitimate Kettering's increased emphasis on community action beyond mere public deliberation. And

Mathews has become a vigorous advocate of the concept of public work in his role as a board member of the National Civic League and in other venues with public administration and government reform practitioners. In the early 1980s, Kettering worked in partnership with the National Academy of Public Administration to convene four regional conferences on ideas for restructuring government institutions. By convening intellectuals and practitioners, Kettering played a major role in incubating public journalism and supporting Project Public Life and the Press. Kettering remains active in efforts to rethink the civic mission of the university, and its NIF work helped spawn the Study Circles Resource Center, founded by Paul Aikers in 1990 and directed by Martha McCoy, who serves as a close associate of Kettering and the National Civic League. Much of Kettering's incubating and network-building occurs through its associates program and Dayton Days meetings, organized around a lively exchange of theoretical analysis and democratic practice. Through its NIF work, Kettering has cultivated many long-term relationships with groups such as the Federation of State Humanities Councils, National Association of Community Leadership Organizations, National Council for Social Studies, National Council for the Advancement of Citizenship, General Federation of Women's Clubs, National Collegiate Honors Councils, Adult Education Committee of the U.S. Catholic Conference, National 4-H Clubs, and North American Association for Environmental Education. Kettering has also been active in the Reinventing Citizenship Project and its various spin-offs, as well as national media projects such as the PBS State of the Union and National Issues Convention.[38]

A third complementary strategy has been Kettering's leadership in "civil investing" seminars among several dozen foundation program officers and directors, beginning in late 1993 in conjunction with the Council on Foundations and the Indiana University Center on Philanthropy. These seminars tapped the growing unease among private funders about the decline of civil society and the patterns of grant giving that might be contributing to it. And they convened many whose own vision and practice had increasingly focused on developing civic capacities, including Bruce Sievers of the Walter and Elise Haas Fund, Edward Skloot and Robert Sherman of the Surdna Foundation, Anna Faith Jones of the Boston Foundation, and Marvin Cohen of the Chicago Community Trust. Participants have engaged in discussions of theoretical literature on civil society and have examined the history and current practice of philanthropy, including the problematic legacy of scientific philanthropy inherited from Progressivism that favored creating social blueprints and replicable models for large-scale improvements. The seminars, as well as research commissioned by Kettering among nonprofit leaders receiving funding, have produced hard-hitting analyses of foundation practices that hinder long-term community building and collaboration among local organizations and service providers: faddish innovation cycles; categorical programs and issue-specific niche funding; professionalized therapeutic interventions "for clients" rather than problem solving "by citizens"; and quantitative indicators and evaluations unable to measure contributions to democratic process and civic capacity. The civil investing seminars have indicated new opportunities for funders to enhance local civic skills and collaborative capacities for sustained action and reflective learning.[39]

During the 1990s, movement-building activities have increased substantially, and network linkages among a broad range of national organizations have become considerably denser. Governing boards of core organizations have an increasing number of overlapping memberships among those leaders who see themselves as building a movement for democratic renewal. Many of the partner organizations in the Alliance for National Renewal and other projects have refined or reoriented their work to place greater emphasis on citizenship and community building and have generated a rich set of practical action guides and models in print, on-line, and in video formats that they have diffused to their local members and to other potential innovators—some of whom have initiated action projects themselves. The civic renewal movement has established its identity as a movement among a critical core of national, state, and local activists and professional practitioners, and it has achieved an important threshold of recognition in the media.[40]

Nonetheless, these important foundational accomplishments over a decade should not be exaggerated, nor the obstacles to further development of a broad movement underestimated. Movement networks often do not penetrate below selected leaders within organizations, nor have they yet been able to catalyze internal transformation of most larger affiliates on a scale that would begin to alter mission and practice in significant ways. Relationships with the key intermediary associations within the healthy communities and civic journalism movements are relatively robust, but in the larger organizational fields of community organizing and community development they are considerably more selective and episodic, and within the civic environmental field they are just beginning to emerge. In these larger organizational fields, as well as in some smaller ones, many individuals have never heard of a distinct civic renewal movement, though many have become aware of a national discourse on civic renewal, and some respond with immediate enthusiasm upon hearing of efforts to build such a movement. Certain key strategic thinkers and practitioners in such fields as community development and civic environmentalism imagine that only a progressive movement of the Left might leverage their work to new levels of impact, though some see themselves belonging simultaneously to both kinds of movements. Linkages between core civic renewal movement entrepreneurs and local groups tend to be strong primarily in areas where the former specialize as sponsors, trainers, and facilitators. Local and state cross-sectoral networks that share a broader movement perspective are sparse. Media coverage of local projects and the emergent movement may be much greater than it was a decade ago, but the movement is far from having established broad public recognition.

The problems of developing more robust networks and a visible national identity are, to some extent, inherent in the civic renewal movement, as we discuss further below. But before turning to these problems and to our own proposal for building the movement in the face of them, we first address the relationship of civic renewal to political parties.

WHY IS THE CIVIC RENEWAL MOVEMENT NONPARTISAN, AND WHY SHOULD IT REMAIN SO?

The civic renewal movement views itself largely as a pluralist and nonpartisan movement cutting across various divides in American politics. Many of its leading proponents trace their activist histories to the progressive, populist, and liberal Left and to a variety of social movements associated with the Left, such as the civil rights, peace, women's, and other social justice movements. Our best estimates would place a considerable majority of the participants at various movement-building meetings and conferences in this camp. The next largest group comes from moderate political backgrounds. A smaller though important group identifies primarily with the conservative Right on issues of mediating institutions and the corrosive role played by the state, as well as the deep moral crisis it sees in American society—though none identify with the fundamentalist far Right or see themselves as militant free-market conservatives.[41]

The choice to build a nonpartisan movement committed to learning openly and self-critically from a pluralistic array of civic practices and models is, in our opinion, strategically wise and politically principled. It does not, however, go uncontested within intellectual and activist circles that identify with the goals of civic renewal. The most articulate argument for systematically linking civic renewal to the renewal of the Democratic party as an instrument of progressive politics is presented by Margaret Weir and Marshall Ganz in their article, "Reconnecting People and Politics."[42] There they argue that, to bring people back into politics, two key tasks need to be accomplished. The first is to rebuild powerful membership organizations in the unions, churches, and other kinds of civic associations. The second is to rebuild party mechanisms that can connect these organizations to meaningful partisan politics and restore the links among fractured elements of a progressive coalition in pursuit of common interests. Powerful membership organizations, according to Weir and Ganz, are "locally widespread, nationally coordinated, and oriented to the accomplishment of public purpose." Unions can perform a key role because of the unique organizational capacities they possess, but only if they invest in worker organizing and join in coalitions with other civic associations as equal partners. They must not dominate coalitions, nor must they be wedded to a narrow definition of their own interests. Indeed, these problems have hampered unions such as the American Federation of State, County, and Municipal Employees (AFSCME) and the National Education Association (NEA), because their weak connections to a broader movement make their defense of the public sector, in which their members work, appear narrow and self-serving. Those urban churches and national congregations that have supported community organizing around the country, as well as suburban congregations that previously supported the civil rights and antiwar movements, provide yet another source of organizational strength. A third key source are civic associations, such as the IAF, the Sierra Club, and the AARP. According to Weir and Ganz, the IAF not only needs to reach out to other groups, as it has done with AFSCME in Baltimore around the living wage campaign, but also needs to revise its stance on the principled avoidance of partisan electoral involvement. This "outsider" strategy no longer makes any sense in an era when the old liberal establishment, against which the earlier Alinsky groups could make their claims, has itself passed into history. And when most decisions that affect local communities today occur at regional, national, and international levels, the IAF's failure to create leadership capable of deliberating over and implementing strategies beyond the local level represents a serious impediment to effective action. If unions, churches, and civic associations can be strengthened as constituency organizations of a progressive coalition, Weir and Ganz argue, then the Democratic party itself, long in decline, can begin to be revitalized as a participatory organization oriented to common purposes, rather than to representing the narrow interests of its fractured constituencies, and as a service organization for entrepreneurial candidates.

Although we share many of the sentiments of Weir and Ganz, we think that their model of the relationship of civic and party renewal, which we shall call *direct linkage,* is seriously flawed. First of all, the attempt to politicize many, if not most, civic organizations by enlisting them in Democratic party campaigns and by mobilizing them for direct representation in party caucuses and conventions would be seriously resisted, because it would undermine their capacities to do much of their work and in many cases would seriously divide their memberships. Many civic organizations depend on foundation funding, which severely restricts their partisan activities. Thus Weir and Ganz argue that local organizations need to generate the revenue to support themselves, but they offer no credible revenue streams that would enable them to do so. Much more important, however, is that groups like the IAF, CDCs, watershed associations, healthy community coalitions, and many other innovative civic projects rely on developing principled, nonpartisan relationships among local civic actors to accomplish their work. Nonpartisanship is also critical in their relationships with administrative agencies that often cat-alyze and fund their efforts. And nonpartisanship facilitates relationships with major political power brokers, such as the Republican mayors who might sup-port the work of CDCs and neighborhood associations and the Republican governors who might support the work of watershed associations and stew-ardship networks, many of whose members are themselves Republicans and Independents. This is also true for relationships with the Republican bankers who work with CDCs or who use their connections to bring other business partners to the table to create a Project QUEST. Imagine, for a minute, how much less effective COPS's relationship with banker Tom Frost would have been if he had had to explain to all of his colleagues why COPS was a major power broker at the state Democratic party convention or was formally en-dorsing a mayoral or gubernatorial candidate. Most likely, the dramatic first meeting that Virginia Ramirez and her fellow community leaders convened with the business leaders of San Antonio would never have taken place, and there would be no Project QUEST.[43]

The problem of direct linkage is compounded further when we consider the role of churches. Congregations, as we have argued throughout this book, provide one of the most important wellsprings of moral energy for civic ac-tion in the country today. They are engaged in community-building activi-ties on many fronts, from community development and social services to en-vironment and health. While they mobilize large numbers of volunteers, they also receive substantial amounts of public and private foundation money to enable them to do their work. In some cases there exist welcome efforts to link urban and suburban congregations in addressing issues of poverty and racism. But congregation members, especially in the suburban congregations that Weir and Ganz would mobilize for Democratic party renewal, are polit-ically quite diverse. While the issues of civil rights and the war in Vietnam of-fered some of them clear moral lines for taking a stand, most of the issues facing our country today, including the core problems of poverty and social justice, are more complex and their solutions much less certain. Such issues do not lend themselves to clear moral crusades, and certainly not partisan ones, especially if relationship-building among politically diverse congrega-tion members is to be mobilized as a resource for sustainable projects in which congregation members themselves participate. Any attempt systematically to mobilize congregations for strictly partisan purposes would, at best, deplete such relationships. At worst it would risk severe internal fighting and exter-nal sanctions from church hierarchies. The Republican right, as Weir and Ganz note, may have developed a model of politicized churches (though its durability now appears open to serious question). But this model is hardly one that the civic renewal movement would wish to emulate. Churches that are highly politicized for narrow partisan purposes represent one of the key threats to civic democracy in America, as they undermine the capacities of communities with diverse values to deliberate reasonably and collaborate productively. Indeed, the civic renewal movement would be wise to create more venues for nonpartisan collaborative problem solving that invited Christian fundamentalists to the table, as has happened in a number of communities, rather than try to draw sharper partisan dividing lines among congregations.

The problems of direct linkage are no less acute when we consider national organizations like the American Association of Retired Persons. The AARP represents enormous untapped potential for civic renewal. Recent efforts to build organizational capacities at the state and local level and to engage members in forms of community service that do not directly serve elders as an interest group are welcome steps. And much further innovation will be needed to help build the capacities for self-help and intergenerational collaboration for an aging population living much longer with chronic illness and disability. But the struggle to transform AARP by investing more heavily in building civic infrastructure—rather than simply providing national member services, public lobbying, and local mobilization in support of elders—will be a long and difficult one, as the former often competes with the latter for resources and attention and represents a significant shift in mindset.[44] Building civic infrastructure will, no doubt, have spillover effects in local and state politics and could help reorient the ways both political parties think about aging policy. But any direct attempt to politicize these efforts by systematically linking local AARP chapters to Democratic party caucuses, conventions, and campaigns would cause enormous strife in the organization at every level. AARP is a nonpartisan organization with a membership widely representative of all political leanings and capable of punishing those who would enlist it for clearly partisan purposes. Partisanship would greatly reduce the capacity of the local chapters to develop collaborations for community problem solving with other civic and public organizations, as well as with office holders from both major parties.

Direct linkage has little relevance to the work of civic renewal that needs to occur in all kinds of institutional and professional settings, from schools, universities, and hospitals to corporations, social service nonprofits, and public agencies. Meeting the major challenges in these settings—such as transforming institutional missions and expert-centered professional cultures, collaborating across organizational and professional boundaries, and facilitating productive work with communities—has little to gain from politicization, and much to lose. But the problem we have with the formulations of Weir and Ganz perhaps goes deeper and reveals the large gap still existing between progressive party politics and the public work of civic renewal. The latter seeks out—wherever possible—collaborative opportunities across the spectrum of interests and ideologies to solve practical problems, build long-term relationships based on trust, and produce things of value to the commonwealth. This is the heart of civic politics, and organized advocacy, partisan campaigns, and policy making should be judged substantially (though certainly not exclusively) on the basis of whether they serve or undermine this work of citizens. Progressive party politics, however, tends to downplay or ignore this level of work in favor of mobilizing popular "constituencies" around "rights" and "interests" that can be served by state regulatory, social welfare, and redistributive policies. To be sure, Weir and Ganz do not fall into the most stylized version of this stance. Nonetheless, nowhere in their article do they mention the kind of collaborative community problem solving and public work that is the stuff of everyday civic politics. Without a far richer basis of such work to build upon—work that generally requires principled nonpartisanship—it is unclear how all the "progressive constituencies" that have pursued their fractionated advocacy agendas in the past will be able to learn how to forge common purposes or new ways of doing politics. It is unlikely that they will learn simply by working together in advocacy coalitions or party caucuses.

Revitalizing Democratic state and local parties as genuine vehicles for participation, deliberation, and accountability is an important task, to be sure, and Weir and Ganz point to opportunities offered by recent court rulings that free state parties to establish their own governance procedures and thus strengthen the role of caucuses and conventions in preprimary endorsements. But the relationship between efforts at party renewal and civic renewal is perhaps better viewed as one of *indirect linkage* rather than direct linkage. Building nonpartisan capacities for community development, neighborhood planning, civic environmentalism, healthy communities, public journalism, community youth development, family-supportive workplaces, universities with a renewed civic mission, and much more represents the infrastructure for a revitalized democracy. It cannot and must not be linked directly and systematically to party renewal and certainly should never be sacrificed to the latter. Building civic capacities can, however, serve indirectly to revitalize the Democratic party—and perhaps both major parties or a third party—by altering the way that the party frames key issues and by providing a stream of individual party activists who have formed their civic identities and learned collaborative skills through various forms of public work and community building. These individual activists may well be networked through other advocacy groups for housing, health, or children that organize directly to send representatives to state party caucuses and conventions but would not attend as official representatives of congregational networks, watershed associations, CDCs, or healthy community coalitions. The stronger the work of civic renewal at the grassroots, and the more that various advocacy organizations adopt community-building models as an essential part of their larger advocacy agendas, the more robust will be the interconnections between civic renewal and party renewal, without threatening to compromise the integrity of the former through direct and systematic linkages to the latter.

While indirect linkage is certainly plausible and, in our view, the more principled way to protect the integrity of the public work of citizens in revitalizing their communities and institutions, it is possible that the profound historical trends of the past century that have eroded Democratic state and local party organizations as vehicles for participation, deliberation, and accountability cannot be fundamentally reversed—even with long-overdue campaign finance reform. The rise of a nonpartisan civil service, the administrative state, and interest groups capable of fine-tuned lobbying and agenda setting independent of party organizations have eroded the capacity of parties to aggregate the interests of an increasingly diverse citizenry. More recent changes in electoral technologies, fund-raising strategies, and presidential nominating procedures have exacerbated these trends. It may be that a historical shift to much greater emphasis on nonpartisan forms of civic deliberation and community problem solving, if increasingly successful, will simply drive another nail in the coffin of the parties of old. What interest groups have done to parties on one level, newer forms of community problem solving and deliberative democracy may do on another, namely, provide a more finely tuned way for citizens with varied interests and values to address complex problems in specific contexts oriented to experimental learning and trust building. The more these succeed and the more they are complemented by policy designs within the administrative state itself, the less relevant state and local parties may become as primary forums for civic deliberation and the aggregation of interests. We would call this shift *displaced linkage,* because civic renewal displaces party structures even further as vital civic associations in their own right. If, indeed, this represents the more plausible scenario, then the tasks of building the civic renewal movement and renovating party structures may be much more zero-sum than we might hope.

Parties, even those much depleted of their former civic substance, still perform crucial functions for political competition and democratic choice. Thus, we think that the most responsible stance is to explore all the avenues for strengthening indirect linkage yet be willing to work within the parameters of displaced linkage, rather than risk compromising the integrity of civic problem solving by more direct linkages to the Democratic party. We would offer the same advice to principled civic activists within the Republican party. Indeed, the critical *political* challenge of the civic renewal movement is perhaps best seen as developing sufficient credibility to compel the two major parties at all levels to compete increasingly over how their policies and candidates can serve the public work of citizens in communities, institutions, and workplaces of all sorts. The challenge is to compel the parties to compete around a vital civic center of American politics where citizens struggle to deliberate reasonably about complex problems that tend not to fit into neat ideological boxes, where they learn how to collaborate pragmatically across the boundaries of partisan camps, and where they fashion robust and sustainable strategies for social justice based on effective inclusion and democratic participation in the productive work of the republic.

Civic Renewal Ideas within the Parties

Within the party system, several groups have begun to place increasing emphasis on civic renewal. Foremost in developing these themes has been the Progressive Policy Institute, the think tank affiliated with the Democratic Leadership Council (DLC). In fact, "The New Progressive Declaration: A Political Philosophy for the Information Age," draws directly upon the work that two of its four coauthors, Will Marshall and William Galston, have done with the Reinventing Citizenship Project and subsequent efforts to build a civic renewal movement. As the declaration argues, the New Progressives constitute "not a party or faction but a broad civic movement dedicated to radical reform," but seeking "to build new common ground, not new partisan divisions." A philosophy of civic empowerment is the core of the new governing philosophy, in which citizens directly participate in producing public goods and where "old civic virtues find fresh expression in new democratic institutions and in a new covenant between citizens and their commonwealth." The New Progressives offer a third choice between what they see as the Left's reflexive defense of the bureaucratic status quo and the Right's destructive bid to dismantle government. This path entails transforming government into a "catalyst for a broader civic enterprise, controlled by and responsive to the needs of citizens and the communities where they live and work." The shift to forms of self-government appropriate to the information age will not occur without a strategy to restore opportunity by fostering new conditions for citizens to create wealth through public and private investment, promote worker access to lifelong learning, and develop innovative ways for managing and organizing every aspect of work. Nor will it occur, according to the New Progressives, without a serious national debate about corporate accountability and governance in the economy or without fresh efforts to reinvent unions and other forms of worker association to enhance economic power and community self-help in a global information society. And key to any strategy based on building the capacities of individual citizens and communities for self-governance and the production of wealth is a renewed national commitment to generate economic opportunities for the urban poor based on work, savings, entrepreneurship, and small business creation. But, as the authors of the declaration argue, there should be no illusions that ideologues, technocrats, and lobbyists of all stripes will not oppose the shift from a government that controls to one that enables. And "ultimately we will have to confront our own demands for public benefits that we are increasingly reluctant to pay for."[45]

Important thinkers on the left of the Democratic party have also begun to incorporate the theme of civil society into their strategic vision for a populist progressivism able to address the needs of ordinary working individuals and families. Most notably, Stanley Greenberg and Theda Skocpol have accepted the message of moderate Democrats like Bill Bradley: "Civil society must be central to democratic renewal. Along with government at all levels, communities, religious institutions, and businesses must be engaged as partners in a larger quest for the good society."[46] Greenberg and Skocpol criticize the economic populists on the Democratic left—the AFL-CIO under John Sweeney's leadership, the Economic Policy Institute, and the Campaign for America's Future launched as a counterweight to the DLC—because these groups focus primarily on workplace issues of unionized blue-collar workers in large transnational corporations. In contrast, Skocpol and Greenberg develop a family-centered agenda to enable working parents to fulfill their civic obligations in raising their children; nurturing civic life in neighborhoods, churches and schools; and caring for elders. They frame the defense of various entitlement programs, from paid parental leave to Social Security, in these terms. Although they are deeply critical of what they see as the DLC's reflexive tendency to favor markets in various policy arenas, they recognize that a winning progressive strategy that renews civil society will have to learn from the existing Democratic right and left alike. This conclusion is shared by E. J. Dionne in his influential 1996 book, *They Only Look Dead: Why Progressives Will Dominate the Next Political Era.*[47]

Civic conservatives within the Republican party have also addressed the problems of community more or less consistently since the publication of Berger and Neuhaus' *To Empower People* in the mid-1970s, and they have drawn upon the work of other important thinkers in these early years, most notably Michael Novak and Robert Nisbet. But, as William Schambra notes, Republican administrations produced little more than a series of false starts. The Ford administration recognized the potency of the paradigm of mediating structures, but its Office of Public Liaison's efforts to reach out to neighborhoods and civic associations degenerated into retail efforts to sell presidential initiatives. President Reagan waxed eloquent about returning initiative to local fraternal lodges and church groups but could manage little more than a Task Force on Private Sector Initiatives that engaged in pointless debates on whether corporations should be expected to foot the bill for welfare state programs. President Bush also proclaimed a grand vision of a nation of communities and voluntary organizations but produced only a modest "points of light" initiative aimed at conferring awards upon exemplary volunteer projects. Along with Michael Joyce, whom he joined at the Bradley Foundation after leaving the Reagan administration, Schambra launched the "new citizenship" program to move beyond these false starts toward genuine civic renewal. Together they have supported local projects and brought together conservative networks engaged in various efforts, from the faith-based groups in urban ghettos affiliated with the National Center for Neighborhood Enterprise to tenant management groups in public housing working with The Empowerment Network. Civic conservatives have emphasized moral reconstruction, as well as vouchers that they view as empowering parents by giving them choice in schools and social services. Civic conservatives have also, however, come to recognize the important work of CDCs and the IAF, and more recently of civic environmentalism. Their critique of the kind of therapeutic professionalism that substitutes for family and community capacities has provided opportunities to explore common ground with Boyte and others farther to their left. And, as Joyce and Schambra note, "the most insightful and effective critique" of the overarching progressive state, to which they see themselves much indebted, came from the New Left of the 1960s and its vision of "supportive community, which could be realized only in small, participatory groups." Like many others in the civic renewal movement, Schambra too has come from this tradition.[48]

WHY A MOVEMENT?

American society needs to revitalize and modernize its civic infrastructure over the coming decades if it is to grapple with the increasingly complex problems of a world undergoing rapid transformation. We believe this to be true even if one takes a less alarmist view of the erosion of civic life than some studies have presented. Ultimately, we need to measure our civic health not against some baseline of involvement of earlier decades, as important as this is, and certainly not against some nostalgic past, but in light of the specific kinds of challenges that the world of today and tomorrow presents. In the face of the increasing complexity of our problems and diversity of actors and interests in a highly differentiated and dynamic society, we will require new organizational and institutional capacities for collaborative problem solving and democratic learning. We will also need to refashion robust identities of "we as citizens" capable of engaging in complex public work and deliberation to build a shared commonwealth, as the old collective identities and solidarities that undergirded previously shared understandings of common interest and public goods during the heyday of the welfare state in America, as well as in Europe, have progressively decomposed in the wake of fundamental structural changes.[49]

Just as the problems of nonpoint pollution and ecosystem restoration require new civic capacities, so will the challenges of sustainable health care in a society of high-tech options, escalating expectations, and aging populations. Just as the problems of poverty and economic development in the inner cities require new forms of community building and empowerment, so will the challenges of dynamic and sustainable regional development in a globalizing postindustrial economy. Other major problems will require civic innovation as well. Democratic school reform depends on collaborative problem solving among parents, teachers, administrators, and students, as well as public deliberation that can orient and sustain reform toward common purposes.[50] Working-time policies to support parental engagement in families and civic life may call for new laws and entitlements to paid parental leave and part-time options, like those in the most effective systems in Europe. These will never succeed, however, unless corporate cultures also transform from within by deliberative strategies capable of balancing complex and often conflicting requirements: individual autonomy and flexibility, work group and gender equity amid temporal diversity and discontinuity, and effective team management in postindustrial business environments. Indeed, this complex balancing of worthy values poses a momentous civic challenge that our work and family institutions have not previously had to confront in this form.[51] In none of these policy arenas will the traditional tools of government mandates, market incentives, professional interventions, or programmatic entitlements be sufficient unless coupled with robust civic capacities appropriate to the tasks.

While one can imagine a variety of initiatives and paths to civic renewal,[52] we are convinced that a broad movement will be necessary to counteract the pervasive cynicism of American political life and the powerful institutional and cultural forces that undermine responsible citizenship. Without a countervailing movement that can progressively mobilize important new sources of symbolic and institutional power, it is difficult to imagine how citizens will be able to alter significantly those dynamics of interest group, expert professional, social service, regulatory, and market actors that erode capacities for self-government and community problem solving. Without a larger movement, civic innovation may continue to progress in some arenas, to be sure, but will probably stall in others and will prove unable to shift basic policy paradigms and professional practices. Of the four arenas we have considered, for instance, civic environmentalism is likely to remain relatively robust and may witness significant breakthroughs due to a combination of broadly distributed public support and associational assets that can be mobilized, as well as regulatory cultures that have manifested substantial learning capacities in response to the limits of command-and-control regulation. But community development remains much more vulnerable to the relative political weakness of cities and urban minorities in a rapidly changing economy, especially in view of the substantial resources that would be required to sustain an effective strategy. Healthy Communities and Health Decisions approaches will undoubtedly see new opportunities. In the absence of broader conceptions of responsible civic action and public work, however, they remain vulnerable to a dysfunctional health policy system, institutionally driven collaborations, and citizens' own unsustainable expectations about the distribution of health as a commodity—which itself has no small impact on the ever-receding goal of universal coverage. Civic journalism is also likely to continue in various forms and perhaps thrive in selective settings, but its limits seem clearly evident unless citizens themselves generate much more interest and capacity on the demand side.

A civic renewal movement can help shift the balances favorably in these and other arenas. Social movements provide the most powerful countervailing forces available to societal actors today. Movements generate moral energy and vision. They challenge citizens to grand and glorious undertakings, and ennoble everyday efforts of mutual support in communities and workplaces. Movements provide a common language that others can easily understand, and they construct plausible frames for re-imagining how citizens can act to change the world. They furnish a grammar of motives to inspire and sustain commitment. They generate new civic identities and locate new opportunities for action deep in the pores of institutional life, as well as in alternative institutional spheres. The interlinked networks and projects of a social movement enable citizens to identify careers of activism across different arenas of engagement, as well as over the stages of their individual life courses. Movements generate a sense of power and efficacy, as well as the moral leverage and cultural authority to compel institutional elites to alter their usual ways of doing business.

The civic renewal movement, though still in its formative stages, holds the potential to generate new wellsprings of moral energy and commitment, especially if it can link the grand task of renovating American democracy with the everyday nobility of producing the commonwealth in communities, institutions, and workplaces of all sorts. The movement can raise the visibility of vital public work and innovative democratic designs beyond segmented arenas and locales, and it can alter the terms of national public discourse. It also has the potential to develop a more robust melding of the civic and the just—one that is appropriate to a highly diverse and differentiated democratic republic much less able to draw upon the old sources of collective solidarity or old tools of redistribution.

However, because the civic renewal movement is not primarily a rights or justice movement, it cannot rely on the metaphors, frames, strategies, or tactical repertoires of recent democratic movements. It cannot inspire action on the basis of unconditional claims to rights or righteous struggles against clearly defined oppressors. It cannot invoke metaphors of unambiguous good and evil or moral resistance in the face of power. It cannot capture and focus public attention through mass protests, marches on Washington, boycotts, strikes, freedom rides, and sit-ins, nor can it count on repression by authorities to galvanize widespread support. It cannot expect dramatic court decisions to energize activists or to secure significant new levers of power and representation. It lacks a constitutional amendment, such as the Equal Rights Amendment, around which to organize to guarantee the power and responsibility of citizens to practice effective self-government. And while legislation could certainly enact "policy designs for democracy" that help build civic capacity in specific arenas, a civic renewal movement cutting across many institutional sectors cannot hope to build its networks through advocacy coalitions and lobbying for specific laws.[53]

A NATIONAL CIVIC CONGRESS:
RECLAIMING THE FOURTH OF JULY FOR SELF-GOVERNMENT

What can be done to develop the movement further and expand its distinctive repertoire in light of these constraints? Undoubtedly, various worthy projects can and will be tested in the coming years. Here we offer a proposal designed to build directly upon the movement's current repertoire and accomplishments, facilitate other movement-building initiatives that might emerge, yet offer significant new opportunities to amplify networks and dramatically capture the public imagination. Our proposal is admittedly ambitious, though not, we trust, inappropriately so in view of the great challenge of democratic renewal. And it is clearly neither politically nor organizationally utopian, even if it does call for the circle of movement entrepreneurs to take a bold step forward together. Indeed, virtually every component, taken separately, has already been tested with reasonable success by some set of civic renewal organizations, and some components have become part of the standard repertoire of the movement. We call our proposal the National Civic Congress, which would convene annually or biannually in Washington, DC, and eventually in state capitals and other cities and towns as well, on or around the weekend of the Fourth of July.

The July Congress is designed to accomplish several goals. First, it would establish the cultural authority and visibility of the public work of citizens in building the commonwealth and solving problems through collaborative and pragmatic action. Second, it would facilitate networking across various arenas and intermediary organizations already engaged in innovative civic practice, and it would enhance their incentives to invest in movement-building activities, thus expanding the leadership of a national movement. Third, it would diffuse lessons and deepen learning within and across networks, as well as generate new opportunities to educate a much broader public about robust forms of public work and innovative problem solving. Fourth, it would provide a national forum for policy intellectuals and civic practitioners to engage in critical discussion of "policy designs for democracy" in various arenas, and it would invite lawmakers and staff to join with them, thus nurturing relationships and helping to modify the frames of policy formation, while not directly lobbying or advocating through the Civic Congress itself. And, finally, it would engage the nation in a festive celebration of the work of contemporary citizens on the holiday of the founding of our democratic republic. It would thereby send a powerful message of practical hope, as well as an invitation and challenge to citizens in all walks of life and all institutional roles to engage productively in the work of building the commonwealth, preserving the Creation, and renewing the legacy of self-government.

Stories of Renewal

A core component of the July Congress would be telling the stories of renewal that are ongoing in communities, workplaces, and institutions across the country. Storytelling, part of the venerable social movement repertoire of bearing witness, can take many forms but should establish the dignity and satisfactions of public work, the diversity and availability of practical models, and the commitment to continue the difficult task of learning in the messy world of collaboration and democracy. Through the Civic Congress, teams of citizen delegates who have worked in innovative partnerships—and this includes everyone from ordinary neighborhood activists, school kids, union stewards, and congregation members to professionals, civil servants, business managers, and elected office holders—assume the responsibility for educating the nation in the arts of civic democracy. They bear witness to working through conflict to reach enough common ground to enable them to produce things of genuine public value. They testify to building relationships of trust to serve them in their future work. They claim the authority and responsibility to meet the challenge that Thomas Jefferson laid down in the early days of the republic, which is no less relevant today and will be no less critical as far as the democratic eye can see into the future: "I know of no safe repository of the ultimate powers of the society but the people themselves; and if we think them not enlightened enough to exercise control with a wholesome discretion, the remedy is not to take it from them, but to inform their discretion by education." Democracy is an art that must be learned and relearned, especially in an increasingly complex world. Through its July gathering, the movement thus assumes a singularly visible role as a congress of civic educators in the unfinished and imperfect, yet no less noble, work of democracy.

Storytelling by diverse teams of citizens can communicate the depth and difficulty of public problem solving in many settings, but it can also celebrate the daily work of ordinary people in producing the commonwealth. The visibility that the July Congress offers to various organizing and community-building intermediaries and their local affiliates would provide a critical incentive for them to invest time and resources, especially when not having one's work represented in the array of groups might prove costly in terms of relative recognition. These incentives can be increased by including special recognition for those projects that have been given awards by the various intermediary organizations themselves during the previous year or two.

These would include winners of the All-America City awards given out by the National Civic League, Neighborhood of the Year awards of Neighborhoods USA, Innovations in Government awards of the Ford Foundation and the Kennedy School (many of which have civic components), James Batten awards of the Pew Center for Civic Journalism, Chesapeake Bay Partner Communities awards, and similar awards for community service, youth leadership, community planning, and program innovation in other arenas. But even where there are no awards programs, intermediaries would play a large role in designating groups and projects that represent the richness of the work in which they are engaged. Funder networks, such as the civil investing group and others among program officers who have helped support community-building projects, not only with money but also with accumulated wisdom, would serve as important partners in selecting participants.

The ability of the July Congress to enhance the visibility and cultural authority of the civic renewal movement depends, of course, on press coverage and other uses of communication media. Stories of renewal provide a critical entry point for the press. Civic journalism editors and reporters would be welcome as full participants. National and local PBS and NPR partnerships could coordinate broadcast coverage, though other media networks would be encouraged to cover the events, and all would be expected to ask probing questions and engage skeptics and critics in discussion. Electronic civic networks could also focus attention on stories of renewal in the weeks leading up to the July Congress, which would, in turn, supply further stories for civic education and leadership development in schools, universities, and other settings.

Designs for Democracy

If practical stories of renewal should be recounted by teams of citizen delegates in a way that makes them accessible and inspiring, the July Congress should also include in-depth critical exchange on key models and policy designs, as well as scholarly analysis of general trends and benchmarks of civic health. Policy design is absolutely essential to renewal, if not in every area of civic life, then certainly in those where citizens engage with complex institutional systems and produce complex public goods. Democracy in contemporary America cannot be revitalized unless policy making itself aims to nurture the virtues of democratic citizenship and the capacities of civic problem solving. And a diverse and nonpartisan movement that does not have available a lobbying and advocacy coalition strategy ought nonetheless to help focus public attention and debate on policy designs that tend to foster democracy, in contrast to those that do not.

The July Congress can draw upon the familiar repertoire of academic and policy conferences, but it can also bring practitioners and lawmakers into the discussions to build networks oriented toward mutual education and ongoing action. Thus, for example, a general session on civic environmentalism might include the National Academy of Public Administration, which produced the important reports to Congress discussed in chapter 3, and might invite key congressional committee and staff members, EPA officials, policy intellectuals, and a range of innovators from watershed councils, state governments, sustainable city projects, environmental groups, businesses, and civic associations. To foster incisive critical reflection, identify key obstacles and limits, and develop relationships that might prove essential to later work, the session could also include skeptics and opponents of collaborative approaches from academia and environmental advocacy groups. And even though consensus on a policy agenda would not be the purpose of this particular session or of the July Congress as a whole, participants could explore the range of options for effective advocacy through other channels. A similar format could be followed for specific environmental policy design sessions on watersheds, forests, toxics, sustainable cities, and for other policy arenas, such as community development, health, family, aging, education, and work.

Indeed, stories and designs of democratic workplaces would be an indispensable component of a July Congress that seeks to make what Michael Sandel calls the "political economy of citizenship" a central theme of civic renewal,[54] and that aims to extend movement networks to a broad range of workplace innovators within unions, professional associations, human resource departments, work-family institutes, consulting firms, schools of management and industrial relations, and the shop floor. If our political economy is to function so that work helps to produce citizens capable of self-government, as some of our deepest political traditions as well as our best contemporary democratic theory contend, then democratic innovations appropriate to the changing world of work must inform civic learning.

Here, too, there is already much to draw upon. The July Congress can feature robust models of worker-management collaboration and employee involvement in unionized and nonunionized settings, where information systems help democratize access to knowledge, continuous learning, decision making, and even technical design itself. The congress can highlight new models of relational organizing in service workplaces, such as the Harvard Union of Clerical and Technical Workers, which has refined strategies of participatory collaboration in the interests of dignity and respect for the contributions of everyone who produces the complex public goods of a university. Indeed, transforming the cultures of service workplaces, where so much of our everyday public interaction in postindustrial society occurs, is absolutely vital to a democratic civic culture based on the mutual recognition of equal citizens, rather than the deference or resentment of inferior servants. The July Congress can also underscore the efforts of professional associations among teachers, nurses, physicians, and others who have assumed new responsibilities for the public mission of their institutions and for an ethic of care and empowerment in their everyday practices. It can accent working-time innovations that combine flexibility with gender equity, employee ownership that promotes participatory decision making, total quality management that incorporates environmental sustainability, and occupational unionism that empowers contingent workers. The July Congress's focus on designs for democracy can, of course, raise all the larger policy questions, from job-training systems to labor law reform, that might enable political economy to promote self-governing citizenship within and outside the workplace. And as a twenty-first-century congress of producers, it can perhaps enable the civic renewal movement to shift popular and policy discourses so that issues of work, narrowly conceived, become opportunities for democratic public work broadly imagined.[55]

Essential partners in the July Congress's work on designs for democracy would be academic networks that have become increasingly focused on community building and civic renewal. These include individual scholars, university institutes, schools of public policy and administration, and academic associations. The July Congress can serve as a coproducer in their ongoing work by helping to develop curricular materials, case study series, edited volumes, and Internet, CD, and video resources on the basis of the annual presentations, which would enrich professional training and orient future research. And it could raise the visibility of important efforts by university leaders in Campus Compact, the American Council of Education, the American Association for Higher Education, and other groups to renew the civic mission of the university itself, as poignantly outlined in the 1999 *Presidents' Fourth of July Declaration on the Civic Responsibility of Higher Education.*[56]

A Festival of Self-Governance

The National Civic Congress would also celebrate the work of citizens in building the commonwealth and thus lay claim to the symbolism of our nation's most important political holiday in order to renew self-government. As many other major movements throughout history have marked significant events by ritual practices and gatherings, the July Congress would reclaim a major national ritual for the civic renewal movement.[57] This can be done with all the fanfare and fireworks, beer and barbecue typical of Fourth of July festivities, as well as with the display booths and curious entertainments one finds at a Good Community Fair or All-America City Awards celebration. But, as in the latter, the festivities would be built around the stories of renewal told by the collaborative teams of delegates themselves. And, for those so inclined, an ecumenical service would anchor the commitment to revitalize the civic foundations of the republic in the deepest and broadest traditions of those faith communities already hard at work.

Since the celebration is designed as a claim to cultural authority for democratic public work and collaborative problem solving within American politics, the July Congress would invite important power holders to attend the sessions, recount to the delegates and public what they may have learned, and express their own commitments to similar modes of civic action and government support. It would aim to establish and publicize as a basic norm of politics that government officials have no more important task than to facilitate the democratic work of citizens themselves. Public officials from both parties who have a proven record of working with innovative civic partnerships—and there are many of them who would be honored to attend—would provide added legitimacy to the efforts of the July Congress to establish this norm.

But the circle needs to be broadened and the challenge made more poignant. Thus, the July Congress might utilize a variant of IAF's accountability nights by inviting the president and the leader of the opposition party in Congress—or, during election years, the presumed nominees or leading candidates for president—to tell how their own policies and governing philosophies will enable the work of citizens to flourish. They would be welcomed to share in the symbolic value of the July Congress, but only to the extent that they engaged its themes and the work of its delegates with a seriousness that goes beyond the usual platitudes of Fourth of July speeches. Teams of delegates could visit Congress in the days and weeks prior, and would issue special invitations to attend the festivities in Washington or back in their home states and to sit in on the sessions that might be most related to their own legislative work.

An Organizing Project

The July Congress is designed as a common project that can help build the civic renewal movement on the basis of relationships of respect, trust, and mutual self-interest among individuals and organizations already engaged in robust civic work, and it can progressively draw in others seeking to reinvent how their communities and institutions function. The key incentives that the July Congress can offer to those inevitably concerned about how movement building will contribute to their own specific work and justify a commitment of scarce time and resources are heightened visibility, increased legitimacy, and useful networks beyond those already available. As the legitimacy of civic approaches is enhanced, so will July Congress participants be more likely to receive further support in their particular arenas. The barrier to entry is relatively low, as participation in the July Congress does not require agreement on a substantive, programmatic agenda, even as it promises to help build selective networks and alter policy frames in ways that might enable groups to become more effective in their policy and advocacy work. Nor does participation require the deployment of substantial new volunteers in a common project, as did the Presidents' Summit for America's Future convened by General Colin Powell. The disincentives to participate felt by groups concerned with sharing the spotlight with too many other parallel projects or competing models would be effectively held in check by the desire not to be left out, especially once the July Congress achieved a certain critical mass of participating groups and public legitimacy. And, of course, funding would lower the barriers to participation significantly.

But organizing must be the critical ingredient. Just as it is impossible to build an independent base of citizen power in a local community without organizing, so it is unlikely that a civic renewal movement will be able to make effective claims on American political life without a concerted strategy of national organizing. The July Congress offers the opportunity to do this in a way that signals large purpose while setting modest and achievable goals. It provides the rationale for identifying leaders in a progressively broader array of institutional arenas year in and year out and for mapping an ever-richer assortment of innovative approaches. It requires one-on-one relationship building based upon common values of civic democracy, as well as negotiating contribution and credit. And as the July Congress spreads beyond its venue in the nation's capital, it would elicit further cross-sectoral network building at the local level.

Delegate selection, governance, and funding of a National Civic Congress pose a set of significant challenges, to be sure. These seem manageable enough, however, if the will exists to organize the congress among a core group of partners who have collaborated on various projects over the previous decade and who see it as an opportunity to raise their work to a new level. Because the July Congress would make no claim to formal authority, set no advocacy agenda, and have no pretense to speak for all citizens or represent all forms of activity in civil society, its organizers and partners would have considerable leeway in selecting teams of delegates whose work they view as relatively robust, diverse, and educative. On the basis of reputation, trust, and relationships developed in the process of further organizing, the July Congress can progressively broaden the array of participants, and could also utilize formal evaluations by independent scholars and consultants to guide selection and help to avoid identifying the movement with superficial faddishness and volunteer hype. The congress can establish strong norms of respectful and constructive dialogue during the sessions, so that the full dignity of the delegate teams' work is upheld even as critical questions are pursued and so that partisan rhetoric is restrained. Funding for such efforts now has several precedents: the National Commission on Civic Renewal, Alliance for National Renewal, Citizens State of the Union, National Issues Convention, and Presidents' Summit for America's Future. Resources for the congress can also be contributed by local projects and intermediaries themselves, or by those who fund specific projects, as is typically the case with such gatherings. An endowment could perhaps be raised to make the July Congress a permanent feature of our political culture and ceremony. And prior to the convening of a formal congress, potential partners could test the strategy through a variety of other coordinated Fourth of July events and projects, including on-line ones that feature stories of renewal and designs for democracy that would eventually be included at a face-to-face gathering.

This proposal for a National Civic Congress on or around the July Fourth weekend is designed to build upon the repertoire and relationships already existing within the civic renewal movement but to provide the movement with a way of leveraging these for much larger impact on American politics. It affords opportunities and incentives to thicken networks across arenas and to establish a visible movement identity in manageable steps, while fully respecting that the work of civic organizing and innovation going on in specific arenas remains the basis for any broader renewal. Because the rhetoric and repertoire of rights and justice movements are largely unavailable for movement building, the July Congress offers a substitute that can nonetheless capture the public imagination in a dramatic way. As a festive but dignified gathering on our nation's most important political holiday, the July Congress offers a powerful image of teams of citizens from all walks of life and every corner of the country working collaboratively to build the commonwealth and solve the difficult problems that beset us amid all the messiness, conflicts, uncertainties, and failures that a free people acting in an imperfect world invariably face. This is an image that has deep resonance among an overwhelmingly nonideological and pragmatic public, but it runs contrary to much of what they see—and hate—about politics. The July Congress lays dramatic claim to cultural authority based on the power of example and the bearing of witness. It asserts in no uncertain terms that, without the public work of citizens themselves, there can be no self-governing democratic republic. And it challenges those with formal political power to account for the ways in which they enable the work of citizens.

The July Congress is called a "congress," and not just another meeting or commission, because it would stake a bold claim to authority within the political culture. Even as it fully respects the genius of institutional design of the American republic, it says, in effect, that alongside the presidency, Congress, courts, agencies, and local governmental bodies, self-governing citizens likewise have their own distinctive gathering through which they directly signal their authority and responsibility to refine the work of democracy, without which all these other institutions could never perform as intended. If we expect these other institutions to educate and form a citizenry by the way they perform their own distinctive functions, as indeed we should insist that they do, then we must recognize the foremost authority and responsibility of citizens themselves to educate the institutions. Who else could we possibly expect to do so? In a system of checks and balances, the work of citizens themselves must provide the essential civic balance for a self-governing republic.

Whether or not this admittedly ambitious proposal for a National Civic Congress might prove feasible in the foreseeable future, the challenges of building a civic renewal movement, and of deepening the kinds of innovation that we have analyzed in this book, will prove daunting. Nonetheless, as we hope that we have demonstrated, there exist substantial networks, models, assets, and wisdom that can be mobilized for these tasks in the coming years. This will undoubtedly require a measure of faith and vision beyond the cynical chic so fashionable in popular discourse or the finely honed skepticism of much academic discourse. Here, if we may be permitted our own personal faith, we join those activists in Save The Bay and COPS and South Carolina Healthy Communities and many other groups in quoting Proverbs: "Where there is no vision, the people perish."

NOTES

ONE. CIVIC INNOVATION AND AMERICAN POLITICS

1. Telephone and personal interviews with Save The Bay staff: Curt Spalding (executive director), December 23, 1999; Andy Lipsky (habitat specialist), December 22, 1999; Christy Law Blanchard (director of communications), December 22, 1999; Stan Dimock (volunteer and internship coordinator), December 22, 1999; Fred Massie (former communication and education director), February 2, 1994, May 1995; Kathryne King (former volunteer and internship coordinator), October 22, 1996; Gayle Gifford (former finance administrator), June 27, 1993; Save The Bay, *A Strategy for Action, 1992–1997; 30 Years of Improving Narragansett Bay: A History of Save The Bay; How to Become a Narragansett Baywatcher; Annual Reports* for the years 1993–98; selected issues of the *Bay Bulletin*, 1993–99; and its website (www.savebay.org). See also Peter Lavigne, *The Watershed Innovators Workshop: Proceedings*, Cummington, MA, June 4–5, 1995 (Portland, OR: River Network, 1995); and Kim Herman Goslant, "Citizen Participation and Administrative Discretion in the Cleanup of Narragansett Bay," *Harvard Environmental Law Review* 12 (1988), 521–68.

2. Quoted in Brett Campbell, *Investing in People: The Story of Project QUEST* (San Antonio, TX: Communities Organized for Public Service and Metro Alliance, 1994), 21; personal interview with Ernesto Cortés, Jr., Cambridge, MA, December 16, 1993; telephone interview with Arthur Mazuca, Project QUEST's director of information services, June 1996. See also Paul Osterman and Brenda Lautsch, *Project QUEST: A Report to the Ford Foundation,* January 1995; Mark Russell Warren, *Social Capital and Community Empowerment: Religion and Political Organization in the Texas Industrial Areas Foundation* (Cambridge, MA: Harvard University, Ph.D. diss., 1995); and Dennis Shirley, *Community Organizing for Urban School Reform* (Austin: University of Texas Press, 1997).

3. Proverbs 29:18.

4. Among these early papers on civic innovation were Carmen Sirianni, "Citizenship, Civic Discovery, and Discursive Democracy: Social Movements and Civic As-

sociations in Citizen Participation Programs," American Political Science Association Annual Meetings, Washington, DC, September 1993; and "Reinventing Citizenship in the United States: Social Learning, Social Capital, and Social Policy," Conference on Social Capital, convened by Robert Putnam, Harvard University and the Rockefeller Foundation, Chatham, MA, July 7–10, 1994.

5. Ronald Ingelhart, "Postmaterialist Values and the Erosion of Institutional Authority," in Joseph Nye, Philip Zelikov, and David King, eds., *Why People Don't Trust Government* (Cambridge, MA: Harvard University Press, 1997), 232, emphasis in original. See also his *Culture Shift in Advanced Industrial Society* (Princeton, NJ: Princeton University Press, 1990), especially 335–70; and Jeffrey M. Berry, *The New Liberalism: The Rising Power of Citizen Groups* (Washington, DC: Brookings, 1999).

6. See Joel Silbey, "The Rise and Fall of American Political Parties, 1790–1993," in L. Sandy Maisel, ed., *The Parties Respond: Changes in American Parties and Campaigns*, 2d ed., (Boulder, CO: Westview Press, 1994), 3–18; Sidney Milkis, *The President and the Parties: The Transformation of the American Party System Since the New Deal* (New York: Oxford University Press, 1993); John Aldrich, *Why Parties? The Origin and Transformation of Party Politics in America* (Chicago: University of Chicago Press, 1995); James Reichley, *The Life of the Parties: A History of American Political Parties* (New York: Macmillan, 1992); David Plotke, "Party Reform as Failed Democratic Renewal in the United States, 1968–1972," *Studies in American Political Development* 10: 2 (fall 1996), 223–88. The phrase "cognitively mobilized nonpartisans" is Ingelhart's.

7. Robert Dahl, *The New American Political (Dis)Order: An Essay* (Berkeley, CA: Institute of Governmental Studies, 1994). See also Richard Harris and Sidney Milkis, *The Politics of Regulatory Change: A Tale of Two Agencies* (New York: Oxford University Press, 1989); Jonathan Rauch, *Demosclerosis: The Silent Killer of American Government* (New York: Times Books, 1994); and Hugh Heclo, "The Sixties' False Dawn: Awakenings, Movements, and Postmodern Policy-making," in Brian Balogh, ed., *Integrating the Sixties: The Origins, Structure, and Legitimacy of Public Policy in a Turbulent Decade* (University Park: Pennsylvania State University Press, 1996), 34–63.

8. John McKnight, *The Careless Society* (New York: Basic Books, 1995), 106. See also Andrew Polsky, *The Rise of the Therapeutic State* (Princeton, NJ: Princeton University Press, 1991); Lisbeth Schorr, *Common Purpose: Strengthening Families and Neighborhoods to Rebuild America* (New York: Doubleday, 1997), 74–75; Peter Dobkin Hall, "Vital Signs: Organizational Population Trends and Civic Engagement in New Haven, Connecticut, 1850–1998," in Theda Skocpol and Morris Fiorina, eds., *Civic Engagement in American Democracy* (Washington, DC: Brookings, 1999), 211–48; and Steven Rathgeb Smith and Michael Lipsky, *Nonprofits for Hire: The Welfare State in the Age of Contracting* (Cambridge, MA: Harvard University Press, 1993).

9. Michael Schudson, *The Good Citizen: A History of American Civic Life* (New York: Free Press, 1998), 293. See also Stephen Holmes and Cass Sunstein, *The Cost of Rights: Why Liberty Depends on Taxes* (New York: Norton, 1999).

10. See Mary Ann Glendon, *Rights Talk: The Impoverishment of Political Discourse* (New York: Free Press, 1991); Marc Landy and Martin Levin, eds., *The New Politics of Public Policy* (Baltimore, MD: Johns Hopkins University Press, 1995); and Claus Offe and Ulrich Preuss, "Democratic Institutions and Moral Resources," in David Held, ed., *Political Theory Today* (Stanford, CA: Stanford University Press, 1991), 143–71, who extend this argument beyond the United States.

11. See Benjamin Barber, *Jihad vs. McWorld* (New York: Times Books, 1995); Robert Kuttner, *Everything for Sale: The Virtues and Limits of Markets* (New York: Knopf, 1997); Stephen Elkin, *City and Regime in the American Republic* (Chicago: University of Chicago Press, 1987); Charles Heying, "Civic Elites and Corporate Delocalization: An Alternative Explanation for Declining Civic Engagement," *American Behavioral Scientist* 40 (1997), 657–68.

12. See Harry Boyte and Nancy Kari, *Building America: The Democratic Promise of Public Work* (Philadelphia, PA: Temple University Press, 1996); Mary Dietz, "'The Slow Boring of Hard Boards': Methodical Thinking and the Work of Politics," *American Political Science Review* 88: 4 (December 1994), 873–86; Claus Offe, "How Can We Trust Our Fellow Citizens?" and Mark E. Warren, "Democratic Theory and Trust," in Mark E. Warren, ed., *Democracy and Trust* (New York: Cambridge University Press, 1999), 42–87 and 310–45, respectively; Robert Dahl, "The Problem of Civic Competence," *Journal of Democracy* 3 (1992), 45–59; Albert O. Hirschman, *Exit, Voice, and Loyalty* (Cambridge: Harvard University Press, 1970). We strongly suspect that the structural effects associated with increasing complexity, differentiation, anonymity, and pluralism over the past half century explain some of the erosion of social capital that may appear as generational effects in survey data, though it is much easier to measure the latter than the former.

13. See James Coleman, "Social Capital in the Creation of Human Capital," *American Journal of Sociology* 94 (1988 Supplement), S95–120; *Foundations of Social Theory* (Cambridge, MA: Harvard University Press, 1990), chapters 5, 8, and 12; Pierre Bourdieu, "The Forms of Capital," in John G. Richardson, ed., *Handbook of Theory and Research for the Sociology of Education* (New York: Greenwood, 1985), 241–58; Robert Putnam, with Robert Leonardi and Raffaella Nanetti, *Making Democracy Work: Civic Traditions in Modern Italy* (Princeton, NJ: Princeton University Press, 1993), chapter 6. See also Alejandro Portes, "Social Capital: Its Origins and Applications in Modern Sociology," *Annual Review of Sociology* 24 (1998), 1–24, for a good critical overview of recent theorizing and research, as well as Michael W. Foley and Bob Edwards, "Is It Time to Disinvest in Social Capital?" *Journal of Public Policy* 19 (1999), 141–73, for a critical analysis of recent literature that is close to our own view in stressing specific social structural contexts in which social capital is generated and utilized, rather than aggregate measures based on survey and other data that are designed to characterize overall national stocks and civic cultures. See also Michael Woolcock, "Social Capital and Economic Development: Toward a Theoretical Synthesis and Policy Framework," *Theory and Society* 27 (1998), 151–208, who argues that "there are different types, levels, or dimensions of social capital, difference performance outcomes associated with different combinations of these dimensions, and different sets of conditions that support or weaken favorable combinations" (159), thus presenting specific kinds of optimizing choices, as is our intent in focusing on civic innovation as we do. While we find the concept of social capital useful in the delimited ways that we lay out below, we do *not* subscribe to a general historical or sociological argument on the primacy of civic or political culture. For useful critiques of this view, see Sidney Tarrow, "Making Social Science Work Across Time and Space: A Critical Reflection on Robert Putnam's Making Democracy Work," *American Political Science Review* 90: 2 (June 1996), 389–97; Robert Jackman and Ross Miller, "A Renaissance of Political Culture?" *American Journal of Political Science* 40: 3 (August 1996), 632–59; and

Dietrich Rueschemeyer, Marilyn Rueschemeyer, and Björn Wittrock, eds., *Participation and Democracy: East and West* (Armonk, NY: Sharpe, 1998).

14. See Theda Skocpol, with Marshall Ganz et al., "How Americans Became Civic," in Skocpol and Fiorina, *Civic Engagement in American Democracy,* 27–80, as well as her analysis of recent shifts in "Advocates without Members: The Recent Transformation of American Civic Life," 461–509 of the same volume. Skocpol emphasizes translocal, albeit locally rooted membership associations, and the historical institutionalist patterns linking these in often symbiotic ways to state structures and policies at various levels. We share some of Skocpol's focus on multitiered associations with linked local, state, and national organizations, though we see a range of other patterns of forming horizontal networks, multi-stakeholder partnerships, and democratic policy designs that respond to a more differentiated and complex organizational and institutional environment than that which existed when most of the classic American translocal but locally rooted associations were created. For the contemporary period, focus on multitiered organizations enrolling large memberships, such as 1 percent or more of the population, can obscure more variegated forms of civic democracy.

15. See William M. Sullivan, *Work and Integrity: The Crisis and Promise of Professionalism in America* (New York: HarperBusiness, 1995), on the concept of "civic professionalism."

16. Nancy Rosenblum, *Membership and Morals: The Personal Uses of Pluralism in America* (Princeton, NJ: Princeton University Press, 1998), is alert to the limits of a fully "congruent" conception of the relationship between secondary associations and public norms and institutions, such that every association needs to be a school of civic virtue. One need not accept anything close to full congruence, however, to recognize the value of citizens' attempts to achieve greater congruence as a way of strengthening and renovating democratic capacities for practical public problem solving in today's world.

17. For useful theoretical analyses of the ecology of associations and publics, see, in particular, Mark E. Warren, *Democracy and Associations* (Princeton: Princeton University Press, 2000); Mustafa Emirbayer and Mimi Sheller, "Publics in History," *Theory and Society* 28 (1999), 145–97. On social movement contributions to social capital, see Debra Minkoff, "Producing Social Capital: National Social Movements and Civil Society," *American Behavioral Scientist* 40: 5 (March/April 1997), 606–19; Mario Diani, "Social Movements and Social Capital: A Network Perspective on Movement Outcomes," *Mobilization: An International Journal* 2 (1997), 129–47.

18. Robert Putnam, *Bowling Alone: The Collapse and Revival of American Community* (New York: Simon and Schuster, 2000); "Democracy in America at Century's End," in Axel Hadenius, ed., *Democracy and Its Critics* (New York: Cambridge University Press, 1997), 27–70; "Bowling Alone: America's Declining Social Capital," *Journal of Democracy* 6: 1 (January 1995), 65–78; "The Strange Disappearance of Civic America," *American Prospect* 24 (winter 1996), 34–48.

19. Sidney Verba, Kay Schlozman, and Henry Brady, *Voice and Equality: Civic Voluntarism in American Politics* (Cambridge, MA: Harvard University Press, 1995). But see Putnam, *Bowling Alone,* 449, n. 30.

20. Frank Baumgartner and Jack Walker, "Survey Research and Membership in Voluntary Associations," *American Journal of Political Science* 32: 4 (November 1988), 908–28.

21. The Pew Research Center for People and the Press, *Trust and Citizen Engagement in Metropolitan Philadelphia: A Case Study* (Philadelphia, PA: Pew Research Center, 1997). This study also included a national comparative group, which displayed roughly similar patterns. On the relation of social and political trust more generally, see Kenneth Newton, "Social and Political Trust in Established Democracies," in Pippa Norris, ed., *Critical Citizens: Global Support for Democratic Governance* (New York: Oxford University Press, 1999), 169–87.

22. Robert Wuthnow, *Loose Connections: Joining Together in America's Fragmented Communities* (Cambridge, MA: Harvard University Press, 1998).

23. Thomas Guterbock and John Fries, *Maintaining America's Social Fabric: The AARP Survey of Civic Involvement* (Washington, DC: AARP, December 1997); Virginia Hodgkinson and Murray Weitzman, *From Belief to Commitment: The Community Service Activities and Finances of Religious Congregations in the United States* (Washington, DC: Independent Sector, 1993); *Nonprofit Almanac 1996–1997: Dimensions of the Independent Sector* (San Francisco: Jossey-Bass, 1996).

24. The National Commission on Civic Renewal, *A Nation of Spectators: How Civic Disengagement Weakens America and What We Can Do About It* (College Park, MD: The National Commission on Civic Renewal, June 1998); *Hopeful Signs in America's Civic Health,* June 17, 1999.

25. Alan Wolfe, *One Nation, After All* (New York: Viking, 1998).

26. James Davison Hunter and Carl Bowman, in collaboration with the Gallup Organization, *The State of Disunion: 1996 Survey of American Political Culture* (Ivy, VA: In Medias Res Educational Foundation, 1996).

27. Everett C. Ladd, "The Data Just Don't Show Erosion of America's 'Social Capital,'" *Public Perspective* 7: 4 (June/July 1996), 1; and *The Ladd Report* (New York: Free Press, 1999), 50. Putnam's response to Ladd in *Bowling Alone,* however, is quite convincing.

28. Michael Schudson, "Keynote Address, James K. Batten Awards and Symposium for Excellence in Civic Journalism," Minneapolis, MN, May 3, 1999.

29. Paul Sabatier and Hank Jenkins-Smith, eds., *Policy Change and Learning: An Advocacy Coalition Approach* (Boulder, CO: Westview Press, 1993), chapters 2, 3, 10. See also Carol Weiss, "Research for Policy's Sake: The Enlightenment Function of Social Research," *Policy Analysis* 3 (fall 1977), 531–45; Charles Lindblom and David K. Cohen, *Usable Knowledge: Social Science and Problem Solving* (New Haven, CT: Yale University Press, 1979); Donald Schön and Martin Rein, *Frame Reflection: Toward the Resolution of Intractable Policy Controversies* (New York: Basic Books, 1994).

30. Helen Ingram and Steven Rathgeb Smith, eds., *Public Policy for Democracy* (Washington, DC: Brookings, 1993), 1. See also Marc Landy, "Public Policy and Citizenship," 19–44 of the same volume; Anne Larason Schneider and Helen Ingram, *Policy Design for Democracy* (Lawrence: University Press of Kansas, 1997).

31. See Paul Light, *Sustaining Innovation: Creating Nonprofit and Government Organizations That Innovate Naturally* (San Francisco: Jossey-Bass, 1998); Peter Senge, *The Fifth Discipline: The Art and Practice of the Learning Organization* (New York: Doubleday, 1990); Chris Argyris, *On Organizational Learning,* 2d ed. (Malden, MA: Blackwell, 1999); William Foote Whyte, *Social Theory for Action: How Individuals and Organizations Learn to Change* (Newbury Park, CA: Sage, 1991); "Social Inventions for Solving Human Problems," *American Sociological Review* 47: 1 (1982), 1–13; Ronald Heifitz, *Lead-*

ership Without Easy Answers (Cambridge, MA: Harvard University Press, 1994); and David Korten, "Community Organization and Rural Development: A Learning Process Approach," *Public Administration Review* (September–October 1980), 480–511. The literature on innovations in American government, such as those that have been part of the joint Ford Foundation and Harvard's Kennedy School of Government program, is also useful. See Sandford Borins, *Innovating with Integrity: How Local Heroes Are Transforming American Government* (Washington, DC: Georgetown University Press, 1998); and Alan Altschuler and Robert Behn, eds., *Innovation in American Government: Challenges, Opportunities, Dilemmas* (Washington, DC: Brookings, 1997).

32. Michael Dorf and Charles Sabel, "A Constitution of Democratic Experimentalism," *Columbia Law Review* 98: 2 (March 1998), 267–473; Robert Reich, "Policy Making in a Democracy," in Robert Reich, ed., *The Power of Public Ideas* (Cambridge, MA: Harvard University Press, 1988), 123–56; Edward P. Weber, *Pluralism by the Rules: Conflict and Cooperation in Environmental Regulation* (Washington, DC: Georgetown University Press, 1998); Elinor Ostrom, "Coping With Tragedies of the Commons," *Annual Review of Political Science* 2 (1999), 493–535; Manik Roy, "Pollution Prevention, Organizational Culture, and Social Learning," *Environmental Law* 22: 1 (1991), 189–251; Ian Ayres and John Braithwaite, *Responsive Regulation: Transcending the Deregulation Debate* (New York: Oxford University Press, 1992); Errol Meidinger, "Administrative Regulation and Democracy," Baldy Center for Law and Policy Working Paper Series (Buffalo, NY: University of Buffalo, 1992); Joshua Cohen and Joel Rogers, "Secondary Associations and Democratic Governance," and "Solidarity, Democracy, Association," in Erik Olin Wright, ed., *Associations and Democracy* (London: Verso, 1995), 7–98, 236–67.

33. Alexis de Tocqueville, *Democracy in America*, vol. 1, trans. Henry Reeve (New York: Schocken Books, 1961), 63–64, *passim*. See also Jane Mansbridge, "Does Participation Make Better Citizens?" *Good Society* 5: 2 (spring 1995), 1–7; Mark E. Warren, "Democratic Theory and Self-Transformation," *American Political Science Review* 86: 1 (March 1992), 12.

34. See Arnold Kaufman, "Human Nature and Participatory Democracy," in Carl Friedrich, ed., *Responsibility: NOMOS III* (New York: Liberal Arts Press, 1960), 178–200; Carole Pateman, *Participation and Democratic Theory* (Cambridge, England: Cambridge University Press, 1970); Benjamin Barber, *Strong Democracy: Participatory Politics for a New Age* (Berkeley: University of California Press, 1984).

35. Jane Mansbridge, *Beyond Adversary Democracy* (New York: Basic Books, 1980).

36. Carmen Sirianni, "Learning Pluralism: Democracy and Diversity in Feminist Organizations," in John Chapman and Ian Shapiro, eds., *Democratic Community: NOMOS XXXV*, (New York: New York University Press, 1993), 283–312.

37. Mansbridge, "Does Participation Make Better Citizens?"

38. On the earlier period, see Mansbridge, *Beyond Adversary Democracy;* and Joyce Rothschild-Whitt, "The Collectivist Organization: An Alternative to Rational Democratic Models," *American Sociological Review* 44 (August 1979), 509–27.

39. Jeffrey Berry, Kent Portney, and Ken Thomson, *The Rebirth of Urban Democracy* (Washington, DC: Brookings, 1993), chapter 11.

40. Personal and telephone interviews with Jerome Delli Priscoli, past president of the Interagency Council on Citizen Participation, Washington, DC, February 1 and March 5, 1994, August 22, 1995; and Stuart Langton, Cambridge, MA, May 2, 1994.

41. The theoretical resources that became available to practitioners are too vast to list here, though we cite some in our analyses. Recent works in the critical theory tradition that stress social learning include James Bohman, *Public Deliberation: Pluralism, Complexity, and Democracy* (Cambridge, MA: MIT Press, 1996); and Jean Cohen and Andrew Arato, *Civil Society and Political Theory* (Cambridge, MA: MIT Press, 1992).

42. See Doug McAdam, *Freedom Summer* (New York: Oxford University Press, 1988); James Max Fendrich, *Ideal Citizens: The Legacy of the Civil Rights Movement* (Albany: SUNY Press, 1993); Jack Whelan and Richard Flacks, *Beyond the Barricades: The Sixties Generation Grows Up* (Philadelphia, PA: Temple University Press, 1989); James Miller, *"Democracy Is in the Streets": From Port Huron to the Siege of Chicago* (New York: Simon and Schuster, 1987), and the preface to the 1994 Harvard University Press edition; Meta Mendel-Reyes, *Reclaiming Democracy: The Sixties in Politics and Memory* (New York: Routledge, 1995); Stuart Burns, *Social Movements of the 1960s: Searching for Democracy* (Boston: Twayne, 1990); Nancy Whittier, *Feminist Generations: The Persistence of the Radical Women's Movement* (Philadelphia, PA: Temple University Press, 1995).

For discussions of the significance of the 1960s for other areas of political and cultural life, see Michael Delli Carpini, *Stability and Change in American Politics: The Coming of Age of the Generation of the 1960s* (New York: New York University Press, 1986); Stephen Macedo, ed., *Reassessing the Sixties: Debating the Political and Cultural Legacy* (New York: Norton, 1997); and Balogh, *Integrating the Sixties.*

43. At Save The Bay, for instance, younger recruits of the 1990s with no previous activist experience, such as habitat specialist Andy Lipsky, learned civic organizing from the 1980s generation, such as executive director Curt Spalding. Spalding himself was recruited from EPA with minimal college activism, but learned his civic organizing from Trudy Coxe and others in the previous cohort. Each added innovative dimensions as they grappled with new challenges and opportunities. Telephone interviews with Curt Spalding, December 23, 1999; and Andy Lipsky, December 22, 1999.

Our disagreement with some of the New Left scholars, while grounded in several basic differences in outlook and interpretation of data, stems partly from differences in sampling methods. We include a broad range of people currently active in various community-building and civic renewal activities, often as leading innovators, and look backward at their biographies, while others have generally selected a sample engaged in a specific organization or event in the 1960s and 1970s and looked forward to their later involvements. Neither method can tell us what statistical proportions of New Left activists have remained engaged in later years, in what kinds of activities, or with what perspectives. But this is not central to our argument, which is not about relative proportions but the existence of a critical core of innovators and their learning trajectories. We thus extend the key analytic insights of this important body of scholarship, while modifying its political assumptions.

44. Samuel Huntington, "The United States," in Michel Crozier, Samuel Huntington, and Joji Watanuki, *The Crisis of Democracy: Report on the Governability of Democracies to the Trilateral Commission* (New York: New York University Press, 1975), 59-118; and *American Politics and the Promise of Disharmony* (Cambridge, MA: Harvard University Press, 1981), 167-220.

45. See Michael Pertschuk, *Revolt Against Regulation: The Rise and Pause of the Con-*

sumer Movement (Berkeley: University of California Press, 1982), 131, on Nader's philosophy of participation.

46. James Morone, *The Democratic Wish: Popular Participation and the Limits of American Government* (New York: Basic Books, 1990).

47. Morone, *Democratic Wish*, 335–36.

48. Of the 467 innovative civic practitioners in our sample, 113 were interviewed at least twice. These interviews averaged approximately forty-five minutes, with a range of ten minutes to three-and-one-half hours. We engaged many other practitioners in informal conversations, often following up on specific written materials or oral presentations. Of the 271 people interviewed whom we do not classify as innovative practitioners, most were citizens, public officials, and nonprofit staff whom we selected to determine the impact of various projects (especially civic journalism projects) on their communities or institutions, or who were journalists not involved in innovation. Constraints of length require us to limit references to some of the interviews, practitioner conferences, action manuals, planning documents, etc., and constraints of confidentiality in some cases limit direct reference to previous political involvements, internal organizational problems, or inter-organizational turf battles, though we have included this material in our broader analysis. The ten cities in which we conducted fieldwork on civic journalism are Austin, TX, Binghamton, NY, Charlotte, NC, Colorado Springs, CO, Madison, WI, Minneapolis, MN, Norfolk, VA (and the five "Hampton Roads" cities), San Francisco, CA, Spokane, WA, and Wichita, KS.

49. On participatory action research, see William Foote Whyte, ed., *Participatory Action Research* (Newbury Park, CA: Sage, 1990); William Foote Whyte and Kathleen King Whyte, *Making Mondragon: The Growth and Dynamics of the Worker Cooperative Complex* (Ithaca, NY: ILR Press, 1988). Given the scope and diversity of our organizational focus, however, we did not attempt to develop a formal action research design.

50. We have served in one or a number of these roles for the National Commission on Civic Renewal; National Civic League's All-America City Awards; Public Broadcasting Service's *Citizens '96* and *State of the Union* series; the *Democracy, Citizenship and Community* series of the American Communications Foundation and the Osgood File, CBS Radio; National Public Radio's *Democracy in America* series; various series on community renewal by the *Dallas Morning News* and the *San Jose Mercury News;* National Issues Forums; Study Circles Resource Center; Kettering Foundation; Alliance for National Renewal; Center for Democracy and Citizenship; Pew Partnership for Civic Change; Pew Center for Civic Journalism; Project on Public Life and the Press; Pew Charitable Trusts; Ford Foundation's media program; Wisconsin Public Television; American Health Decisions; Hastings Center for Bioethics; U.S. Environmental Protection Agency; U.S. Department of Housing and Urban Development; and U.S. Department of Health and Human Services. Our work has typically involved mutual exchange of information, case material, and critical evaluation as part of a collaborative learning and strategic planning process.

TWO. COMMUNITY ORGANIZING AND DEVELOPMENT

1. See William Julius Wilson, *The Truly Disadvantaged: The Inner City, the Underclass, and Public Policy* (Chicago: University of Chicago Press, 1987); and John

Kasarda, "Inner-City Concentrated Poverty and Neighborhood Distress: 1970–1990," *Housing Policy Debate* 3 (1993), 253–302.

2. Quoted in Peter Marris and Martin Rein, *Dilemmas of Social Reform: Poverty and Community Action in the United States,* 2d ed. (Chicago: University of Chicago Press, 1982), 210.

3. Marris and Rein, *Dilemmas of Social Reform,* 260, 269. See also Richard Boone, "Reflections on Citizen Participation and the Economic Opportunity Act," *Public Administration Review* 32 (September 1972), 444–56; Paul Peterson and J. David Greenstone, "Racial Change and Citizen Participation: The Mobilization of Low-Income Communities through Community Action," in Robert Havemann, ed., *A Decade of Federal Antipoverty Programs* (New York: Academic Press, 1977), 241–78.

4. Lyndon Johnson, quoted in James Sundquist, "Origins of the War on Poverty," in James Sundquist, ed., *On Fighting Poverty* (New York: Basic Books, 1969), 23; John Wofford, "The Politics of Local Responsibility," 73–74 in the same volume; and *CAP Program Guide,* quoted in Ralph Kramer, *Participation of the Poor: Comparative Community Case Studies in the War on Poverty* (Englewood Cliffs, NJ: Prentice Hall, 1969).

5. See Marris and Rein, *Dilemmas of Social Reform,* epilogue; Morone, *Democratic Wish,* chapter 6; Jill Quadagno, *The Color of Welfare: How Racism Undermined the War on Poverty* (New York: Oxford University Press, 1994), chapter 2; and Nelson Polsby, *Political Innovation in America* (New Haven, CT: Yale University Press, 1984), 128–45, on the program's vulnerabilities deriving from the circumstances of its creation.

6. See Frank Riessman and Arthur Pearl, *New Careers for the Poor* (New York: Free Press, 1965).

7. See Kramer, *Participation of the Poor,* chapter 1.

8. See Kramer, *Participation of the Poor;* and Peter Eisinger, "Comment on Peterson and Greenstone," in Havemann, *Federal Antipoverty Programs.*

9. See Dale Rogers Marshall, *The Politics of Participation in Poverty* (Berkeley: University of California Press, 1971); Nancy Naples, *Grassroots Warriors: Activist Mothering, Community Work, and the War on Poverty* (New York: Routledge, 1998); David Austin, "Resident Participation: Political Mobilization or Organizational Cooptation?" *Public Administration Review* 32 (September 1972); John Strange, "Citizen Participation in Community Action and Model Cities Programs," *Public Administration Review* 32 (October 1972), 655–69; "Citizen Action in Model Cities and CAP Programs: Case Studies and Evaluation," *Public Administration Review* 32 (September 1972); Karen Davis and Cathy Schoen, *Health and the War on Poverty* (Washington, DC: Brookings, 1978); Edward Zigler and Susan Muenchow, *Head Start* (New York: Basic Books, 1992), chapter 5; Lucie White, "On the Vision and Practice of Participation in Project Head Start," in Gary Bellow and Martha Minow, eds., *Law Stories* (Ann Arbor: University of Michigan Press, 1998), 197–218; and Joe Soss, "Lessons of Welfare: Policy Design, Political Learning, and Political Action," *American Political Science Review* 93: 2 (June 1999), 363–80, on the continuing impacts of participatory design within Head Start.

10. See Greenstone and Peterson, *Race and Authority in Urban Politics;* Kramer, *Participation of the Poor;* and Austin, "Resident Participation," 416 ff.

11. See Arthur Stinchcombe, "Social Structure and Organizations," in James March, ed., *Handbook of Organizations* (Chicago: Rand McNally, 1965), 153–93.

12. On the first, see especially Greenstone and Peterson, *Race and Authority in Urban Politics;* on the second, see Quadagno, *Color of Welfare,* chapters 1–2.

13. Quadagno, *Color of Welfare,* 57.

14. James Sundquist with David Davis, *Making Federalism Work: A Study of Program Coordination at the Community Level* (Washington, DC: Brookings, 1969), 118 and chapter 2. See also Lawrence Brown and Bernard Frieden, "Rulemaking by Improvisation: Guidelines and Goals in the Model Cities Program," *Policy Sciences* 7: 4 (1976), 455–88; Robert Aleshire, "Power to the People: An Assessment of Community Action and Model Cities Experience," *Public Administration Review* 32 (September 1972), 428–43; Sherry Arnstein, "Eight Rungs on the Ladder of Citizen Participation," *Journal of the American Institute of Planners* 25 (1969), 216–24; and Marshall Kaplan, *The Model Cities Program* (New York: Praeger, 1970).

15. Aleshire, "Power to the People," 438.

16. Brown and Frieden, "Rulemaking by Improvisation," 484, are especially insightful about practical improvisation in response to problem solving and conflict resolution among community groups, as well as the development of local counterstrategies in the face of federal obstacles, especially under the Nixon administration. On the substantial development of citizen capacities to collaborate and learn from experience through Model Cities, and the legislative and bureaucratic context in which the entire effort evolved, see Charles Haar, *Between the Idea and the Reality: A Study in the Origin, Fate, and Legacy of the Model Cities Program* (Boston: Little, Brown, 1975).

17. Daniel Patrick Moynihan, *Maximum Feasible Misunderstanding: Community Action in the War on Poverty* (New York: Free Press, 1969). See the especially incisive critique of Moynihan in Berry, Portney, and Thomson, *Rebirth of Urban Democracy,* 22–30.

18. For example, Greenstone and Peterson, *Race and Authority in Urban Politics.*

19. Peter Berger and Richard John Neuhaus, *To Empower People: From State to Civil Society,* 2d ed., ed. Michael Novak (Washington, DC: AEI Press, 1996).

20. See, for instance, Frances Fox Piven and Richard Cloward, *Regulating the Poor* (New York: Vintage, 1971), chapter 9; *Poor People's Movements: How They Succeed and Why They Fail* (New York: Pantheon, 1977); Ira Katznelson, *City Trenches: Urban Politics and the Patterning of Class in the United States* (New York: Pantheon, 1981); Stephen Rose, *The Betrayal of the Poor: The Transformation of Community Action* (Cambridge, MA: Schenkman, 1972).

21. Polsky, *Rise of the Therapeutic State;* McKnight, *Careless Society.*

22. Heather Booth, quoted in Harry Boyte, *The Backyard Revolution: Understanding the New Citizen Movement* (Philadelphia, PA: Temple University Press, 1980), 39.

23. Quoted in Sanford Horwitt, *Let Them Call Me Rebel: Saul Alinsky, His Life and Legacy* (New York: Knopf, 1989), 472. See also Saul Alinsky, *Reveille for Radicals* (New York: Vintage, 1946, 1969).

24. Manuel Castells, *The City and the Grassroots: A Cross-Cultural Theory of Urban Social Movements* (Berkeley: University of California Press, 1983), 65, and chapters 6 and 13. See also Donald Reitzes and Dietrich Reitzes, *The Alinsky Legacy: Alive and Kicking* (Greenwich, CT: JAI Press, 1987); Joan Lancourt, *Confront or Concede: The Alinsky Citizen-Action Organizations* (Lexington, MA: Lexington Books, 1979).

25. For comparative studies on the relative effectiveness of congregational models, see Richard Wood, *Faith in Action: Religion, Race, and the Future of Democracy* (Berkeley: University of California, Ph.D. diss., 1995); and Roger Karapin, "Community-Organizations and Low-Income Citizen Participation in the U.S.: Strategies, Organization and Power Since the 1960s," paper presented at the Annual Meetings

of the American Political Science Association, New York, September 1–4, 1994. Due to limitations of space, we cannot analyze other important models in detail here. For a useful overview, see Gary Delgado, *Beyond the Politics of Place: New Directions in Community Organizing in the 1990s, A Report to the Ford Foundation* (Oakland, CA: Applied Research Center, 1994).

26. Jim Drake, organizing director for the Northeast region of IAF, provided recent organizational figures, Cambridge, MA, April 1998.

27. Boyte, *Common Wealth: A Return to Citizen Politics,* (New York: Free Press, 1989), 76–77, and chapter 6; Clifford Green, ed., *Churches, Cities, and Human Community: Urban Ministry in the United States, 1945–1985* (Grand Rapids, MI: Eerdmans, 1996), which examines the history of urban missions and community organizing within various denominations and the ways in which learning occurred within specific congregations, denominations, and interfaith networks even before the major shifts by the IAF.

28. Samuel Freedman, *Upon This Rock: The Miracles of a Black Church* (New York: Harper Collins, 1993); Timothy Ross, *The Impact of Community Organizing on East Brooklyn, 1978–1995* (College Park: University of Maryland, Ph.D. diss., 1996); Jim Rooney, *Organizing the South Bronx* (Albany: SUNY Press, 1995); and Industrial Areas Foundation, *Organizing for Family and Congregation* (Franklin Square, NY: IAF, 1978).

29. Mark Russell Warren, *Social Capital and Community Empowerment: Religion and Political Organization in the Texas Industrial Areas Foundation* (Cambridge, MA: Harvard University, Ph.D. diss., 1995).

30. Quoted in Mary Beth Rogers, *Cold Anger: A Story of Faith and Power Politics* (Denton: University of North Texas Press, 1990), 175.

31. Quoted in Rogers, *Cold Anger,* 176. See also Joseph Sekul, "Communities Organized for Public Service: Citizen Power and Public Policy in San Antonio," in David Johnson, John Booth, and Richard Harris, eds., *The Politics of San Antonio: Community, Progress and Power* (Lincoln: University of Nebraska Press, 1983), 175–90.

32. Quoted in Warren, *Social Capital and Community Empowerment,* 170.

33. See Charles Kieffer, *The Emergence of Empowerment: The Development of Participatory Competence Among Individuals in Citizen Organizations,* 2 vols. (Ann Arbor: University of Michigan, Ph.D. diss., 1981); Larry McNeil, "The Soft Arts of Organizing," *Social Policy* (winter 1995), 17–22; and Bernard Loomer, "Two Conceptions of Power," *Criterion* 15: 1 (winter 1976), 12–29. See also Susan Stall and Randy Stoecker, "Community Organizing or Organizing Community? Gender and the Crafts of Empowerment," *Gender and Society* 12: 6 (December 1998), 729–56, who, however, neglect the significance of relational strategies within congregation-based organizing since Alinsky's death, and the fact that relational models of women's organizing underlie many contemporary community building strategies not primarily attached to protest or social movements.

34. Personal interview with Ernesto Cortés, Jr., Cambridge, MA, December 16, 1993. See also Ernesto Cortés, Jr., "Reweaving the Fabric: The Iron Rule and the IAF Strategy for Power and Politics," in Henry Cisneros, ed., *Interwoven Destinies: Cities and the Nation* (New York: Norton, 1993), 294–319; Rogers, *Cold Anger,* part 1.

35. Field notes from Greater Boston Interfaith Organization meetings, Saint Paul Cathedral, Boston, January 13, 1999; Saint Anne Church, Somerville, MA, July 15, 1998; First Baptist Church, Cambridge MA, April 19, 1998.

36. Virginia Ramirez, quoted in Warren, *Social Capital and Community Empowerment*, 273, which provides the most careful scholarly study of the relation of organizers and leaders in the IAF. For a contrasting view, see Peter Skerry, *Mexican Americans: The Ambivalent Minority* (New York: Free Press, 1993), 166 ff.

37. Kurt Schmoke, Conference on Building Healthier Communities: Ten Years and Learning, Arlington, VA, November 14, 1998; personal interviews and discussions with current BUILD lead organizer Jonathan Lange, Waltham, MA, April 22, 1994; Gerald Taylor, Washington, DC, March 4, 1994, and Racine, WI, December 3–4, 1996. See also Marion Orr, *Black Social Capital: The Politics of School Reform in Baltimore, 1986–1998* (Lawrence: University of Kansas Press, 1999); Harold McDougall, *Black Baltimore* (Philadelphia, PA: Temple University Press, 1993), chapters 6–7.

38. Dennis Shirley, *Community Organizing for Urban School Reform* (Austin: University of Texas Press, 1997), 56.

39. Edna Rodriguez, quoted in Shirley, *Community Organizing for Urban School Reform*, 194–95. Shirley also shows how IAF learned from its earlier failures on school reform efforts in Chicago.

40. Wood, *Faith in Action*. See also Rev. David Mann, *Pastor, Priest, Organizer* (San Jose, CA: n.d.); personal interview with Heidi Swarts, Somerville, MA., August 11, 1994, who was a leader in the PICO San Francisco Organizing Project in the 1980s, and former feminist and anti-pornography organizer in Pittsburgh. The number of federations for PICO and other congregation-based networks are based on figures provided by their national offices in December 1999.

41. See Delgado, *Beyond the Politics of Place;* John D. McCarthy and Jim Castelli, *Working for Justice: The Campaign for Human Development and Poor Empowerment Groups* (Washington, DC: Life Cycle Institute, Catholic University, November 1994); Mark Gornick, "Putting Faith to Work: The Role of Congregations in Community Building," in James Gibson, Joseph McNeely, and Alice Shabecoff, eds., *Building Community in America* (unpublished ms., 1998); Meredith Ramsay, "Redeeming the City: Exploring the Relationship Between Church and Metropolis," *Urban Affairs Review* 33: 5 (May 1998), 595–626; Gamaliel Foundation, *Jubilee: A Time for Metropolitan Equities and the Common Good* (Chicago: Gamaliel Foundation, 1999).

42. See Frederick Perella, Jr., "Roman Catholic Approaches to Urban Ministry, 1955–85," in Green, *Churches, Cities, and Human Community*, 179–211; and McCarthy and Castelli, *Working for Justice*.

43. Quoted in Jeremy Brecher, *"Canst Thou Draw Out Leviathan with a Fishhook?": A Community-Based Response to an Out-of-Control Economy* (Washington, DC: Grassroots Policy Project, 1995), 23. Here we draw on personal interviews and discussions with Robert Woodson, Sr., director of the National Center for Neighborhood Enterprise, Washington, DC, March 4, 1994, July 18, 1994, and January 24, 1996; Kathleen Hurty, Office of Ecumenical Networks, National Council of Churches of Christ in the USA, South Hadley, MA, June 15, 1996; Dorothy Rose and John Landesman of the Syracuse interfaith network, South Hadley, MA, June 15, 1996; Bobby Austin, Director of the National Task Force on African American Men and Boys, Waltham, MA, April 1997. See also Jim Wallis, *The Soul of Politics* (New York: Harcourt Brace, 1994); Bobby Austin, *Repairing the Breach: Report of the National Task Force on African American Men and Boys* (Chicago: Noble Press, 1996); John DiIulio, "The Church and the Civil Society Sector," *Brookings Review* 15: 4 (fall 1997), 27–31; Virginia Hodgkinson and Mur-

ray Weitzman, *From Belief to Commitment: The Community Service Activities and Finances of Religious Congregations in the United States* (Washington, DC: Independent Sector, 1993). Verba, Schlozman, and Brady, *Voice and Equality,* 518–21, emphasize the importance of religious institutions in developing civic skills, and especially their capacity to counteract other tendencies toward participatory inequality linked to class, education, and job skills.

44. Herbert Rubin, "Renewing Hope in the Inner City: Conversations with Community-Based Development Practitioners," *Administration and Society* 27: 1 (1995), 147.

45. John Mollenkopf, *The Contested City* (Princeton, NJ: Princeton University Press, 1983), 180.

46. Mollenkopf, *Contested City,* chapters 5 and 7. See also Carol Steinbach, "Community-Based Development Organizations: A New Industry Emerges," in Gibson, McNeely, and Shabecoff, *Building Community in America;* Neal Peirce and Carol Steinbach, *Corrective Capitalism: The Rise of America's Community Development Corporations* (New York: Ford Foundation, 1987); Severyn Bruyn and James Meehan, eds., *Beyond the Market and the State: New Directions in Community Development* (Philadelphia, PA: Temple University Press, 1987).

47. See Gregory Squires, ed., *From Redlining to Reinvestment: Community Responses to Community Disinvestment* (Philadelphia, PA: Temple University Press, 1992); Christopher Walker and Mark Weinheimer, *Community Development in the 1990s* (Washington, DC: Urban Institute, 1998), 62.

48. See Edward Goetz, *Shelter Burden: Local Politics and Progressive Housing Policy* (Philadelphia, PA: Temple University Press, 1993); Rachel Bratt, *Rebuilding a Low-Income Housing Policy* (Philadelphia, PA: Temple University Press, 1989); Pierre Clavel, Jessica Pitt, and Jordan Yin, "The Community Option in Urban Policy," *Urban Affairs Review* 32: 4 (March 1997), 435–58; Kathryn Tholin, *Community Development Financial Institutions: Investing in People and Communities* (Chicago: Woodstock Institute, 1994); and Margaret Weir, "Power, Money, and Politics in Community Development," in Ronald Ferguson and William Dickens, eds., *Urban Problems and Community Development* (Washington, DC: Brookings, 1999), 149–53, 174, who refers to the "network strategy" that was enabled by the incentives of the LIHTC and the sanctions of the CRA.

49. See Carol Steinbach, "Community Development Corporations in United States Civil Society," paper presented to the Conference on Civil Society in the United States, Washington, DC, Georgetown University, June 3–4, 1999; Sara Stoutland, "Community Development Corporations: Mission, Strategy, and Accomplishments," in Ferguson and Dickens, *Urban Problems and Community Development,* 193–240.

50. Telephone interviews with Pablo Eisenberg, executive director of the Center for Community Change, February 10, 1994; Karen Stokes, executive director of the Coalition for Low-Income Community Development, February 26, 1994; personal interview with Joseph McNeely, executive director of the Development Training Institute, Reston, VA, February 25, 1995; Avis Vidal, "CDCs as Agents of Neighborhood Change: The State of the Art," in Keating, Krumholz, and Starr, *Revitalizing Urban Neighborhoods,* 154–59; Langley Keyes, Alex Schwartz, Avis Vidal, and Rachel Bratt, "Networks and Nonprofits: Opportunities and Challenges in an Era of Federal Devolution," *Housing Policy Debate* 7: 2 (1996), 201–29; Ronald Ferguson and Sara Stout-

land, "Reconceiving the Community Development Field," in Ferguson and Dickens, *Urban Problems and Community Development*, 33–75.

51. Walker and Weinheimer, *Community Development in the 1990s*, 56, 71.

52. YouthBuild was developed by Dorothy Stoneman, a long-time community organizer in Harlem, on the basis of the Youth Action Program she founded in the 1970s, and later modified in Boston, before extending it nationwide. It is now funded by HUD and other sources, though the YouthBuild USA Affiliated Network functions as a nonprofit to transfer best practices and learning in a way most consistent with the model of empowerment and public work. Personal discussions with, and presentations by, Dorothy Stoneman, Racine, WI, March 1–3, 1996; and Ronald Ferguson and Philip Clay, *YouthBuild in Developmental Perspective: A Formative Evaluation of the YouthBuild Demonstration Project* (Cambridge, MA: Kennedy School of Government, Harvard University, September 1996). See also P. Jefferson Armistead and Matthew Wexler, *Community Development and Youth Development: The Potential for Convergence* (New York: Ford Foundation and International Youth Foundation, April 1997), and other publications in this series; and *CYD Journal* 1:1 (winter 2000).

53. Steinbach, "Community-Based Development Organizations: A New Industry Emerges"; Bennett Harrison and Marcus Weiss, *Workforce Development Networks: Community-Based Organizations and Regional Alliances* (Newbury Park, CA: Sage, 1998); and Avis Vidal, "Can Community Development Re-Invent Itself? The Challenges of Strengthening Neighborhoods in the Twentieth Century," *Journal of the American Planning Association* 63: 4 (autumn 1997), 429–38.

54. See Stoutland, "Community Development Corporations," 219–26, for a good overview of issues and literature on the long-standing question of the tension between resident participation and staff dominance.

55. Tony Robinson, "Inner-City Innovator: The Non-Profit Community Development Corporation," *Urban Studies* 33: 9 (1996), 1660–61. See also Clavel, Pitt, and Yin, "The Community Option in Urban Policy," 444–45; Rubin, "Renewing Hope in the Inner City"; Edward Goetz and Sidney Mara, "Community Development Corporations as Neighborhood Advocates: A Study of Political Activism of Nonprofit Developers," *Applied Behavioral Science Review* 3: 1 (1995), 1–20; Jordan Yin, "The Community Development Industry System: A Case Study of Politics and Institutions in Cleveland, 1967–1997," *Journal of Urban Affairs* 20: 2 (1998), 137–57, on the complex dynamics between organizing, corporate, and city-sponsored activities. For a critical view of CDCs that sees them as disorganizing their communities by accommodating to capital markets, dampening confrontational organizing, and encouraging victim blaming, see Randy Stoecker, "The CDC Model of Urban Redevelopment: A Critique and an Alternative," *Journal of Urban Affairs* 19: 1 (1997), 1–22, as well as the compelling responses by Rachel Bratt and Dennis Keating.

56. Personal interview with Michael Eichler, Racine, WI, December 3, 1996. See also Ross Gittell and Avis Vidal, *Community Organizing: Building Social Capital as a Development Strategy* (Thousand Oaks, CA: Sage, 1998).

57. Telephone interviews with John McKnight, April 21, 1994, and November 19, 1996; personal discussions with Curt Johnson, United Way of America, in flight from Kansas City to Washington, DC, May 18, 1997; Dan Duncan, president, Mesa (Arizona) United Way, and a former Alinsky organizer, Kansas City, MO, May 17, 1997. See John Kretzmann and John McKnight, *Building Communities from the Inside Out*

(Evanston, IL: Center for Urban Affairs, Northwestern University, 1993); Janice Hirota, Prudence Brown, and Nancy Martin, *Building Community: The Tradition and Promise of Settlement Houses* (Chicago: Chapin Hall Center for Children, 1996); United Way of America, *United Ways' Community Capacity-Building Stories* (Washington, DC: United Way of America, 1995); *Storymaking: United Way and the Transformation of Community* (1996); and *Community Impact through Neighborhood Partnerships* (1997).

58. Personal discussions with Jeff Armistead, senior vice president at LISC; and Carey Shea, former program director of the LISC Community Building Initiative, Racine, WI, December 3, 1996.

59. Field notes and site visits, 1997 NCBN Spring Conference, "Putting Community Building To Work: Making the Jobs Connection," Kansas City, MO, May 15–18, 1997; telephone interview, October 1996, with Gregory Watson, executive director of the Dudley Street Neighborhood Initiative, an important comprehensive community-building initiative. See also Joan Walsh, *Stories of Renewal: Community Building and the Future of Urban America* (New York: Rockefeller Foundation, 1996); G. Thomas Kingsley, Joseph McNeely, and James Gibson, *Community Building: Coming of Age* (Baltimore, MD: Development Training Institute and Urban Institute, 1997); Lisbeth Schorr, *Common Purpose: Strengthening Families and Neighborhoods to Rebuild America* (New York: Doubleday, 1997), chapter 9; Anne Kubisch et al., *Voices from the Field: Learning from the Early Work of Comprehensive Community Initiatives* (Washington, DC: Aspen Institute, 1997); Rebecca Stone, ed., *Core Issues in Comprehensive Community-Building Initiatives* (Chicago: Chapin Hall Center for Children, 1996); Peter Medoff and Holly Sklar, *Streets of Hope: The Fall and Rise of an Urban Neighborhood* (Boston: South End Press, 1994).

60. See Gerri Spilka and Tom Burns, *The Comprehensive Community Revitalization Program in the South Bronx: Final Assessment Report* (Philadelphia, PA: OMG Center for Collaborative Learning, March 1998); Mitchell Sviridoff and William Ryan, *Investing in Community: Lessons and Implications of the Comprehensive Community Revitalization Program*, rev. ed. (New York: Surdna Foundation, April, 1996).

61. Richard Cowden, quoted in Carl Vogel, "Open for Business," *The Neighborhood Works* 20: 1 (January–February 1997), 8. We also draw upon our discussions with George Latimer, director of the Special Actions Office, Office of the Secretary of HUD, Washington, DC, July 15, 1994. See also the President's Community Empowerment Board, *Building Communities Together: Guidebook for Community-Based Strategic Planning for Empowerment Zones and Enterprise Communities* (Washington, DC: Government Printing Office, May 1995 Update).

62. See Marilyn Gittell, Kathe Newman, Janice Brockmeyer, and Robert Lindsay, "Expanding Civic Opportunity: Urban Empowerment Zones," *Urban Affairs Review* 33: 4 (March 1998), 530–58; Special Issue on EZ/ECs Two-Year Anniversary, *The Neighborhood Works* 20: 1 (January–February 1997); Weir, "Power, Money, and Politics in Community Development," 164–68; National Civic League, *Building Communities Together: Strategic Planning Guide for Empowerment Zone/Enterprise Community Initiative, Round II* (Washington, DC: Department of Housing and Urban Development, 1998); Andrew Cuomo and Dan Glickman, *What Works in the Empowerment Zones and Enterprise Communities,* vol. 2 (Washington, DC: U.S. Department of Housing and Urban Development and Department of Agriculture, 1998).

63. Quoted in Arthur Naparstek, Dennis Dooley, and Robin Smith, *Community*

Building in Public Housing: Ties That Bind People and Their Communities (Washington, DC: U.S. Department of Housing and Urban Development, April 1997); personal discussions with, and presentations by, HOPE VI resident leaders, National Community Building Network Conference, Kansas City, MO, May 16, 1997. See also *A Guide to Best Practices* (Washington, DC: HUD, 1998), developed by the Center for Visionary Leadership working with a task force of public housing authority officials, resident leaders, and nonprofit intermediaries.

64. See Berry, Portney, and Thomson, *Rebirth of Urban Democracy;* Ken Thomson, Joanne Bissetta and Thomas Webb, *Participation Works* (Medford, MA: Lincoln Filene Center, 1994).

65. See especially Carl Abbott, *Portland: Planning, Politics, and Growth in the Twentieth Century* (Lincoln: University of Nebraska Press, 1983).

66. Department of Housing and Urban Development, *The Model Cities Program: A History and Analysis of the Planning Process in Three Cities—Atlanta, Seattle, Dayton* (Washington, DC: Government Printing Office, 1968).

67. See Steven Haeberle, *Planting the Grassroots: Structuring Citizen Participation* (New York: Praeger, 1989).

68. See Joseph Sekul, *The C.O.P.S Story: A Case Study of Successful Collective Action* (Austin: University of Texas, Ph.D. diss., 1984), 157–61; John Booth, "Political Change in San Antonio: 1970–82," in Johnson, Booth, and Harris, eds., *Politics of San Antonio,* 193 ff.; Heywood Sanders, "Communities Organized for Public Service and Neighborhood Revitalization in San Antonio," in Robert H. Wilson, ed., *Public Policy and Community: Activism and Governance in Texas* (Austin: University of Texas Press, 1997), 36–68.

69. Personal interviews with John Parr, Denver, CO, October 19, 1996; William Potapchuk, Washington, DC, November 8, 1996. See also Neal Peirce, with Curtis Johnson and Stuart Hall, *Citistates* (Washington, DC: Seven Locks Press, 1993), 283; and Christopher Howard, Michael Lipsky, and Dale Rogers Marshall, "Citizen Participation in Urban Politics: Rise and Routinization," in George Peterson, ed., *Big-City Politics, Governance, and Fiscal Constraints* (Washington, DC: Urban Institute Press, 1994), 177–78.

70. This account is based on personal interviews, formal presentations, group discussions, and a review of official documents and community outreach materials in Portland, OR, May 20–23, 1998. The individuals included Nancy Biasi, executive assistant to the commissioner, City of Portland, formerly the director of the Office of Neighborhood Associations (also Washington, DC, November 8, 1996); Diane Linn, director of Office of Neighborhood Involvement; Vera Katz, mayor; J. Lauren Norris, Office of Neighborhood Involvement and Bureau of Environmental Services; Linda Robinson, East Multnomah Soil and Water Conservation District; Jay Mower, coordinator of the Columbia Slough Watershed Association; Susan Barthel, Bureau of Environmental Services; Peter Teneau, member of the Columbia Slough Watershed Association; Cindy Silveira, resident of Southeast Uplift and community activity coordinator of the Southwest Washington Medical Center Foundation; Michael Harrison, chief planner for Neighborhood and Community Planning; Lee Leighton, president of the Sellwood-Moreland Improvement League; Lenard Gard, Southwest Neighborhoods, Inc.; Kathy Brazell, Outer Southeast organizer; Multnomah County district attorneys Laurel Abraham, Jay Hayden, and Wayne Pearson; and Charles

Moose, chief, Portland Police Bureau. See also *Report and Recommendations of the Task Force on Neighborhood Involvement* (Portland, February 7, 1996); *Guidelines for Neighborhood Associations, District Coalitions, Neighborhood Business Associations, Communities Beyond Neighborhood Boundaries, Alternative Service Delivery Structures, and the Office of Neighborhood Involvement*, adopted by the City Council of Portland, January 7, 1998; *Community Watershed Stewardship Program: Framework Plan* (Portland, OR: Portland Bureau of Environmental Services, 1995); Bruce Adams, "The Portland Way," in Bruce Adams and John Parr, eds., *Boundary Crossers: Case Studies of How Ten of America's Metropolitan Regions Work* (College Park, MD: Burns Academy of Leadership, University of Maryland, 1997); Christopher Leo, "Regional Growth Management Regime: The Case of Portland, Oregon," *Journal of Urban Affairs* 20: 4 (1998), 363–94; Barbara Boland, "Community Prosecution: Portland's Experience," in David Karp, ed., *Community Justice: An Emerging Field* (Lanham, MD: Rowman and Littlefield, 1998), 253–77; Alexander Welsch and Charles Heying, "Watershed Management and Community Building: A Case Study of Portland's Community Watershed Stewardship Program," *Administrative Theory and Praxis* 21: 1 (March 1999), 88–102; Michael Irwin, "Periodic Atlas of the Metroscape: Social Capital of Local Communities," *Metroscape* (spring 1998), 13–19; the National Academy of Public Administration, *Building Stronger Communities and Regions: Can the Federal Government Help?* (Washington, DC: National Academy of Public Administration, 1998), 34–36; Walker and Weinheimer, *Community Development in the 1990s*, 93, 96.

71. See Susan Fainstein and Clifford Hirst, "Neighborhood Organizations and Community Planning: The Minneapolis Neighborhood Revitalization Program," in Keating, Krumholz, and Star, *Revitalizing Urban Neighborhoods*, 96–111; Rip Rapson, "The Neighborhood Revitalization Program in Minneapolis," presentation to the Conference on Governance, Washington, DC, November 8, 1996; and Keyes et al., "Networks and Nonprofits," 213–15.

72. See Edward Goetz and Mara Sidney, "Local Policy Subsystems and Issue Definition: An Analysis of Community Development Policy Change," *Urban Affairs Review* 32: 4 (March 1977), 490–512; and "Revenge of the Property Owners: Community Development and the Politics of Property," *Journal of Urban Affairs* 16: 4 (1994), 319–34. On the politics of regional fair housing efforts by its chief legislative proponent, see Myron Orfield, *Metropolitics: An Agenda for Community and Stability*, rev. ed. (Washington, DC and Cambridge, MA: Brookings Institution and Lincoln Institute of Land Policy, 1997), chapter 7.

73. We draw this account from several formal presentations by Jim Diers and other staff of the Seattle Department of Neighborhoods, Neighborhoods USA Conference, Portland, OR, May 21–22, 1998; telephone interview with Shireen Deboo in the matching grants program, October 4, 1999; and from follow-up conversations with Diers, as well as materials provided by his office. The Department of Neighborhoods website (www.ci.seattle.wa.us/don) contains a comprehensive listing of projects funded since 1988, and of the great diversity of civic associations involved, as well as the detailed neighborhood plans developed by citizens over the past five years. See also Wendelyn Martz, *Neighborhood-Based Planning: Five Case Studies* (Chicago: American Planning Association, 1995), 18–21; Margaret Gordon, Hubert Locke, Laurie McCutcheon, and William Stafford, "Seattle: Grassroots Politics Shaping the Environment," in H. V. Savitch and John Clayton Thomas, eds., *Big City Politics in Transi-*

298 NOTES TO PAGES 76–79

tion (Newbury Park, CA: Sage, 1991), 216–34; and Barrett A. Lee, R. S. Oropesa, Barbara J. Metch, and Avery Guest, "Testing the Decline of Community Thesis: Neighborhood Organizations in Seattle, 1929 and 1979," *American Journal of Sociology* 89: 5 (1984), 1161–88.

74. John Clayton Thomas, *Between Citizen and City: Neighborhood Organizations and Urban Politics in Cincinnati* (Lawrence: University Press of Kansas, 1986). See also Carmine Scavo, "The Use of Participative Mechanisms in Large U.S. Cities," *Journal of Urban Affairs* 15: 1 (1993), 93–109; Sallie Marston, "Citizen Action Programs and Participatory Politics in Tucson," in Ingram and Smith, *Public Policy for Democracy*, 119–35; Elaine Sharpe, *Citizen Demand-Making in the Urban Context* (Birmingham: University of Alabama Press, 1986). Residential community associations have grown enormously, from 1,000 in 1960 to 205,000 in 1998, with an average of 40–160 dwelling units each. Although such associations are generally created by developers, members rarely terminate them when developers leave the scene, because they effectively provide many low-level public goods (and undoubtedly some bads as well), not unlike some previous forms of social capital that have been depleted during the same period. See Robert C. Ellickson, "New Institutions for Old Neighborhoods," *Duke Law Journal* 48 (1998), 75–110.

75. Host city organizers provide substantial resources that permit NUSA to operate with a small national staff and volunteer leadership. We base this analysis on several presentations and personal conversations with two recent presidents of NUSA, George Manning and Milton Dohoney, as well as field observations, extensive conversations, and review of audio tapes from the 1998 and 1999 NUSA conferences.

76. National League of Cities, National Conference, "Building Civic Democracy and Responsibility," Charlotte, NC, May 2–3, 1997; the NLC's CD-ROM, *Examples of Programs for Cities*, 2d ed. (1998); personal discussions with Antoinette Samuel of the National League of Cities, Denver, CO, April 17–20, 1997, and April 16–19, 1998; Peter Hawley, American Planning Association, Boston, April 8, 1998, Portland, OR, May 21, 1998; Ed Ferguson, National Association of Counties, Denver, CO, April 19, 1997, April 17–18, 1998. See also Dan Kemmis, *The Good City and the Good Life: Renewing the Sense of Community* (Boston: Houghton Mifflin, 1995); Martz, *Neighborhood-Based Planning;* the 63rd Annual Conference of Mayors, Best Practices in City Government, June 1995; Architects/Designers/Planners for Social Responsibility, "Introduction," *Newvillage* 1 (1999); Norman Krumholz and Pierre Clavel, *Reinventing Cities: Equity Planners Tell Their Stories* (Philadelphia, PA: Temple University Press, 1994); Norman Krumholz and John Forester, *Making Equity Planning Work: Leadership in the Public Sector* (Philadelphia, PA: Temple University Press, 1990); John Forester, *The Deliberative Practitioner: Encouraging Participatory Planning Processes* (Cambridge, MA: MIT Press, 1999); John Friedmann, *Planning in the Public Domain* (Princeton, NJ: Princeton University Press, 1987).

77. Telephone interview with Suzanne Morse, August 5, 1997; Tom Dewar, David Dodson, Virginia Paget, and Rona Roberts, *"Just Call It Effective"*: *Civic Change, Moving From Projects to Progress* (Richmond, VA: University of Richmond, 1998); Harwood Group, *Planned Serendipity* (Charlottesville, VA: Pew Partnership, 1998); Pew Partnership for Civic Change, *Civic Partners* (Charlottesville, VA: Pew Partnership, 1997).

78. Personal interviews with John Parr, former NCL president, Denver, CO, October 19, 1996; Chris Gates, NCL president, Denver, CO, October 18, 1996; Derek

Okubo, Denver, CO, October 18, 1996; William Potapchuk, Washington, DC, November 8, 1996; and Cathy Dec, Denver, CO, October 18, 1996. Our analysis of the All-America City Awards is based on a formal review of approximately 240 applications, as well as field observations of the accompanying four-day deliberations, as a participant of the screening committees for the 1997 and 1998 awards, Denver, CO, April 17–20, 1997, and April 16–19, 1998; field observations of formal group presentations among finalists at the All-America City Awards, Cleveland, OH, June 1995. Our analysis of NCL's community visioning work also draws upon a review of material produced by local partners of several of these visioning projects, as well as *The Community Visioning and Strategic Planning Handbook* (Denver, CO: National Civic League, 1995); David Chrislip and Carl Larson, *Collaborative Leadership* (San Francisco: Jossey-Bass, 1994). See also National Civic League, *The Civic Index: Measuring Your Community's Civic Health,* 2d ed. (Denver, CO: National Civic League, 2000).

79. See Joel Baum and Christine Oliver, "Institutional Embeddedness and the Dynamics of Organizational Populations," *American Sociological Review* 57: 4 (August 1992), 540–59; and Joel Baum, "Organizational Ecology," in Stewart Clegg, Cynthia Hardy, and Walter Nord, eds., *Handbook of Organization Studies* (London: Sage, 1996), 77–114. See also Charles Frombrun, "Structural Dynamics Within and Between Organizations," *Administrative Science Quarterly* 31 (1986), 403–21; "Crafting an Institutionally Informed Ecology of Organizations," in Glen Carroll, ed., *Ecological Models of Organizations* (Cambridge, MA: Ballinger, 1988), 223–39.

80. On this latter point, see Susan Clarke and Gary Gaile, *The Work of Cities* (Minneapolis: University of Minnesota Press, 1998), 70 ff.

81. See Karp, *Community Justice;* Wesley Skogan, *Community Policing, Chicago Style* (New York: Oxford University Press, 1997); Susan L. Miller, *Gender and Community Policing: Walking the Talk* (Boston: Northeastern University Press, 1999); Mark Moore, "Security and Community Development," in Ferguson and Dickens, *Urban Problems and Community Development,* 293–337; Archon Fung, *Street-Level Democracy: Social Experimentation in Theory and Urban Practice* (Cambridge, MA: MIT, Ph.D. diss., 1999).

82. See Jack Brittain and Douglas Wholey, "Competition and Coexistence in Organizational Communities: Population Dynamics in Electronics Components Manufacturing," in Carroll, *Ecological Models of Organizations,* 195–222; and Baum, "Organizational Ecology," for a useful classification and literature review of types of organizational interaction.

83. See Clarence Stone, "Urban Regimes and the Capacity to Govern: A Political Economy Approach," *Journal of Urban Affairs* 15: 1 (1993), 1–28; and *Regime Politics: Governing Atlanta, 1946–1988* (Lawrence: University Press of Kansas, 1989).

84. See Marc Bendick, Jr., *Rebuilding Inner-City Communities: A New Approach to the Nation's Urban Crisis* (New York: Committee for Economic Development, 1995); Larry Ledebour and William Barnes, *All in It Together: Cities, Suburbs, and Local Economic Regions* (Washington, DC: National League of Cities, February 1993); Cisneros, *Interwoven Destinies;* Michael Porter, "New Strategies for Inner-City Economic Development," *Economic Development Quarterly* 11: 1 (February 1997), 11–27; and Bennett Harrison and Amy Glasmeier, "Why Business Alone Won't Redevelop the Inner City: A Friendly Critique of Michael Porter's Approach to Urban Revitalization," *Economic Development Quarterly* 11: 1 (February 1997), 28–38, who locate many of Porter's key insights within the community development legacy of learning over several decades.

For a theoretical analysis of how business exchange values depend on a variety of use values tied to urban place (daily round, agglomeration economies, relations of commitment and trust, etc.), see Todd Swanstrom, "Beyond Economism: Urban Political Economy and the Postmodern Challenge," *Journal of Urban Affairs* 15: 1 (1993), 55–78.

85. See Richard DeLeon, *Left Coast City: Progressive Politics in San Francisco, 1975–1991* (Lawrence: University Press of Kansas, 1992); Anthony Robinson, *Community Mobilization and Regime Transformation in San Francisco's Tenderloin* (Berkeley: University of California, Ph.D. diss., 1994); Pierre Clavel, *The Progressive City* (New Brunswick, NJ: Rutgers University Press, 1986); Pierre Clavel and Wim Wievel, eds., *Harold Washington and the Neighborhoods: Progressive City Government in Chicago* (New Brunswick, NJ: Rutgers University Press, 1991); Barbara Ferman, *Challenging the Growth Machine: Neighborhood Politics in Chicago and Pittsburgh* (Lawrence: University of Kansas Press, 1996); Marion Orr, "Urban Regimes and Human Capital Policies: A Study of Baltimore," *Journal of Urban Affairs* 14: 2 (1992), 173–87; Richard Hula, Cynthia Jackson, and Marion Orr, "Urban Politics, Governing Nonprofits, and Community Revitalization," *Urban Affairs Review* 32: 4 (March 1997), 459–89; Alan DiGaetano, "Urban Governing Alignments and Realignments in Comparative Perspective: Developmental Politics in Boston, Massachusetts, and Bristol, England, 1980–1996," *Urban Affairs Review* 32: 6 (July 1997), 844–70; Denise Nickel, "The Progressive City? Urban Redevelopment in Minneapolis," *Urban Affairs Review* 30: 3 (January 1995), 355–77.

86. See Weir, "Power, Money, and Politics in Community Development," 154–68. On various other constraints, see David L. Imbroscio, *Reconstructing City Politics: Alternative Economic Development and Urban Regimes* (Thousand Oaks, CA: Sage, 1997).

87. Alice O'Connor, "Swimming Against the Tide: A Brief History of Federal Policy in Poor Communities," in Ferguson and Dickens, *Urban Problems and Community Development* (Washington, DC: Brookings, 1999), 77–138, stresses this latter failure to learn. See also David Rusk, *Inside Game/Outside Game: Winning Strategies for Saving Urban America* (Washington, DC: Brookings, 1999); Julia Koschinsky, "Challenging the Third-Sector Housing Approach: The Impact of Federal Policies (1980–1996)," *Journal of Urban Affairs* 20: 2 (1998), 117–35.

88. See Peter Dreier and John Atlas, "U.S. Housing Policy at the Crossroads: Rebuilding the Housing Constituency," *Journal of Urban Affairs* 18: 4 (1996), 341–70; Peter Dreier, "The New Politics of Housing: How to Rebuild the Constituency for a Progressive Housing Policy," *Journal of the American Planning Association* 63: 1 (winter 1997), 5–27.

89. On innovative regional governance practices, see William Dodge, *Regional Excellence: Governing Together to Compete Globally and Flourish Locally* (Washington, DC: National League of Cities, 1996); National Academy of Public Administration, *Building Stronger Communities and Regions;* Allan Wallis, "The Third Wave: Current Trends in Regional Government," *National Civic Review* (summer-fall 1994), 290–309. For business strategies to support community building, see Bendick, *Rebuilding Inner-City Communities,* 50–53; George Peterson and Dana Sunblad, *Corporations as Partners in Strengthening Urban Communities.* Urban Institute Report (New York: The Conference Board, 1994).

90. Harold Wolman, "Introduction," in Harold Wolman and Elizabeth Agius, eds.,

National Urban Policy: Problems and Prospects (Detroit, MI: Wayne State University Press, 1996), 26. See also Vidal, "CDCs as Agents of Neighborhood Change," 159 ff.; Norman Krumholz and Philip Star, "Neighborhood Revitalization: Future Prospects," in Keating, Krumholz, and Star, *Revitalizing Urban Neighborhoods*, 235–48; Alex Schwartz, Rachel Bratt, Avis Vidal, and Langley Keyes, "Nonprofit Housing Organizations and Institutional Support: The Management Challenge," *Journal of Urban Affairs* 18: 4 (1996), 389–407; Kingsley, McNeely, and Gibson, *Community Building: Coming of Age*, for specific strategic recommendations to advance the community-building agenda.

91.   Bendick, *Rebuilding Inner-City Communities*, 2. See also Rebecca Blank, *It Takes a Nation: A New Agenda for Fighting Poverty* (New York: Russell Sage Foundation, with Princeton University Press 1997) 284–93; and Schorr, *Common Purpose*.

THREE. CIVIC ENVIRONMENTALISM

1.   DeWitt John, *Civic Environmentalism: Alternatives to Regulation in States and Communities* (Washington, DC: Congressional Quarterly Press, 1994). See also William Shutkin, *The Land That Could Be: Environmentalism and Democracy in the Twenty-First Century* (Cambridge, MA: MIT Press, 2000).

2.   See Richard Harris and Sidney Milkis, *The Politics of Regulatory Change: A Tale of Two Agencies,* 2d ed. (New York: Oxford University Press, 1996), chapter 3.

3.   See Joseph Saxe, *Defending the Environment: A Strategy for Citizen Involvement* (New York: Knopf, 1971); George Hoberg, *Pluralism by Design: Environmental Policy and the American Regulatory State* (New York: Praeger, 1992).

4.   Berry, Portney, and Thomson, *The Rebirth of Urban Democracy,* 42–43. See also Robert Gottlieb, *Forcing the Spring: The Transformation of the American Environmental Movement* (Washington, DC: Island Press, 1993), 134–35, 253, 357–58.

5.   See Walter Rosenbaum, "Slaying Beautiful Hypotheses with Ugly Facts: EPA and the Limits of Public Participation," *Journal of Voluntary Action Research* 6: 6 (1978), 161–73; Paul Sabatier, "Social Movements and Regulatory Agencies: Towards a More Adequate—and Less Pessimistic—Theory of 'Clientele Capture,'" *Policy Sciences* 6: 3 (1975), 301–42.

6.   William Ruckelshaus, "The Citizen and the Environmental Regulatory Process," *Indiana Law Journal* 47 (1971–72), 638.

7.   See Marc Landy, Marc Roberts, and Stephen Thomas, *The Environmental Protection Agency: Asking the Wrong Questions* (New York: Oxford University Press, 1990, 1994), chapter 2; and Walter Rosenbaum, "The Bureaucracy and Environmental Policy," in James Lester, ed., *Environmental Politics and Policy: Theories and Evidence* (Durham, NC: Duke University Press, 1989), 214–16, 224.

8.   See Evan Ringquist, *Environmental Protection at the State Level: Politics and Progress in Controlling Pollution* (Armonk, NY: Sharpe, 1993); and Barry Rabe, "Power to the States: The Promise and Pitfalls of Decentralization," in Norman Vig and Michael Kraft, eds., *Environmental Policy in the 1990s,* 3d ed. (Washington, DC: Congressional Quarterly Press, 1997), 31–52.

9.   See Barry Boyer, "Funding Public Participation in Agency Proceedings: The Federal Trade Commission Experience," *Georgetown Law Journal* 70 (1981–82), 51–172. The FTC provided a model for the EPA on these issues. See also Carl To-

bias, "Of Public Funds and Public Participation: Resolving the Issue of Agency Authority to Reimburse Public Participants in Administrative Proceedings," *Columbia Law Review* 82 (1982), 906–55.

10. See Walter Rosenbaum, "The Paradoxes of Public Participation," *Administration and Society* 8: 3 (November 1976), 355–83; "Public Involvement as Reform and Ritual: The Development of Federal Participation Programs," in Stuart Langton, ed., *Citizen Participation in America* (Lexington, MA: Lexington Books, 1978), 81–96; and "Slaying Beautiful Hypotheses with Ugly Facts."

11. Personal and telephone interviews with Jerome Delli Priscoli, past president of the ICCP, February 1, 1994, and Washington, DC, March 5, 1994, August 22, 1995; personal interview with Stuart Langton, Cambridge, MA, March 1994.

12. See ICF, Inc., *Analysis of Community Involvement in Hazardous Waste Site Problems: A Report to the Office of Emergency and Remedial Response* (Washington, DC: U.S. EPA, July 1981); and Stephen A. Cohen, Thomas Ingersoll, and James Janis, "Institutional Learning in a Bureaucracy: the Superfund Community Relations Program," *Proceedings of the National Conference on the Management of Uncontrolled Hazardous Waste Sites* (Washington, DC: Hazardous Materials Control Institute, 1981), 405–10.

13. Landy, Roberts, and Thomas, *Environmental Protection Agency*, especially chapter 9.

14. Personal interview with Jerome Delli Priscoli, Washington, DC, August 22, 1995. See also Jeffrey Berry, "Maximum Feasible Dismantlement," *Citizen Participation* (November/December 1981), 3–5. Participants in the ICCP continued to collaborate over the course of the 1980s, and in 1990 helped form the International Association of Public Participation Practitioners (IAP3, since renamed the International Association for Public Participation, or IAP2), which has remained a vital network and forum for reflecting on best practices and sharing techniques within and outside of government.

15. See Eugene Bardach and Robert Kagan, *Going by the Book: The Problem of Regulatory Unreasonableness* (Philadelphia, PA: Temple University Press, 1982).

16. John, *Civic Environmentalism*, 7, 261.

17. See Richard Harris, "Politicized Management: The Changing Face of Business in American Politics," in Richard Harris and Sidney Milkis, eds., *Remaking American Politics* (Boulder, CO: Westview Press, 1989), 261–86; Michael Kraft and Norman Vig, "Environmental Policy in the Reagan Presidency," *Political Science Quarterly* (fall 1984), 415–39; Stuart Langton, ed., *Environmental Leadership* (Lexington, MA: Lexington Books, 1984), 5–11; and Edward P. Weber, *Pluralism by the Rules: Conflict and Cooperation in Environmental Regulation* (Washington, DC: Georgetown University Press, 1998), who analyzes the complex learning and emergence of cooperation games among environmental lobbies, industry, and regulators at state and federal levels in terms of increasing recognition of transaction costs of command and control and the threat to interests held dear by each set of actors, such as industry's heightened stake in flexibility and timeliness in competitive international markets.

18. Conservation Foundation, *Water Quality Training Institute Handbook* (Conservation Foundation: Washington, DC, 1974), 1.

19. David Godschalk and Bruce Stiftel, "Making Waves: Public Participation in State Water Planning," *Journal of Applied Behavioral Science* 17: 4 (1981), 597–614.

20. See Godschalk and Stiftel, "Making Waves"; Stephen A. Cohen, *Citizen Par-*

ticipation in Bureaucratic Decision Making: With Special Emphasis on Environmental Policy (Buffalo: State University of New York, Ph.D. diss., 1979); Ethan Paul Seltzer, *Citizen Participation in Environmental Planning: Context and Consequence* (Philadelphia: University of Pennsylvania, Ph.D. diss., 1983).

21. Mary Lou Soscia and Karen Flagstad, "EPA's National Estuary Program," *EPA Journal* (July–August 1987), 16–20; Tudor Davies, "Answering Questions About a Key Resource: An Interview," *EPA Journal* (July–August 1987), 5–8. For an extensive overview of statutory and institutional levers and barriers that set the context for the emergence of collaborative watershed strategies over several decades, see Robert W. Adler, "Addressing Barriers to Watershed Protection," *Environmental Law* 25: 4 (1995), 973–1106.

22. See Marjorie Hutter, "The Chesapeake Bay: Saving a National Resource Through Multi-State Cooperation," *Virginia Journal of Natural Resources Law* 4 (1985), 185–207; Citizens Program for the Chesapeake Bay, *Choices for the Chesapeake: An Action Agenda, Workshop Recommendations* (October 1983).

23. See Anacostia Watershed Society, *Calendar of Events,* spring 1997; Troy Abel and J. Thomas Hennessey, Jr., "State and Local Opportunities in Environmental Policy: Cleaning Up the Potomac and Anacostia Rivers," *Public Works Management and Policy* 2: 2 (October 1997), 160–71; and Steve Lerner, *Eco-Pioneers: Practical Visionaries Solving Today's Environmental Problems* (Cambridge, MA: MIT Press, 1997), 353–72, from which the quotation from Robert Boone is taken.

24. See Kerry Hodges, ed., *Chesapeake Bay Communities: Making the Connection* (Washington, DC: U.S. Environmental Protection Agency for the Chesapeake Bay Program, April 1996); Chesapeake Bay Program, *A 'Who's Who' in the Chesapeake Bay Program* (Washington, DC: U.S. Environmental Protection Agency for the Chesapeake Bay Program, August 1996); G. Page and R. Davis, *Community-Based Restoration of Submerged Aquatic Vegetation in the Chesapeake Bay* (Baltimore, MD: Alliance for the Chesapeake Bay, 1998); *Small Watershed Grants Program: Summary of 1998 Projects to Be Funded* (Baltimore, MD: Alliance for the Chesapeake Bay, 1998); Jennifer Greenfeld and Brian LeCouteur, *Chesapeake Bay Community Action Guide* (Washington, DC: Metropolitan Washington Council of Governments, 1994); Erik Meyers, Robert Fischman, and Anne Marsh, "Maryland Chesapeake Bay Critical Areas Program: Wetlands Protection and Future Growth," in Douglas Porter and David Salvesen, eds., *Collaborative Planning for Wetlands and Wildlife* (Washington, DC: Island Press, 1995), 181–201; Robert Costanza and Jack Greer, "The Chesapeake Bay and Its Watershed: A Model for Sustainable Ecosystem Management?" in Lance Gunderson, C. S. Holling, and Stephen Light, eds., *Barriers and Bridges to the Renewal of Ecosystems and Institutions* (New York: Columbia University Press, 1995), 169–213; Shari Taylor Wilson, "The Chesapeake Bay Restoration Effort Moves Upstream with Tributary Strategies," *Journal of Environmental Law* 4 (1994), 154 ff.; Marc K. Landy, Megan M. Susman, and Debra S. Knopman, *Civic Environmentalism in Action: A Field Guide to Regional and Local Initiatives* (Washington, DC: Progressive Policy Institute, January 1999), 35–46; Francis X. Clines, "For Chesapeake Oysters, Future May Lie in Past," *New York Times,* August 2, 1999, A11.

25. Archon Fung, Bradley Karkkainen, and Charles Sabel, eds., *Information-Based Environmental Regulation: The Beginning of a New Regulatory Regime?* (New York: Columbia Law School, October 29–30, 1998). See also *Cookbook of Innovations in Coastal*

Protection (Washington, DC: Office of Wetlands, Oceans and Watersheds, U.S. EPA, 1994).

26. Personal and telephone interviews with Elizabeth Kraft, former director of the LWVEF Groundwater Education Project, Washington, DC, December 9, 1994; April 21, 1995, November 1996; Rebekka Fennell, former director of LWVEF, November 1996, and Arlington, VA, November 14, 1998; Lisa Edouard, natural resources assistant project manager, Washington, DC, December 7, December 9, 1994; and Charles Abdalla, Pennsylvania State University Cooperative Extension Services, Overland Park, KS, September 25, 1995. See especially Christine Mueller, *Protect Your Groundwater: Educating for Action* (Washington, DC: LWVEF, 1994).

27. Bob Green, presentation to the First Annual National Community Involvement Conference/Training, sponsored by the Environmental Protection Agency, Boston, August 5, 1998. We have also drawn from presentations and follow-up discussions with Brad Cross, Texas Natural Resources Conservation commissioner; Diane Schrameyer, project director of the RSVP of Lehigh, Northampton, and Carbon Counties, PA; and Jan Shubert of EPA's Office of Ground Water and Drinking Water. See also Lillian Smith Madarchik and Winifred Dowling, *Volunteers and the Environment: How-To Manual for Ground Water Protection Projects* (El Paso, TX: RSVP of the City of El Paso, 1992).

28. See the River Network and the Rivers, Trails and Conservation Assistance program of the National Park Service, *1998–1999 River and Watershed Conservation Directory* (Portland, OR: To the Point Publications, 1998); Christina Akers, "Service Learning and the Environment," unpublished paper, Brandeis University, May 1999.

29. Carl Pope, quoted in Trebbe Johnson, "The Second Creation Story: Redefining the Bond Between Religion and Ecology," *Sierra* (November–December 1998), 50–57. See also Cheryl Cook, Enid Gorman, and Lorette Picciano-Hanson, eds., *A Directory of Environmental Activities and Resources in the North American Religious Community* (New York: Joint Appeal by Religion and Science for the Environment, 1992); Virginia Hodgkinson and Murray Weitzman, *From Belief to Commitment: The Community Service Activities and Finances of Religious Congregations in the United States* (Washington, DC: Independent Sector, 1993), 47; Lerner, *Eco-Pioneers*, 373–83; and Leslie Paul Thiele, *Environmentalism for a New Millennium: The Challenge of Coevolution* (New York: Oxford University Press, 1999), 188–95.

30. Glenn Tremblay, "The School as the Hub of the Community," *Volunteer Monitor* 5: 1 (spring 1993); National Public Radio, June 21, 1997. The *Volunteer Monitor* provides extensive resources and examples of school-based and other forms of volunteer monitoring. Global Rivers Environmental Education Network (GREEN), which provides extensive curricula resources, has recently become part of Earth Force, a national network for youth environmental education and community problem solving.

31. See *The Strategy for Improving Water-Quality Monitoring in the United States: Final Report of the Intergovernmental Task Force on Monitoring Water Quality* (Washington, DC: U.S. Government Printing Office, 1995), 18. See also *National Directory of Voluntary Environmental Monitoring Programs* (Washington, DC: Office of Water), http://www.epa.gov/OWOW/monitor/dir2.html; and the published proceedings of the National Citizens Volunteer Water Quality Monitoring conferences during the 1990s.

32. Eve Endicott, ed., *Land Conservation Through Public/Private Partnerships* (Washington, DC: Island Press, 1993), 3. See also Jean Hocker, "Patience, Problem Solv-

ing, and Private Initiative: Local Groups Chart a New Course for Land Conservation," in Henry Diamond and Patrick Noonan, eds., *Land Use in America* (Washington, DC: Island Press, 1996), 245–59. Land trusts go back to the late nineteenth century.

33. Angela Graziano, "Preserving Wildlife Habitat: The U.S. Fish and Wildlife Service and the North American Waterfowl Management Plan," in Endicott, ed., *Land Conservation Through Public/Private Partnerships*, 85–103.

34. See Peter Lavigne, *The Watershed Innovators Workshop: Proceedings*, Cummington, MA, June 4–5, 1995 (Portland, OR: River Network, 1995); Don Elder, *Four Corners Watershed Innovators Initiative: Florida Meeting Report*, Titusville, FL, March 13–16, 1997 (Portland, OR: River Network, 1997); Natural Resources Law Center, *The Watershed Source Book: Watershed-Based Solutions to Natural Resource Problems* (Boulder: University of Colorado, 1995). The *1998–1999 River and Watershed Conservation Directory* lists, by our count, 281 watershed associations and councils, and 535 kindred groups, such as "friends" or "stewards" of specific watersheds. Our own crosscheck against other directories, state studies, and interviews with state river networks reveals this to be an underestimate on the order of 15 percent or more for watershed associations and councils, and 100 percent or more for friends groups. Putnam, in *Bowling Alone* (471, n. 54), relies on the directories of the National Wildlife Federation to make the case that there has been a decline in local environmental groups. But the NWF directories are not designed to survey local groups and are thus radically incomplete. The *1999 Conservation Directory*, 44th ed., Rue Gordon and Jamie Anderson, eds. (Vienna, VA: National Wildlife Federation, 1999), for instance, lists *none* of the 154 watershed groups in Oregon listed in the directory of For the Sake of the Salmon, and only three of the 153 groups in California. NWF listings for other states and for other types of local environmental groups are similarly off by *factors* of ten, fifty, even one hundred and more. The vast majority of even the most famous and widely discussed cases are not listed.

35. See Kenneth Gould, Allan Schnaiberg, and Adam Weinberg, *Local Environmental Struggles: Citizen Activism in the Treadmill of Production* (New York: Cambridge University Press, 1996), chapter 2. Of course, development often appeals to many town residents themselves, since it enables them to build better schools, bring in new jobs, and increase their property values.

36. Telephone interview with Karen Vigmostad, former director of the Rouge River Watershed Council and senior policy specialist for public participation, Michigan Department of Natural Resources, March 25, 1997; personal interviews with Jay Mower, coordinator of the Columbia Slough Watershed Association, and Peter Teneau, member of the Columbia Slough Watershed Association, Portland, OR, May 22, 1998; Kirk Johnson, "The Henry's Fork Watershed Council: Community-Based Participation in Regional Environmental Management," in Marie Hoff, ed., *Sustainable Community Development: Studies in Economic, Environmental, and Cultural Revitalization* (Boca Raton, FL: Lewis Publishers, 1998), 165–76; Marie Hoff, "The Willapa Alliance: The Role of a Voluntary Organization in Fostering Regional Action for Sustainability," 177–92, in the same volume; Derek Busby and Don Elder, *Four Corners Watershed Innovators Initiative: Florida Background Report* (Portland, OR: River Network, March 5, 1997); and www.savethesound.org.

37. Freeman House, *Totem Salmon: Life Lessons from Another Species* (Boston: Beacon Press, 1999), 157.

38. See Ronnie Lipschutz, with Judith Mayer, *Global Civil Society and Global Environmental Governance: The Politics of Nature from Place to Planet* (Albany: State University of New York Press, 1996), chapter 4; Ted Bernard and Jora Young, *The Ecology of Hope: Communities Collaborate for Sustainability* (Gabriola Island, British Columbia: New Society Publishers, 1997), chapter 8; Fran Vitulli, Sari Sommarstrom et al., *Four Corners Watershed Innovators Workshop: California Background Report* (Portland, OR: The River Network, March 18, 1998); Daniel Press, "Environmental Regionalism and the Struggle for California," *Society and Natural Resources* 8 (1995), 289–306; and Blaine Anton Vogt, *Border Fish: Salmon Crises, Environmental Imaginaries, and the Politics of Sustainability* (Waltham, MA: Brandeis University, Ph.D. diss., 2000).

39. See Mark Smith, Ed Himlan et al., *Four Corners Watershed Innovators Workshop: Massachusetts Background Report* (Portland, OR: The River Network, October 5, 1998); Lavigne, *Watershed Innovators Workshop*.

40. Telephone interview with Sarah Humphries, executive director of Rivers Council of Washington, July 26, 2000. See Ken Slattery, Joy Huber, and Phil Shelton, *Four Corners Watershed Innovators Initiative: Washington Background Report* (Portland, OR: The River Network, September 19, 1997); Don Elder, *Four Corners Watershed Innovators Initiative: Washington Meeting Report*, Olympia, WA, October 2–4, 1997 (Portland, OR: The River Network, 1997); Lavigne, *Watershed Innovators Workshop*, 85. On the challenges of sustaining watershed partnership strategies, see the Four Corners final report by Stephen M. Born and Kenneth D. Genskow, *Exploring the Watershed Approach: Critical Dimensions of State-Local Partnerships* (Portland, OR: The River Network, September 1999).

41. Telephone interview with Kathy Luscher, River Network, September 19, 1997; River Network, *Watershed 2000* (Portland, OR: River Network, 1996); *Annual Report 1996* (Portland, OR: River Network, 1996); *Starting Up: A Handbook for New River and Watershed Organizations* (Portland, OR: River Network, 1996); David Bolling, *How to Save a River: A Handbook for Citizen Action* (Washington, DC: Island Press, 1994).

42. See Endicott, *Land Conservation through Public/Private Partnerships;* Steven Yaffee, Ali Phillips et al., *Ecosystem Management in the United States: An Assessment of Current Experience* (Washington, DC: Island Press, 1996).

43. See Kristen Nelson, Nancy Manring, James Crowfoot, and Julia Wondolleck, "Maximizing Organizational Effectiveness," in Crowfoot and Wondolleck, *Environmental Disputes*, 152–82; and Julia Wondolleck and Steven Yaffee, *Making Collaboration Work: Lessons from Innovation in Natural Resource Management* (Washington, DC: Island Press, 2000).

44. Data on organizational structure and size are derived from several sources: Gordon and Anderson, *1999 Conservation Directory; 1998–1999 River and Watershed Conservation Directory;* Sandra Jaszczak, ed., *Encyclopedia of Associations*, 32nd ed. (Detroit: Gale Research, 1997); John Hendee and Randall Pitstick, "Growth and Change in U.S. Forest-Related Environmental Groups," *Journal of Forestry* 92: 6 (June 1994), 24–31. For growth trends in membership and budgets between 1970 and 1995, see Christopher Bosso, "Seizing Back the Day: The Challenge of Environmental Activism in the 1990s," in Vig and Kraft, *Environmental Policy in the 1990s*, 62–63.

45. See Mark Roseland, *Toward Sustainable Communities: Resources for Citizens and their Governments* (Gabriola Island, British Columbia: New Society Publishers, 1998); Daniel Mazmanian and Michael Kraft, eds., *Toward Sustainable Communities: Transi-*

tion and Transformations in Environmental Policy (Cambridge, MA: MIT Press, 1999); Daniel Sitarz, ed., *Sustainable America: America's Environment, Economy and Society in the Twenty-First Century* (Carbondale, IL: EarthPress, 1998), chapter 10; Lerner, *Eco-Pioneers*, chapter 12; John Parr, "Chattanooga: the Sustainable City," in Adams and Parr, *Boundary Crossers: Case Studies.* On the challenges of building regional capacities, see Kai Lee, *Compass and Gyroscope: Integrating Science and Politics for the Environment* (Washington, DC: Island Press, 1993); Rosemary Mazaika, "The Grande Ronde Model Watershed Program: A Case Study," *Administrative Theory and Praxis* 21: 1 (March 1999), 76–87; W. Michael McDavit, "The Lake Tahoe Collaborative Partnership: Expanding the Role of Community in Environmental Protection," *Policy Perspectives* (1999), 37–56; Michael McGinnis, "On the Verge of Collapse: The Columbia River System, Wild Salmon and the Northwest Power Planning Council," *Natural Resources Journal* 35 (winter 1995), 63–92.

46. See LaJuana Wilcher, "Looking Forward in the Office of Water," *EPA Journal* 16: 11–12 (Nov./Dec. 1990), 60–63; and Landy, Roberts, and Thomas, *Environmental Protection Agency.*

47. Personal and telephone interviews with staff at the Office of Regional, State, and Local Relations, U.S. EPA, Washington, DC: Shelly Metzenbaum, director, February 3, 1994; Thomas Pfeiffer, March 14, 1994; Deborah Martin, February 3, 1994; personal discussions with Marilyn Katz, program analyst at the EPA Office of Sustainable Ecosystems and Communities (OSEC), and Mardi Klevs, regional team manager of Region 5 (Chicago), which has restructured around CBEP quite extensively, Boston, August 5, 1998. See also *Community-Based Environmental Protection: A Resource Book for Protecting Ecosystems and Communities* (Washington, DC: U.S. EPA, Office of Policy, Planning and Evaluation, September 1997); Ecosystem Protection Workshop, *Toward a Place-Driven Approach: The Edgewater Consensus on an EPA Strategy for Ecosystem Protection* (Washington, DC: U.S. EPA, March 1994).

48. See Daniel Mazmanian and Jeanne Nienaber, *Can Organizations Change? Environmental Protection, Citizen Participation and the Corps of Engineers* (Washington, DC: The Brookings Institution, 1979), 132–57; Gerald Cormick and Jane McCarthy, *Environmental Mediation: A First Dispute* (Seattle, WA: Office of Environmental Mediation, 1974).

49. See Ann Riley, "The Greening of Federal Flood-Control Policies: The Wildcat–San Pablo Creeks Case," in Rutherford Platt, Rowan Rowntree, and Pamela Muick, eds., *The Ecological City: Preserving and Restoring Urban Biodiversity* (Amherst: University of Massachusetts Press, 1994), 217–30; Mazmanian and Nienaber, *Can Organizations Change?* 103 ff.

50. Stuart Langton, *An Organizational Assessment of the U.S. Army Corps of Engineers in Regard to Public Involvement Practices and Challenges* (Fort Belvoir, VA: U.S. Army Corps of Engineers Institute for Water Resources, May 1996). See also James Creighton, Jerome Delli Priscoli, and C. Mark Dunning, eds., *Public Involvement Techniques: A Reader of Ten Years' Experience at the Institute for Water Resources* (Fort Belvoir, VA: U.S. Army Corps of Engineers Institute for Water Resources, May 1983); and *Public Involvement and Dispute Resolution: A Reader on the Second Decade of Experience at the Institute for Water Resources* (Fort Belvoir, VA: U.S. Army Corps of Engineers Institute for Water Resources, 1998); and personal and telephone interviews with Jerome Delli Priscoli, Washington, DC, February 1 and March 5, 1994, August 22, 1995, who has

headed the Corp's public participation and dispute resolution programs at the Institute for Water Resources since 1976. For further critical insight into the Corps' failed coastal policies, with recommendations for community involvement, see Orrin Pilkey and Katherine Dixon, *The Corps and the Shore* (Washington, DC: Island Press, 1996).

51. See John Hendee, Robert Lucas, Robert Tracy, Tony Staed et al., *Public Involvement and the Forest Service* (Seattle, WA: Pacific Northwest Forest and Range Experiment Station, May 1973); Rupert Cutler, *A Study of Litigation Related to Management of Forest Service Administered Lands and Its Effect on Policy Decisions* (East Lansing: Michigan State University, Ph.D. diss., 1972); "Public Involvement in USDA Decision-Making," *Journal of Soil and Water Conservation* 33: 6 (1978), 264–66.

52. See Margaret Shannon, *Managing Public Resources: Public Deliberation as Organizational Learning* (Berkeley: University of California, Ph.D. diss., 1989); Paul Culhane, *Public Lands Politics: Interest Group Influence on the Forest Service and the Bureau of Land Management* (Baltimore, MD: Johns Hopkins University Press, 1981).

53. Julia Wondolleck, *Public Lands Conflict and Resolution: Managing National Forest Disputes* (New York: Plenum, 1988).

54. See Wondolleck, *Public Lands Conflict and Resolution;* Paul Mohai, "Public Participation and Natural Resource Decision-making: The Case of the RARE II Decisions," *Natural Resources Journal* 27 (1987), 123–55; Jo Ellen Force and Kevin Williams, "A Profile of National Forest Planning Participants," *Journal of Forestry* 87: 1 (January 1989), 33–38.

55. See George Hoberg, "From Localism to Legalism: The Transformation of Federal Forest Policy," in Charles Davis, ed., *Western Public Lands and Environmental Politics* (Boulder, CO: Westview Press, 1997), 47–73; Paul Hirt, *A Conspiracy of Optimism: Management of the National Forests Since World War Two* (Lincoln: University of Nebraska Press, 1994), chapters 11–12.

56. See Hanna Cortner and Margaret Moote, *The Politics of Ecosystem Management* (Washington, DC: Island Press, 1999); Edward P. Weber, "A New Vanguard for the Environment: Grass-Roots Ecosystem Management as a New Environmental Movement," *Society and Natural Resources* (forthcoming); Greg Brown and Charles Harris, "The Implications of Work Force Diversification in the U.S. Forest Service," *Administration and Society* 25: 1 (May 1993), 85–113; "The U.S Forest Service: Toward the New Resource Management Paradigm," *Society and Natural Resources* 5 (July/September 1992), 231–45.

57. Gregg Walker and Steven Daniels, "The Clinton Administration, the Northwest Forest Conference, and Managing Conflict: When Talk and Structure Collide," *Society and Natural Resources* 9 (1996), 77–91.

58. Michael Dombeck, quoted in Dave Webster, "Pursuing Collaborative Stewardship," *American Forests* 103: 2 (summer 1997), 30.

59. See Elinor Ostrom, "Coping with Tragedies of the Commons," *Annual Review of Political Science* 2 (1999), 493–535; Sara Singleton, *Constructing Cooperation: The Evolution of Institutions of Comanagement* (Ann Arbor: University of Michigan Press, 1998); James Acheson, *The Lobster Gangs of Maine* (Hanover, NH: New England University Press, 1988); C. Gibson, M. A. McKean, and Elinor Ostrom, eds., *People and Forests: Communities, Institutions, and the Governance of Forests* (Cambridge, MA: MIT Press, 2000).

60. Quoted in Steven Sellin, Michael Schuett, and Deborah Carr, "Has Collabo-

NOTES TO PAGES 115-18

rative Planning Taken Root in the National Forests?" *Journal of Forestry* 95: 5 (May 1997), 26. See also Steven Yaffee and Julia Wondolleck, "Building Bridges Across Agency Boundaries," in Kathryn Kohm and Jerry Franklin, eds., *Creating a Forestry for the Twenty-First Century: The Science of Ecosystem Management* (Washington, DC: Island Press, 1997), 381–96; Yaffee et al., *Ecosystem Management in the United States;* Timothy Duane, "Community Participation in Ecosystem Management," *Ecology Law Quarterly* 24: 4 (1997), 771–97.

61. Presentations by, and discussions with, Kristin Ramstad, State of Oregon Department of Urban Forestry, Jane Glazer, Urban Forestry commissioner, Heritage Trees of Portland, and others at the Twenty-Third Annual Neighborhoods USA Conference, Portland, OR, May 21, 1998; Joseph Poracsky and Michael Houck, "The Metropolitan Portland Urban Natural Resource Program," in Platt et al., *The Ecological City,* 251–67; USDA Forest Service and Center for Urban Forestry, *An Ecosystem-Based Approach to Urban and Community Forestry* (Philadelphia, PA: Center for Urban Forestry, 1994); Rita Schoeneman, USDA Forest Service national program manager for Urban and Community Forestry, "FY 1997 Report"; Brian Donahue, *Reclaiming the Commons: Community Farms and Forests in a New England Town* (New Haven, CT: Yale University Press, 1999); Morgan Grove and Mark Hohmann, "Social Forestry and GIS," *Journal of Forestry* 90: 12 (December 1992), 10–15.

62. Quoted in William Stevens, *Miracle under the Oaks: The Revival of Nature in America* (New York: Pocket Books, 1995), 212. See also www.chiwild.org.

63. See Susan Hadden, *A Citizen's Right to Know: Risk Communication and Public Policy* (Boulder, CO: Westview Press, 1989); Walter Rosenbaum, "The Politics of Public Participation in Hazardous Waste Management," in James Lester and Ann Bowman, eds., *The Politics of Hazardous Waste Management* (Durham, NC: Duke University Press, 1983), 176–95; Andrew Szasz, *Ecopopulism: Toxic Waste and the Movement for Environmental Populism* (Minneapolis: University of Minnesota Press, 1994), which discusses the crucial role of the media in creating an icon of Love Canal. An extensive review of the scientific studies that casts much doubt on the actual dangers to health existing at Love Canal, and at the inactive hazardous waste disposal sites that became the centerpiece of Superfund's long-term remediation program (in contrast to its emergency response program), is provided by Aaron Wildavsky, *But Is It True? A Citizen's Guide to Environmental Health and Safety Issues* (New York: Cambridge University Press, 1995), chapters 4–5.

64. See Citizen's Clearinghouse for Hazardous Waste, *Ten Years of Triumph* (Arlington, VA: CCHW, 1993); Lois Gibbs, "Environmental Community Organizing," in Langton, *Environmental Leadership,* 63–78; *Dying from Dioxin: A Citizen's Guide to Reclaiming Our Health and Rebuilding Democracy* (Boston: South End Press, 1995); Temma Kaplan, *Crazy for Democracy: Women in Grassroots Movements* (New York: Routledge, 1997). See also Phil Brown and Edwin Mikkelsen, *No Safe Place: Toxic Waste, Leukemia, and Community Action* (Berkeley: University of California Press, 1990).

65. Personal interview with John O'Connor, Cambridge, MA, March 21, 1994; Gary Cohen and John O'Connor, *Fighting Toxics: A Manual for Protecting Your Family, Community, and Workplace* (Washington, DC: Island Press, 1990). See also Bruce Williams and Albert Matheny, *Democracy, Dialogue, and Environmental Disputes: The Contested Languages of Social Regulation* (New Haven, CT: Yale University Press, 1995). The Highlander Center has also played a critical role in training grassroots activists.

66. See Robert Bullard, *Dumping in Dixie: Race, Class, and Environmental Quality* (Boulder, CO: Westview Press, 1990); Robert Bullard, ed., *Unequal Protection: Environmental Justice and Communities of Color* (San Francisco: Sierra Club Books, 1994); and *Confronting Environmental Racism: Voices from the Grassroots* (Boston: South End Press, 1993); Marianne Lavelle and Marcia Coyle, "Unequal Protection: The Racial Divide in Environmental Law," *National Law Journal,* September 21, 1992, 2–12. For studies that cast doubt on some of the empirical claims of the environmental justice movement, see Vicki Been with Francis Gupta, "Coming to the Nuisance or Going to the Barrios? A Longitudinal Analysis of Environmental Justice Claims," *Ecology Law Quarterly* 24: 1 (1997), 1–56; Christopher Foreman, Jr., *The Promise and Peril of Environmental Justice* (Washington, DC: Brookings, 1998), chapter 4; Evan Ringquist, "Environmental Justice: Normative Concerns and Empirical Evidence," in Vig and Kraft, *Environmental Policy in the 1990s,* 231–54.

67. See Karl Grossman, "The People of Color Environmental Summit," in Bullard, *Unequal Protection,* 272–97; Robert Bullard, ed., *People of Color Environmental Groups: 1994–95 Directory* (Atlanta, GA: Environmental Justice Resource Center, Clark Atlanta University, 1994); Stella Capek, "The 'Environmental Justice' Frame: A Conceptual Discussion and Application," *Social Problems* 40: 1 (February 1993), 5–24; Dorceta E. Taylor, "The Rise of the Environmental Justice Paradigm: Injustice Framing and the Social Construction of Environmental Discourses," *American Behavioral Scientist* 43:4 (January 2000), 508–80. The Washington Office on Environmental Justice was founded in 1994 as a national clearinghouse.

68. Personal interview with John O'Connor, Cambridge, MA, March 21, 1994.

69. Robert Bullard, presentation and discussion at Environmental Justice Panel, American Sociological Association Annual Meetings, Washington, DC, August 20, 1995.

70. Telephone interview with Robert Knox, assistant director of the Office of Environmental Justice, March 1, 1994; presentation by, and group discussion with, Clarice Gaylord, director of the Office of Environmental Justice, Washington, DC, September 12, 1994; *Summary of Previous Grant Awards for Environmental Justice through Pollution Prevention* (Washington, DC: U.S. EPA, 1997, 1998, 1999); *Office of Environmental Justice Small Grants Program: FY 1994, FY 1995, FY 1996, FY 1997, FY 1998 Recipients* (Washington, DC: U.S. EPA, Office of Environmental Justice, 1994–1998); *Environmental Justice Small Grants Program: Emerging Tools for Local Problem Solving* (Washington, DC: U.S. EPA, 2000).

71. Personal interview with Henry Topper, lead staff from OPPT on the Baltimore partnership, Boston, August 5, 1998; presentations by, and further discussions with, Henry Topper, Paul Cusamano, and Reverend Richard Andrews of Brooklyn United Methodist Church, who serves on the partnership executive committee, at the EPA National Community Involvement Conference, Boston, August 5, 1998; Baltimore Community Environmental Partnership, *Air Committee Technical Report, Community Risk-Based Air Screening: A Case Study in Baltimore, MD: Internal Draft Document* (Washington, DC: U.S. EPA, Office of Pollution Prevention and Toxics, February 8, 1999).

72. See Kimberly Thompson, "Cleaning Up Dry Cleaners," in John Graham and Jennifer Kassalow Hartwell, eds., *The Greening of Industry: A Risk Management Approach* (Cambridge, MA: Harvard University Press, 1997), 93–135; Environmental Protection Agency, "The DfE Dry Cleaning Project," in *Design for the Environment: Building*

Partnerships for Environmental Improvement (Washington, DC: EPA, Office of Pollution Prevention and Toxics, 1995); and Lerner, *Eco-Pioneers,* 85–86.

73. Personal interviews with Henry Topper, Office of Pollution Prevention and Toxics, U.S. EPA, Washington, DC, March 2 and November 9, 1994. See also *Summary of Focus Group Discussions with Screen Printers and Lithographers for the Design for the Environment Printing Project* (Washington, DC: Prepared by Abt Associates for U.S. EPA, Office of Pollution Prevention and Toxics, June 1994).

74. See Frances Lynn and Jack Kartez, "Environmental Democracy in Action: The Toxics Release Inventory," *Environmental Management* 18: 4 (1994), 511–21; Shameek Konar and Mark Cohen, "Information as Regulation: The Effect of Community Right to Know Laws on Toxic Emissions," *Journal of Environmental Economics and Management* 32 (1997), 109–24; James Hamilton, "Pollution as News: Media and Stock Market Reactions to the Toxics Release Inventory Data," *Journal of Environmental Economics and Management* 28 (1995), 98–113; Archon Fung and Dara O'Rourke, "Reinventing Environmental Regulation from the Grassroots Up: Explaining and Expanding the Success of the Toxics Release Inventory," in Fung, Karkkainen, and Sabel, *Information-Based Environmental Regulation.*

75. Personal interview with Sanford Lewis, director of the Good Neighbor Project, Waltham, MA, August 27, 1997. See also Sanford Lewis, "Good Neighbor Agreements: A Tool for Environmental and Social Justice," *Social Justice* 23: 4 (1996), 134–51; *The Good Neighbor Handbook* (Waverly, MA: Good Neighbor Project, 1993). Further arguments for strengthening stakeholder involvement in Project XL can be found in Rena Steinzor, "Regulatory Reinvention and Project XL: Does the Emperor Have Any Clothes?" *Environmental Law* 26 (October 1996). See Manik Roy, "Pollution Prevention, Organizational Culture, and Social Learning," *Environmental Law* 22 (1991), 189–251, for an astute analysis of how learning is contingent on notions of "good citizenship," right-to-know requirements, and social networks linking actors within the firm to the broader community.

76. Quoted in Nevin Cohen, Caron Chess, Frances Lynn, and George Busenberg, *Fostering Environmental Progress: A Case Study of Vulcan Chemical's Community Involvement Group* (New Brunswick, NJ: Center for Environmental Communication, Rutgers University, August 1995), 18, 24. See also their *Improving Dialogue: A Case Study of the Community Advisory Panel of Shell Oil Company's Martinez Manufacturing Complex* (New Brunswick, NJ: Center for Environmental Communication, Rutgers University, August 1995); Caron Chess, Michal Tamuz, and Michael Greenberg, "Organizational Learning About Environmental Risk Communication: The Case of Rohm and Haas' Bristol Plant," *Society and Natural Resources* 8 (1995), 57–66.

77. See Marc Landy and Mary Hague, "The Coalition for Waste: Private Interest and Superfund," in Michael Greve and Fred Smith, eds., *Environmental Politics: Public Costs and Private Rewards* (New York: Praeger, 1992), 67–87; Landy, Roberts, and Thomas, *Environmental Protection Agency,* chapter 5. See also John Hird, *Superfund: The Political Economy of Environmental Risk* (Baltimore, MD: Johns Hopkins University Press, 1994).

78. See U.S. Environmental Protection Agency, Office of Emergency and Remedial Response, *Community Relations in Superfund: A Handbook* (Washington, DC: U.S. EPA, Office of Emergency and Remedial Response, Interim Version 1988; Final Version, 1992). For further refinements in the 1990s, see *Community Advisory Group*

Toolkit: For the Community (Washington, DC: U.S. EPA, Office of Solid Waste and Emergency Response, September 1998).

79. See Ellison Folk, "Public Participation in the Superfund Cleanup Process," *Ecology Law Quarterly* 18 (1991), 173–221; Michael Edelstein, *Contaminated Communities* (Boulder, CO: Westview Press, 1988).

80. See Hird, *Superfund*, 225–26, 248.

81. See Landy and Hague, "The Coalition for Waste," 74 ff.; and Barry Rabe, "Legislative Incapacity: Congressional Policymaking and the Case of Superfund," *Journal of Health Politics, Policy, and Law* 15 (fall 1990), 571–90.

82. Christopher Foreman, Jr., *The Promise and Peril of Environmental Justice.*

83. Telephone and personal interviews with Gregory Watson, executive director of the Dudley Street Neighborhood Initiative, October 1996; Ernesto Cortés, Jr., Cambridge, MA, December 16, 1993; John O'Connor, Cambridge, MA, March 21, 1994. See also Lerner, *Eco-Pioneers,* chapter 22; Shutkin, *The Land That Could Be,* chapter 4.

84. Personal interview with Daniel Fiorino, senior policy analyst, Waste and Chemical Policy Division, U.S. EPA, Washington, DC, February 28, 1994; telephone interview with Deborah Martin, Office of Regional, State, and Local Relations, February 3, 1994. See also Barry Rabe, *Beyond NIMBY: Hazardous Waste Siting in Canada and the United States* (Washington, DC: Brookings, 1994); Richard Minard, Jr., "Comparative Risk Assessment and the States: History, Politics, Results," in J. Clarence Davies, ed., *Comparing Environmental Risks: Tools for Setting Government Priorities* (Washington, DC: Resources for the Future, 1996), 23–61.

85. Kathy Milberg, quoted in Keith Schneider, "Rules Easing for Urban Toxic Cleanup," *New York Times,* September 20, 1993, A12.

86. On the latter point, see Marc Landy, "The New Politics of Environmental Policy," in Landy and Levin, *New Politics of Public Policy,* 207–27.

87. On environmental values in the broader public, see Riley Dunlap, "Trends in Public Opinion Toward Environmental Issues," in Riley Dunlap and Angela Mertig, eds., *American Environmentalism: The U.S. Environmental Movement, 1970–1990* (New York: Taylor and Francis, 1992), 89–116; Willett Kempton, James Boster, and Jennifer Hartley, *Environmental Values in American Culture* (Cambridge, MA: MIT Press, 1995); Robert Paehlke, "Environmental Values and Public Policy," in Vig and Kraft, *Environmental Policy in the 1990s,* 75–94; Thiele, *Environmentalism for a New Millennium,* 209–20.

88. On the organizational instability and factionalism of radical Green and direct action groups, see Paul Lichterman, *The Search for Political Community: American Activists Reinventing Commitment* (New York: Cambridge University Press, 1996); Barbara Epstein, *Political Protest and Cultural Revolution: Nonviolent Direct Action in the 1970s and 1980s* (Berkeley: University of California Press, 1991); Greta Gaard, *Ecological Politics: Ecofeminists and the Greens* (Philadelphia, PA: Temple University Press, 1998).

89. See Martin Lewis, *Green Delusions: An Environmentalist Critique of Radical Environmentalism* (Durham, NC: Duke University Press, 1992).

90. See Stuart Hill, *Democratic Values and Technological Choices* (Stanford, CA: Stanford University Press, 1992); Adolf Gundersen, *The Environmental Promise of Democratic Deliberation* (Madison: University of Wisconsin Press, 1995); Minard, "Comparative Risk Analysis and the States." For a philosophical discussion, see Andrew Light and Eric Katz, *Environmental Pragmatism* (New York: Routledge, 1996).

91. See, for instance, Mark Dowie, *Losing Ground: American Environmentalism at the Close of the Twentieth Century* (Cambridge, MA: MIT Press, 1995).

92. For a good case study of the limits of community collaboration where national environmental groups are excluded, see Duane, "Community Participation in Ecosystem Management"; and Mark Sagoff, "The View from Quincy Library: Civic Engagement in Environmental Problem Solving," in Robert K. Fullinwider, ed., *Civil Society, Democracy, and Civic Renewal* (Lanham, MD: Rowman and Littlefield, 1999), 151–83. For high-level criticism within the Sierra Club board by its former chairman, see Michael McClosky, "The Skeptic: Collaboration Has Its Limits," *High Country News* 28: 9 (13 May 1996), 7, which does not, however, represent the position of the board. See also Donald Snow, "Empire or Homelands? A Revival of Jeffersonian Democracy in the American West," in John A. Baden and Donald Snow, eds., *The Next West: Public Lands, Community, and Economy in the American West* (Washington, DC: Island Press, 1997), chapter 9, for a poignant argument that the "risk of the local" posed by community conservation is now the only plausible response to many of the region's pressing needs, especially in view of the unaffordable and politically unsupportable centralized management of natural resources. Snow is a long-time environmental activist and leader in the West, and sees the emerging consensus-based groups as a "new environmental movement."

93. On some of the organizational developments in the Sierra Club, National Audubon Society, and National Wildlife Federation over the past several decades, see Gottlieb, *Forcing the Spring,* 148–61; Christopher Bosso, "Seizing Back the Day," and "The Color of Money: Environmental Groups and the Pathologies of Fund Raising," in Allan Cigler and Burdett Loomis, eds., *Interest Group Politics,* 4th ed. (Washington, DC: Congressional Quarterly Press, 1995), 101–30. Both authors, however, largely ignore the civic environmental activism at the grassroots that does not point to radical alternatives. For increasing leadership support among some of the large mainstream environmental organizations for community-based approaches, see Thiele, *Environmentalism for a New Millennium,* 133, 160, 208; and Shutkin, *The Land That Could Be,* 198–99, 239. See also Douglas Wheeler, "The Ecosystem Approach: New Departures for Land and Water, Keynote Address," *Ecology Law Quarterly* 24: 4 (1997), 623–30.

94. Personal discussions with Marge Baker, executive director of the National Institute for Dispute Resolution, Washington, DC, November 7, 1996, Reston, VA, February 24, 1995; Bruce C. McKinney, William D. Kimsey, and Rex M. Fuller, "A Nationwide Survey of Mediation Centers," *Mediation Quarterly* 14: 2 (winter 1996), 155–66; Lawrence Susskind, Sarah McKearnan, and Jennifer Thomas-Larmer, eds., *The Consensus Building Handbook* (Thousand Oaks, CA: Sage, 1999); Crowfoot and Wondolleck, *Environmental Disputes.*

95. See Adler, "Addressing Barriers to Watershed Protection"; Jan G. Laitos and Thomas A. Carr, "The Transformation of Public Lands," *Ecology Law Quarterly* 26 (1999), 216–21; and Richard Haeuber, "Setting the Environmental Policy Agenda: The Case of Ecosystem Management," *Natural Resources Journal* 36: 1 (winter 1996), 1–28.

96. See Carmen Sirianni, Harry Boyte, Jerome Delli Priscoli, and Benjamin Barber, *Can the White House Help Catalyze Civic Renewal?* (Washington, DC: Reinventing Citizenship Project, June 1994); Harris and Milkis, *Politics of Regulatory Change,* chap-

ter 10. Useful strategies for transforming EPA culture are provided by DeWitt John and Marian Mlay, "Community-Based Environmental Protection: Encouraging Civic Environmentalism," in Ken Sexton, Alfred Marcus, K. William Easter, and Timothy Burkhardt, eds., *Better Environmental Decisions: Strategies for Governments, Businesses, and Communities* (Washington, DC: Island Press, 1999), 353–76; and National Academy of Public Administration, *Principles for Federal Managers of Community-Based Programs* (Washington, DC: NAPA, August 1997).

97. See Rena Steinzor, "Reinventing Environmental Regulation: The Dangerous Journey from Command to Self-Control," *Harvard Environmental Law Review* 22: 1 (1998), 103–202; and Bradford Mank, "The Environmental Protection Agency's Project XL and Other Regulatory Reform Initiatives: The Need for Legislative Authorization," *Ecology Law Quarterly* 25: 1 (1998),1–88; Daniel Press and Daniel Mazmanian, "The Greening of Industry: Achievement and Potential," in Vig and Kraft, *Environmental Policy in the 1990s,* 255–77; Elizabeth Fastiggi, *Catalyzing Environmental Results: Lessons in Advocacy Organization-Business Partnerships* (Boston: Alliance for Environmental Innovation, 1999).

98. See National Academy of Public Administration, *Setting Priorities, Getting Results: A New Direction for the Environmental Protection Agency.* A National Academy of Public Administration Report to Congress (Washington, DC: NAPA, 1995); DeWitt John et al., *Resolving the Paradox of Environmental Protection: An Agenda for Congress, EPA and the States.* A Report for Congress by a Panel of the National Academy of Public Administration (Washington, DC: NAPA, September 1997). The NAPA project was commissioned by the Senate and House Committees that appropriate funds for EPA. NAPA is a nonprofit, nonpartisan, collegial organization chartered by Congress to improve government at all levels. The NAPA project director was DeWitt John, and the associate director was Richard Minard, both prominent proponents of civic approaches. Marc Landy, whose work has been key in bringing themes of citizenship to the fore in environmental policy design, also served as a panel member. For other important sets of policy proposals that converge around civic environmentalism as a key component of regulatory reform and sustainable development, see The President's Council on Sustainable Development, *Sustainable America: A New Consensus for Prosperity, Opportunity, and a Healthy Environment for the Future* (Washington, DC: President's Council on Sustainable Development, February 1996), which was pushed in this direction only after community groups and local sustainable development projects mobilized; Sitarz, *Sustainable America,* which is drawn from proposals in various of the President's Council documents and working groups; Debra Knopman, *Second Generation: A New Strategy for Environmental Protection* (Washington, DC: Progressive Foundation, April 1996), which is associated with the Democratic Leadership Council; The Aspen Institute, *The Alternative Path: A Cleaner, Cheaper Way to Protect and Enhance the Environment* (Washington, DC: Aspen Institute, 1996); Marian R. Chertow and Daniel C. Esty, *Thinking Ecologically: The Next Generation of Environmental Policy* (New Haven, CT: Yale University Press, 1997), which is the product of Environmental Reform: The Next Generation Project, and involved participants from industry, agencies, academia, and several national environmental organizations; and Enterprise for the Environment, *The Environmental Protection System in Transition: Toward a More Desirable Future* (Washington, DC: Center for Strategic and International Studies, 1997), which was published in collaboration with NAPA and the Keystone Center. Enter-

prise for the Environment was chaired by William Ruckelshaus and included three other former EPA administrators (Douglas Costle, Lee Thomas, and William Reilly) on its steering committee, deputy administrator Fred Hansen, several members of Congress and governors, representatives from Save The Bay, The Nature Conservancy, and other national environmental organizations, and industry leaders. Its civic environmentalism, crafted by leading innovators, is complemented by a strategy for corporate environmental stewardship. Prestigious policy forums such as these, which enable professionals from different settings to participate, and where professional norms govern dialogue, are often critical to policy learning across various advocacy coalitions, as Sabatier and Jenkins-Smith argue in *Policy Change and Learning*.

99. See Michael Kraft, "Environmental Policy in Congress: Revolution, Reform or Gridlock?" in Vig and Kraft, *Environmental Policy in the 1990s*, 3d ed., 119–42; and Walter Rosenbaum, "The EPA at Risk: Conflicts over Institutional Reform," 143–67 in the same volume.

FOUR. COMMUNITY HEALTH AND CIVIC ORGANIZING

1. See Alice Sardell, *The U.S. Experiment in Social Medicine: The Community Health Center Program, 1965–1986* (Pittsburgh, PA: University of Pittsburgh Press, 1988), chapter 3; Jude Thomas May, Mary Durham, and Peter Kong-ming New, "Professional Control and Innovation: The Neighborhood Health Center Experience," in Julius Roth, ed., *Research in the Sociology of Health Care*, vol. 1 (Greenwich, CT: JAI Press, 1980), 105–36.

2. H. Jack Geiger, "The Meaning of Community-Oriented Primary Care in the American Context," in Eileen Connor and Fitzhugh Mullan, eds., *Community Oriented Primary Care: New Directions for Health Services Delivery* (Washington, DC: National Academy Press, 1983), 60–90; "Community Health Centers: Health Care as an Instrument of Social Change," in Victor Sidel and Ruth Sidel, eds., *Reforming Medicine: Lessons of the Last Quarter Century* (New York: Pantheon, 1984), 11–32; Robert Hollister, Bernard Kramer, and Seymour Bellin, "Neighborhood Health Centers as a Social Movement," in Robert Hollister, Bernard Kramer, and Seymour Bellin, eds., *Neighborhood Health Centers* (Lexington, MA: Lexington Books, 1974), 19.

3. H. Jack Geiger, "A Health Center in Mississippi: A Case Study in Social Medicine," in Lawrence Corey, Steven Saltman, and Michael Epstein, eds., *Medicine in a Changing Society* (St. Louis, MO: Mosby, 1972), 157–67; "Community Control or Community Conflict?" in Hollister, Kramer, and Bellin, *Neighborhood Health Centers*, 133–42; "Community Shares in Policy Decisions for Rural Health Centers," *Journal of the American Hospital Association* 43 (1969), 109–112.

4. Daniel Zwick, "Some Accomplishments and Findings of Neighborhood Health Centers," *Milbank Memorial Fund Quarterly* 50: 4 (October 1972), 387–420; Howard Freeman, K. Jill Kiecolt, and Harris Allen II, "Community Health Centers: An Initiative of Enduring Utility," *Milbank Memorial Fund Quarterly* 60: 2 (1982), 245–67.

5. Sardell, *U.S. Experiment in Social Medicine*, chapters 6–7; the National Association of Community Health Centers, *Health Care Access and Equality: The Story of Community and Migrant Health Centers and their National Association* (Washington, DC: NACHC, 1990).

6. As Sardell argues in *The U.S. Experiment in Social Medicine,* defining CHCs as poor people's medicine allowed the issue of their funding to remain low enough in salience to succeed at successive stages through effective bureaucratic advocacy, even though a strong, independent interest group favoring their expansion did not exist.

7. See Paul Torrens, "Administrative Problems of Neighborhood Health Centers," *Medical Care* 9: 6 (November–December 1971), 487–97; John Hatch and Eugenia Eng, "Community Participation and Control: Or Control of Community Participation," in Sidel and Sidel, *Reforming Medicine,* 223–44; Jude Thomas May, Mary Durham, and Peter Kong-ming New, "Structural Conflicts in the Neighborhood Health Center Program: The National and Local Perspectives," *Journal of Health Politics, Policy, and Law* 4: 4 (1980), 581–604; and Michael Lipsky and Morris Lounds, "Citizen Participation and Health Care: Problems of Government Induced Participation," *Journal of Health Politics, Policy, and Law* 1 (1976), 85–111.

8. Geiger, "Community-Oriented Primary Care in the American Context," 67.

9. See Karen Davis and Cathy Schoen, *Health and the War on Poverty: A Ten-Year Appraisal* (Washington, DC: Brookings, 1978), 122 ff.; Geiger, "Community-Oriented Primary Care in the American Context," 65 ff.; and Paul Nutting and Eileen Connor, *Community-Oriented Primary Care: A Practical Assessment* (Washington, DC: National Academy of Sciences Press, 1984).

10. Geiger, "Community-Oriented Primary Care in the American Context," 72. See also Donald Light, "The Rhetorics and Reality of Community Health Care: The Limits of Countervailing Powers to Meet the Health Care Needs of the Twenty-first Century," *Journal of Health Politics, Policy, and Law* 22: 2 (April 1997), 105–45.

11. Morone, *Democratic Wish,* chapter 7.

12. Russell Roth, quoted in Paul Starr, *The Social Transformation of American Medicine* (New York: Basic Books, 1982), 402.

13. P.L. 93–641, Section 1512(3).

14. See Barry Checkoway, ed., *Citizens and Health Care: Participation and Planning for Social Change* (New York: Pergamon, 1981); *Making Public Participation Work: Case Studies of Innovative Health Planning Agencies* (Hyattsville, MD: Bureau of Health Planning, 1980).

15. Morone, *Democratic Wish,* 278 ff.; James Morone and Theodore Marmor, "Representing Consumer Interests: the Case of American Health Planning," *Ethics* 91: 3 (April 1981), 431–450; Bill Hanson, "An Ethnography of Power Relations: Consumers and Providers on a Health Systems Council," in Julius Roth, ed., *Research in the Sociology of Health Care,* vol. 1 (Greenwich, CT: JAI Press, 1980), 137–78.

16. Morone and Marmor, "Representing Consumer Interests."

17. James Morone, "The Real World of Representation: Consumers and the HSAs," in Committee on Health Planning Goals and Standards, Institute of Medicine, *Health Planning in the United States: Selected Policy Issues,* vol. 2 (Washington, DC: National Academy Press, 1981), 258, 267.

18. Quoted in Terry Shannon, *Report on Consumer Participation in the Health Planning Program,* Adopted by the National Council on Health Planning and Development (Hyattsville, MD: National Council on Health Planning and Development, Subcommittee on Implementation and Administration, February 6, 1981), appendix 1, 29.

19. See Shannon, *Report on Consumer Participation,* 26, who estimates fifty thousand people were currently involved in 1981 in the HSAs, the subarea councils es-

tablished by 126 of them, and their various subcommittees, with an annual turnover rate of one-third; Dorothy Ellenburg, *What's Wrong with Consumer Participation?* Report to the Subcommittee on Implementation and Administration (Hyattsville, MD: National Council on Health Planning and Development, 1980); Committee on Health Planning Goals and Standards, Institute of Medicine, *Health Planning in the United States*, vol. 1, chapter 4; Morone, "The Real World of Representation," 266–67.

20. Shannon, *Report on Consumer Participation.*

21. Bruce Vladek, "Interest-Group Representation and the HSAs: Health Planning and Political Theory," *American Journal of Public Health* 67: 1 (January 1977), 23–29.

22. This was Vladek's other major criticism of the health reform act.

23. See Daniel Sigelman, "Health Costs, Consumer Constituencies, and Community Change," in Checkoway, *Citizens and Health Care*, 222–37; Morone, *Democratic Wish*, 286 ff. The citizen movement, however, included voices that made absolutist claims to "the right of every person to the level and type of health care he or she needs, at whatever age, in whatever condition," and without need to deliberate about trade-offs, and presumed this to be the only way in which a strong citizen movement could maintain itself. See Dorothy Ellenburg, "Special Interest vs. Citizen Control: Who Owns Health Planning?" in Committee on Health Planning Goals and Standards, Institute of Medicine, *Health Planning in the United States*, vol. 2, 219. And, of course, citizen groups in particular communities often aligned with provider groups to save or expand facilities, regardless of measures of overcapacity. Citizen representatives on HSAs, however, including those with histories of community activism, generally resisted both types of claims in the name of a broader public interest, which they described as having discovered through the deliberations of HSA boards and on-the-job learning. The large geographical area covered by HSAs also partially insulated them from the logic of local self-dealing. See Drew Altman, Richard Greene, and Harvey Sapolsky, *Health Planning and Regulation: The Decision-Making Process* (Washington, DC: AUPHA Press, 1981), chapter 4.

24. Helen Halpin Schauffler and Jessica Wolin, "Community Health Clinics under Managed Competition: Navigating Uncharted Waters," *Journal of Health Politics, Policy, and Law* 21: 3 (fall 1996), 461–88.

25. A nice example of the latter is the Codman Square Health Center in Boston. Field notes from meeting with William Walzak, founder and director of the Codman Square Health Center, and Patrice Keegan, director of its Civic Health Institute, Waltham, MA, April 29, 1997.

26. Telephone interviews with David Swankin, executive director of Citizen Advocacy Center (CAC), November 1994; and Richard Morrison, vice president of CAC, and former executive director, Virginia Board of Health Professions, November 1994.

27. Morone, *Democratic Wish*, 314.

28. See Altman, Greene, and Sapolsky, *Health Planning and Regulation*, 45. Morone's influential treatment of the HSAs in *The Democratic Wish*, which was published in 1990 shortly before the next major effort at national health reform under the Clinton administration, omitted the participatory learning that he had observed in his fieldwork a decade earlier, though he had conducted no further study since then. Instead, he stressed how the HSA experience fit the purported historical cycles of democratic wish making followed by the reinforcement of bureaucratic authority,

discussed in chapter 1. This framing of the policy legacy played no small part in the lack of attention given to the participatory components in the regional health alliances in the Clinton plan, as the failure of the democratic wish became the common wisdom of liberal health reform intellectuals. Morone later took up the issue of the alliances in a way that emphasized the hazards of citizen participation and proposed no constructive lessons on how to prevent an extended "brawl" and a "spectacular scramble for board seats," other than to focus on administrative detail. See James Morone, "Organizing Reform," *The American Prospect* 17 (spring 1994), 11–12. See also "The Bureaucracy Empowered," in James Morone and Gary Belkin, eds., *The Politics of Health Care Reform* (Durham, NC: Duke University Press, 1994), 162, where Morone argues astutely that as "the state pushes further into the details of medicine, the hard choices are hidden deeper in the technique. Political leaders find few opportunities and no rewards for publicly grappling with cost-control trade-offs or the limits of medicine." But Morone then provides a narrow conception of the democratic accountability needed to deal with this dilemma. He refers to this as Americans "forcing leaders to account for how they juggle costs, quality and access [as] the key to significant and sustained reform," as if there were no need for core institutional and civic processes in which citizens themselves are enabled to have these conversations and become collectively responsible for such hard choices. Both the HSAs and the Health Decisions projects represent substantial learning on exactly this set of critical issues.

29. Telephone interview with Dr. Ralph Crawshaw, February 3, 1994, and subsequent personal discussions, Portland, OR, October 13–14, 1994; personal interview with Michael Garland, Washington, DC, December 7, 1994. See also Brian Hines, *Oregon—and American—Health Decisions: A Guide for Community Action on Bioethical Issues* (Washington, DC: Office of Health Planning, Department of Health and Human Services, 1985).

30. Hines, *Oregon—and American—Health Decisions;* Ralph Crawshaw, Michael Garland, Brian Hines, and Caroline Lobitz, "Oregon Health Decisions: An Experiment with Informed Community Consent," *Journal of the American Medical Association* 254 (1985), 3213–16.

31. Personal interview with Michael Garland, Portland, OR, May 20, 1998. On the transplant controversy, see Howard Leichter, "Rationing of Health Care: Oregon Comes Out of the Closet," in Howard Leichter, ed., *Health Policy Reform in America: Innovations from the States* (Armonk, NY: Sharpe, 1992), 125.

32. Oregon Health Decisions, *Quality of Life in Allocating Health Resources: Principles Adopted by the Citizens Health Care Parliament, September 23–24, 1988* (Portland: Oregon Health Decisions, December 1988); personal interview with Michael Garland, Portland, OR, May 20, 1998. See also Benjamin Barber, *Strong Democracy: Participatory Politics for a New Age* (Berkeley: University of California Press, 1984).

33. See Thomas Oliver and Pamela Paul-Shaheen, "Translating Ideas into Actions: Entrepreneurial Leadership in State Health Care Reforms," *Journal of Health Politics, Policy, and Law* 22: 3 (June 1997), 721–87.

34. Biographical information on the commissioners was drawn from Oregon Health Services Commission, *Prioritization of Health Services: A Report to the Governor and Legislature* (Portland: Oregon Health Services Commission, 1991), appendix B, and from personal interviews with Michael Garland, Washington, DC, December 7,

1994; Paige Sipes-Metzler, executive director of the Health Services Commission, Portland, OR, October 14, 1994; and Romana Hasnain, Waltham, MA, February 15, 1994.

35. The Oregon Basic Health Services Act, Senate Bill 27, quoted in Oregon Health Services Commission, Prioritization of Health Services.

36. See Romana Hasnain and Michael Garland, *Health Care in Common: Report of the Oregon Health Decisions Community Meetings Process* (Portland: Oregon Health Decisions, April 1990); Annette Kirby, *The Needs Assessment Process of Senate Bill 27: Analysis of Attendance at Community Meetings* (Portland: Oregon Health Decisions, March 1990); Oregon Health Services Commission, *Prioritization of Health Services*, E-1; personal interviews with Michael Garland, Portland, OR, May 20, 1998; and Romana Hasnain, Waltham, MA, February 15, 1994. Hasnain directed the training of the community meeting facilitators and recruited them from church and other civic groups and the health community. Community action agencies, advocacy groups, and professional associations helped in the work of the HSC and with outreach for the public hearings and the community meetings.

37. For a fuller discussion of the rankings and the process, see Oregon Health Services Commission, *Prioritization of Health Services;* Michael Garland, "Light on the Black Box of Basic Health Care: Oregon's Contribution to the National Movement Toward Universal Health Insurance," *Yale Law and Policy Review* 10: 2 (1992), 409–30; and Robert Kaplan, *The Hippocratic Predicament: Affordability, Access, and Accountability in American Medicine* (New York: Academic Press, 1993), chapter 6. On the controversy over the federal waiver needed for state Medicaid revisions, see Howard Leichter, "Rationing Health Care in Oregon: Making the Implicit Explicit," in Howard Leichter, ed., *Health Policy Reform in America: Innovations from the States,* 2d ed. (Armonk, NY: Sharpe, 1997), 138–62; and Jean Thorne, "The Federal-State Relationship in Health Care Reform: A View from the Trenches," 126–37 in the same volume.

38. The Medicaid component of the Oregon Plan, originally projected to include 120,000 new eligibles, had reached 115,000 by August 1996. See Marsha Gold, "Markets and Public Programs: Insights from Oregon and Tennessee," *Journal of Health Politics, Policy, and Law* 22: 2 (April 1997), 633–66.

39. Personal interview with Paige Sipes-Metzler, executive director of the Health Services Commission, Portland, OR, October 14, 1994; Daniel Fox and Howard Leichter, "Rationing Care in Oregon: The New Accountability," *Health Affairs* 10: 2 (summer 1991), 22; Kaplan, *Hippocratic Predicament,* 172–73; 159 ff.; David Pollack, Benston McFarland, Robert George, and Richard Angell, "Prioritization of Mental Health Services in Oregon," *Milbank Quarterly* 72: 3 (1994), 515–550. See also David Falcone, with Dell Ensley and Cecilia Moore, "Political Culture, Political Leadership, Sustained Advocacy, and Aging Policy Reform: The Oregon and North Carolina Experiences," in Leichter, *Health Policy Reform in America,* 73–101, who demonstrate how the participatory and community-oriented political culture in Oregon has helped bring about innovative assisted living programs as an alternative to nursing home care, and has reduced Medicaid costs for long-term elder care well below national averages, even while providing a wider range of long-term care programs.

40. Bruce Vladek, "Unhealthy Rations," *The American Prospect* (summer 1991), 101–3.

41. Lawrence Brown, "The National Politics of Oregon's Rationing Plan," *Health Affairs* 10: 2 (summer 1991), 41.

42. This short summary hardly does justice to the range and depth of criticisms and responses. For some further critics, see W. John Thomas, "The Oregon Medicaid Proposal: Ethical Paralysis, Tragic Democracy, and the Fate of a Utilitarian Health Care Program," *Oregon Law Review* 72 (1993), 47–156; Sara Rosenbaum, "Poor Women, Poor Children, Poor Policy: The Oregon Medicaid Experiment," in Martin Strosberg, Joshua Wiener, Robert Baker, and I. Alan Fein, eds., *Rationing America's Medical Care: The Oregon Plan and Beyond* (Washington, DC: Brookings, 1992), 91–106; Norman Daniels, "Justice and Health Care Rationing: Lessons from Oregon," 185–95 of the same volume; Amitai Etzioni, "Health Care Rationing: A Critical Evaluation," *Health Affairs* 10: 2 (summer 1991), 88–95. For some further proponents, see Daniel Callahan, "Symbols, Rationality and Justice: Rationing Health Care," *American Journal of Law and Medicine* 18: 1–2 (1992), 1–13; Willard Gaylin, "Faulty Diagnosis: Why Clinton's Health-Care Plan Won't Cure What Ails Us," *Harper's Magazine* (October 1993), 57–64; Bruce Jennings, "Counsel and Consensus: Norms of Argument in Health Policy," in Frank Fischer and John Forester, eds., *The Argumentative Turn in Policy Analysis and Planning* (Durham, NC: Duke University Press, 1993), 101–14; Leonard Fleck, "Just Caring: Oregon, Health Care Rationing, and Informed Democratic Deliberation," *Journal of Medical Philosophy* 19 (1994); Ezekiel Emanuel, *The Ends of Human Life: Medical Ethics in a Liberal Polity* (Cambridge, MA: Harvard University Press, 1991), 210–11. As of 1998, Oregon had reduced the percentage of uninsured from 15 percent to 11 percent, but had hit a variety of roadblocks, as had other reforming states. See Pamela Paul-Shaheen, "The States and Health Care Reform: The Road Traveled and Lessons Learned from Seven That Took the Lead," *Journal of Health Politics, Policy, and Law* 23: 2 (April 1998), 319–61.

43. Telephone and personal interviews with Ellen Severoni, president, California Health Decisions and former chair of AHD, February 3, 1994; Mary Strong, founder of the New Jersey Citizens Committee on Biomedical Ethics, and one of the key founders of AHD, Cambridge, MA, May 1994; Bruce Jennings, executive director, Hastings Center, January 31, 1994; Bruce Jennings, *A Grassroots Movement in Bioethics: Community Health Decisions, A Hastings Center Report, Special Supplement* (Briarcliff Manor, NY: Hastings Center, June–July 1988), 1–16.

44. Telephone interview with Beverly Tyler, executive director of Georgia Health Decisions, February 8, 1994; Georgia Health Decisions, *Project Documentation* (Atlanta: Georgia Health Decisions, 1993); *Georgians Speak Out on Health Care: What They Want and What They Are Willing to Do* (Atlanta: Georgia Health Decisions, 1993); *Citizen Panels: Video Tapes* (Atlanta: Georgia Health Decisions, August 14, 1993); American Health Decisions, *A Guide to Ethnic Minority Neighborhood Outreach* (Orange, CA: American Health Decisions, 1994).

45. Telephone and personal interviews and informal discussions with Ellen Severoni, February 3, 1994; Treacy Colbert, former vice president of CHD, Los Angeles, August 1995; Beau Carter, "California Stakeholder Groups Join in Partnership Model for Health Policy," *Bureau of National Affairs Managed Care Reporter*, March 3, 1996; and various publications and internal documents of CHD, including *California Health Decisions Fiscal Years 1994–97 Strategic Plan* (Orange, CA: September 21, 1993); *The California Health Care Divide: Californians Talk About Medi-Cal and Their Health Care Values,* prepared by the Harwood Group for CHD (1993); *Condition Critical,* interim and final reports (1993); and *Public Values and Perspectives on Managed Care,* pre-

pared by Michael Perry and Evan Stark of Lake Snell Perry and Associates (October 1998).

46. Theda Skocpol, *Boomerang: Clinton's Health Security Effort and the Turn Against Government in Politics* (New York: Norton, 1996), 187, 110; and "Is the Time Finally Ripe? Health Insurance Reforms in the 1990s," *Journal of Health Politics, Policy, and Law* 18: 3 (fall 1993), 548, where she argues that "reformers need to engage in a dialogue with citizens, involving them in a process of reform that is certain to happen, not all at once in a back-room bargain, but over many years of adjustment and learning within a democratic polity." Skocpol herself, however, neglects the Health Decisions experience, as well as the specific arguments on public deliberation of those such as Daniel Yankelovich, Willard Gaylin, and Daniel Callahan who have sought to build upon the work of Health Decisions and other models, like the National Issues Forums. See Daniel Yankelovich, "The Debate That Wasn't: The Public and the Clinton Plan," *Health Affairs* 14: 1 (spring 1995), 7–23. One point of contention is that Skocpol believes that health reform requires promising generous new benefits to organized groups and middle-class citizens already well treated by the U.S. health care system, rather than engaging them in a responsible civic conversation about limits and trade-offs. Another is perhaps best captured by Margaret Weir, who argues that Skocpol's characterization of public reasoning as one of "finding plausible analogies" more adequately describes public deliberation than does the process of extended civic education sketched by Yankelovich, which challenges citizens to move beyond wishful thinking to a point where they can engage in sophisticated choicework involving necessary trade-offs. After all, Weir argues, "Roosevelt did not explain that social security was a generational transfer in which citizens had to give up current income. He said it was like having your own savings account." Would that the complex problems of health reform could plausibly be based on an analogy so simple, or that a more educated citizenry operating in a more differentiated institutional environment could buy it! See Margaret Weir, "Comment on Heclo and Skocpol," in Henry J. Aron, ed., *The Problem That Won't Go Away: Reforming U.S. Health Care Financing* (Washington, DC: Brookings, 1996), 56; Theda Skocpol, "The Rise and Resounding Demise of the Clinton Health Security Plan," 48–49 of the same volume.

47. Our analysis of American Health Decisions as a network is based on formal interviews conducted between 1994 and 1998, many informal conversations, work on several common projects, and extensive field notes taken during the following meetings and conferences: "Empowering the Public in an Era of Health Reform: AHD Annual Meeting and Working Conference," Portland, OR, October 13–15, 1994; AHD Board Meeting, Chicago, May 6, 1996; meeting at the Office of the Secretary, Department of Health and Human Services, of representatives of AHD and the American Civic Forum with Assistant Secretary for Health Peter Edelman, Assistant Secretary for Health Dr. Phillip Lee, Deputy Assistant Secretary for Health Michael McGinnis, and Ashley Files, Washington, DC, December 8, 1994. Two AHD publications were also especially helpful: Bruce Jennings, *Voices of Value: What Americans Expect from a Health Care System* (Orange, CA: AHD, 1995), and Michael Garland, *Community Responsibility for Health Policy: Tools, Structures, and Financing* (Orange, CA: AHD, 1995).

48. Telephone interview with Leonard Duhl, October 5, 1998; Leonard Duhl, *Toward the Common Good: A Therapist for Changing Communities*, unpublished autobi-

ography, November 22, 1997. See also Leonard Duhl, "The Healthy City: Its Function and Its Future," *Health Promotion* 1: 1 (1986), 55–60. On Robert Kennedy's vision of civic democracy, see Michael Sandel, *Democracy's Discontent: America in Search of a Public Philosophy* (Cambridge, MA: Harvard University Press, 1996), 299–304.

49. Mary Pittman, presentation at the Healthy Communities Conference, Washington, DC, November 7, 1996, and personal discussions.

50. Personal interview with John Parr, former president of NCL, Denver, CO, October 19, 1996; telephone interview with Leonard Duhl, October 5, 1998; field notes from December 8, 1994 meeting in the office of the secretary of HHS. See also John Ashton, ed., *Healthy Cities* (Milton Keynes, England: Open University Press, 1992); John Davies and Michael Kelly, eds., *Healthy Cities: Research and Practice* (London: Routledge, 1993).

51. This account is based on presentations by, and discussions with, Judith Kurland, Waltham, MA, November 5, 1997; Ted Landsmark, Washington, DC, November 7, 1996; Bradlee Seeman, interim director of Healthy Boston, Washington, DC, November 7, 1996; Roberta Miller, Marsha Morris, and Mary Skelton, *Healthy Boston Evaluation: Final Report* (Boston: Office of Community Partnerships, May 15, 1996); Jerry Mogul, "When the Funding Runs Dry: Sustaining the Healthy Boston Coalitions," in Christopher Freeman Adams, ed., *Voices from America: Ten Healthy Community Stories Across the Nation* (Chicago: Hospital Research and Education Trust, 1998), 42–47.

52. This account is based on personal interviews with Peter Lee, former program director, South Carolina Department of Health and Environmental Control, Boston, December 30, 1998; Julia Weaver, former director of the Healthy Communities Program of the National Civic League, Denver, CO, October 17, 1996; as well as presentations by Peter Lee, Healthy Communities Conference, Charleston, SC, December 7, 1997; James Walker, Jr., vice president of human resources, South Carolina Hospital Association; Tena Hoyle and Christi Sanford, Community Health Partners, at the same conference; Robert Carlton, director of youth development at DHEC, Washington, DC, November 7, 1996.

53. Telephone interview with Tyler Norris, the first director of CHCI, October 8, 1998; personal interview with Julia Weaver, its second director, Denver, CO, October 17, 1996; presentation by the coordinators of six of the community partnerships, as well as by Michele Sturm, director of the Colorado Healthy Communities Council, Conference on Building Healthier Communities: Ten Years and Learning, Arlington, VA, November 14, 1998; CHCI materials, partnership newsletters, and community indicator reports generously supplied by Michele Sturm.

54. See Joan Twiss, "California's Healthy Cities: Governance in Action," *National Civic Review* 86: 1 (spring 1997), 81–91; Joseph Hafey, Joan Twiss, and Lela Folkers, "California," in Ashton, *Healthy Cities*, 186–94.

55. Telephone interview with Beverly Flynn, December 8, 1998; Melinda Rider and Beverly Flynn, "Indiana," in Ashton, *Healthy Cities*, 195–204; Beverly Flynn, "Healthy Cities within the American Context," in Davies and Kelly, *Healthy Cities*, 112–26; Beverly Collora Flynn, Dixie Wiles Ray, and Melinda Rider, "Empowering Communities: Action Research through Healthy Cities," *Health Education Quarterly* 21: 3 (fall 1994), 395–405.

56. Telephone interview with Tom Wolff, December 10, 1998; personal interview

with Peter Lee, Boston, December 30, 1998; *Healthy Communities Massachusetts News,* October 1998; Tom Wolff, *Healthy Communities Massachusetts: One Vision of Civic Democracy* (Amherst: AHEC/Community Partners, n.d.). Representatives from approximately twenty-five state networks gathered to develop strategies to build the state organizations in Arlington, VA, on November 13, 1998.

57. Telephone interview with Tyler Norris, executive director of CHCC, October 8, 1998; fieldnotes at three national CHCC conferences, Washington, DC, November 7, 1996; Charleston, SC, December 7-9, 1997; and Arlington, VA, November 13-15, 1998.

58. Tyler Norris, speech at the conference on Building Healthier Communities: Ten Years and Learning, Arlington, VA, November 14, 1998. We have drawn upon our personal interview with Julia Weaver, former director (1995-1997) of NCL's Healthy Communities Project, Denver, CO, October 17, 1996; telephone interview with Tyler Norris, its first director (1990-1995), October 8, 1998; and personal interview with John Parr, former NCL president at the time of the initial projects, Denver, CO, October 19, 1996.

59. We have drawn upon our field notes from the Third and Fourth Annual CCN Networking Conferences, held respectively in Charleston, SC, December 7-9, 1997, and Arlington, VA, November 13-15, 1998, which included extensive formal presentations by the evaluation and governance teams, as well as dialogues among CCN and Healthy Communities leaders; extensive personal discussions with Richard Bogue, a key team member; personal interviews with Ramon Sanchez, community coordinator, Genesis Center for Health and Empowerment, in Des Plaines, IL, which is part of the Metropolitan Chicago CCN, and Dr. Julie Blankemeier, the director of Genesis, Charleston, SC, December 8, 1997. Romana Hasnain-Wynia, director of health services research and evaluation at HRET, previously served as trainer for the community meetings facilitators for Oregon Health Decisions. See also Richard Bogue and Claude Hall, Jr., eds., *Health Network Innovations: How Twenty Communities Are Improving Their Systems Through Collaboration* (Chicago: American Hospital Publishing, 1997); Richard Bogue, Mazda Antia, Rita Harmata, and Claude Hall, Jr., "Community Experiments in Action: Developing Community-Defined Models for Reconfiguring Health Care Delivery," *Journal of Health Politics, Policy, and Law* 22: 4 (August 1997), 1051-76; Gloria Bazzoli et al., "Public-Private Collaboration in Health and Human Service Delivery: Evidence From Community Partnerships," *Milbank Quarterly* 75: 4 (1997), 533-61.

60. See Kathryn Johnson, Wynne Grossman, and Anne Cassidy, eds., *Collaborating to Improve Community Health: Workbook and Guide to Best Practices in Creating Healthier Communities and Populations* (San Francisco: Jossey-Bass, 1996); *The Healthcare Forum: Our Vision* (San Francisco: Healthcare Forum, 1993); Healthcare Forum, in collaboration with DYG, Inc. and the National Civic League, *What Creates Health? Individuals and Communities Respond* (San Francisco: Health Care Forum, 1994). We have also examined the detailed programs of five (1994-1998) Healthier Communities Summits. In 1998 the Healthcare Forum merged with the AHA.

61. See CDC/ATSDR Committee on Community Engagement, *Principles of Community Engagement* (Atlanta, GA: Centers for Disease Control and Prevention, 1997); Dr. David Satcher, "Prevention Begins at Home: A Dialogue with the Surgeon General," Conference on Building Healthier Communities: Ten Years and Learning, Ar-

lington, VA, November 14, 1998; Kathleen Roe, Cindy Berenstein, Christina Goette, and Kevin Roe, "Community Building Through Empowering Evaluation: A Case Study of HIV Prevention Community Planning," in Meredith Minkler, ed., *Community Organizing and Community Building for Health* (New Brunswick, NJ: Rutgers University Press, 1997), 308–22. On Dr. Julius Richmond and parent participation in Head Start, see Zigler and Muenchow, *Head Start*, and other references in chapter 2 above. See also E. Zigler, C. S. Piotrkowski, and R. Collins, "Health Services in Head Start," in *American Review of Public Health* 15 (1994), 511–34. The parent participation figure in Head Start in 1988 is from Smith and Lipsky, *Nonprofits for Hire*, 7.

62. Parish nursing draws from the neighborhood health center movement of the 1960s, women's organizing, assets-based community development, and a vision of professional and lay partners "cocreating health." See Phyllis Ann Solari-Twadell and Mary Ann McDermott, eds., *Parish Nursing: Promoting Whole-Person Health within Faith Communities* (Newbury Park, CA: Sage, 1999); American Nurses Association and Health Ministries Association, *Standards of Practice for Parish Nurses* (Washington, DC: American Nurses Publishing, 1998).

63. Telephone interview with Gary Gunderson, director of operations of the Interfaith Health Center, December 3, 1998. See also Gary Gunderson, *Deeply Woven Roots* (Minneapolis, MN: Fortress Press, 1997); *Strong Partners: Realigning Religious Health Assets for Community Health* (Atlanta, GA: Carter Center, 1998); *Faith and Health* (Atlanta, GA: Carter Center, fall 1998, summer 1999). On the Dallas–Fort Worth partnership, see Ron Anderson and Paul Bamboulian, "Comprehensive Community Health Programs: A New Look at an Old Approach," in David Korn, Christopher McLaughlin, and Marian Osterweis, eds., *Academic Health Centers in the Managed Care Environment* (Washington, DC: Association of Academic Health Centers, 1995); Gerry Gunnin, "The Interfaith Health Partnership of North Texas," Conference on Building Healthier Communities, Arlington, VA, November 15, 1998.

64. Institute of Medicine, *Improving Health in the Community: A Role for Performance Monitoring* (Washington, DC: National Academy Press, 1997).

65. See Mary Zimmerman, "The Women's Health Movement: A Critique of Medical Enterprise and the Position of Women," in Beth Hess and Myra Marx Ferree, eds., *Analyzing Gender* (Newbury Park, CA: Sage, 1987), 442–72; Sheryl Ruzek, *The Women's Health Movement* (New York: Praeger, 1978); Marc Rodwin, "Patient Accountability and Quality of Care: Lessons from Medical Consumerism and the Patients' Rights, Women's Health and Disability Rights Movements," *American Journal of Law and Medicine* 20: 1–2 (1994), 147–67.

66. Personal interview with Irving Zola, Waltham, MA, October 26, 1993; Nancy Crew, Irving Zola, and Associates, *Independent Living for Physically Disabled People* (San Francisco: Jossey-Bass, 1983); Irving Kenneth Zola, "Towards the Necessary Universalizing of a Disability Policy," *Milbank Quarterly* 67, supplement 2, part 2 (1989), 401–28; G. L. Albrecht, *The Disability Business: Rehabilitation in America* (Newbury Park, CA: Sage, 1992); Richard Scotch, "Politics and Policy in the History of the Disability Rights Movement," *Milbank Quarterly* 67, supplement 2, part 2 (1989), 380–400, who notes how many of the leaders of the independent living movement came out of the participatory democratic movements of the 1960s. See also Frank Riessman and David Carroll, *Redefining Self-Help* (San Francisco: Jossey-Bass, 1995); and Alfred H. Katz, *Self-Help in America: A Social Movement Perspective* (New York: Twayne, 1993).

67. Henrie Treadwell et al., *Timely Opportunities: What Works in Community Care for the Elderly: Lessons Learned from W. K. Kellogg Foundation Programming* (Battle Creek, MI: W. K. Kellogg Foundation, November 1995); James Callahan, Jr., and Susan Lanspery, eds., *Supportive Services Programs in Senior Housing: Making Them Work*, Conference Proceedings, Washington, DC, October 15, 1993; Joel Handler, "Community Care for the Frail Elderly: A Theory of Empowerment," *Ohio State Law Journal* 50 (1989), 541–60; Nancy Kari, P. Hayle, and Peg Michels, "The Politics of Autonomy: Lessons from the Lazarus Project," in L. Gamroth, J. Semradek, and E. Tornquists, eds., *Enhancing Autonomy in Long-Term Care: Concepts and Strategies* (New York: Springer, 1995); David Li, "Developing Integrated Service Networks for Elder Care in New Hampshire: A Volunteer-Based Resource," unpublished paper, Heller Graduate School, Brandeis University, December 1996.

68. See Dan Wohlfeiler, "Community Organizing and Community Building among Gay and Bisexual Men: The STOP AIDS Project," in Minkler, *Community Organizing and Community Building for Health*, 230–43; Suzanne Kobasa, "AIDS Volunteering," in Dorothy Nelkin et al., eds., *A Disease of Society* (New York: Cambridge University Press, 1991); Nicholas Freudenberg and M. A. Zimmerman, "The Role of Community Organizations in Public Health Practice: The Lessons from AIDS Prevention," in Nicholas Freudenberg and M. A. Zimmerman, eds., *AIDS Prevention in the Community: Lessons from the First Decade* (Washington, DC: American Public Health Association, 1995).

69. See Steven Rathgeb Smith, "Civic Problem Solving and Substance Abuse: Seminar Report," sponsored by Join Together and the Robert Wood Johnson Foundation, Washington, DC, September 29–30, 1997. For a variety of other health-related models of community participation, see Embry Howell, Barbara Devaney, Marie McCormick, and Karen Thiel Raykovich, "Back to the Future: Community Involvement in the Healthy Start Program," *Journal of Health Politics, Policy, and Law* 23: 2 (April 1998), 291–317; "Community Empowerment, Participatory Education and Health," special issue of *Health Education Quarterly* 21: 2–3 (summer–fall 1994). On the strengthening of general norms of personal and social empowerment in health care, see David Mechanic, "Changing Medical Organization and the Erosion of Trust," *Milbank Quarterly* 74: 2 (1996), 171–89.

70. See especially Roz Lasker and the Committee on Medicine and Public Health, *Medicine and Public Health: The Power of Collaboration* (New York: New York Academy of Medicine, 1997), which is the result of a collaborative project by the American Medical Association and the American Public Health Association, and has been distributed to two hundred thousand health professionals nationwide. On the challenges that managed-care markets pose for CHCs, see Schauffler and Wolin, "Community Health Clinics under Managed Competition."

71. See Robert Thompson, "What Have HMOs Learned about Clinical Prevention Services? An Examination of the Experience at Group Health Cooperative of Puget Sound," *Milbank Quarterly* 74: 4 (1996), 469–509; Lasker, *Medicine and Public Health*, 118–20; Ezekiel Emanuel and Linda Emanuel, "Preserving Community in Health Care," *Journal of Health Politics, Policy, and Law* 22: 2 (April 1997), 158–62; Emanuel, *Ends of Human Life*, 206–7.

72. Mark Schlesinger and Bradford Gray, "A Broader Vision for Managed Care, Part 1: Measuring the Benefit to Communities," *Health Affairs* 17: 3 (May/June 1998),

157. See also Schlesinger, Gray et al., "A Broader Vision for Managed Care, Part 2: A Typology of Community Benefits," *Health Affairs* 17: 5 (September/October 1998), 26–49.

73. See especially Schlesinger and Gray, "A Broader Vision for Managed Care, Part 1," 159–62; Light, "Rhetorics and Reality of Community Health Care," 132–34; and Larry Gamm and Keith Benson, "The Influence of Governmental Policy on Community Health Partnerships and Community Care Networks," *Journal of Health Politics, Policy, and Law* 23: 5 (October 1998), 771–94.

74. Bruce Jennings and Mark Hanson, "Commodity or Public Work? Two Perspectives on Health Care," *Bioethics Forum* (fall 1995), 3–11. See also Emanuel and Emanuel, "Preserving Community in Health Care"; and Nancy Kari, Harry Boyte, and Bruce Jennings et al., *Health as a Civic Question* (Minneapolis, MN: Center for Democracy and Citizenship, November 1994). Deborah Stone, "Managed Care and the Second Great Transformation," *Journal of Health Politics, Policy, and Law* 24: 5 (October 1999), 1213–18, speaks of the "transformation of the citizen into a fiscal sinkhole" and "voracious predators on the common weal" in the new health market discourse, but articulates neither the public work nor deliberative democratic components of a robust civic alternative.

75. Schlesinger, "Paradigms Lost," especially 971–86; Schlesinger and Gray, "A Broader Vision for Managed Care, Part 1," 159–62. See also Bruce Spitz, "Community Control in a World of Regional Delivery Systems," *Journal of Health Politics, Policy, and Law* 22: 4 (August 1997), 1021–50, for further evidence of support for community control, but the profound challenges of institutionalizing it in combination with state and market actors.

76. Daniel Callahan, *False Hopes: Why America's Quest for Perfect Health Is a Recipe for Failure* (New York: Simon and Schuster, 1998).

77. See Lipsky and Lounds, "Citizen Participation and Health Care," for an early analysis of some of these constraints. For an analysis of the broadest range of current local action initiatives in 642 cities, see Jeffrey Prottas and Anne Standley, "Improving Access to Care: Grassroots Initiatives," unpublished paper, Heller Graduate School, Brandeis University, Waltham, MA, September 1999; and Anne Standley and Jeffrey Prottas, *Action Where It Counts: Communities Responding to the Challenge of Health Care for the Uninsured* (Boston: Access Project, June 1999).

78. Christopher Gates, "President's Report," National Civic League Annual Meeting, Arlington, VA, November 13, 1998. Compare Light, "Rhetorics and Realities of Community Health Care," 128 ff., who emphasizes the dynamic of cooptation in the rhetoric of community health by large corporate actors.

79. Telephone interview with Tyler Norris, October 8, 1998; field observations at the 1997 and 1998 CHCC conferences.

80. Schlesinger and Gray, "A Broader Vision for Managed Care, Part 1," 164, which, along with its companion piece, provides the most extensive discussion of policy options for expanding community benefits under managed care.

81. Emanuel and Emanuel, "Preserving Community in Health Care," 177–78. For models of citizen participation in institutional and community-level benefit or guideline review boards, see Ezekiel Emanuel and Lee Goldman, "Protecting Patient Welfare in Managed Care: Six Safeguards," *Journal of Health Politics, Policy, and Law* 23: 4 (August 1998), 635–59; and Susan D. Goold, "Allocating Health Care: Cost-

Utility Analysis, Informed Democratic Decision Making, or the Veil of Ignorance?" *Journal of Health Politics, Policy, and Law* 21: 1 (spring 1996), 69–98.

82. Stephen Shortell, Robin Gillies, David Anderson, Karen Morgan Erickson, and John Mitchell, *Remaking Health Care in America: Building Organized Delivery Systems* (San Francisco: Jossey-Bass, 1996).

83. See Light, "Rhetorics and Realities of Community Health Care," 138 ff.

84. See Carmen Sirianni, "The Civic Lessons of Health Reform: The Clinton Failure and Beyond," unpublished paper, Brandeis University, Heller Graduate School, November 1999; Yankelovich, "The Debate That Wasn't"; and Gaylin, "Faulty Diagnosis."

85. See Haynes Johnson and David Broder, *The System: The American Way of Politics at the Breaking Point* (New York: Little, Brown, 1996), 90, *passim;* John Immerwahr, Jean Johnson, and Adam Kernan-Schloss, *Faulty Diagnosis: Public Misconceptions About Health Care Reform* (New York: Public Agenda Foundation, April 1992). We also draw upon video tapes of various public events, including the signature town meeting in Tampa, FL, ABC *Nightline*, September 23, 1993, which kicked off the campaign after the plan's announcement; Thomas Friedman, "Coffee and Clinton: A Hard Sell on the Health Plan," *New York Times*, September 27, 1993, A15; field notes from the planning meeting at AARP, "Post Health Care Reform Consumer Education and Advocacy: Strengthening the Consumer Voice in a Changing Health Care System," Washington, DC, November 22, 1994, where various pro-reform interest groups that worked closely with the White House, such as Families USA and Citizen Action, discussed their "victim bank" strategies.

86. Jacob Hacker, *The Road to Nowhere: The Genesis of President Clinton's Plan for Health Security* (Princeton, NJ: Princeton University Press, 1997), 142, astutely refers to this as a "core disjunction" of the structural details of the plan and the public campaign to sell it, which were "radically disconnected" from one another. See also Lawrence R. Jacobs and Robert Y. Shapiro, *Politicians Don't Pander: Political Manipulation and the Loss of Democratic Responsiveness* (Chicago: University of Chicago Press, 2000).

87. See Skocpol, *Boomerang,* and Sven Steinmo and Jon Watts, "It's the Institutions, Stupid! Why Comprehensive National Health Insurance Always Fails in America," *Journal of Health Politics, Policy, and Law* 20: 2 (summer 1995), 329–72.

FIVE. PUBLIC JOURNALISM

1. Michael Schudson, "What Public Journalism Knows About Journalism, But Doesn't Know About 'Public,'" in Theodore Glasser, ed., *The Idea of Public Journalism* (New York: Guilford, 1999), 118–33.

2. John Dinges, quoted in Jay Rosen, *Getting the Connections Right: Public Journalism and the Troubles in the Press* (New York: Twentieth Century Fund Press, 1996), 70. For major statements of the philosophy of public journalism from which we draw this composite, see also Jay Rosen, *What Are Journalists For?* (New Haven, CT: Yale University Press, 1999); Davis Merritt, *Public Journalism and Public Life: Why Telling the News Is Not Enough* (Hillsdale, NJ: Lawrence Erlbaum, 1995); Arthur Charity, *Doing Public Journalism* (New York: Guilford Press, 1995). Of course, not every practitioner or even theorist would agree with every element in our composite.

3. Carnegie Commission on Educational Television, *Public Television: A Program for Action* (New York: Bantam Books, 1967), 92–93.

4. For arguments on the decline of the public mission of public television, see William Hoynes, *Public Television for Sale: Media, the Market, and the Public Sphere* (Boulder, CO: Westview Press, 1994); Patricia Aufderheide, "Public Television and the Public Sphere," *Critical Studies in Mass Communication* 8 (1991), 168–83; Lewis A. Friedland, "Public Television and the Crisis of Democracy: A Review Essay," *Communication Review* 1: 1 (1995), 111–28; Twentieth Century Fund, *Quality Time? The Report of the Twentieth Century Fund Task Force on Public Television* (New York: Twentieth Century Fund Press, 1993).

5. See Lewis A. Friedland, *Cable-Broadband Communications: The Control of Information in Post-Industrial Society* (Waltham, MA: Brandeis University, Ph.D. diss., 1985); K. Visnawath, John R. Finnegan, B. Rooney, and J. Potter, "Community Ties in a Midwest Community and Use of Newspapers and Cable TV," *Journalism Quarterly* 67 (1990), 899–911; Patricia Aufderheide, "Cable Television and the Public Interest," *Journal of Communication* 42 (winter 1992), 52–65; Laura R. Linder, *Public Access Television: America's Electronic Soapbox* (Westport, CT: Praeger, 1999).

6. See John H. McManus, *Market-Driven Journalism: Let the Citizen Beware?* (Thousand Oaks, CA: Sage, 1994); and Phyllis Kaniss, *Making Local News* (Chicago: University of Chicago Press, 1991). For the effect of local news programming on perceptions of community, see Jack M. McLeod, Zhongshi Guo, Katie Daily, and William P. Eveland, *Community Issues and Civic Attitudes: The Influence of Public Perceptions of Local News* (Chicago: Midwest Association for Public Opinion Research, 1994).

7. See Leo Bogart, "The State of the Industry," in Philip S. Cook, Douglas Gomery, and Lawrence W. Lichty, eds., *The Future of News: Television, Newspapers, Wire Services, Newsmagazines* (Washington DC: Woodrow Wilson Center Press, 1992), 87–88.

8. Leo Bogart, *Press and Public: Who Reads What, When, Where, and Why in American Newspapers*, 2d ed. (Mahwah, NJ: Lawrence Erlbaum Associates, 1989), 23–27.

9. Thomas C. Leonard, *News for All: America's Coming-of-Age with the Press* (New York: Oxford University Press, 1995).

10. See Don R. Le Duc, *Cable Television and the FCC: A Crisis in Media Control* (Philadelphia, PA: Temple University Press, 1973); Friedland, *Cable-Broadband Communications*.

11. See W. Russell Neuman, *The Future of the Mass Audience* (New York: Cambridge University Press, 1991). For the range of experiments with new forms of "electronic democracy," see Jeffrey B. Abramson, F. Christopher Arterton, and Gary R. Orren, *The Electronic Commonwealth: The Impact of New Media Technologies on Democratic Politics* (New York: Basic Books, 1988).

12. The results are described in Doug Underwood, *When MBAs Rule the Newsroom* (New York: Columbia University Press, 1995).

13. Kevin G. Barnhurst, *Seeing the Newspaper* (New York: St. Martin's Press, 1994).

14. Personal interview with Jennie Buckner, Charlotte, NC, April 30, 1997; telephone interview with Clark Hoyt, April 6, 1998.

15. Jay Rosen, "Journalism as Political Action: The Case of the *Columbus (Ga.) Ledger-Enquirer*" (New York: New York University, unpublished manuscript, 1991). See also Rosen, *What Are Journalists For?* 27–32.

16. Rosen, "Journalism as Political Action," 55. Jack Swift's untimely death in 1990 effectively ended the earlier experiment in Columbus, GA.

17. Personal interview with Jennie Buckner, Charlotte, NC, April 30, 1997.

18. Personal interview with Jennie Buckner, Charlotte, NC, April 30, 1997. See also James K. Batten, *America's Newspapers: What Are Our Prospects?* (Riverside, CA: Press-Enterprise Lecture Series, 1989); *Newspapers and Communities: The Vital Link* (Lawrence: University of Kansas, 1990). Batten died of cancer in 1995, but the last years of his life and career were spent pursuing these themes.

19. See James W. Carey, "The Problem of Journalism History," *Journalism History* 1 (1974); *Media, Myths, and Narratives: Television and the Press* (Newbury Park, CA: Sage, 1988); *Communication As Culture: Essays on Media and Society* (Boston: Unwin Hyman, 1989); "The Mass Media and Democracy: Between the Modern and the Postmodern," *Journal of International Affairs* 47: 1 (1993), 1–21; "The Press, Public Opinion, and Public Discourse," in Theodore L. Glasser and Charles T. Salmon, eds., *Public Opinion and the Communication of Consent* (New York: Guilford Press, 1995), 373–402.

20. James W. Carey, "The Press and the Public Discourse," *Kettering Review* (winter 1992), 12–13. There have been several dissents from Carey's interpretation. Schudson, in "What Public Journalism Knows About Journalism, But Doesn't Know About 'Public,'" argues that Dewey simply restated Lippmann's paradox of modernity while invoking a nostalgic vision of community. Peters similarly claims that Lippmann has been given short shrift by public journalists. See John Durham Peters, "Public Journalism and Democratic Theory: Four Challenges," in Glasser, *Idea of Public Journalism,* 99–117.

21. James W. Carey, "The Chicago School and the History of Mass Communication Research," in Eve Stryker Munson and Catherine A. Warren, eds., *James Carey: A Critical Reader* (Minneapolis: University of Minnesota Press, 1997), 31.

22. James W. Carey, "Communications and Economics," in Munson and Warren, *James Carey: A Critical Reader,* 71–72.

23. Jay Rosen, *The Impossible Press: American Journalism and the Decline of Public Life* (New York: New York University, Ph.D. diss., 1986).

24. Daniel Yankelovich, *Coming to Public Judgment: Making Democracy Work in a Complex World* (Syracuse, NY: Syracuse University Press, 1991).

25. Harwood Group, *Citizens and Politics: A View from Main Street* (Dayton, OH: Kettering Foundation, 1991). This study was heavily influenced by Yankelovich and the Kettering Foundation.

26. David Broder, "Democracy and the Press," *Washington Post,* January 3, 1990, A15. See also Rosen, *What Are Journalists For?* 3.

27. See Thomas E. Patterson, *Out of Order* (New York: Alfred A. Knopf, 1993), 163–65.

28. Personal interview with Steve Smith, Washington, DC, October 5, 1997.

29. Davis Merritt, "Must Restore Meaning to Election Campaigns," *Wichita Eagle,* November 13, 1988, 15A.

30. Personal interview with Davis Merritt, Wichita, KS, July 23, 1997.

31. Personal interview with Sheri Dill, Wichita, KS, April 10, 1997.

32. Personal interviews in Wichita with Margalee Wright, former mayor and city councilwoman, April 11, 1997; James Roseboro, president of the predominantly African American Northeast Heights Neighborhood Association, April 12, 1997; Beth King, College Hill Neighborhood Association, April 12, 1997; reporters Jon Roe, April 10, 1997; Anita Schrodt, April 9, 1997; telephone interview with Ed Arnone, June

18, 1999. See also Merritt, *Public Journalism and Public Life;* John Bare, "A New Strategy," in Edward Lambeth, Esther Thorson, and Phillip Meyer, eds., *Assessing Public Journalism* (Columbia, MO: University of Missouri Press, 1998), 83–108; Rosen, *Getting the Connections Right,* 35–43.

33. Personal interview with Davis Merritt, Wichita, KS, July 7, 1997.

34. Iverson began working at the station in 1980, and had been largely responsible for a number of innovative weekly news magazines, as well as a documentary output that in quality and quantity rivaled that of any public station in the United States. For Wisconsin Public Television's leading role in PBS news and public affairs, see Lewis Friedland, "Public Television as Public Sphere: The Case of the Wisconsin Collaborative Project," *Journal of Broadcasting and Electronic Media* 39 (May 1995), 147–76.

35. Quoted in Jan Schaffer and Edward D. Miller, eds., *Civic Journalism: Six Case Studies,* reported by Staci Kramer (Washington, DC: Pew Center for Civic Journalism, 1995), 12; footage on the companion video produced by the Pew Center.

36. Frank Denton and Esther Thorson, *Civic Journalism: Does It Work?* (Washington, DC: Pew Center for Civic Journalism, 1995); Esther Thorson, Lewis Friedland, and Peggy Anderson, *Civic Lessons: Report on Four Civic Journalism Projects Funded by the Pew Center for Civic Journalism* (Philadelphia, PA: Pew Charitable Trusts, 1996).

37. Lewis Friedland, Mirjana Sotirovic, and Katie Daily, "Public Journalism and Social Capital: The Case of Madison, Wisconsin," in Lambeth et al., *Assessing Public Journalism,* 191–220.

38. In addition to extensive field observation over the 1990s, we draw upon telephone interviews with Byron Knight, station manager of Wisconsin Public Television, January 17, 19, 24, 2000, from whom these quotations are taken; James Steinbach, assistant station manager, February 1997, January 24, 2000; Maria Alvarez Stroud, director of outreach, January 13, 2000.

39. Telephone interview with Cole Campbell, March 6, 1998; Cole Campbell, seminar at the American Press Institute, in Cheryl Gibbs, ed., *Speaking of Public Journalism* (Dayton, OH: Kettering Foundation, 1997), 24–33.

40. For a comprehensive analysis of the place of moral reflection in investigative journalism, see James S. Ettema and Theodore Lewis Glasser, *Custodians of Conscience: Investigative Journalism and Public Virtue* (New York: Columbia University Press, 1998).

41. Personal interview with Tom Warhover, Norfolk, VA, March 27, 1997.

42. Personal interviews with Tony Germinotta, March 28, 1997; Kerry Sipe, March 28, 1997; Esther Diskin, March 26, 1997, all in Norfolk, VA.

43. Personal interview with Mike Knepler, Norfolk, VA, March 29, 1997.

44. Personal interview with Dennis Hartig, Norfolk, VA, March 27, 1997. See also Boyte and Kari, *Building America,* 170–71.

45. Personal interview with Dennis Hartig, Norfolk, VA, March 27, 1997.

46. Personal interview with Dennis Hartig, Norfolk, VA, March 27, 1997.

47. Our analysis is based on an extensive review of the Public Life, Public Safety and Education pages of the *Norfolk Virginian-Pilot* from March 1997 to June 1998.

48. Personal interviews in Norfolk, VA, with Dennis Hartig, March 27, 1997; and Mike Knepler, March 29, 1997.

49. Personal interview with Karen Weintraub, Norfolk, VA, March 27, 1997.

50. Personal interview with Dennis Hartig, Norfolk, VA, March 27, 1997.

51. Personal interview with Julian Acken, Virginia Beach, VA, March 29, 1997. The Virginia Beach Neighborhood Leadership Institute is one of several to have been developed along the model of the Hampton Neighborhood Institute in the five-city area. Personal interview with Jim Bellun, Virginia Beach, VA, March 29, 1997, who is the official in charge of the program.

52. Personal interview with Jim Morrill, Charlotte, NC, April 20, 1997.

53. Telephone interview with Rich Oppel, August 25, 1998; telephone interview with Ed Miller of the Poynter Institute, July 6, 1998. For a comprehensive account of the early project, see Edward D. Miller, *The Charlotte Project: Helping Citizens Take Back Democracy* (St. Petersburg, FL: The Poynter Institute for Media Studies, 1994).

54. Personal interview with John Drescher, Charlotte, NC, May 1, 1997.

55. Personal and telephone interviews with Trisha Greene O'Connor, Charlotte, NC, June 12, 1997.

56. Jennie Buckner, quoted in *Civic Journalism: A Practical Guide,* Edward Fouhy, executive producer (Washington, DC: Pew Center for Civic Journalism, 1995 video).

57. Personal interviews in Charlotte, NC, with Jennie Buckner, April 30, 1997; and Ted Mellnik, May 7, 1996, and March 8, 1997.

58. Personal interview with Charlayne Price-Patterson, Charlotte, NC, June 8, 1996.

59. For the most complete account of public journalism and commercial television, including Charlotte, see David Kurpius, *Commercial Local Television News and Public Journalism: A Case Study of the Range of Organizational Routines of Coverage* (Madison: University of Wisconsin, Ph.D. diss., 1997). For Charlotte, see especially pp. 67–70, 149–51.

60. For 1995–97, we reviewed special projects coverage by the *Observer,* including all of the coverage of Taking Back Our Neighborhoods and other daily public journalism coverage of issues like cruising, education, local culture wars, race, urban design, and regional environmentalism, as well as its election coverage. See also Schaffer and Miller, *Civic Journalism: Six Case Studies,* 4–11.

61. On Charlotte's civic infrastructure, see "Charlotte: A Company Town," in Bruce Adams and John Parr, eds., *Boundary Crossers: Case Studies of How Ten of America's Metropolitan Regions Work* (College Park, MD: Burns Academy of Leadership, University of Maryland, 1997); and William J. McCoy, "Building Coalitions for the Future in Charlotte-Mecklenburg," *National Civic Review* (spring 1991), 120–34.

62. Personal interview with Burt Green, Charlotte, NC, May 9, 1996.

63. Field observations from Seversville Community Meeting, Charlotte, NC, May 14, 1996.

64. Field observations from Seversville Community Meeting, focus group, and personal interview with Wallace Pruitt, Charlotte, NC, May 14, 1996. Others at the focus group agreed that they had seen significant change since Taking Back Our Neighborhoods.

65. Personal interview with Burt Green, Charlotte, NC, May 9, 1996.

66. Personal interview with Pat Garrett, Charlotte, NC, May 9, 1996.

67. Personal interview with Jane Burts, Charlotte, NC, May 8, 1996.

68. Personal interview with Dennis Nowicki, Charlotte, NC, May 7, 1996.

69. Personal interview with Isaac Applewhite, Charlotte, NC, May 10, 1996.

70. Personal interviews at Uptown Rotary Meeting, Charlotte, NC, May 14, 1996.

The only significant pocket of negative reaction we found was from a group of city planners, architects, and others who had already been working to bring back North Charlotte.

71. Personal interview with Fannie Flono, Charlotte, NC, May 1, 1997.

72. Personal interview with Wallace Pruitt, Charlotte, NC, May 14, 1996. The series eventually covered ten neighborhoods, including Seversville. We did additional fieldwork in the racially mixed Commonwealth-Morningside neighborhood.

73. Personal interviews in Charlotte, NC, with Liz Chandler, May 6, 1996 and June 11, 1997; Gary Wright, May 7, 1996; Ames Alexander May 2, 1997; and Jennie Buckner, May 7, 1996. Buckner believes the phrase "public journalism" gets in the way of others accepting the practices. She refers to the ASNE "timeless values" study done by the Harwood group as a good example of the kind of values framework that she is trying to instill in her newsroom, in part because it embodies the core values of public journalism without necessarily labeling them as such. See Richard C. Harwood, *Timeless Values: Staying True to Journalistic Principles in the Age of New Media* (Washington, DC: American Society of Newspaper Editors, 1995).

74. Personal interviews in Charlotte, NC, with Jennie Buckner, April 30, 1997; May 7, 1996; Rick Thames, May 6, 1996.

75. Personal interview with Jennie Buckner, Charlotte, NC, April 30, 1997.

76. Personal interview with Jennie Buckner, Charlotte, NC, April 30, 1997.

77. Personal interview with Cheryl Carpenter, Charlotte, NC, June 10, 1997.

78. Personal interview with Jim Walser, Charlotte, NC, May 2, 1997.

79. Personal interview with Jennie Buckner, Charlotte, NC, May 7, 1996.

80. Personal interview with Cheryl Carpenter, Charlotte, NC, June 10, 1997.

81. Personal interview with Cheryl Carpenter, Charlotte, NC, June 10, 1997.

82. Personal interview with Cheryl Carpenter, Charlotte, NC, June 10, 1997.

83. Personal interview with Cheryl Carpenter, Charlotte, NC, June 10, 1997.

84. Personal interview with Cheryl Carpenter, Charlotte, NC, June 10, 1997.

85. We base our analysis here on material in the archives of the PPLP, which are in the process of being permanently housed at the Kettering Foundation in Dayton, OH; field notes from PPLP seminars, Reston, VA, March 23–26, 1995; Washington, DC, June 27, 1998; personal interviews with Jay Rosen, Chicago, July 18, 1997; Lisa Austin, Washington, DC, October 5, 1997; telephone interview July 25, 1994. See also Rosen, *What Are Journalists For?*

86. Personal interviews with Ed Fouhy, Washington, DC, July 28, 1997; Jan Schaffer, Washington, DC, July 29, 1997; field observations at James K. Batten Symposium, Washington, DC, September 13, 1995. See also Rosabeth Moss Kanter, "When a Thousand Flowers Bloom: Structural, Collective, and Social Conditions for Innovation in Organization," *Research in Organizational Behavior* 10 (1988), 169–211, for a conceptual analysis of this strategy.

87. Jan Schaffer. "Transforming Journalism for Today: Reinventing It for Tomorrow," *Civic Catalyst*, fall 1999, 2, 16.

88. Our analysis is drawn from the Pew Center for Civic Journalism archives, which Sandra Nichols analyzed for us, and from fieldnotes from Pew Center events and workshops, including the following: Association of Educators in Journalism and Mass Communication (AEJMC), Chicago, IL, August 31, 1997; "Civic Laboratories: Journalism under the Microscope," National Press Club, Washington, DC, August 28, 1997; "Civic

Journalism Retreat," Poynter Institute for Media Studies, St. Petersburg, FL, November 7–9, 1997; "Redefining the News: The Evolution of Civic Journalism," Civic Journalism Interest Group of AEJMC, Wichita State University, Wichita, KS, March 27–29, 1998; "Journalists: Custodians or Catalysts for the Community?" cosponsored by Investigative Reporters and Editors, Baltimore, MD, April 9–11, 1999; AEJMC Annual Meetings, New Orleans, LA, August 5, 1999; PBS convention, Democracy Project founding, New Orleans, LA, June 4, 1994; personal interviews with Ed Fouhy, Washington, DC, July 28, 1997; Jan Schaffer, Washington, DC, July 29, 1997.

89. We base our analysis here on discussions with many practitioners and a review of other community renewal projects, as well as our telephone interviews with Richard Harwood, September 22, 1998; D. Neil Richardson, September 1999; see Harwood, *Timeless Values.*

90. Field observations and personal interviews with Steve Smith and various editors and reporters at the *Colorado Springs Gazette,* Colorado Springs, July 25–26, 1997 (and Steve Smith, Washington, DC, October 5, 1997), including Terri Fleming, managing editor; Katherine Sosbe, training and development manager; John Steepleton, public editor; Cliff Foster, city editor; Barb Reichert, sports editor; Susan Edmondson, entertainment editor; Jeff Thomas, business editor; reporters Wendy Lawton and Bill McKeown. See also Steve Smith, "The Tyranny of 'Or'; the Power of 'And,'" *Civic Catalyst,* summer 1998, 11; *The Gazette Journalism Handbook* (Colorado Springs: Colorado Springs Gazette and the Harwood Group, 1997), and other training materials. Smith resigned his position as editor in late 1999 when a new publisher took over.

91. Telephone interview with Dennis Foley, ombudsman, *Orange County Register,* January 12, 2000. See also Dennis Foley, "Newsroom Conversations, New Approaches to News," *Civic Catalyst,* spring 1998, 8–9; "Reaching Out to Readers: They Do Notice," *Civic Catalyst,* spring 1999, 14–15.

92. Telephone interview with Cole Campbell, editor, *St. Louis Post-Dispatch,* March 6, 1998; personal discussions, Washington, DC, February 5, 1998, and Racine, WI, January 14–16, 2000. Cole Campbell left the *Post-Dispatch* to join the Poynter Institute in the spring of 2000.

93. Field observations and personal interviews in Spokane, WA, at the *Spokesman-Review,* November 5–7, 1999, including Chris Peck, editor; Doug Floyd, public editor; Peggy Kuhn, managing editor; Richard Wagner, city editor; Rebecca Nappi, reporter; and Colin Mulvaney, photojournalist. See also Elana Ashanti Jefferson, *Soapbox: A Guide to Civic Journalism at the Spokesman-Review* (Spokane, WA: Spokesman-Review, n.d.), which reflects on the cumulative practice at the paper since the early 90s. For Peck's work as chair of the ASNE Ethics and Values Committee in 1996, see Chris Peck, "Does Civic Journalism Move the Needle? ASNE Surveys Key Practitioners," *Civic Catalyst,* January 1996, 8; Chris Peck, "Civic Journalism: Savior of Newspapers in the Twenty-First Century?" *Civic Catalyst,* fall 1999, 12–14.

94. See Paul Voakes, *The Newspaper Journalists of the 1990s* (Washington, DC: American Society of Newspaper Editors, 1997); and Walter K. Lindenmann, *Views of Print and Broadcast Media Executives Toward Journalism Education* (New York: Virginia Commonwealth University and Associated Press Managing Editors, 1997).

95. Personal discussions with John Dinges, July 18, 1994; *Civic Catalyst,* December 1994, 5.

96. See Jan Schaffer, Stanley Cloud, and Kathleen Fitzgerald, *The Citizens Elections*

Project: Case Studies (Washington, DC: Pew Center for Civic Journalism, 1996); *Civic Catalyst,* March 1995, 5; June 1995, 1; October 1995, 1; April 1996, 3; July 1996, 2.

97. Earvin Duggan, speech to the 1994 PBS Convention, New Orleans, LA, June 4, 1994; Ellen Hume, presentation on the Democracy Project, Public Broadcasting Service, Alexandria, VA, May 2, 1996.

98. Our analysis of Citizens '96 and State of the Union is based on field notes of the meetings of the National Advisory Board, Wisconsin Public Television producers, and national PBS partners, Alexandria, VA, October 25, 1995, January 24, May 2, July 18, 1996; logs of advisors' conference calls throughout 1996 and 1997; a complete set of broadcast tapes airing on PBS between January 1996 and September 1997; and a review of public outreach materials used in local town meetings. Especially noteworthy is the study guide, *Working in the USA: Making a Living, Making a Difference,* produced by the Study Circles Resource Center, to accompany the Labor Day 1997 special, "That's Why They Call It Work."

99. Our analysis is based on the full set of PBS broadcast tapes and other materials of the NIC and discussions with a variety of foundation and journalism partners before and after the event. On the deliberative opinion poll as a design, see James Fishkin, *The Voice of the People: Public Opinion and Democracy* (New Haven, CT: Yale University Press, 1995). For a useful exchange of views on the strengths and limits of such polls, see the symposium in *Good Society* 9: 1 (1999), 1-29.

100. Max Frankel, "Fix-It Journalism," *New York Times Magazine,* May 21, 1995, 28, 30. Curiously, Frankel had called Buzz Merritt before writing the column with the question, "What is your agenda for the city of Wichita?" Merritt said that he had no particular agenda and that this was not what public journalism was about. He offered to overnight a copy of his short book, *Public Journalism and Public Life,* but Frankel replied, "No thank you." Merritt never was mentioned in the column. See Rosen, *What Are Journalists For?* 219.

101. See David Remnick, "Scoop," *New Yorker,* January 29, 1996, 42; Michael Kelly, "Media Culpa," *New Yorker,* November 4, 1996, 45-49; Michael Gartner, "Public Journalism, Seeing Through the Gimmicks," *Media Studies Journal* (winter 1997), 69-76. Kelley and Gartner relied particularly on the complaints of losing Democratic senatorial candidate Harvey Gantt's campaign manager that Gantt's views could not get in the paper, despite extensive coverage of Gantt's campaign. In an unintended irony, both of these traditional journalists got major facts wrong. For example, although only twelve articles were published by the partnership among hundreds during the election season, the critics portrayed the joint coverage as the *only* campaign coverage. Gantt's campaign manager's complaints concerned the exclusion of the issue of race from the campaign. But the campaign's own strategy was based on the exclusion of race, and it was never introduced by the Gantt campaign—he had hoped the liberal *Observer* would introduce it *sub rosa* in its horserace coverage. Most tellingly, in an interview with us, the registrar of voters of Charlotte-Mecklenburg county (and no friend of Jesse Helms, Gantt's opponent) said that the coverage was the best that he had seen in thirty years; that in his more than seventy public talks in the area since the campaign, he heard unalloyed support for public journalism; and that he believed the postelection criticism by Gantt's manager was sour grapes to cover up a poorly run campaign. And citizens of North Carolina lined up at the polls with the *Observer*'s special edition on the election. Personal interview with Bill McCoy, Char-

lotte-Mecklenburg registrar of voters, Charlotte, NC, May 10, 1996. See also Jennie Buckner, "Public Journalism, Giving Voters a Voice," *Media Studies Journal* (winter 1997), 65–68.

102. Our presentation of the criticisms of civic journalism draws upon a review of many articles in the *Columbia Journalism Review, American Journalism Review,* and especially the summary by its editor, Rem Rieder, himself a critic, in "Public Journalism: Stop the Shooting," *American Journalism Review* (November–December 1995), 6, as well as the analysis by Michael X. Delli Carpini, *Reframing News: Press Coverage of Public Journalism* (Dayton, OH: Kettering Foundation, 1998); and Rosen, *What Are Journalists For?*

103. See David O. Loomis, "Is Public Journalism Cheap Journalism: Putting Public Journalists' Money Where Their Mouths Are," presented at Public Journalism: A Critical Forum at the University of South Carolina, Columbia, SC, October 11–13, 1998.

104. See "House of Cards Tumbles Out of Asbury Park Civic Journalism Project," *Civic Catalyst,* fall 1997, 1; William Glaberson, "Press: From a Wisconsin Daily, a Progress Report on a New Kind of Problem-Solving Journalism," *New York Times,* February 27, 1995, C6.

105. Hodding Carter, III, quoted in Rosen, *Getting the Connections Right,* 63–64.

106. Max Frankel, "Word and Image: Pay-Pay-Pay-Per-View," *New York Times Sunday Magazine,* November 8, 1998, 36.

107. See Charlotte Ryan, *Prime Time Activism: Media Strategies for Grassroots Organizing* (Boston: South End Press, 1991); Robert McChesney, *Rich Media, Poor Democracy: Communication Politics in Dubious Times* (Urbana: University of Illinois Press, 1999); Schudson, "What Public Journalism Knows About Journalism, But Doesn't Know About 'Public,'" 122; and David Pritchard, "The Future of Media Accountablity," in David Pritchard, ed., *Holding the Media Accountable: Citizens, Ethics, and the Law* (Bloomington: Indiana University Press, 2000). For broad theorizations of the public sphere that appreciate the complexity of many overlapping forms of conversation and argumentation, see Craig Calhoun, ed., *Habermas and the Public Sphere* (Cambridge, MA: MIT Press, 1992); Seyla Benhabib, "Toward a Deliberative Model of Democratic Legitimacy," in Seyla Benhabib, ed., *Democracy and Difference* (Princeton, NJ: Princeton University Press, 1996), 67–94; and Michael Walzer, "Deliberation, and What Else?" in Steven Macedo, ed., *Deliberative Politics: Essays on Democracy and Disagreement* (New York: Oxford University Press, 1999), 58–69.

108. Our analysis of grassroots community information projects and networks, which must remain very abbreviated here, draws upon personal and telephone interviews with twenty prominent national and local innovators, field observations at eleven conferences and planning meetings, and project documentation. See also Douglas Schuler, *New Community Networks: Wired for Change* (Reading, MA: Addison-Wesley, 1996); Jan Gray, Stephen Silha, and Marion Woyvodich, *Good News/Good Deeds: Citizen Effectiveness in the Age of Electronic Democracy* (Seattle, WA: GoodNews/Good Deeds, 1999); Mario Morino, *Assessment and Evolution of Community Networking* (Great Falls, VA: Morino Institute, 1994); Lewis A. Friedland, "Electronic Democracy and the New Citizenship," *Media, Culture and Society* 18: 2 (April 1996), 185–212; Libraries for the Future and the Benton Foundation, *Local Places, Global Connections: Libraries in the Digital Age* (Washington, DC: Benton Foundation, 1996), and *Buildings, Books, and*

Bytes: Libraries and Communities in the Digital Age (Washington, DC: Benton Foundation, 1996).

109. See Patricia Aufderheide, *Communications Policy and the Public Interest* (New York: Guilford Press, 1999); Robert B. Horwitz, "Broadcast Reform Revisited: Reverend Everett C. Parker and the WLBT Case (Office of Communications of the United Church of Christ v. FCC)," *Communication Review* 2: 3 (1997), 311–48. The most important work on the transformation of the communications infrastructure globally, and its effects on the entire political and economic system, is Manuel Castells, *Information Age, Economy, Society, and Culture*, 3 vols. (Cambridge, England: Blackwell Publishers, 1996, 1997, 1998). On the problems of information equity, see Mark Cooper, *Universal Service: A Historical Perspective and Policies for the Twenty-First Century* (Washington, DC: Benton Foundation/Consumer Federation of America, 1996); S. Goslee, *Losing Ground Bit by Bit: Low-Income Communities in the Information Age* (Washington, DC: Benton Foundation, 1998); National Telecommunication and Information Administration, *Falling Through the Net II: New Data on the Digital Divide* (Washington, DC: NTIA, 1998).

SIX. THE CIVIC RENEWAL MOVEMENT

1. See the Final Report of the National Commission on Civic Renewal, *A Nation of Spectators: How Civic Disengagement Weakens America and What We Can Do About It* (College Park, MD: The National Commission on Civic Renewal, June 1998); Carmen Sirianni and Lewis Friedland, "Civic Innovation and American Democracy," *Change*, January/February 1997, 14–23; David Broder, "'Citizenship Movement' Is Trying to Combat Cynicism," *Washington Post*, Sunday, November 27, 1994, C7; William Raspberry, "Community, Heal Thyself," *Washington Post*, March 18, 1996. See also the series edited by Nancy Kruh, "People's Movement," *Dallas Morning News*, March 5–12, 1995, which included various staff reports on "The We Decade: Rebirth of Community," "The Community Builders: Faces of a Social Movement," and "Roots of Renewal"; and the CBS Radio *Osgood File*, Democracy, Community, and Citizenship Series and Network Access Project: Democracy Update (1995–97), on tape, produced by the American Communications Foundation. As a senior advisor to the National Commission on Civic Renewal, Sirianni was an insistent proponent of recognizing and legitimating the emergence of a nascent "civic renewal movement." It should be noted that various others either prefer, or interchangeably use, phrases such as "community renewal movement," "community building movement," "communitarian movement," or "civil society movement," though the definitions and boundaries can vary considerably.

2. See, for instance, Aldon Morris and Carol McClurg Mueller, eds., *Frontiers in Social Movement Theory* (New Haven, CT: Yale University Press, 1992); Enrique Laraña, Hank Johnston, and Joseph Gusfield, eds., *New Social Movements: From Ideology to Identity* (Philadelphia, PA: Temple University Press, 1994); Hank Johnston and Bert Klandermans, eds., *Social Movements and Culture* (Minneapolis: University of Minnesota Press, 1995); Alberto Melucci, *Challenging Codes: Collective Action in the Information Age* (New York: Cambridge University Press, 1996); Jean Cohen, "Strategy or Identity: New Theoretical Paradigms and Contemporary Social Movements," *Social Research* 52: 4

(1985), 663–716; and Donatella della Porta and Mario Diani, *Social Movements: An Introduction* (Malden, MA: Blackwell, 1999), who emphasize the fluid, polycentric, and negotiated relationships among movement identities, which is an insight important to our own analysis of the civic renewal movement's relationships to other movements.

3. See David Snow, E. Burke Rocheford, Jr., Steven Worden, and Robert Benford, "Frame Alignment Processes, Micromobilization, and Movement Participation," *American Sociological Review* 51: 4 (August 1986), 464–81.

4. Among the core texts we draw upon here are Harry Boyte, Benjamin Barber, Will Marshall, and Carmen Sirianni, *Civic Declaration: A Call for a New Citizenship* (Dayton, OH: Kettering Foundation, December 1994); John Gardner, *National Renewal* (Washington, DC, and Denver, CO: Independent Sector and National Civic League, September 1995); Alliance for National Renewal, *What Is the Alliance for National Renewal?* (Denver, CO: National Civic League, 1996); The National Commission on Civic Renewal, *A Nation of Spectators;* Amitai Etzioni, Mary Ann Glendon, and William Galston, "The Responsive Communitarian Platform: Rights and Responsibilities," in Amitai Etzioni, *The Spirit of Community: The Reinvention of American Society* (New York: Simon and Schuster, 1993), 251–67; David Mathews, *Politics for People: Finding a Responsible Public Voice* (Urbana: University of Illinois Press, 1994); Kathryn Stoff Hogg, ed., *Reinventing Citizenship: The Practice of Citizen Politics* (Minneapolis, MN: Center for Democracy and Citizenship, 1995); and G. Thomas Kingsley, Joseph McNeely, and James Gibson, *Community Building: Coming of Age* (Baltimore, MD, and Washington, DC: The Development Training Institute and the Urban Institute, 1996).

Our reading of these texts is also informed by extensive fieldnotes of meetings, phone logs, interviews, and early drafts that were important to their collaborative production. For evidence of dissemination and reception, we have surveyed a broad range of literature and practical "toolkits" produced by organizations in the fields of community and youth service, civic education, and community leadership development that have drawn upon these core texts in fashioning or refashioning themes for a wider audience.

5. This quotation is from the opening paragraph of Boyte, Barber, Marshall, and Sirianni, *Civic Declaration,* 5. Hereafter we will not cite each reference from one of the group of texts. The term *citizen* is used here and in all other texts as an inclusive term denoting effective and authoritative engagement in community problem solving and public work by both those who are legal citizens and those who do not enjoy such formal status. The movement does not directly address the issues of the rights of noncitizens. Some participants in the movement prefer the term *community* because it does not elicit concerns of potential exclusion, though others (ourselves included) believe that *citizen* has a more robust normative resonance that is important to preserve.

6. The second example is taken from a personal interview with Derek Okubo of the National Civic League, Denver, CO, October 19, 1996, who facilitated the collaborative process in Colorado. The first example is taken from a telephone interview with Mary Jacksteit, cofounder of the Common Ground Network for Life and Choice, February 9, 1995, and from a telephone interview with David Cohen, codirector of the Advocacy Institute, August 17, 1994, who also contributed to the Civic Declaration and worked with the Reinventing Citizenship Project. See also Mary Jack-

steit and Adrienne Kaufmann, *Finding Common Ground in the Abortion Conflict: A Manual* (Washington, DC: Common Ground Network for Life and Choice, 1995).

7. Mathews, *Politics for People*, 1, 32.

8. In the everyday discourse among leaders of the civic renewal movement, one rarely, if ever, hears identity-specifying prefaces used to claim privileged insight to political truth or special rights of representation. In reviewing our field notes from numerous meetings on civic renewal and community building over a six-year period, we found, even to our own astonishment, not a single instance that we would classify as forthright identity politics, though inclusiveness was assumed as a fundamental value, and efforts to ensure diversity were the norm. In this sense, the civic renewal frame aligns itself with what Alan Wolfe describes as the "benign multiculturalism" of most Americans, in *One Nation, After All*, 154–63. See also Carmen Sirianni, "Feminist Pluralism and Democratic Learning: The Politics of Citizenship in the National Women's Studies Association," *NWSA Journal* 5: 3 (fall 1993), 367–84; Nancy Rosenblum, "Navigating Pluralism: The Democracy of Everyday Life (and Where It Is Learned)," in Stephen L. Elkin and Karol Edward Soltan, eds., *Citizen Competence and Democratic Institutions* (University Park: Pennsylvania State University Press, 1999), 67–88; and Neil Smelser and Jeffrey Alexander, eds., *Diversity and Its Discontents: Cultural Conflict and Common Ground in Contemporary American Society* (Princeton, NJ: Princeton University Press, 1999).

9. This conception of relational power derives from several sources and extends beyond the civic renewal movement. It has important roots in the work of democratic thinkers such as Mary Parker Follett, whose contributions were recognized by Dorothy Emmet in the 1950s and then taken up by feminist thinkers and activists in the late 1960s and early 1970s. See Mary Parker Follett's 1920 classic, *The New State: Group Organization: The Solution of Popular Government* (University Park: Pennsylvania State University Press, 1998); Dorothy Emmet, "The Concept of Power," *Proceedings of the Aristotelian Society* 54 (1953–54); Nancy Hartsock, "Political Change: Two Perspectives on Power," *Quest: A Feminist Quarterly* 1: 1 (summer 1974); and *Money, Sex, and Power* (Boston: Northeastern University Press, 1983).

The IAF, the first and most important community-organizing network to stress relational power in the 1970s, derived it from Bernard Loomer, "Two Faces of Power," *Criterion* 15: 1 (1976), 12–29, who draws upon theological sources but also relies upon analogies with women's experiences of acting in the world, which IAF has self-consciously utilized in its development of women leaders (see chapter 2). Indeed, Loomer contrasts the "purely masculine stance in life" with that "traditionally associated with the feminine" in a way that suggests that he is drawing upon views that had become increasingly widespread in the women's movement at that time. The extent to which this view of power added important novel elements can be seen by contrasting the well-known treatments by Peter Bachrach and Morton Baratz, "The Two Faces of Power," *American Political Science Review* 56 (1962), 947–52, and Steven Lukes, *Power: A Radical View* (London: Macmillan, 1974). It is also profoundly different from the Foucauldian view of power, which excludes the possibility of democratic and productive uses of relational power. For a good overview, see Mark Bevir, "Foucault, Power, and Institutions," *Policy Studies* 47 (1999), 345–59.

10. The civic renewal movement is hardly unique among movements in its emphasis on stories of success to generate the sense of efficacy and optimism needed to

motivate and sustain participation. See Snow and Benford, "Frame Alignment Processes, Micromobilization, and Movement Participation," 471. But the civic renewal movement places much greater emphasis than do protest and justice movements on stories of practical problem solving and learning from best practice. This is evident in conference trainings, websites, practice guides, videos, journalistic features, and even in high-level meetings to educate federal officials. On theoretical issues of civic competence, see Elkin and Soltan, *Citizen Competence and Democratic Institutions*.

11. David Snow and Robert Benford, "Master Frames and Cycles of Protest," in Morris and Mueller, *Frontiers in Social Movement Theory*, 133–55. See also William Gamson, "The Social Psychology of Collective Action," 53–77 in the same volume; Doug McAdam, "Culture and Social Movements," in Laraña, Johnston, and Gusfield, *New Social Movements*, 36–57.

12. Snow and Benford, "Master Frames and Cycles of Protest," 149. See also Thomas Rochon, *Culture Moves: Ideas, Activism, and Changing Values* (Princeton, NJ: Princeton University Press, 1998).

13. For some theoretical discussions of civil society, see the references in chapter 1. For a provocative critique of the role this concept has played in recent years by one of the leaders of the civic renewal movement, see Harry Boyte, "Off the Playground of Civil Society," *Good Society* 9: 2 (1999), 1–7, who argues that the term often trivializes civic action as moralism and voluntarism and diverts focus from the robust public work needed in core institutions.

14. Kingsley, McNeely, and Gibson, *Community Building: Coming of Age*, 3.

15. This phrase arose in the civil service and has been borrowed by movement thinkers from Jerome Delli Priscoli, head of public participation programs for the Army Corps of Engineers, former president of the Interagency Council on Citizen Participation (ICCP) in the 1970s, and more recently of the International Association for Public Participation (IAP2), an important movement network. Field notes, Reinventing Citizenship Project, Washington, DC, March 4, 1994.

16. Gardner, *National Renewal*, 7–8. Government's catalytic role in civic problem solving is almost always, to our knowledge, combined with enforcing norms of inclusiveness and helping civic groups expand their boundaries, as in the case of the offices of neighborhood associations in Portland and Seattle.

17. National Commission on Civic Renewal, *A Nation of Spectators*, 11. For important theoretical critiques of those civil society thinkers who downplay the essential role of political and legal institutions, see Christopher Beem, *The Necessity of Politics: Reclaiming American Public Life* (Chicago: University of Chicago Press, 1999); and Jean L. Cohen, "Does Voluntary Association Make Democracy Work?" in Smelser and Alexander, *Diversity and Its Discontents*, 263–91.

18. On injustice frames and micromobilization against unjust authorities, see William Gamson, Bruce Fireman, and Steven Rytina, *Encounters with Unjust Authority* (Homewood, IL: Dorsey, 1982); and William Gamson, *Talking Politics* (New York: Cambridge University Press, 1992). The phrase "cold anger," in contrast to Gamson's "hot cognitions," is taken from Rogers's study of the IAF, *Cold Anger*.

The civic renewal frame is closer to what some social movement theorists call the frames of "consensus movements" that diffuse personal responsibility for such goals as peace and environmental protection, rather than sharply define an oppositional "we" and "they." But the civic renewal frame focuses explicitly on the methods and

skills for translating conflict into productive collaboration and raises normative issues about the everyday responsibilities of "we as citizens" that are beyond the descriptive classification of consensus movements as those with "widespread support
for their goals and little or no organized opposition from the population of a geographic community." Thus, unlike some consensus movements whose primary work
is conducted in legislative halls, political offices, and the mass media, the civic renewal frame stresses that the contributions of ordinary people are critical to success.
The civic renewal movement thus cannot be classified as a consensus movement in
the usual sense, though one might argue that it is a variant lying somewhere between
the poles of consensus and conflict and synthesizing the two for new purposes. On
consensus movements, see John D. McCarthy and Mark Wolfson, "Consensus Movements, Conflict Movements, and the Cooptation of Civic and State Infrastructures,"
in Morris and Mueller, *Frontiers in Social Movement Theory,* 273–95 (the quotation is
from 273–74); Michael Schwartz and Shuva Paul, "Resource Mobilization versus the
Mobilization of People: Why Consensus Movements Cannot Be Instruments of Social Change," 205–23 in the same volume; John Lofland, "Consensus Movements:
City Twinning and Derailed Dissent in the American Eighties," *Research in Social Movements, Conflicts and Change* 11 (1989), 163–96; and *Polite Protesters: The American Peace
Movement in the 1980s* (Syracuse, NY: Syracuse University Press, 1993), chapter 2. On
some of the factors shaping "contentious cooperation," see Marco G. Giugni and Flo-
rence Passey, "Contentious Politics in Complex Societies: New Social Movements between Conflict and Cooperation," in Marco G. Giugni, Doug McAdam, and Charles
Tilly, eds., *From Contention to Democracy* (Lanham, MD: Rowman and Littlefield,
1998), 81–107.

19. On the importance of networks in social movements, see especially David
Knoke, *Political Networks: The Structural Perspective* (New York: Cambridge University
Press, 1990), chapter 3 (with Nancy Wisely); della Porta and Diani, *Social Movements,*
chapter 5; Mayer Zald and John McCarthy, "Social Movement Industries: Competition and Cooperation among Movement Organizations," in Louis Kriesberg, ed., *Research in Social Movements, Conflict and Change,* vol. 3 (Greenwich, CT: JAI Press, 1980),
1–20. See also Stanley Wasserman and Katherine Faust, *Social Network Analysis: Methods and Applications* (New York: Cambridge University Press, 1994), chapter 5; and
David Knoke and Ronald Burt, "Prominence," in Ronald Burt and M. J. Minor, eds.,
Applied Network Analysis (Newbury Park, CA: Sage, 1983), 195–222.

20. Aldon Morris, *The Origins of the Civil Rights Movement* (New York: Free Press,
1984), 114, 149–55, 236–39. See also Belinda Robnett, "African-American Women
in the Civil Rights Movement, 1954–65: Gender, Leadership, and Micromobilization,"
American Journal of Sociology 101 (1996), 1661–93; Charles Payne, "Ella Baker and
Models of Social Change," *Signs: Journal of Women in Culture and Society* 14 (1989),
885–99.

21. Telephone interview with Harry Boyte, June 2, 1998, and personal discussions; personal interview with Dorothy Cotton, Minneapolis, MN, September 21,
1995. See also Sara Evans and Harry Boyte, *Free Spaces: The Sources of Democratic Change
in America* (Chicago: University of Chicago Press, 1986, 1992), 62–68. Cotton has remained active in African American youth work. She participated in the Reinventing
Citizenship Project, the American Civic Forum, and the Civic Practices Network, and
was a member of the partner network of Project Public Life (see below). She also

gave the keynote address at the national planning conference to establish AmeriCorps in the spring of 1993.

22. Telephone interviews with Harry Boyte, June 2, 1998; and Heather Booth, August 28, 1994. See also Harry Boyte, *The Backyard Revolution*, and *Community Is Possible: Repairing America's Roots* (New York: Harper and Row, 1984); Evans and Boyte, *Free Spaces;* Harry Boyte, Heather Booth, and Steve Max, *Citizen Action and the New American Populism* (Philadelphia, PA: Temple University Press, 1986); Harry Boyte and Frank Riessman, eds., *The New Populism: The Politics of Empowerment* (Philadelphia, PA: Temple University Press, 1986).

23. Personal and telephone interviews with Harry Boyte, June 2, 1998; Dennis Donovan, Washington, DC, May 19, 1997, and Somerville, MA, September 1998; Melissa Bass, Waltham, MA, September 17, 1999; Nancy Kari, September 8, 1994, and January 23, 1995; Anthony Massengale, Washington, DC, February, March, November, 1994; Peg Michels, February, March, November 1994; Catherine Milton, Corporation for National and Community Service, San Francisco, May 1, 1995. See also Boyte and Kari, *Building America*, chapter 9; Melissa Bass, *Toward a New Theory of Democratic Practice and Education: An Evaluation of Public Achievement* (Minneapolis: Humphrey Institute for Public Affairs, University of Minnesota, Masters Paper, 1995); *A Public Achievement Guidebook* (Minneapolis, MN: Center for Democracy and Citizenship, 1996); Melissa Bass with Harry Boyte et al., *By the People: An AmeriCorps Citizenship and Service Training Guide* (Minneapolis: Minnesota Commission on National and Community Service and the Center for Democracy and Citizenship, 1995), later adopted as the official AmeriCorps citizenship training manual. The themes emerging from the center have been important in other youth development and higher education projects. See, for instance, the Citizenship Symposium, Lake Bluffs, IL, September 1, 1993; *Active Citizenship Today* (Washington, DC: Close-Up Foundation and the Constitutional Rights Foundation, 1993); the two conferences on youth, civic, and community development, Wingspread Conference Center, Racine, WI, March 1–3, December 2–4, 1996; Elizabeth Hollander, Harry Boyte et al., *The Wingspread Declaration on the Civic Responsibilities of Research Universities* (Racine, WI, 1999). Our interviews and informal conversations with hundreds of innovators over the past six years, as well as our reading of scholarly and other literature, have demonstrated to us how influential such books as *Free Spaces* and *Commonwealth* have been, even in arenas far afield, such as some of the early reframings of civic environmentalism or libraries as civic spaces.

24. Telephone interview with Harry Boyte, June 2, 1998; Paul DuBois, "The American News Service," presentation to Alliance for National Renewal meeting, Washington, DC, February 24, 1995; Frances Moore Lappé and Paul Martin DuBois, *The Quickening of America: Rebuilding Our Nation, Remaking Our Lives* (San Francisco: Jossey-Bass, 1994). Some three hundred newspapers have subscribed to the American News Service, including leading ones such as the *Los Angeles Times*, the *Boston Globe*, and the *Christian Science Monitor.*

25. Telephone interview with Suzanne Morse, August 5, 1997. The board of the Pew Charitable Trusts and its president, Rebecca Rimel, have provided top-level support for various civic renewal projects, and Rimel has argued that "this country's greatest challenge is to renew its spirit of civic responsibility and to more fully develop its public stewardship." Quoted in a press release announcing the Pew Civic Entrepre-

neur Initiative, June 9, 1997. Benjamin Barber and Dorothy Cotton were the other coauthors of the White Paper.

26. Etzioni, Glendon, and Galston, "The Responsive Communitarian Platform," 262, emphasis in the original; personal discussions with Amitai Etzioni, Washington, DC, December 7, 1994. The Communitarian Network has served as the critical vehicle for developing and diffusing within intellectual and policy circles the critique of "rights without responsibilities." Although some of its emphases have been contested within the civic renewal movement, its intellectual influence and vitality can be gleaned from its journal, *The Responsive Community,* as well as from the many publications of its leaders and affiliates. See, for instance, Amitai Etzioni, *The New Golden Rule* (New York: Basic Books, 1996); Etzioni, ed., *New Communitarian Thinking: Persons, Virtues, Institutions and Communities* (Charlottesville: University of Virginia Press, 1995).

27. See Carmen Sirianni, Harry Boyte, Jerome Delli Priscoli, and Benjamin Barber, *Civic Partnership Council: A Proposal* (Minneapolis, MN: Center for Democracy and Citizenship, June 6, 1994). This analysis is based on various sources, including field notes of the Reinventing Citizenship Project's meetings, Washington, DC, March 4 and June 6, 1994; its formal reports; and logs of telephone and personal conversations and formal planning meetings with key participants. See also Howard Fineman, "Citizen Bill," *Newsweek,* February 6, 1995, 16–17.

28. This account is based on field notes of two meetings in Washington, DC, on July 18 and December 9, 1994, as well as logs of telephone and conference calls and several planning meetings. Sirianni coordinated the teams of practitioners and academics. See also Boyte, Barber, Marshall, and Sirianni, *The Civic Declaration;* Carmen Sirianni, Lewis Friedland, and Melissa Bass, "The Civic Practices Network: Social Learning for a New Citizenship," *Good Society* 6: 1 (winter 1996), 31–35.

29. Field notes and transcripts of the four plenary sessions in Washington, DC, January 25, May 19, September 15–16, 1997, January 21, 1998; the National Commission on Civic Renewal, *A Nation of Spectators.* The quotation from William Bennett is from the Third Plenary session, 88–89.

30. This is a paraphrase by John Parr, personal interview conducted in Denver, CO, on October 19, 1996.

31. This account is based on personal interviews conducted in Denver, CO, on October 17–19, 1996, with John Parr and Chris Gates, and extensive conversations with each of them between 1994 and 1998. Ben Barber, director of the Whitman Center at Rutgers University, was especially influential in Bradley's thinking on civil society, as was Jay Westbrook, author of the influential book, *John Dewey and American Democracy* (Ithaca, NY: Cornell University Press, 1991), who had served as a fellow in Bradley's office. Personal and telephone discussions with Erika Gabrielson, March, June, and November 10, 1994. See also Scott Fosler and Renee Berger, *Public-Private Partnerships: An Opportunity for Urban Community* (Washington, DC: Committee for Economic Development, 1982); and Bill Bradley, "America's Challenge: Revitalizing Our National Community," in E. J. Dionne, Jr., ed., *Community Works: The Revival of Civil Society in America* (Washington, DC: Brookings, 1998), 107–14.

32. In addition to the sources on the National Civic League cited in chapters 2 and 4, we draw upon field observations at the 102nd National Conference on Governance: Citizens and Local Government—New Roles and Responsibilities in Communities, Washington, DC, November 7–9, 1996; the NCL Annual Meetings, No-

vember 1996 and November 1998; and personal discussions with Gloria Rubio-Cortés, NCL vice president and chief operating officer, Washington, DC, November 12, 1998, and Reston, VA, February 24, 1996; Michael McGrath, NCL director of publications, Denver, CO, October 18, 1996.

33. John Gardner, quoted in William Raspberry, "Community, Heal Thyself," *Washington Post*, March 18, 1996, 3. See also Richard Scheinin, "The Greater Society," *San Jose Mercury News*, January 21, 1995, 1, 11F; John Gardner, *Self-Renewal: The Individual and the Innovative Society* (New York: Harper and Row, 1964); *Excellence* (New York: Norton, 1984); *On Leadership* (New York: Free Press, 1990).

34. We base our analysis here upon field notes from various meetings, including Alliance for National Renewal Meeting, Washington, DC, February 24, 1995; November 7, 1996; Cleveland, OH, June 23, 1995; ANR Board Retreat, Reston, VA, February 23–25, 1996; ANR Strategic Planning Meeting, Washington, DC, May 27, 1998; ANR National Meeting, Washington, DC, November 13, 1998; Christopher Gates, "President's Report," NCL Annual Meeting, November 13, 1998; personal interview with Christine Benero, former director of ANR, Washington, DC, June 2, 1999; personal discussions with Gloria Rubio-Cortés, ANR Deputy Director, November 12, 1998. We also draw upon participant lists, comprehensive project descriptions, selective cases studies, a comprehensive review of study guides, and field observations of annual strategy meetings at the Study Circles Resource Center, South Hadley, MA, June 15–16, 1996, September 1997; personal discussions with Curt Johnson, director of community building at United Way of America, in flight from Kansas City to Washington, DC, May 18, 1997; and field notes from various national media projects in which we collaborated with ANR partners. For the list of ANR member organizations, see the *1999 Alliance for National Renewal Guide* (Denver, CO: National Civic League, 1999). For an ANR view of the culture of the movement, see Richard Louv, *The Culture of Renewal: Ten Characteristics of the Community Renewal Movement* (Denver, CO: National Civic League, 1996).

35. Personal interviews with David Mathews, May 27, 1999; and Estus Smith, Dayton, OH, May 28, 1999, who is director of the NIF Institute; Robert Daley, "David Mathews: A Biographical Sketch," June 8, 1998, unpublished draft; Annabel Dunham Hagood, *Full Circle: The Domestic Policy Association* (Birmingham: University of Alabama, unpublished ms., 1983); correspondence in the Kettering archives. The Johnson Foundation hosted the early meetings for NIF trainers at its Wingspread conference center in Racine, Wisconsin, which has been an important venue for planning many innovative civic efforts over the past several decades and for building networks within and across various action arenas.

36. National Issues Forums, *The National Issues Forums Network 1992–1993 Estimates* (Dayton, OH: National Issues Forums Institute, 1993); Leonard Oliver, *The National Issues Forums: Reports from the Field: Executive Summary and A Complete Volume of Case Histories* (Dayton, OH: Domestic Policy Association, 1986); Kim Downing, *National Issues Forums: Network Study* (Dayton, OH: Kettering Foundation, April 1996); David Mathews and Noëlle McAffee, *Making Choices Together: The Power of Public Deliberation* (Dayton, OH: Kettering Foundation, 1999); D. A. Hamlin, *A Practical Interpretation of Values: National Issues Forums, 1982–1992* (New Brunswick, NJ: Rutgers University, Walt Whitman Center, April 1992); Doble Research Associates, *Responding to the Critics of Deliberation* (Englewood Cliffs, NJ: Doble Research Associates, July

1996); John Dedrick, *The Results of the National Issues Forums: A Review of Selected Documents, 1981–1991* (New Brunswick, NJ: Rutgers University, Walt Whitman Center, July 1991); John Gastil, *Democratic Citizenship and the National Issues Forums* (Madison: University of Wisconsin, Ph.D. diss., 1994); John Gastil, Gina Adam, and Hank Jenkins-Smith, *Understanding Public Deliberation* (Albuquerque: University of New Mexico Institute for Public Policy, 1995); Judith Alamprese, *National Issues Forums Literacy Program: Linking Literacy and Citizenship in Adult Basic Education* (COSMOS Corporation, 1995). We have also examined a wide array of guidebooks designed around specific issues and constituencies.

37. We have reviewed the full set of the *Kettering Review* beginning with the first (winter 1983) issue. On newspaper coverage of the Harwood *Main Street* study, see *Connections* (October 1991), 4. Beyond its regular subscriber list, the *Kettering Review* is distributed for free at a great number of conferences in the fields of civic education and community building.

38. We draw upon our field notes of meetings at the Kettering Foundation in Dayton and Washington, DC, 1995–99; a complete set of weekly "Letters From Home," by Robert Daley, former director of public relations and communications, which provide a comprehensive overview of meetings, visitors, and projects from 1988 to 1996; a partial set of the Kettering magazine, *Connections,* from December 1989 to December 1996; personal interview with David Mathews, May 27, 1999; presentation by David Mathews at the 102nd National Conference on Governance: Citizens and Local Government—New Roles and Responsibilities in Communities, Washington, DC, November 7, 1996.

39. See Bruce Sievers, "Can Philanthropy Solve the Problems of Civil Society?" *Kettering Review* (December 1997), 62–70; Patrick Scully and Richard Harwood, *Strategies for Civil Investing: Foundations and Community Building* (Dayton, OH: the Harwood Group for the Kettering Foundation, January 1997); Kettering Foundation, *Learning About Civil Society: A Graphic Record of the Civil Investing Seminars,* rev. ed. (Dayton, OH: Kettering Foundation, March 1999).

40. In addition to our field observations, review of participant lists, and informal conversations at various conferences and media projects cited above, we have selectively examined board memberships, practitioner journals, and media coverage of specific projects. We have surveyed websites and interviewed editors and webmasters of leading civic renewal and community-building websites about users and usage trends. We have kept extensive logs of telephone and e-mail communications on usage of the Civic Practices Network, as well as more selective oversight of several other websites developed by our ONline@UW project. In some cases, such as the Pew Partnership for Civic Change, which had recorded 500 newspaper articles about its local partners' projects as of August 1997, we have been provided with a quantitative profile of media coverage.

41. These are rough estimates based on interviews, extensive informal conversations, field notes at meetings and conferences, and organizational affiliations in conference participant lists.

42. Margaret Weir and Marshall Ganz, "Reconnecting People and Politics," in Stanley Greenberg and Theda Skocpol, eds., *The New Majority: Toward a Popular Progressive Politics* (New Haven, CT: Yale University Press, 1997), 148–71. See also Theda

Skocpol, *The Missing Middle: Working Families and the Future of American Social Policy* (New York: Norton, 2000), 165–69.

43. As Dennis Shirley also notes, "radical nonpartisanship" has been indispensable to IAF organizing. See *Community Organizing for Urban School Reform*, 90, 267 ff., 281–82.

44. Personal interviews and conversations with AARP staff Mike McKeown, Portland, OR, October 13–14, 1994, and Washington, DC, November 22, 1994; Robert Jackson, Portland, OR, October 13–14, 1994; Robert Hoffman, Washington, DC, November, 7, 1996; former staff Kathy Dec, Denver, CO, October 18, 1996; and Stuart Langton, Cambridge, MA, May 2, 1994, who served as the consultant to the board and its president in developing the "field enhancement" strategy. We also had a chance to discuss these issues at AARP as part of a formal response to the release of the report by Guterbock and Fries, *Maintaining America's Social Fabric: The AARP Survey of Civic Involvement*, May 27, 1998. See also Charles Morris, *The AARP* (New York: Times Books, 1996).

45. Will Marshall, Al From, William Galston, and Doug Ross, "The New Progressive Declaration: A Political Philosophy for the Information Age," in Will Marshall, ed., *Building the Bridge: Ten Big Ideas to Transform America* (Lanham, MD: Rowman and Littlefield, 1997), 17–35. See also *The New Democrat* (March/April 1995; spring 1999). On the evolution of the DLC, see Dionne, *They Only Look Dead*, 68 ff.; Margaret Weir, "Political Parties and Social Policymaking," in Weir, *Social Divide*, 27 ff; and Kenneth Baer, *Reinventing Democrats: The Politics of Liberalism from Reagan to Clinton* (Lawrence, KS: University Press of Kansas, 2000).

46. Stanley Greenberg and Theda Skocpol, "A Politics for Our Time," in Greenberg and Skocpol, *New Majority*, 16; Skocpol, "A Partnership with American Families," 104–29, in the same volume; Greenberg, "Popularizing Progressive Politics," 279–98 in the same volume; and see Skocpol, *Missing Middle*, 169–70, for an argument for creating a Movement for America's Families.

47. Dionne, *They Only Look Dead*. Unfortunately, in the 2000 election Gore's choice of populist rhetoric largely excluded the more robust civic themes of either wing of the party, which—in our view—enjoy substantial resonance with exactly those swing voters he needed to win in greater numbers.

48. We draw upon field notes from the conference, "Populism in the 1990s," Chevy Chase, MD, March 3, 1994, which Schambra jointly sponsored with Boyte, and which brought together civic conservatives, liberals, and community organizing activists; William Schambra, "By the People: The Old Values of the New Citizenship," *Policy Review* (summer 1994), 32–38; Michael Joyce and William Schambra, "A New Citizenship, A New Civic Life," in Lamar Alexander and Chester Finn, Jr., eds., *The New Promise of American Life* (Indianapolis, IN: Hudson Institute, 1995), 139–63 (the quotation is from p. 161). This volume contains other contributions of the civic conservatives, as does Don E. Eberly, ed., *Building a Community of Citizens* (Lanham, MD: University Press, 1994); and the twentieth-anniversary edition of Berger and Neuhaus, *To Empower People*. On some of the lines of division within both the Right and the Left around the significance of what he calls the "civil society movement," see Don E. Eberly, *America's Promise: Civil Society and the Renewal of American Culture* (Lanham, MD: Rowman and Littlefield, 1998), chapter 2.

49. On this latter point, see Claus Offe, "Democracy Against the Welfare State?" in *Modernity and the State: East, West* (Cambridge, MA: MIT Press, 1996), 147–82.

50. See Shirley, *Community Organizing for Urban School Reform*; Deborah Meier, *The Power of Their Ideas: Lessons for America from a Small School in Harlem* (Boston: Beacon, 1995); Seymour Fliegel with James MacGuire, *Miracle in East Harlem: The Fight for Choice in Public Education* (New York: Times Books, 1993); David Mathews, *Is There a Public for Public Schools?* (Dayton, OH: Kettering Foundation, 1997).

51. On the politics of time, see Carmen Sirianni, "The Self-Management of Time in Postindustrial Society," in Karl Hinrichs, William Roche, and Carmen Sirianni, eds., *Working Time in Transition: the Political Economy of Working Hours in Industrial Nations* (Philadelphia, PA: Temple University Press, 1991), 231–74; Mindy Fried, *Taking Time: Parental Leave Policy and Corporate Culture* (Philadelphia, PA: Temple University Press, 1998); Arlie Hochschild, *The Time Bind: When Work Becomes Home and Home Becomes Work* (New York: Metropolitan Books, 1997).

52. See, for instance, Putnam, *Bowling Alone*, chapter 24; Peter Levine, *The New Progressive Era: Toward a Fair and Deliberative Democracy* (Lanham, MD: Rowman and Littlefield, 2000).

53. On contentious social movement repertoires, see Sidney Tarrow, *Power in Movement: Social Movements and Contentious Politics*, 2d ed. (New York: Cambridge University Press, 1998); Mark Traugott, ed., *Repertoires and Cycles of Collective Action* (Durham, NC: Duke University Press, 1995); and della Porta and Diani, *Social Movements*, chapter 7.

Of course, some components of rights and justice movement repertoires are available and utilized in local organizing within specific arenas, especially in early stages, as many of our cases in the previous chapters indicate. And lobbying by community development or watershed coalitions is key to getting enacted policy designs that support their community-based work. But these strategies are not available to a broad-based movement cutting across many sectors and networks and seeking to focus public attention on models of civic collaboration.

As should be apparent by this point, the relationship between the civic renewal movement and various rights and justice movements is complex, sometimes complementary, but also fraught with tensions, and is likely to remain so, even if these tensions become progressively more productive over time. We do not see the civic renewal movement as displacing rights and justice movements, which serve a variety of legitimate purposes that the former cannot directly serve. But we do see it as attempting to partially dislodge these other movements from certain ways of framing problems and solutions, in the interests of a more robust and sustainable melding of the civic and the just. Without the latter, we do not see the possibility of many of the legitimate aspirations for justice ever adding up to transform American society in a more egalitarian direction, or even stemming increases in inequality, though this is a much larger argument to be made on another occasion. Our approach stands in striking contrast to self-marginalizing Leftist accounts of the new organizing, however, which see these broader civic renewal themes as little more than updated "can-do Americanism" and a "domesticated concept of revolt," and find little more in the "radiant vocabulary" of common good and civic trust than attempts to cover over the thuggishness and greed of America's elite. See JoAnn Wypijewski, "A Stirring in the Land," *Nation*, September 8/15, 1997, 17–25; and Benjamin DeMott,

NOTES TO PAGES 275-76

"Seduced by Civility: Political Manners and the Crisis of Democratic Values," *Nation,* December 9, 1996, 11–19.

54. Michael Sandel, *Democracy's Discontent: America in Search of a Public Philosophy* (Cambridge, MA: Harvard University Press, 1996), articulates this concept in a way that we find quite useful, despite our disagreement on various aspects of his overall historical and theoretical framework. See also Anita Allen and Milton Regan, Jr., eds., *Debating Democracy's Discontent* (New York: Oxford University Press, 1998).

55. On public work broadly conceived, see Boyte and Kari, *Building America.* For a selection from the large literature on workplace innovations over the past generation, see Charles Heckscher, *The New Unionism: Employee Involvement in the Changing Corporation* (Ithaca, NY: Cornell University Press, 1996); Thomas Kochan and Paul Osterman, *The Mutual Gains Enterprise: Forging a Winning Partnership Among Labor, Management, and Government* (Boston: Harvard Business School Press, 1994); Shoshana Zuboff, *In the Age of the Smart Machine: The Future of Work and Power* (New York: Basic Books, 1988); Barney Olmsted and Suzanne Smith, *Creating a Flexible Workplace,* 2d ed. (New York: American Management Association, 1996); Joseph Blasi with Douglas Lynn Kruse, *The New Owners* (New York: HarperBusiness, 1989); John Hoerr, *We Can't Eat Prestige: The Women Who Organized Harvard* (Philadelphia, PA: Temple University Press, 1997); Susan Eaton, "'The Customer Is Always Interesting': Unionized Harvard Clericals Renegotiate Work Relationships," in Cameron Macdonald and Carmen Sirianni, eds., *Working in the Service Society* (Philadelphia, PA: Temple University Press, 1996), 291–332; Dorothy Sue Cobble, "The Prospects for Unionism in a Service Society," 333–58 in the same volume.

56. See Thomas Ehrlich and Elizabeth Hollander, *Presidents' Fourth of July Declaration on the Civic Responsibility of Higher Education,* endorsed by the Presidential Leadership Colloquium convened by Campus Compact and the American Council of Education, at the Aspen Institute, Aspen, CO, July 1, 1999 and signed by nearly four hundred college presidents as of 2000; Campus Compact, *Educating Students for Active Citizenship and Engaging with Communities: Practices in Higher Education.* Both are available on-line through the Campus Compact website (www.compact.org). See also Thomas Erlich, *Civic Responsibility and Higher Education* (Phoenix, AZ: Oryx Press, 2000). For an analysis of the role of youth in the civic renewal movement, see Carmen Sirianni, Melissa Bass, and Lewis Friedland, *Youth Leadership for Civic Renewal: Mapping Networks, Catalyzing Action,* Final Report to the Pew Charitable Trusts, Public Policy Program (Waltham, MA: Heller Graduate School for Social Policy, Brandeis University, October 9, 2000).

57. On the changing rituals of the Fourth of July in American history, as well as its potential for being invested with new meaning, see John Bodnar, *Remaking America: Public Memory, Commemoration, and Patriotism in the Twentieth Century* (Princeton, NJ: Princeton University Press, 1992); Fred Somkin, *Unquiet Eagle: Memory and Desire in the Idea of American Freedom, 1815–60* (Ithaca, NY: Cornell University Press, 1967); and John Frie, *Counterfeit Community: The Exploitation of Our Longings for Community* (Lanham, MD: Rowman and Littlefield, 1998), 112–14, who notes how the Fourth has become a public ritual that promotes consumerism and the legitimation of elite democracy.

INDEX

AARP (American Association of Retired Persons), 264
ABCD Institute (Asset-Based Community Development Institute), 63, 64, 81
Acken, Julian, 207
ACORN (Association of Community Organizations for Reform Now), 81, 148
ACT (Allied Communities of Tarrant; Forth Worth), 47–48
activism, Leftist, 26–28, 287n43
Adams, Samuel, 44
Adams County (Penn.), 94
Addams, Jane, 237
Addis, Kay Tucker, 203
Adopt-a-Watershed, 103
Adult Education Committee of the U.S. Catholic Conference, 259
advocacy coalitions, 20, 272
Advocate Medical Group, 175
AEJMC (Association for Educators in Journalism and Mass Communication), 222
AFL-CIO, 268
African American movement, 31, 240
AFSCME (American Federation of State, County, and Municipal Employees), 68, 262
AHA (American Hospital Association), 174
AHD (American Health Decisions), 139, 162–66
AIDS/HIV, 167, 179
Aiken (S.C.), 171

Aikers, Paul, 259
Alexander, Ames, 209
Alinsky, Saul, 6, 31–32, 44, 118; *Reveille for Radicals*, 43. *See also* IAF
All-America City Award, 78, 274, 276
Alliance for Chesapeake Bay, 93–94
Alliance for Community Media, 232
Alliance for National Renewal. *See* ANR
Alliance for Redesigning Government, 256
Alliance Schools (Tex.), 53–54
Allied Communities of Tarrant (ACT; Forth Worth), 47–48
Alternative Views, 188
AMA (American Medical Association), 144, 146, 151
American Academy of Pastoral Counseling, 176
American Association for Higher Education, 276
American Association of Retired Persons (AARP), 264
American Civic Forum, 250–51
American Council of Education, 276
American Enterprise Institute, 246
American Farmland Trust, 108, 135
American Federation of State, County, and Municipal Employees (AFSCME), 68, 262
American Health Planning Association, 149
American Library Association, 255–56
American Medical Association. *See* AMA
American Newspaper Publishers Association (ANPA), 189

Compositor:	Integrated Composition Systems
Text:	10/12 Baskerville
Display:	Baskerville
Printer and binder:	Friesens, Altona, Manitoba, Canada